DISCARDED

HARVARD POLITICAL STUDIES
Published under the Direction of the
Department of Government in
Harvard University

HARVARD POLITICAL STUDIES

A Brief History of the Constitution and Government of Massachusetts. By Louis Adams Frothingham.

The Political Works of James I. Edited by Charles Howard McIlwain.

Politica Methodice Digesta of Johannes Althusius. Edited by Carl Joachim Friedrich.

Municipal Charters. By Nathan Matthews.

A Bibliography of Municipal Government. By William Bennett Munro.

Town Government in Massachusetts, 1630–1930. By John F. Sly.

Interstate Transmission of Electric Power. By Hugh Langdon Elsbree.

American Interpretations of Natural Law. By Benjamin Fletcher Wright, Jr.

Sanctions and Treaty Enforcement. By Payson Sibley Wild, Jr.

Foreign Relations in British Labour Politics. By William Percy Maddox.

Administration of the Civil Service in Massachusetts. By George C. S. Benson.

International Socialism and the World War. By Merle Fainsod.

The President's Control of the Tariff. By John Day Larkin.

Federal Commissioners. By E. Pendleton Herring.

Government Proprietary Corporations in the English-Speaking Countries. By John Thurston.

The Physiocratic Doctrine of Judicial Control. By Mario Einaudi.

The Failure of Constitutional Emergency Powers under the German Republic. By Frederick Mundell Watkins.

The Treasury and Monetary Policy, 1933–1938. By C. Griffith Johnson, Jr.

The Art and Technique of Administration in German Ministries. By Arnold Brecht and Comstock Glaser.

The Political Life of the American Medical Association. By Oliver Garceau.

Nazi Conquest through German Culture. By Ralph F. Bischoff.

The Regulation of Railroad Abandonments. By Charles R. Cherington.

The City of Reason. By Samuel H. Beer.

Presidential Agency: The Office of War Mobilization and Reconversion. By Herman Miles Somers.

Philosophical Foundations of English Socialism. By Adam B. Ulam.

The Labor Problem in the Public Service. By Morton Robert Godine.

MUDDY WATERS

THE ARMY ENGINEERS

AND

THE NATION'S RIVERS

ARTHUR MAASS

Foreword by Harold L. Ickes

Harvard University Press
Cambridge · Massachusetts

1951

UG
23
M27

Copyright 1951 by the President
and Fellows of Harvard College

Distributed in Great Britain by
Geoffrey Cumberlege
Oxford University Press
London

Printed
in the United States of America

Preface

THE CORPS OF ENGINEERS DEVELOPS THE NATION'S rivers for navigation, for flood control, and for many allied purposes. I propose to evaluate the work of the Corps in these fields. Any evaluation presupposes the existence of standards or criteria against which the work of the agency may be measured. These criteria are stated in the Introduction; and the main body of the book, Chapters II, III, and IV, is devoted to an analysis of Engineer Corps water functions in the light of the stated criteria. Chapter I is a statement of the Army project planning procedure; and Chapter V, a fairly elaborate case history of the Kings River Project in the Great Central Valley of California, serves to illustrate many of the conclusions reached in the study.

There has been a lot of talk about the Army Engineers — on the floors of Congress and in administrators' circles in Washington — and within the last two years there have been frequent references to the rivers and harbors work of the Corps in popular journals and the daily press. Little of the talk and few of these references, however, have been supported fully by citations from the record. This book is the result of a rather extensive examination of the record and consists very largely of citations therefrom. I apologize if the resulting documentary nature of the writing requires careful reading in places. To reduce this deficiency and, at the same time, to maintain the documentary integrity of the study, the lengthy notes have been placed at the end of the volume.

This book was completed in first draft before either the President's Water Resources Policy Commission in 1950 or the Hoover Commission Task Force on Natural Resources in 1948 prepared its report. This first draft was made available on request to the staff of the Hoover Commission Task Force and, somewhat indirectly, to that of the Water Policy Commission. The proposals of the Hoover group have been included in the book; those of the Water Policy Commission appeared too late for full coverage. But I am happy to report that very few of the Commission's conclusions differ essentially from those of this study.

Some of the material in this book has appeared in the last two years in articles by the author in *Harper's*, *Public Administration Review*, *American Political Science Review*, and *California Law Review*.

To the friends who have given aid in preparing this study I have already given thanks. With pride I list their names: Dr. Hugh Elsbree, Library of Congress; Professor Merle Fainsod, Harvard University; Professor Carl Friedrich, Harvard University; Mr. Robert Hartley, Brookings Institution; Dr. Pendleton Herring, Social Science Research Council; Mr. Maynard Hufschmidt, Department of the Interior; Mr. William Pincus, U. S. Bureau of the Budget; Professor Laurence Radway, Dartmouth College, who is coauthor of the first chapter; Mr. James Rowe, Washington, D. C.; President Gilbert White, Haverford College, whose excellent study, *Human Adjustment to Floods* (University of Chicago Press, 1945), has been used broadly in Chapter IV; and Mr. Joel Wolfsohn, Department of the Interior.

I was very anxious to induce Mr. Ickes to prepare a foreword. First, I have always admired him as a symbol of all that was great and American in the New Deal — up-building, fearlessness, inherent honesty, concern for the democratic man, capitalizing on the great diversities of our natural environment to make a stronger nation. Second, I am intensely interested in doing what little I can to bring about a change in the Army's programs for resources development. A foreword to the book by Harold Ickes increases its effectiveness manifold.

ARTHUR MAASS

Harvard University
June, 1951

Contents

	FOREWORD BY HAROLD L. ICKES	ix
	INTRODUCTION: GAUGING ADMINISTRATIVE RESPONSIBILITY	1
1	THE CIVIL FUNCTIONS OF THE CORPS OF ENGINEERS	20
2	ADJUSTMENT OF GROUP INTERESTS	37
3	RESPONSIBILITY TO THE EXECUTIVE AND LEGISLATIVE ESTABLISHMENTS	61
4	RESPONSIBILITY TO PROFESSION	134
5	THE KINGS RIVER PROJECT IN THE BASIN OF THE GREAT CENTRAL VALLEY	208
	ABBREVIATIONS AND STATUTE REFERENCES	263
	NOTES	265

Maps

1	Existing and Potential Inland Navigation, Central United States. From the Report of the President's Water Resources Policy Commission (Volume II)	168
2	Proposed Lake Erie–Ohio River Canal	169
3	Water Resource Development, Cumberland and Tennessee River Basins	191
4	Existing and Proposed Major Water Developments in the State of California (California State Department of Public Works)	210

Foreword

ONE WAY TO DESCRIBE THE CORPS OF ARMY ENGINEERS would be to say that it is the most powerful and most pervasive lobby in Washington. The aristocrats who constitute it are our highest ruling class. They are not only the political elite of the army, they are the perfect flower of bureaucracy. At least, this is the reflection that their mirrors disclose to them. Within the fields that they have elected to occupy, they are the law — and therefore above the law. Senator Douglas of Illinois said on the floor of the Senate on March 29, 1950, "They [the Army Engineers] become the Congress of the United States." And on page 248 of the Report to the House of Representatives of its Appropriations Committee in 1950, its chairman, Representative Clarence Cannon of Missouri, wrote, "The Chief of Engineers has committed the Government and is continuing to commit the Government to the expenditure of funds far in excess of amounts contemplated by the Congress."

Since the greatest power of government under the American system is the power to appropriate money, it would seem that Senator Douglas employed derogatory and belittling language in referring to the Army Engineers as he did. Yet the senior senator from Illinois is customarily one of the most courteous of men. According to Representative Cannon, these gentlemen make monetary commitments which the Congress must later make good and thus they arrogate to themselves powers above those of the Congress. They regard themselves as "the engineer consultants (if and when they choose to consult) and contractors" of the Congress and therefore as independent of any other executive agency of however high degree. When they demean themselves to report to anyone in the Government, it is to the Congress. Their record shows that they not only regard themselves as independent of the Secretary of the Army and the Secretary of Defense, but even of the President.

When Herbert Hoover was in the White House, the Corps of Engineers casually brushed him aside, although he himself was a member of their profession. Franklin D. Roosevelt once considered transferring the civil activities of the Corps to the Department of the Interior where they belong, but did not succeed. Specific and direct orders from President Roosevelt were disregarded with a casualness that was not pretended. In his turn, President Truman has tried to impress upon the Corps of Army Engineers that he is, by the Constitution, the Commander in Chief of the Armed Forces of the Nation. He was strong enough to fire General Douglas MacArthur but, so far, the Army Engineers have successfully defied him.

A small, powerful, and exclusive clique of about two hundred Army officers controls some fifty thousand civilian employees. They constitute the core of the Corps. But let no one make the mistake of assuming that the officers who make up this tight little army machine recognize any civilian engineer, however eminent, as an equal. The civilian engineers may include a few men who are regarded as equivalent in rank to an army sergeant or corporal but, in mass, these civilians are rated in the minds of their self-conscious superiors as little better than privates. A civilian engineer may not expect rank or recognition or decoration. These are the exclusive prerogatives of the inbred two hundred.

The Corps of Engineers has grown strong on the basis of the work of competent civilian engineers for over a century. This is not to imply that the officer engineers lack competence; it is merely to suggest that, necessarily, a few officer engineers could not hope to accomplish what has been done by more numerous and, on the average, just as able civilians. Not only have the Army Engineers long regarded themselves as above the civilian control that the top generals seem to recognize and to prefer as conforming to American concepts; to an amazing measure they are above such controls. They cannot be dismissed from office except through the drastic action of a court-martial. Their worst fate is to be transferred to a military post, and that is rarely done except as a warning to others that they should always strive to please their own army superiors in the Corps. The conviction that an Army Engineer can be disciplined only by the Corps binds all the more closely together this exclusive and ingrowing clique.

The Army Engineers are doubtless brave soldiers, when they work at their trade, but to a surprising and disproportionate degree, they have gradually accepted and adapted themselves to the safer and less rigorous field of flood control. They have taken on, over the years, always with the taxpayer standing by with open purse, such warlike and dangerous undertakings as the regulation and develop-

FOREWORD

ment of domestic and industrial water supplies, the creation and supervision of navigation facilities, the irrigation of farm lands, and the development of hydroelectric power. They have even been reaching out greedily for the function of land drainage. Every little drop of water that falls is a potential flood to the ubiquitous Army Engineers and they therefore assume it to be their duty to control its destiny from the cradle to the grave.

My first contact with the Army Engineers was on the occasion when President Roosevelt, shortly after his inauguration in 1933, turned to me during a Cabinet meeting and directed me to have an investigation made of suspicious circumstances which had been called to his attention by the late Senator George W. Norris of Nebraska and which apparently involved the Army Engineers and the Alabama Power Company at Muscle Shoals. It was subsequently disclosed that there had been collusion between these two brothers under the skin, as the result of which public power generated at the dam was being supplied to the private utility during peak-load hours.

That amazing American phenomenon, the pork barrel, emerged in complete and functioning order from the teeming Corps of Army Engineers. The theory behind it is that the harder the people scratch to pay their taxes, the more money there will be for the Corps of Army Engineers to scratch out of the Treasury with the aid of Congress in order to maintain its control of that body by building, or promising to build, more or less justifiable or downright unjustifiable projects in the various states and districts for which senators and representatives may claim credit during the next election campaign. What matters it if many of these projects are against the wishes of, or even in defiance of orders from, the President himself? An Army Corps' "Operation Santa Claus" is a two-pronged affair — the Engineers lobbying directly for an appropriation by the Congress while inciting local constituencies to bring pressure to bear upon their senators and representatives.

The power-hungry Army Engineers will commit Federal funds without interest and without thought of repayment for projects that it has been settled National policy to build only upon an obligation to repay. For instance, they fought brazenly for the right to build Pine Flat Dam on the Kings River in California and won. Originally, this was to be a reclamation project. Under the Reclamation Law, the water users benefited by Pine Flat Dam would repay in installments the estimated value of the water used by them for irrigation purposes. This would go into a revolving fund, out of which additional reclamation projects in future might be financed without undue drains upon the Treasury.

Under the pretext of "flood control" and despite both oral and written orders to the contrary from President Roosevelt, the Army Engineers defiantly lobbied through the Congress a bill giving it the authority to build this dam, although its real purpose was to provide irrigation water and generate power. The fact is, Kings River drains into Tulare Lake and there is no question of building a harbor or of deepening or widening a waterway since Lake Tulare has no outlet to the sea. This project is by nature a reclamation project; and it will cost from fifty million to seventy million dollars to build it in the middle of Central Valley, whose general development has already made great strides under the direction of the Bureau of Reclamation. The unjustifiable trespass by the Corps of Engineers upon this project merely means the addition of another cook when the brew was already in the hands of an expert chef.

Themselves spoilsmen in spirit, the Army Engineers never worry about land speculators. In this project, they are working hand and glove with the Kings River Water Users Association which has not done anything in return for, or in repayment of, this great public irrigation benefit. Nor are the Army Engineers interested in enforcing the 160-acre provisions of the Reclamation Act, passed during the administration of President Theodore Roosevelt for the purpose of preventing such land monopolies as that of the Kern County Land Company in California, which controls irrigated and irrigable land to the amount of 53,000 of the total of 58,000 acres in the county. The company is generously willing to allow the Federal Government to provide supplemental water to it free of cost.

It is to be doubted whether any Federal agency in the history of this country has so wantonly wasted money on worthless projects as has the Corps of Army Engineers. It is beyond human imagination. Gradually, even the Army Engineers themselves have come to learn, at the cost of hundreds of millions of dollars of the taxpayers' money, that the way to control a flood is to prevent it by containing rising spring freshets behind dams with spillways in the upper tributaries of the rivers so that the flow can be regulated. On the upper Missouri at Fort Peck, Montana, with Public Works money the Army the Congress of the United States" to read deeply enough into the Constitution to discover whether it contains even a slight intimation that the legislative branch of the government was set up by the founding fathers to pass laws, the execution of any part of which would be the exclusive duty and responsibility of a minor executive agency.

How surprised the signers of the Constitution would have been if someone had suggested that the time would come when a newly created Corps of Army Engineers would refuse to submit to the authority of the Department in which it was placed, or even to that of the President himself. The President was intended to be and, with the rare exception of the Corps of Army Engineers, generally is regarded by all branches, agencies, and individual officers of the government to be the head of the Executive Branch of the Government. Moreover, despite their disingenuous, but purposeful, protestations to the contrary, the Engineers do, when they feel like it, make policy without even consulting Congress or reporting to it.

No more lawless or irresponsible Federal group than the Corps of Army Engineers has ever attempted to operate in the United States, either outside of or within the law. If the people of the country were but half aware of the general subserviency of their representatives and senators in the Congress to this insubordinate and self-seeking clique, they would quickly demand that the Congress reassume its dignity and prestige which have been borrowed surreptitiously by the Army Engineers within which to masquerade. In order to put a stop to the reckless and wastrel behavior of the Corps of Engineers, the people should provide a Congress willing and strong enough to take back its usurped and misused power. The President cannot act without the support of the Congress. The Congress has not acted because of the torporific effect of the pork barrel. For too many years the Corps of Army Engineers has been an insubordinate secret society whose slogan has been "One for all and all for one." Nothing could be worse for the country than this wilful and expensive Corps of Army Engineers closely banded together in a self-serving clique in defiance of their superior officers and in contempt of the public welfare. The United States has had enough of "mutiny *for* the bounty."

HAROLD L. ICKES

Washington, D. C.
June, 1951

FOREWORD

Engineers, some years ago, built a great earth dam. It is not generally known, but as it was being filled, a serious fault developed. The Army Engineers hurried without fanfare to Washington to beg for more money in order to make good on their own bad engineering. Unofficial expert opinion was to the effect that, if this break had occurred when the dam was full, or nearly full, it would have caused one of the most disastrous floods in history.

Not only have the Army Engineers invaded the jurisdiction of the Bureau of Reclamation, they have carried on undercover campaigns for other projects that will never pay any return to the Federal Government for money lavishly expended. They persuaded the Congress to approve a Federal handout of millions of dollars to assist local groups in building the Cherry Valley Reservoir in California for irrigation and power purposes, title to which remains in the names of the private owners. In one Middle Western state, the Corps arbitrarily decided that the Reclamation laws do not apply and cheekily recommended that it be authorized to furnish cut-rate irrigation service contrary to law, thereby creating inequities between states in different parts of the country. It would seem obvious that one reclamation district should not be given free irrigation water or cut-rate service by the Army Engineers, while another is required to pay the going rate for its water and its surveys.

As Dr. Maass realizes, the Corps of Engineers has not coördinated its activities with those of other agencies of the executive branch. He adds what ought to be a truism, but not so far as this introvert agency is concerned: "An administrative agency should be responsible for formulating, as well as executing, public policy. The agency has a responsibility to seek a legislative policy that is clear, consistent, feasible, and consonant with community values. The Corps of Engineers contends that it is not, and should not be, concerned with policies. The development of policies and programs is regarded as the sole duty of Congress. The Corps considers itself as no more than the executing agent of specific Congressional directives — 'the engineer consultants to, and contractors for, the Congress of the United States.'"

This conception of the Corps' duty would make of it an administrative monstrosity. Some obsequious lackey of the Army Engineers ought to supply an ice bag for the nigh-bursting head of the Engineers and advise "the Engineer consultants to, and contractors for,

INTRODUCTION

Gauging Administrative Responsibility[1]

Method of Approach

THE FOLLOWING DISCUSSION IS AN EFFORT TO ESTABlish criteria which will be useful in determining the extent to which any administrative agency conducts itself as a responsible instrument of government. It is not primarily addressed to the related problem of how best to sustain the state of mind that issues in responsible administrative conduct. The emphasis here is rather on appraising degrees of responsibility on the basis of criteria applicable to particular functioning agencies.

Much has been written on the "principles" of administrative responsibility. Students have engaged in lively controversy over their nature and validity. But these principles are frequently equivocal; and though mutually incompatible, they are often equally applicable to the same administrative situation. It is therefore believed desirable to use the more modest language of "criteria" of responsibility, some of which may indeed conflict with others, but all of which must be weighted and applied together in any attempt to gauge the responsibility of a specific administrative agency.

Of course, these criteria have not been formulated *in vacuo*. They rest on certain points of view or biases which must be made explicit. Necessarily these biases are cast in normative terms. But they are held as tools for the task, not as dogma for the ages. In particular, the analysis assumes large-scale federal organization in the context of contemporary American society; and this context is taken to include both constitutional government in its presidential form and prevailing democratic ideology.

RESPONSIBILITY — A GENERAL AND HISTORICAL VIEW

To appreciate the general nature and importance of administrative responsibility it is necessary to understand the significance of bureaucracy in the modern state. Logically, of course, constitutional government presupposes a functioning bureaucracy; for until an administrative machine exists there cannot be efforts to subject it to popular influence and control. But more than this, bureaucracy is the very core of constitutional democracy in the sense that no modern government can long survive without an efficient administrative organization. "It is . . . not a question of *either* democracy *or* bureaucracy, of *either* constitutionalism *or* efficient administration," but of "a combination of the two, of a working balance between them, in short, of a responsible bureaucracy."

Historically, the responsibility of officials has been enforced more often, and perhaps more easily, through religious than through secular sanctions. The only way to escape religious responsibility and its restraints is to emancipate oneself from religious faith itself. This is what happened in Renaissance Italy. Deviations from the religious norm seemed necessary to meet the practical requirements of government. They were made in the name of *raison d'état*. The Christian mind, still clinging to its ideological traditions, attempted to rationalize such conduct by deifying the political order. In the seventeenth century, government by and responsible to divine law thus became government by and responsible to kings ruling by divine right. But ultimately the religious sanction lost its force, and modern government has on the whole been obliged to seek other means for enforcing responsibility. These means are summed up in the term "modern constitutionalism," which is essentially "an effort to produce responsible conduct of public affairs without religious sanctions."

Constitutional democracy thus seeks to restrain bureaucracy by secular devices. And administrative responsibility under such a regime has been termed the sum total of the constitutional, statutory, administrative, judicial, and professional practices by which public officers are restrained and controlled in their official actions. But it is not possible to identify the *criteria* for gauging administrative responsibility by relying on such general language. It becomes necessary, therefore, to relate the general concept of responsibility to the specific functions of power (i.e. responsibility to whom?) and purpose (i.e. responsibility for what?).

Responsibility for What?

Working Bias: An administrative agency should be responsible for formulating as well as executing public policy.

It has been popular in the past for American political scientists to assume that administrative officials are responsible only for the execution of policy and not at all for the formulation of policy. The distinction between policy making and policy execution may have a great deal of practical value as a relative matter. By accepting such a distinction, we have been enabled, for example, to develop many of the detailed techniques for the conduct of personnel, budget, and related functions in government. But as an absolute form, any such distinction between politics (the making of policy) and administration (the execution of policy) is unrealistic and leads to incomplete, if not incorrect, analyses of the conduct of responsible government. Public policy is being formed as it is being executed, and it is being executed as it is being formed. Politics and administration are not two mutually exclusive processes; they are, rather, two closely linked aspects of the same process.

Administrative hierarchies have a profound influence on public policy formulation in two ways: (1) in the exercise of the discretionary powers allowed in everyday operations; (2) in the process of developing specific proposals for legislative consideration.

With respect to everyday operations, the extent to which an administrative agency determines policy depends largely on the nature of the discretionary powers which the legislature has assigned to the agency. These powers may be classified according to the legislature's disposition regarding its mandate:

(1) Technical discretion. Here the legislature states the desired results or assumes that the administrator knows them. Its mandate is clear, and the administrator plays the role of a technical expert in fulfilling it.

(2) Discretion in social planning. Here the legislature does not know in fine detail what results it seeks. Its mandate is vague or

general, and the administrator is authorized both to work out definite rules for action and to plan goals for government activities.

(3) *Discretion in reconciliation of interests.* Here the legislature in effect asks the administrator to break a political deadlock. Its mandate is in dispute, and the administrator acquires a certain discretion to mediate and to facilitate negotiations between pressure groups.

Administrative hierarchies may also formulate specific proposals for legislative approval, amendment, or rejection. That they do in fact play such a role has been established by careful studies of the origin of legislation in both federal and state governments. That they should play such a role is coming to be accepted by most political scientists and practitioners, though the ritual of partisan politics often appears to require denunciation of bureaucratic influence on legislation. Accordingly the administrator has a responsibility to seek a legislative policy that is clear, consistent, feasible, and consonant with basic community values.[2] It is his obligation to anticipate problems, to devise alternative policies for meeting them, to estimate the probable consequences of each alternative, and, through the chief executive, to transmit this information to the legislature along with his own recommendations.

The bureaucrat is peculiarly well equipped for this task by virtue of his opportunity to develop professionally accepted techniques and standards; his opportunity to observe at first hand how policies work out in practice; his capacity for tempering enthusiasm for theory with a shrewd appreciation of what is practical and what is not; and his ability to represent interests which are not well represented by organized pressure groups, for example, the consumers.

Responsibility to the People at Large

Working Bias: An administrative agency cannot and should not normally be held directly responsible to the people at large.

In the last century direct official responsibility to the entire electorate was encouraged by requiring that many administrative officials be elected at the polls. But the long ballot secured hardly more than an ill-defined and intermittent responsibility to the general public at the expense of an unfortunate dispersion of authority and an undue responsiveness to private interests. Popular election has given way therefore to an integrated administration governed by the power of appointment and the principle of hierarchical subordination. Other devices for holding the bureaucracy directly accountable to the electorate, such as the recall, the initiative, and the referendum, have not been conspicuously successful, and none is used in the Federal Government. In general it is becoming clear that direct control by the public at large cannot insure administrative responsibility and that the influence of John Doe can be exerted effectively only through the legislature, the executive, and special interest associations.

More recently, some governmental programs have come to depend significantly on voluntary coöperation of the general public for their administration. Good examples are selective service and consumer rationing. In such cases the information function of the government agency becomes of central importance. The people at large need to be informed of available administrative services. They must also be notified of what is expected of them in conformance to government rules and regulations. The agency's intelligence service must in turn pick up from the public the attitudes and information necessary to the successful development and execution of policy — "where the shoe pinches," how it can be made to fit better, what is felt to be unnecessary red tape, and so on. Thus it is possible to state one criterion for gauging administrative responsibility to the people at large — the extent to which the voluntary coöperation of the general public is sought for programs whose success depends significantly on such coöperation. Application of this criterion requires an evaluation of methods for disseminating, collecting, and utilizing the type of information discussed above.

Responsibility to the People — Pressure Groups

Working Bias: An administrative agency should be responsible to pressure groups so far as necessary to equalize opportunities for safeguarding interests, to acquire specialized knowledge, and to secure consent for its own program.

It has been argued that the responsibility of all government is the free and effective adjustment of group interests. Certainly the administrator as well as the legislator operates within a context of intense intergroup activity. Indeed, the legislator often confers upon the administrator a specific responsibility for consulting with groups and reconciling their respective interests. He may do this either because group conflict is so intense that he is unable or unwilling to make the necessary reconciliation, or because the issues are so complex that he lacks the time and information to resolve them and has, therefore, to delegate to administrators the authority to make the necessary rules and regulations. In either case the responsibility of the administrator is clear: to recognize what the legislature has required of him and to conduct his operations accordingly. The extent to which he does this is, then, the first of the possible criteria of responsibility which relates the administrator to pressure groups.

But the administrator will undoubtedly have to work with special interests even in the absence of a specific legislative mandate. His agency and the laws which he administers are usually the product of the pressures and rivalries of organized groups. Naturally, these groups will continue to seek a voice in the development of programs which affect them; and as the scope of the administrator's activities continues to increase, group attention will tend to shift from legislator to bureaucrat in conformity to the adage, "where power rests, there influence will be brought to bear."

This growing tendency for interest groups to participate in the formulation and execution of policy, irrespective of legislative provision, can be supported on at least three grounds: first, that such group representation is desirable to equalize opportunities for protecting and promoting respective interests; second, that the preparation of detailed regulations on complicated matters requires exact knowledge which even the best informed official may not possess and which interest groups can supply; third, that group participation in policy decisions makes possible the winning of consent for the agency's program. This last proposition is not, of course, intended to imply that the agency should attempt to win consent at any price. The desires of the legislature, the chief executive, and other agencies, relevant professional standards, and the dictates of ordinary morality set limits which must be respected in any program which pretends to further the public interest. But within these limits there is ample margin for the agency to seek consent by anticipating the reaction of affected interest groups, by keeping them informed of agency activities, and by permitting them to be notified in advance, to be heard, and to be informed of the basis of emerging policy.[3] In this manner the official can avoid foolish mistakes; he can resolve differences with less "loss of face" on the part of all; and he can impart to the people organized as pressure groups both a sense that they are respected and a conviction that they are playing a valuable role in the process by which they are governed.

The effectiveness with which an agency discharges the aforementioned obligations to special interests furnishes the three criteria of responsibility which follow:

(1) The extent to which an agency equalizes opportunities to safeguard interests. Do the groups dealt with represent all major interests affected by the program? Is each given equitable treatment? Have steps been taken to assure that group spokesmen fairly reflect the views of those whom they claim to represent?

(2) The adequacy of the means employed and the results achieved in securing from interest groups technical knowledge necessary to policy decisions.

(3) The extent to which an agency succeeds in winning group consent in the sense discussed above. This includes an appraisal of its methods and its effectiveness in forecasting the reaction of interested groups to contemplated measures and in exchanging with these groups factual data and attitudes of mutual concern.[4]

Application of these criteria, so far as they involve an appraisal of the methods by which an agency maintains contact with interest groups, requires some study of the precise *form* of the relationship between agency and interest group. Often, groups are represented in the very structure of government, as when an organization is created to benefit a special category of citizens. The Veterans Administration, Women's Bureau, and Bureau of Indian Affairs are generally cited as examples of such clientele agencies. When a number of different interest groups is involved, resort is sometimes made to "staffing for point of view," i.e. appointing officials on the basis of special vocational affiliation or experience. A more direct device is interest representation on multiheaded boards; and occasionally interest groups are even authorized to nominate members of such boards. Finally, public power may actually be delegated to private organizations, although this practice is not generally in accord with our constitutional traditions.[5]

Perhaps more often, however, interest groups maintain merely an advisory or consultative status in their relations to administrative agencies. They present their views in the process of legal or less formal procedures of investigation, notice, and hearing. Some agencies create special staff units to maintain contact with outside groups and present their grievances and suggestions. A common technique is to establish advisory committees composed of the relevant special interests. Wartime experience with such advisory bodies, particularly in the War Production Board and the Office of Price Administration, was on the whole successful, and from that experience improved techniques for the utilization of advisory bodies have been developed.

A general bias is here stated in favor of the advisory devices. An incentive should be placed upon the administrator to win group assent; and group representatives should be free to withdraw or criticize as they see fit. To build interest representation into the governmental structure, at least on a piecemeal basis, is to invite the extremes of hierarchical suppression of group demands or of undue responsiveness thereto. Furthermore, the advisory relationship should be formalized or legalized, since an informal relationship opens the way to invisible exertion of pressure with consequent danger of action that is irresponsible in the eyes of all third parties. It is conceded, however, that these results need not necessarily follow in each situation; that a general preference for formalized consultation may derive from an uncritical acceptance of traditional democratic ideology; and that each case must be examined on its own merits. With this approach, a finding that pressure groups have been directly integrated into the administrative structure, or at the other extreme, that complete informality exists in the relationship between bureaucrat and group spokesman, should be regarded only as a red flag indicating possible lack of responsibility ahead.

Responsibility to the Legislature

Working Bias: An administrative agency should be responsible to the legislature, but only through the chief executive, and primarily for broad issues of public policy and general administrative performance.

Representative bodies are the institutional embodiment of democratic theory, and an administration responsible to the legislature is of the very essence of democratic government. Yet many political scientists fear that representative bodies are losing both power and prestige because of the compelling necessity to delegate to administrators broad discretion in the initiation and execution of public policy. There is no reason, however, why delegation of power need necessarily result in loss of power provided the legislature devises techniques for holding the administration responsible for the exercise of its discretion. If it is true that Congress has lost power and prestige, that is because Congress has not adapted its organization and procedures to the needs of the time, not because such adaptation is inherently impossible within our present form of government.[6]

Moreover, it has been pointed out that the problem of responsible government today is not so much that of legislative-executive relations as of the relationships between the legislature and chief executive on the one hand, and the administrative agency, often allied with pressure groups and legislative blocs, on the other. The administrative agency must be answerable in some sense to *both* the chief executive and the legislature. The real question is how to structure such dual responsibility under our present constitutional system. Should the agency be responsible directly to the legislature, or should it be responsible to the legislature through the chief executive?

The advocates of direct responsibility point out that the legislature creates, defines the powers of, and appropriates the money for each administrative agency. Also, they note that many agencies exercise sublegislative and quasi-judicial functions which they feel should be supervised by legislature and courts respectively. And perhaps most important, they argue that the direct responsibility of an agency cannot end with the chief executive because the chief executive himself cannot be made answerable to the legislature in quite the same sense as under parliamentary government. In its relationships with the President, Congress lacks the ultimate sanction: authority to force resignation when the President no longer commands the confidence of the Congress.

Advocates of indirect responsibility argue that it is of supreme importance to focus responsibility sharply, and that if the legislature attempts to hold each agency directly accountable, responsibility for the coördinated conduct of government programs in broad areas of public policy will become too diffused to be made effective. It is contended: (1) that there must be unity of ultimate command and clearly formulated lines of authority in any such hierarchical organization as a public bureaucracy. Lack of clarity gives rise to uncertainty, conflict, and irresolution, making it difficult to enforce responsible conduct. It is asserted that this can best be prevented by running the line of authority from agency to chief executive to legislature. (2) That careful coördination of the often conflicting programs of different agencies is required if the official is to be kept from an unduly narrow view of the public interest. The legislature alone cannot accomplish such coördination, particularly if it attempts to hold each single agency directly responsible. However, the chief executive, if assisted by adequate staff, is in a position to develop clear and balanced programs for areas of public policy which cut across organizational lines. He is also in a better position to insure effective execution of such programs. (3) That legislators must have balanced programs responsibly placed before them if they are to be able to make intelligent policy decisions. It is the chief executive who is best equipped to prepare such programs and assume responsibility for placing them before the elective body. (4) That the legislature is not equipped to hold the many individual officers and agencies of government to a detailed responsibility. On the other hand, the interposition of the chief executive can reduce the pressure on the legislature. He can devise procedures for settling matters too trivial for legislative attention, for eradicating administrative parochialism, and for controlling the executive agencies in such a manner as to simplify the task of legislative surveillance. (5) That direct responsibility to the legislature nearly always means direct responsibility to individual members of particular legislative committees which happen to have jurisdiction. In such cases the legislature often finds it difficult to check its own entrenched and uncoördinated minorities. This is less likely to occur when the legislature considers integrated policies submitted by the chief executive. (6) That the difficulties of executive-legislative relationships under a system of separated powers are reduced by the presentation, through the chief executive, of an internally consistent and coherent legislative program. (7) That sublegislative powers are really similar to the policy making powers of regular executive agencies, and as such should be exercised under direct responsibility to the chief executive, while judicial functions should be independent of both legislature and executive. (8) That a single responsible chief executive to manage the departments in accordance with statute is an essential part of our republican system and was clearly intended by the framers of the Constitution.

On balance, it is believed that the advocates of indirect responsibility have the better of the argument. Of course, there is no question but that a determined legislature can in fact control individual agencies directly if it wishes to pay the price; the general position taken here requires rather the evolution of a custom of legislative self-restraint where direct controls are concerned. Nor is it meant to imply that the legislature should be denied the *authority* to prescribe the duties and procedures of administrative agencies in detail. No more is meant than that the requirements for a truly effective responsibility today will call for sparing use of such authority.[7] The legislature can neither determine a national policy nor maintain effective supervision over the executive branch unless it focuses on the great issues and rests content with having laid out general lines of policy for the executive branch. To impose mandatory and minute specifications for the organization and operation of the administrative machine is to absolve "first the bureau chief, then the Secretary of the department, and then the President . . . from part of his executive responsibility, and in consequence the Congress is foreclosed from adequately criticizing the conduct of the business." Accordingly, administrative agencies should be responsible to the legislature, but only through the chief executive, and primarily for the broader questions which arise in formulating and executing policy.

If an agency can be controlled effectively only when Congress focuses on major issues of integrated policy, a major criterion of its responsibility is the success with which that agency, in reporting to Congress through the President, points up the broad policy questions which require legislative determination and plays down administrative details. The remaining criteria of indirect responsibility to the legislature can be derived in the process of examining the nature of the business which draws legislator and bureaucrat together.

First, agencies give legislative committees professional assistance and advice that leads to the drafting of statutes. Here the criterion of their responsibility is the effort which they make, by producing competent advice, to encourage the passage of laws containing a careful definition of the agencies' obligations and authorities. An official cannot proceed to a wise and democratic use of his discretion unless the legislature has indicated the general nature of the standards which should guide his action; and it is his responsibility to present the professional information available to him to the legislature, through the chief executive, in a way to insure the writing of competent standards into law. A corollary of this criterion is the extent to which the agency presses for revision of vague or overly ambitious statutes when it has access to technical information for the determination of more satisfactory standards. Yet another corollary is the response of legislative committees to the agency's recommendations. However, this last criterion does not have wide application. It is based on the assumption that committees generally respond more favorably to recommended legislation that incorporates professionally determined standards than to other recommendations. Though this may be true, there are so many other factors which enter into legislative response that it will usually be difficult to isolate this one.

Second, agencies are required to come before appropriation committees annually to present their plans for the ensuing year, to account for activities and expenditures for the current and past years, and generally to satisfy these committees that the legislature's purposes are actually guiding their operations. Review of the budget is the most important of the regular legislative controls over the executive branch. Even though changes in items may be relatively small, it should not be thought that this review is ineffective. Departments and budget officers are keenly aware of legislative attitudes and prepare their budgets to meet them.[8] In this activity, the criterion of responsibility is the effectiveness with which the agency (1) reports and justifies projected work, and (2) reports and accounts for accomplishments. A corollary measure is the treatment accorded the agency's budget by the appropriations committees, but here again there are too many other factors conditioning legislative response to permit any but extremely guarded conclusions.

Third, an agency is constantly subject to legislative investigations; and though it may never have undergone such an investigation, the threat of one is a continued sanction by which the legislature insures conformity to its own policies and safeguards against abuses which run counter to community values. The agency must always be prepared to answer; its record must be good; and it must be prepared to spread that record before the legislature. The criterion of responsibility is thus the willingness and ability of an agency to provide investigating committees with a complete, accurate, and clear record of its activities. A corollary, again to be used with extreme care because of the vagaries of "politics," is the extent to which an investigating committee indicates satisfaction with its findings.

Fourth, the accounts of agencies are regularly audited by an independent instrumentality of the legislature. The criterion of responsibility is here self-evident.

Fifth, agencies conduct business with the legislature which involves the appointment and removal of personnel, both personnel whom the agency appoints directly and personnel whom it recommends to the President to be confirmed with the consent of the Senate. The criteria of responsibility here are also difficult to apply because of the supervention of "political" factors, but they can be enumerated as the success of the agency in obtaining confirmation of appointments which it has in fact initiated, absence of legislative efforts to impeach or by other means remove or place obstacles on the removal of agency personnel, and general evidence of legislative satisfaction with the agency's staff.

Finally, agencies often maintain a network of informal contacts with individual legislators and committees. In some form such relationships are inevitable, and in fact indispensable. But in their pathological form, a single legislator or committee may occupy a position of influence so commanding in matters affecting the agency that responsibility to the remainder of the legislature is prevented. Accordingly, a final criterion of responsibility to the legislature is whether an agency conducts its relationships therewith in a manner to prevent minority control over its affairs.

Responsibility to the Chief Executive[9]

Working Bias: An administrative agency should be directly responsible for conforming to the general program of the chief executive and for coördinating its activities with other agencies of the executive branch.

To the extent that the chief executive is held responsible by the legislature and by the public for the administration of a government-wide program, he will in turn try to establish the responsibility of administrative agencies to himself.[10] In so doing he must define the duties for which they are held accountable and the means by which this accountability is to be effectuated.

Both in formulating and in executing programs, agencies usually operate under the general policies or philosophy of the Administration. The broad lines of such policy are normally laid down by the chief executive. But he cannot be expected to provide detailed direction on all matters. He is entitled to expect that, within the limitations of specific legislative determinations, agencies will adapt their activities to his general policy directives and to the broad philosophy of his Administration.[11] The extent to which such adaptations are made is one major criterion of an agency's responsibility to the chief executive.

Moreover, nearly all agencies operate in fields in which they also affect the programs and interests of other organizations immediately subordinate to the chief executive. If the purposes set by the President are to be achieved with maximum effectiveness, it is essential that these agencies act in concert. To be sure, it is becoming fashionable to observe that a sophisticated executive may prefer something less than complete coördination of his establishment on the ground that occasional conflict between subordinates enables him to keep posted and insures that policy conflicts will be brought before him for resolution. But a decision to adopt this strange substitute for an effective intelligence service should rest with the superior, not with the subordinate. Generally, an agency subordinate to the chief executive has an obligation not to take action which has not been carefully checked with other interested agencies through the established means for coördination. Thus, a second major criterion of responsibility to the chief executive is the extent to which an agency coördinates its work with that of other agencies. A closely related criterion is the extent to which controversial matters of detail, unworthy of legislative attention, are settled within the executive branch.

The remaining criteria of responsibility to the chief executive relate to the means for attaining concerted conformance to his program. They involve techniques for departmental and overhead organization designed to provide public leadership. These techniques include not only unity of ultimate command and clearly formulated lines of authority, but also the existence of effective staff organs at appropriate levels in the administrative hierarchy. Some progress has been made in recent years in securing such staff organs, especially for administrative staff services (budget and personnel) and long-term planning. The development of policy general staff has lagged behind. By direction of the President, the Bureau of the Budget performs a central clearance function for the programs of executive agencies. But though central clearance has proved effective in a large number of instances, the procedure is notoriously less adequate for those important cases which involve highly controversial subjects. On broader issues interdepartmental committees have been used to eliminate conflicts in policy. Such committees, however, especially when unsupported by secretariat, are too often stultified by the "veto power" and by the presence of members more concerned with defending their positions than with reaching genuine agreement.

More recently, there has grown a general awareness that negative and piecemeal review of individual proposals flowing up from agencies to the chief executive cannot produce an integrated governmental program at the time it is required. It is becoming clear that top level executives require policy staff organs to formulate general programs which subordinate units cannot evolve because of limited terms of reference, inertia, organizational or professional bias, or inadequate factual information. Such a policy general staff, by supplying common premises for action, can help insure coördination "before the event," that is, by prior indoctrination.

From this discussion it is possible to derive the following additional criteria of responsibility to the chief executive: (1) the existence of unity of ultimate command and clearly formulated lines of authority within an agency; (2) the availability and effectiveness of administrative staff organs, intra-agency committees, and liaison or other devices for insuring concerted conformance with the chief executive's policies; (3) the extent and genuine sincerity of agency coöperation with staff, liaison, interdepartmental, or other coördinating mechanisms established by the chief executive; (4) the extent to which an agency conforms to the chief executive's program in information transmitted to the legislature or to the public;[12] (5) as a measure of successful adjustment of program conflicts, the extent to which evidence of such conflicts with other agencies fails to appear in information transmitted to the legislature or to the public;[13] (6) so far as can be ascertained by rough estimate, the extent to which an agency demonstrates a "sense of administrative discipline" in its conduct.[14]

Responsibility to Political Parties

Working Bias: An administrative agency cannot be held independently responsible to the organization or policies of political parties.

If responsibility to political parties exists at all in the Federal Government, it is largely indirect and can be included within the criteria already developed. For example, for some purposes the political party can be considered an interest group. Furthermore, political parties dictate the organization of the legislature and the selection of the chief executive and his top aides, so that the manner in which responsibility to the legislature and chief executive is effected will reflect whatever responsibility to political parties exists. In contrast to cabinet government and to British society, the structure of American government and of American society has not encouraged the development of party organization or policy to which administrative agencies can be held responsible.

Responsibility to Profession

Working Bias: An administrative agency should be responsible for maintaining, developing, and applying such professional standards as may be relevant to its activities.

An administrative agency can be held responsible for adherence to the standards of technical knowledge, craftsmanship, and professionalism applicable to the function administered. In other words, it can be said that objective standards of professional performance are one technique for insuring responsible conduct. Where such standards exist, the official often sacrifices his personal preference to the compulsion of professional group opinion. Should he fail to do so, he faces a loss of professional status or possibly affirmative action by executive, legislative, or judicial agents based on use of professional standards as a measure of conduct.

It is generally agreed that the professional sanction does not of itself provide an adequate guarantee of responsibility in our society. Some students have even emphasized the special dangers of any heavy reliance on professional standards. It is held that there can be no real responsibility unless it is an obligation to someone else (X being responsible to Y for Z), and that this condition cannot be fulfilled by the relationship of a man and a science or by an inward personal sense of moral obligation. It is also feared that professional responsibility leads to group introversion, undue emphasis on technique, and inflexibility. It is felt that agency traditions based on a sense of narrow monopoly of expertness often harden into a pattern that resists alteration. Finally, there is the traditional democratic aversion to the efficiency which is one of the objectives of professional standards. The maxim that "men who think first and foremost of efficiency are seldom democrats" is of hoary, if not wholly palatable, vintage.

But most of the objections cited above are not really objections to reliance on professional standards. They are objections to the fact that the bureaucracy often has a monopoly of skill in modern government, and that the indispensability of skilled administrators tends to make such a bureaucracy autonomous. Professionalization may actually play an important role in transforming the quasi-autonomous bureaucracy into a subservient tool. Conversely, responsibility is often most conspicuously absent where objective professional standards either do not exist or are not applied.

For present purposes it is enough that the professional responsibility recognized by an agency must be supplemented by responsibility to interest groups, legislature, and chief executive, and that it must be convincing to persons not associated with the profession or agency concerned. Whether or not it will be convincing depends in part on the status of the profession involved, i.e. the extent to which the profession has developed or can be made to develop objective standards which are generally recognized and respected, and in part on evidence that the agency recognizes and has taken steps to insure fidelity to such standards by its personnel.

Accordingly the criteria for gauging the responsibility of an agency to professional standards include: (1) the extent to which it recognizes such generally accepted standards and utilizes them to formulate policies and to anticipate problems which a technically qualified man knows will arise; (2) the extent to which it makes an effort to develop additional standards, especially when it possesses a near monopoly of skill in its field; and the extent to which such standards gain the respect of competent professional personnel outside the agency; (3) the extent to which it takes into account the professional education and experience of personnel in its recruitment, advancement, and separation policies; (4) the nature and extent of in-service training programs designed to improve professional skills; and (5) the nature and extent of its coöperation with outside organizations which attempt to keep their members up-to-date on professional developments and to promote devotion to the highest professional standards.

Beyond the standards of any one profession or craft, there are also standards common to the whole body of public servants considered as a distinctive social group — i.e. as "bureaucracy." These standards usually reflect (a) the fiduciary relationship in which bureaucracy generally stands to political authority and (b) the norms of the wider social order. Consequently in a democracy they will include the demand for honesty, efficiency, courtesy, and impartiality in public acts, and an insistence that administration, both as to policy and procedure, be conducted in accordance with the prevailing democratic values.[15] The extent to which these requirements are met furnishes the major criteria of the responsibility of public officials regarded as a single identifiable profession.

Responsibility to the Courts

Administrative responsibility to the courts will not be discussed in any detail, nor will criteria for this type of responsibility be developed. Administrative law has recently been the subject of so many specialized studies that the limited examination that might be made here would add nothing.

Failure to develop criteria for judicial responsibility is not intended to detract from its importance. All responsibility of public officials is, of course, responsibility under law; and in the United States it is generally to the regular courts that administrative agencies must prove, when challenged, that they have not abused their discretion, overstepped their jurisdiction, or committed an error of law, fact, or procedure. It should be noted, however, that such administrative abuses as excessive red tape or offensive conduct toward the public are beyond the reach of the courts. Moreover, judicial review is largely a negative, *post hoc,* and unduly ritualized check addressed to errors of commission, whereas administrative irresponsibility in the modern state is just as likely to arise from errors of omission.

For these reasons it is necessary to supplement the legal accountability of administrative agencies with responsibility to the people

GAUGING ADMINISTRATIVE RESPONSIBILITY

organized as interest groups, to the legislature, to the chief executive, and to relevant professional standards. Ordinarily, the analysis of a genuinely responsible agency will reveal a high positive correlation on all the criteria developed in connection with these relationships. But such a multiplicity of responsibilities may occasionally impose mutually contradictory obligations on an agency; and in such cases, as was suggested at the outset, the criteria of responsibility herein developed may well conflict. In this event there is a residual responsibility for the agency to evidence rational policy and good faith in seeking a resolution of the impasse, primarily through the chief executive.

ONE

The Civil Functions of the Corps of Engineers

"Essayons" — motto of the Corps of Engineers

IN THIS STUDY WE ARE CONCERNED WITH THE CIVIL functions administered by a military department, the planning and construction of river and harbor improvements by the Corps of Engineers, United States Army. Few Government services have a longer history than the Engineer Corps. The Continental Congress originally authorized the organization of a Corps of Engineers in 1775. This Corps was disbanded in 1783, and the present Corps of Engineers may be said to have originated in the Act of March 16, 1802, fixing the new military establishment.[1] This Act authorized the President to organize and establish a Corps of Engineers consisting of five officers and ten cadets to be stationed at West Point, New York, and to "constitute a Military Academy." The headquarters of the Corps was moved to Washington within a few years, but the Military Academy remained under the charge of the Corps of Engineers until 1866, when Congress transferred the institution to the Army at large under the direction of the Secretary of War. West Point was the first, and remained the only, technical engineering school in the United States until Rensselaer Polytechnical School was founded in 1825. This early association of the Engineers with West Point may account for the fact that among the officers in the United States Army today the Engineer Corps is considered the elite. Traditionally,

CIVIL FUNCTIONS OF ENGINEERS

only the highest eight per cent of the graduating class at the Military Academy is allowed to choose the Engineer Corps, and the Corps is given high preference by most of the graduates in indicating desired assignments.

The Corps of Engineers is both a civil and military engineering and construction agency. As a military unit, the Corps is broadly responsible for military construction, military engineering supply, and military engineering training programs. As a civil construction agency, the Corps is responsible for the design, construction, operation, and maintenance of navigation and flood control improvements and related works.

From its inception the Engineer Corps has been concerned with civil functions. The Corps was the engineering department of the Government which planned and executed the national internal improvements program initiated in the 1820's. Among the first projects undertaken were improvements of the navigation of the Ohio and Mississippi Rivers, the building of the Chesapeake and Ohio Canal, and the continuation of the Cumberland Road. In 1852 Congress placed rivers and harbors work generally under the Corps of Engineers, and in 1917, provided that the laws relating to the improvement of rivers and harbors apply to works of improvement for flood control.[2] Flood control work for the nation as a whole was more definitely assigned to the Army Engineers by the provisions of the Flood Control Act of 1936.[3] The Corps has been known, particularly with reference to its civil functions, as the United States Engineer Department (USED).

These civil functions are of great magnitude. As to investment, the Federal Government has appropriated over six billion dollars to the Corps of Engineers for the improvement of rivers and harbors and the elimination of flood hazards; an additional six billion dollars is required to complete currently authorized programs; and additional programs of the Corps not yet authorized, but under investigation, may add billions more.[4]

The organization and appropriations for civil functions are entirely separate and distinct from those for military work.[5] In the performance of his civil duties the Chief of Engineers is nominally responsible directly to the Secretary of War. He does not report to the Chief of Staff nor to any General or Special Staff Section. And as a matter of fact, the Secretary of War exercises little, if any, real supervision or review over the conduct of Engineer civil functions.

At Washington headquarters the Chief of Engineers is assisted by a civil works staff and by a Board of Engineers for Rivers and Harbors.[6] The latter is a permanent advisory board whose major function is to review for the Chief all examination, survey, and review reports of proposed projects. The Board consists of seven officers of the Corps, detailed by the Chief of Engineers; one is resident member, the other six are usually Division Engineers or officers on duty in the Office of the Chief.

The field staff of the Engineer Department is organized on a decentralized basis into District and Division Offices. The continental United States is divided into forty-two Districts, each of which is headed by an officer of the Corps who bears the title of District Engineer. The forty-two continental District Offices are in turn grouped into twelve Divisions, each under the command of a Division Engineer. The Engineer Districts and Divisions are generally located to embrace complete watersheds.

Several branches of rivers and harbors work are conducted in the field through special organizations. The most important of these is the Mississippi River Commission which is charged with improvements for flood control and navigation on great stretches of the Father of Rivers. The Commission consists of seven members, the majority of whom are not Engineer Corps officers on active duty. It conducts its operations, however, through the regular Division and District Offices; and the President of the Mississippi River Commission is at the same time Division Engineer of the Mississippi Valley Division.

In all, there are roughly 215 Army Engineer officers engaged in civil functions, supervising some 40,000 full-time employees. No enlisted men are involved.

Project Planning Preliminary to Authorization

Familiarity with the planning process from the time of inception of a project to the time it goes under construction is essential to an evaluation of the work of the USED. Thus, the remainder of this chapter is concerned with a factual statement of this process. The casual reader may prefer to scan it and turn directly to the analysis of Chapters II, III, and IV.

The Corps of Engineers may not undertake any navigation or flood control project until it is specifically authorized by Congress in a legislative enactment. Thus, the first steps in project planning deal with the process preliminary to authorization.

INCEPTION OF A PROJECT

The request for the conduct of an examination and survey of a proposed project is first presented by local interests or officials to the Congressman or Senator representing the district in which the desired improvement is located. The request is presented to a Member of Congress for the reason that the right to conduct an examination of any particular area is dependent upon specific authorization in law. Thus, the Member of Congress to whom the request is presented seeks to have the project written into the survey authorization section of an omnibus rivers and harbors or flood control bill. This he does by presenting the item to the committees which prepares such legislation — the Public Works Committees of the House and Senate.[7]

Until very recently it has been the general rule of the Congressional committees never to refuse requests by Congressmen to include preliminary examinations in omnibus bills on the theory that every community should be given an equal opportunity to have its proposals for improvements examined on their merits.[8] In 1947, however, the newly organized House Committee on Public Works adopted a resolution which altered this philosophy. In order to reduce the number of preliminary examinations to be undertaken by the Corps, the Committee sought to inquire into the need for these examinations before recommending their authorization to the full legislative body. The Members of Congress seeking approval must appear before the Committee, and the Chief of Engineers is called upon to estimate the cost of making the preliminary examinations and to furnish other pertinent data. However, the Senate Committee on Public Works failed to follow its House counterpart in any action that might limit the authorization of water investigations, so that the House action has been ineffective.[9]

PRELIMINARY EXAMINATION

The purpose of the preliminary examination is to ascertain, without too detailed an investigation, the economic feasibility of a proposed improvement.[10] This step is taken so as to avoid the necessity of conducting a complete survey in case the benefits to be obtained from a project are definitely not felt to justify the expenditure to be involved. When a preliminary examination indicates a reasonable possibility that an improvement may be economically justified, a favorable recommendation for a survey is warranted.

Commencement of a preliminary examination is not necessarily coincident with its authorization. The money for the conduct of preliminary examinations and surveys is appropriated in lump sum.[11] As the number of authorized investigations is invariably greater than the number that can be conducted under available appropriations, the actual initiation of an examination depends upon the order of priority given it by the Chief of Engineers.

The original examination is made at the location of the proposed improvement by the District Engineer Office. As soon as practicable after a preliminary examination report has been assigned, the District Engineer is required to consult "the Senator or Representative responsible for the item authorizing the report . . . concerning the character and extent of the improvement desired, and for the purpose of obtaining the names of the parties at whose instigation the investigation was initiated." [12] After consulting the interested Congressman or Senator, all "persons known to be interested in the improvement, and those whose local knowledge renders their opinion of value, should be given full opportunity to express their views." To obtain the views of these interested parties, the District Engineer, in almost all cases, arranges for public hearings.[13] At these hearings, Members of Congress, State and local officials, and representatives of local, State, regional, and national interest groups appear before the District Engineer to justify, and in some cases oppose, proposed projects. In addition, representatives of interested Federal agencies sometimes attend and participate in hearings. In the hearing, an attempt is made to develop information on the improvements desired; the local coöperation that may be expected; and the interests that would be benefited and the value of the benefits.

The public hearing is followed by a field reconnaissance of the

CIVIL FUNCTIONS OF ENGINEERS

area under consideration. The reconnaissance party consists of engineering personnel qualified to plan the most practicable scheme of improvement and to gather data upon which may be determined the type, location, approximate cost, and benefits to be anticipated from works required. During the reconnaissance, every effort is made to interview parties who may be in a position to furnish information useful in the preparation of the report.

In the conduct of preliminary examinations, especially on reservoir projects, the Corps of Engineers coöperates with other Federal and with State agencies. The nature of coöperation with Federal agencies is developed in greater detail in Chapter III. It is largely the Departments of Interior and Agriculture, and the Federal Power Commission which are involved.[14] As for State agencies, the District and Division Engineers are directed to consult freely with designated State representatives in the preparation of reports.[15] Joint hearings with State agencies are authorized where such agencies have a particular interest and desire to participate. By law, all completed preliminary examination and survey reports must be submitted by the Chief of Engineers to the affected States for comment before they are submitted to Congress, and the views of the States must accompany the report of the Chief of Engineers.

The contents of preliminary examination reports are uniform as to outline and are prescribed by the *Orders and Regulations* of the Corps of Engineers.[16] Each report contains a conclusion either that the data available are sufficient to show that the improvement is not justified at this time and that a survey is therefore not required, or that the prospects for a justified improvement are such that a survey is warranted to determine more definitely the best plan of improvement and its justification.

All preliminary examination reports must be reviewed by the Division Engineer before they are transmitted to Washington. The Division Engineer is assisted in the review by his staff of "office" engineers. If the Division Engineer disagrees in whole or in part with the report, he may return it to the District Engineer with suggestions for revision. The District Engineer must reëxamine his conclusions in the light of the Division Engineer's views; however, he need not revise his report if he does not agree with the Division Engineer. Thus, the report of the Division Engineer, which accompanies that of the District Engineer, is made in the form of an indorsement with only such presentation of detail as may be essential for the explanation of views and recommendations which remain divergent from those of the District Engineer. In the matter of technical engineering work, which is supposed to be capable of precise analysis, important differences of opinion are not allowed in written reports. It should be noted, however, that the preliminary examination report does not contain much engineering detail.

When the Division Engineer submits to higher authority an unfavorable examination report, he must issue a public notice stating the nature of his recommendations and that, "since it is the policy of the Engineer Department before arriving at conclusions of an important nature in its reports to Congress to afford interested parties an opportunity to be heard," all parties have the privilege of a written or oral appeal to the Board of Engineers for Rivers and Harbors.

Division Engineers will furnish all Senators and Representatives of the area affected an advance copy of the public notice with a covering letter advising the scheduled date of the general release of the notice, and a list of the names and addresses of the other parties to whom the notice will be issued. In order to comply with the long-standing policy that members of Congress must be the first to be aware of the status of examinations, surveys, and reviews, the notice to Senators and Congressmen will be furnished far enough in advance of the general release to permit the members of Congress to announce to their constituents the submission of the report and to supplement the Department's release if they so desire.[17]

The Board of Engineers for Rivers and Harbors, the advisory review board for the Chief of Engineers, passes upon all preliminary examination and survey reports submitted by Division Engineers. As stated above, the Board grants hearings to, and gives consideration to written arguments presented by, interested parties, including Senators and Representatives. Though the Board usually sits in Washington, it takes testimony at the location of proposed projects on occasion. If the Board of Engineers reports unfavorably upon a preliminary examination upon which the Division Engineer has reported favorably, it issues a notice to the interested parties to the effect that "the Board is not convinced that the benefits expected to accrue from the proposed improvement warrant the undertaking of a survey at this time." This notice invites interested parties to submit statements and arguments bearing upon the necessity for the improvement and to request a hearing if such is desired. In the light of the additional information submitted in response to this notice, the Board will, at a later date, reconsider its original determination. The purpose of this procedure is to give the interested parties an opportunity to present their cases before the Board, an opportunity of which they might not have taken advantage, since the Division Engineer's report was favorable.

The Board submits its recommendations, along with those of the Division and District Engineers, to the Chief of Engineers, who is responsible for the final recommendation. Though he usually accepts the conclusions reached by his advisory board, the Chief of Engineers is free to act independently.[18]

If the Chief of Engineers agrees to a favorable preliminary examination, then his report takes the form of an authorization for a more detailed survey. Favorable preliminary examinations need not be submitted to affected States, the Executive Office of the President, nor to the Congress, as the project is still under investigation.

If the Chief of Engineers agrees to an unfavorable preliminary examination, his report must be submitted to the affected States and, whenever the project is located in a western river basin, to the Department of Interior for comment. It may be submitted also to the Federal Power Commission and to the Department of Agriculture if they are interested parties.[19] The views of the States and of the Federal agencies are considered by the Chief of Engineers, and are made a part of the report.

An unfavorable report must be submitted to Congress. As in the case of most reports to Congress by executive agencies, those of the Corps are cleared first with the Executive Office of the President (Bureau of the Budget) to determine their relationship to the program of the President. As unfavorable preliminary examinations have always been in accord with the President's program, this is not a significant procedure at this stage of project planning. The unfavorable report is submitted to Congress largely for information, for that body will not authorize a project on the basis of such a report. However, an unfavorable examination may result in further legislative action in the form of a committee resolution calling for review by the Engineer Department of its conclusions. In accordance with law and prior to the Eightieth Congress (1947), the House Committees on Rivers and Harbors and on Flood Control and the Senate Committee on Commerce had each adopted procedures whereby any Representative or Senator might, after a report of the Chief of Engineers had lain on the committee table for at least twelve months, present a resolution which, if adopted by the committee, required the "Board of Engineers for Rivers and Harbors . . . to review the report with a view to determining whether any modification should be made at this time in the recommendations heretofore made." [20] It should be noted that all unfavorable reports of the Chief of Engineers state that the proposed improvement is not recommended "at this time," leaving the way open to further investigation at a later date if authorized.

When the Congressional committees were reorganized in 1947, the new House Committee on Public Works revised the twelve-months delay requirement. It provided by resolution "that hereafter, following the submission by the War Department of an unfavorable report . . . an interval of three years shall elapse before a new investigation of the area covered in said unfavorable report is ordered, unless facts are presented which could not have been foreseen when the unfavorable report was submitted to Congress and which the Committee deems sufficient to warrant earlier action." [21] The committee inquires into the need for a review, requires the appearance of the Member of Congress seeking the review, and requires the Chief of Engineers to report on estimated cost and other pertinent data. Again, the Senate Committee on Public Works failed to adopt a restrictive resolution. It merely "agreed that proponents of Committee resolutions should submit appropriate evidence showing need for reviews of reports on river and harbor and flood control projects" and authorized the committee chairman, without even the necessity of a committee vote, "to certify and pass upon Committee resolutions for review of flood control and river and harbor reports and forward the resolutions to the Chief of Engineers." [22]

The review report, if ordered, is conducted in the same manner as the original preliminary examination.[23] The Chief of Engineers gives the review an order of priority among the preliminary examinations to be assigned. When undertaken, all levels of the USED participate in preparing the report.

SURVEY

The purpose of the survey is to determine more definitely the most suitable plan for improvement and whether such improvement

CIVIL FUNCTIONS OF ENGINEERS

is economically justifiable.[24] A favorable preliminary examination — one which indicates that there is a reasonable possibility that an improvement may be economically justified — constitutes an automatic authorization for a survey. However, the commencement of a survey is dependent upon the availability of funds which are allotted by the Office of the Chief of Engineers from lump sum appropriations in accordance with priorities it establishes.

The survey is conducted in a manner similar to the preliminary examination in that it is executed in the field at the District level, reviewed at the Division level and again at the Bureau level by the Board of Engineers, and recommended to the Congress by the Chief of Engineers.

Hearings are not usually held at the District level, though contacts with interested parties and Government agencies are maintained, and the District Engineer must report any modifications of the desires of local interests that may have been presented subsequent to the submission of the report on the preliminary examination.

Expensive detailed surveys of dam sites and reservoirs, or other improvement works, and subsurface investigations are not, as a rule, undertaken until the economic data obtained by the field forces are analyzed, and new cost estimates are made, based upon the latest available information. If the cost-benefit ratio appears to be unfavorable and there appears to be little possibility that the improvements can be economically justified, detailed surveys and subsurface investigations are not made. If, on the other hand, the cost-benefit ratio appears to be favorable, then considerable engineering detail is developed.

As in the case of preliminary examination reports, the contents of survey reports are prescribed by regulations.[25] They include a detailed description of existing conditions; a description of the plan or alternate plans of improvement considered; estimates of economic cost, computed as an annual charge; estimates of economic benefit, computed on an annual basis; a comparison of benefits and costs; allocations of cost among Federal agencies and local interests and among different water uses; and recommendations as to what, if any, Federal project should be authorized by the Congress.

The reviews of surveys by Division Engineers and the Board of Engineers for Rivers and Harbors are similar to those for preliminary examinations. If the Division Engineer submits an unfavorable report, he must inform interested parties. The Board grants hearings. Differences in engineering detail are ironed out.

The Chief of Engineers is responsible for the final recommendations to Congress. As in the case of preliminary examinations, he submits his proposed reports to interested States and Federal agencies for comment, and clears with the Executive Office of the President to determine their relation to the program of the President. If the Executive Office informs the Engineer Department that a proposed report is not in accord with the program of the President, the Chief of Engineers (through the Secretary of War) may transmit the report to Congress nonetheless, including in the letter of transmittal a statement of the Executive Office position.

When a survey report has been submitted to Congress, the Senate or House Committee on Public Works may, by committee resolution, direct the Corps of Engineers to reëxamine all or any part of it with a view to determining whether any modifications should be made. In this case, the review report is conducted in a manner similar to the survey report.[26]

Authorization of Project by Congress

After a project has been surveyed, no further action may be taken until Congress specifically authorizes construction. Authorization for preliminary examination and survey does not constitute authorization for construction; Congress must consider the project on the basis of the information contained in the survey report.

The survey reports are usually submitted by the Chief of Engineers, through the Secretary of War, to the House Committee on Public Works, where they are considered by the subcommittees on rivers and harbors and on flood control when these subcommittees prepare omnibus authorization bills. In general, it may be said that the Committee will not consider for authorization any project which has not received a favorable survey report from the Engineer Corps, though there is no rule establishing this procedure. The following statement of Judge Mansfield, then chairman of the House Committee on Rivers and Harbors, is illustrative:

"You know, Mr. Small, we have been trying to follow the example that you set for us when you were chairman of this committee, not to permit anything to be brought up unless it had the approval of

CIVIL FUNCTIONS OF ENGINEERS 31

the engineers of the War Department. We have tried to hew close to the line in that respect." [27]

However, on occasion unrecommended projects have crept into omnibus authorization bills, if not through committee action, then through action taken on the floor of the House without any opposition from committee leadership. Furthermore, the Committee has recommended authorization of projects based on survey reports which had not been submitted formally to the Congress by the Chief of Engineers at the time of committee approval of the project. In an attempt to put an end to this latter procedure, Congress declared in 1946 that it would not authorize a project unless a report has been submitted previously by the Chief of Engineers.[28]

The subcommittees conduct public hearings on the projects at which many interested parties appear. Officers of the Engineer Corps defend and justify each favorable report. In addition, the Members of Congress from the districts in which projects are located usually appear to corroborate and supplement the testimony of the Engineer officer. At the hearings on the rivers and harbors bill of 1937, fifty-five Congressmen from twenty-two States and Alaska testified; at hearings on the omnibus flood control bill in 1939, there were seventy-three Representatives from twenty-seven States.[29] Senators, though less frequently than Representatives, appear before House subcommittees on projects in which they are interested. Some of the more important regional and national interest groups which testify will be described in the next chapter.

After hearings, the subcommittees draw up a bill and accompanying report for presentation to the full Committee and to the whole House. As a rule, the omnibus authorization bill defines the improvements by mention of the survey reports, which have been printed as House or Senate Documents. For example:

Red River Basin

The Denison Reservoir on Red River in Texas and Oklahoma for flood control and other purposes as described in House Document No. 541, 75th Congress, 3rd Session, with such modifications thereof as in the discretion of the Secretary of War and the Chief of Engineers may be advisable, is adopted and authorized at an estimated cost of $54,000,000 . . .[30]

After the bill has passed the House of Representatives, it is referred to the Senate Committee on Public Works, whose subcommittee on flood control and improvement of rivers and harbors holds hearings on controversial projects in the bill and on proposed additional projects. The Senate subcommittee usually increases the House version of the bill considerably, adding projects turned down by the House subcommittees and items not considered by them. Though the Senate subcommittee in the past has not adhered to it as closely as the House, it may be stated as the rule that only projects which have received favorable reports from the Engineer Corps will be included in authorization bills. The following quotation from a speech by Senator Bailey, then chairman of the committee which handled river and harbor legislation, illustrates the point:

> I cannot get a river and harbor proposition or a flood control proposition through my committee by introducing the bill or trading with my fellow Senators. I couldn't get it through by personal influence or political manipulation. All that a Senator is allowed to do in this matter is to offer a resolution providing for an investigation by the Board of Engineers of the War Department. If the Board of Engineers of the War Department finds that the project which I am sponsoring is sound economically and in accord with the national policy, then I can get somewhere in the Committee and on the floor of the Senate and over on the House side. Now this is a self-imposed restraint, but it is an indispensable restraint. I could make a confession for all these members of Congress here behind this table. They wouldn't know what to do or where to turn or where to stop but for that restraint.
>
> For my part I fully share what Mr. Green said by way of praise of our Engineers of the Army. Last year one Senator tried to get by them. I am proud of the fact that the committee turned him down, notwithstanding he was a very fine fellow. Every now and then some Senator undertakes to break the precedent, but I am going to pledge to my country and to the Congress and to the committee that as long as I am chairman of that committee, I am going to see to it that before a dollar is ever spent on river and harbor and flood control projects they are approved by the Board of Engineers in the Army of the United States.[31]

The Senate considers the bill, as reported by the Public Works Committee, in the usual manner. Many amendments providing for additional projects are offered on the floor by individual Senators, and often a number of these are accepted both by the Senate and

CIVIL FUNCTIONS OF ENGINEERS 33

by the conference committee appointed to settle differences between the House and Senate versions of the bill.

PROJECT PLANNING SUBSEQUENT TO AUTHORIZATION

Planning does not stop with the authorization of a project by Congress. There are at least four additional steps in the planning procedure which must be completed before "the dirt begins to fly." Two of these steps, the preparation of detailed plans and specifications and the preparation and awarding of bids, relate largely to the details of project construction and are not of first interest in this study. The other two steps are described below.

DEFINITE PROJECT REPORT

Definite project reports are required for all authorized major improvements to establish definitely the most suitable plans for their accomplishment, to provide a firm basis for the preparation of contract specifications, and to serve as a basis for the programming of construction.[32] Studies made in connection with definite project reports serve in many cases to crystallize plans of improvement which theretofore have been only of a general nature. Since many authorizations for flood control improvements are comprehensive in character, and provide that the particular reservoirs and related works in the plan are to be selected and approved by the Chief of Engineers, the definite project report is used as a medium for selecting the definite projects to be constructed.

Prior to World War II, the Engineer Department did not attempt to prepare any plans more detailed than those contained in the survey report until after money had been appropriated and allotted for construction of a project. However, in order to build up a backlog of useful projects for immediate initiation at the end of the War, Congress in 1942 authorized the Chief of Engineers to prepare in advance detailed plans for authorized projects.[33] Money has been specifically allotted to the Corps of Engineers for this purpose in each annual appropriation measure since that time, and it appears that the procedure of preparing detailed plans prior to the appropriation and allotment of funds for construction has become permanent.

With his annual budget estimates, the Chief of Engineers presents a list of authorized projects on which it is proposed to prepare detailed plans with the funds requested under that heading. After the money has been provided by the Congress, the Chief of Engineers makes an allotment to the District Office for the definite project report.[34]

A considerable amount of field investigation and engineering detail is required in the preparation of the report.[35] Since it forms the basis for contract plans and specifications, the report must establish all controlling elements of design, including all important dimensions and elevations. The study of foundations, hydrology, and other design factors must be carried far enough to avoid the necessity for subsequent fundamental changes. For important flood control or multiple purpose projects, particularly where there is doubt concerning local support for such projects, public hearings may be held, but this is not the rule.

All definite project reports are reviewed by the Division Engineer before they are transmitted to the Office of the Chief of Engineers, where they are given final approval, or are disapproved and returned to the District and Division Engineers for revision. The Board of Engineers for Rivers and Harbors does not review these reports.

APPROPRIATION PROCESS

The appropriation process is involved in all stages of project planning. Money is appropriated for conducting the preliminary examination, survey, definite project report, and detailed plans and specifications. However, it is immediately prior to the letting of contracts and the commencement of construction that the first very large allotment of funds must be available, and for this reason the appropriation process is discussed at this point.

Funds for navigation and flood control projects are appropriated annually by Congress in the Army Department Civil Functions Appropriation Bill. They are voted in lump sum and are available until expended. The lump sum appropriations are allotted to authorized projects by the Chief of Engineers. However, the discretion of the Chief in making allocations after funds have been voted is very much limited by the program of projects which he has presented to the Executive Office of the President (Budget Bureau) and to the Congress in justification for the appropriation — which program, or revision thereof, the Budget Bureau and the Congress have approved in making the money available.

CIVIL FUNCTIONS OF ENGINEERS 35

The actual appropriation procedure, both executive and legislative, is similar in the case of Army Department civil functions to that for other Government functions and need not be described. However, the manner in which the Chief of Engineers constructs his budget is of some special interest. Each year the District Engineers are required to submit six-year programs of additional funds required for completion of authorized navigation and flood control projects. The projects in the programs, in addition to being distributed over a six-year period, are assigned recommended priorities. On the basis of these priorities, the Chief prepares a consolidated program and budget for the Engineer Department. However, in preparing his final budget requests the Chief of Engineers is given advance advice from the Executive Office of the President as to the total amounts to be included. The following excerpt from a Congressional hearing illustrates this point:

> Mr. Terry. When you submit an estimate to the Budget you usually submit the sort of figure they give you.
> General Schley. Yes sir; we were told by the Budget before we submitted a list that it should total $30,000,000 . . .
> Mr. Terry. Then you submitted to the Budget . . . the figure of $30,000,000.
> General Schley. At their direction.[36]

In addition to the construction programs and estimates of required appropriations, each District Engineer, in preparing his portion of the *Annual Report of the Chief of Engineers,* must estimate for each project in his district "the amount that can be profitably expended" in the second fiscal year following that for which the report is prepared (thus, the annual report for 1946 contains estimates of amounts that can be profitably expended in fiscal year 1948). The proposed expenditures published in the annual report agree with the construction programs and estimates of appropriations prepared by the District Office. But it should be pointed out that these estimates, though they are published and available for public inspection, do not agree with the final budget request of the President.

This concludes a factual recitation of the planning history of a typical river or harbor project from the time of its inception to the time "the dirt begins to fly." The history constitutes the controlling facts in the conduct of Engineer Department civil works and, as such, is the basis for an analysis and interpretation of Engineer Department activities.

TWO

Adjustment of Group Interests

". . . the pitiless pressures which are the price of our freedom . . ."
— Walter Lippmann[1]

THE GROUNDWORK HAS BEEN LAID NOW FOR AN EVALUation of how the Corps of Engineers meets the requirements of administrative responsibility. The requirements were stated in the Introduction, and that which is to be evaluated — the Engineer Department procedure for planning water development projects — was set out in the first chapter.

How does this planning process adapt itself to an adjustment of group interests? Does the process reveal an effective responsibility of the Engineers to the public organized as interest groups?

The planning process appears to be specifically organized in response to the need for an adjustment of group interests at the several levels at which these interests may become articulate. A recapitulation of the process in these terms reveals a minimum of thirty-two stages at which group interests may be able to present their views to the Corps and Congress. Of these thirty-two stages, fifteen may involve contacts between interest groups and the Engineer Department. At three of these fifteen stages, public hearings are regularly provided for; at two additional stages, Engineer Department instructions require consultation with local interests; and at the remaining ten, the extent of consultation varies with particular circumstances, but the necessity for a constant awareness of the current attitudes of local interests is emphasized in all Engineer publications.

Since Congress, as a general rule, will not authorize the construction of a project unless that project has received a favorable recommendation from the Engineers in the form of a survey or review report, it may be said that Congress has, in part, transferred the responsibility for adjusting group interests from its own body to the executive agency. The Engineer Department has recognized the nature of this transfer and has developed its planning procedure in response thereto. The following statement, submitted by the Chief of Engineers to the House Committee on Appropriations in 1947, serves to illustrate this point:

> The authorization of a river and harbor or flood control project follows a definitely prescribed, democratic course of action. It is based upon the activation of the desires of local interests, who are most vitally interested. Local interests, as individuals or groups through the actions of their representatives in Congress, make request for an item to be included in a rivers and harbors or flood control bill . . . The District Engineer, mindful of the need for developing all public opinion, holds an open public hearing at which not only those interests that are active in obtaining the authorization of the proposed work but also all other views are obtained and encouraged. Having thus developed the desires of the local citizens, the district engineer makes a study . . .[2]

The individuals and groups which take advantage of the many opportunities to present their views before the Engineers have developed interesting patterns of relations with the Corps. These are developed in the pages that follow.

As for Representatives and Senators, the general relations between Congress and the Engineers will be developed in more detail in Chapter III. It might be mentioned here, however, that, though Congress as a group has disassociated itself largely from the process of project planning by transferring the responsibility for adjusting group interests in that process to the Engineer Department, individual Members of Congress have not been so abstentious. Representatives and Senators, knowing they cannot obtain Congressional authorization for the projects they are sponsoring without favorable reports from the Engineers, have attempted to pressure the Corps into approving these projects both by (1) appealing to District Engineers and to the Board of Engineers for Rivers and

Harbors in Washington in public hearings, and (2) devising what amounts to a new method of legislation — legislation by committee resolution — by which they can compel the Engineer Corps to reconsider "unfavorable" conclusions.

The importance which Members of Congress attach to their appearances at Engineer Department hearings is indicated in the following statements:

Rep. Dockweiler (Calif.). I have appeared before the Board of Army Engineers in behalf of a harbor in my district and I made what I thought was a pretty good case for improvement of Santa Monica Harbor . . . And I think the conclusion of the Board of Army Engineers was that no work should be done there because there was not enough business there . . .

Of course we must abide by the decision of somebody, and the Army Engineers decided against me in that case.[3]

Rep. Harris (Ark.). Mr. Speaker, the Army engineers, of the Vicksburg district, who are doing a fine work in that area [sic], held a public meeting at Hot Springs, Ark., Friday, December 12, investigating the construction by the Federal Government of Blakely Mountain Dam and Reservoir, on the Ouachita River. I had accepted their invitation to appear before the engineers at that meeting, but, due to the emergency and declaration of war, I did not have the privilege. My remarks, however, were read for me and I insert them here in the *Record.*

"Colonel Sturgis and gentlemen, on behalf of the people of the Seventh District of Arkansas, I am glad to appear before you in the interest of the construction of the Blakely Mountain Dam and Reservoir for flood control and power development. Needless to say the greater part of the Ouachita River in Arkansas runs through my district, affecting directly 8 of the 11 counties . . .

"I wish to express my appreciation and the appreciation of the people throughout this whole area for the fine work the Army Engineers are doing in the development of these projects for flood control and power facilities as well. The people are intensely interested and not only asking but pleading for this protection and development . . ."[4]

It is difficult to evaluate the importance of the review resolution as a technique for pressuring the Corps of Engineers to give its approval to projects which the Members of Congress desire. A 1935 manuscript in the files of the National Resources Planning Board concludes:

Such data as are available are rather impressive as showing the importance of the committee resolution in getting rivers and harbors projects expanded in scope or modified in terms of reducing the local contribution required. In recent years, especially the last two or three Congresses, the number of committee resolutions requesting review has increased each year. During the 74th Congress, first session, the Committee on Rivers and Harbors passed 117 resolutions calling for reviews of reports on rivers and harbors projects. Just about one-third of the 204 projects authorized in the current rivers and harbors act (1935) originated as favorable reports, transmitted to Congress by the Corps of Engineers. Nearly two-thirds of the improvements authorized in the current act represent projects which were originally turned down by the Corps of Engineers or projects which have been modified by them upon review under committee resolutions.[5]

This statement may overestimate the current significance of the resolution as a legislative device. However, it should be noted that of the eighty-three investigations completed by the Corps in fiscal year 1946, twenty were authorized by regular legislation and sixty-three were reëxaminations submitted in response to committee resolutions.[6]

Thus, a tremendous pressure is put upon the executive agency by individual Members of Congress — a pressure which might be expected to lead so easily to strained relations. But just the opposite is true. As we shall see later, relations between the Engineer Corps and the Congress are uncommonly cordial.

Municipal, county, water district, and State officials; local industries; and local and State organized interest groups take fullest advantage of the opportunities to be heard by District Engineers and the Board of Engineers. Chambers of commerce, boards of trade, representatives of local manufacturing concerns, flood control district officials, municipal engineers — these are among the "local interests" whose desires "activate the democratic course" of the authorization process.

In addition, every large geographic region in which river and harbor developments are of importance is represented by at least one powerful regional pressure group. These groups are often quite active in the entire planning process; and a statement of the objectives of two groups, one interested in navigation and the other, flood control, is desirable.

ADJUSTMENT OF GROUP INTERESTS

The Atlantic Deeper Waterways Association was founded in 1907 to further the development and expansion by the Federal Government of an intracoastal waterway system along the Atlantic seaboard from New England to Florida.[7] The Atlantic Intracoastal Waterway, a protected two-thousand-mile water route inside the Atlantic coastline, is divided into twelve so-called links or sections, of which eleven had been substantially completed by 1941. Thus, after thirty-four years of constant agitation, the Association prided itself on having attained the near completion of that one project which it originally set out to accomplish.

The Association, however, remained active. It worked for construction of the "missing link" in the original project — the New Jersey Ship Canal, which would stretch thirty-five miles from the Raritan to the Delaware River. This "missing link" was authorized finally in the Rivers and Harbors Act of 1945,[8] and the Association is now concentrating its efforts on obtaining appropriations to build the project. The Association has favored extensions of the Intracoastal Waterway northward from Boston to Portland, Maine, and southward in Florida. The construction of both the ship and barge canals across Florida and of the inland waterway north of the Caloosahatchee River on the west coast of Florida are advocated. In addition, the Association has promoted numerous local harbor, channel, and river improvements along the Atlantic coast.

The membership of the organization consists of municipal, State, and some few national executive officials and legislators; trade associations, chambers of commerce, maritime business interests; and others from the Atlantic coast States. From its inception in 1907 until 1946 its president was J. Hampton Moore, who was a Member of Congress from Philadelphia at the time he accepted the office, and who remained in the Congress until 1920, when he resigned to become mayor of Philadelphia. Former Representatives and Senators, including former members of the Congressional committees which handle rivers and harbors legislation, have served as officers of the Association.[9]

Representatives of the Atlantic Deeper Waterways Association keep in constant touch with the Army Engineers. They attend hearings conducted by the District Engineers and by the Board of Engineers on projects in which they are interested. For example, in May

1942, in April 1935, and at several prior dates the Association was granted a hearing before the Board of Engineers to present its views on pending reports on the "missing link."

Relations between the Association and the Corps of Engineers are maintained, not only through appearances of representatives of the Association before hearings conducted by the Engineers, but also through appearances of Army Engineers before annual conventions of the Association. In addition, the Chief of Engineers sends to each convention a detailed report outlining the progress of river and harbor and flood control improvements along the Atlantic coast. Recognition by the Association of the excellent coöperation offered by the Engineers is expressed in formal resolutions adopted at each convention. The following resolution, as an example, was adopted at the thirty-fourth annual convention at Miami, Florida, in 1941:

> The improvement of our rivers and harbors has, for more than a century, been delegated to the Corps of Engineers of the United States Army. Many notable engineering achievements have been accomplished. Their work has been marked by engineering skill and fidelity in execution. The officers of the Corps have supervised the expenditure of public funds not only with economy, but with the purpose of securing the best results. The planning and construction of works for the improvement and maintenance of our rivers and harbors should continue with these efficient public servants. We congratulate the Corps of Engineers upon the work done by it in developing and improving the inland waterways of the country during the past year.[10]

Although we are primarily concerned with the relations between interest groups and the Corps of Engineers, it might be well to note the very excellent relations between this particular group and the Congress. Representatives of the Atlantic Deeper Waterways Association appear at most Congressional hearings on projects relating to the Intracoastal Waterway. Joseph H. McGann, then clerk of the House Rivers and Harbors Committee, in addressing the twenty-fifth annual convention of the Association on the subject of Congressional action on projects having to do with the Atlantic Waterway, said, "I might say that Mr. Moore [president] and Mr. Small [vice-president at large] appeared at nearly all of these hearings. If one was absent the other was present, the one who was absent filing a written brief." [11] The fact that Messrs. Moore and Small were former Members of Congress, the latter having been chairman of the

ADJUSTMENT OF GROUP INTERESTS

Rivers and Harbors Committee, greatly facilitated their appearances before Congressional committees. To illustrate:

> Chairman (Mr. Mansfield). Mr. Small, I appeared before you many years ago in a similar capacity, when you were chairman of this committee.
>
> Mr. Small. I hope you will refrain from mentioning how many years ago, though. [Laughter] [12]
>
> Chairman (Mr. Mansfield). I might say that when I first came to Congress the two foremost advocates in Congress of waterway improvement were the two former Congressmen we have just heard, Mr. Small and Mr. Moore, one from the Democratic side and one from the Republican side.[13]

As for the total general effectiveness of this organization, the purpose for which it was created, the construction of the Atlantic Intracoastal Waterway, has been very nearly achieved. But as Representative Mansfield has indicated in a letter to J. Hampton Moore, the influence of the organization has extended beyond this purpose.

> The influence of your Association has extended far beyond the area benefited by the Intracoastal Waterway. At the time of your organization the interest of the public in waterway improvement was at a very low ebb. Expenditures made for navigation and flood control improvements during the five years previous to 1907 averaged less than $23,000,000 annually. From that time on, however, interest in this work grew and appropriations increased until, during the past five years [1934–1939], these expenditures have averaged over $210,000,000 annually. The credit due to your organization for the part it played in creating this public sentiment for waterway improvement cannot be overestimated.[14]

For the purposes of good will, the Congressman may have overstated the case for the Association, but its general importance is not to be overlooked.

The Ohio Valley Conservation and Flood Control Congress was organized in 1933 by representatives of twenty-five chambers of commerce of the Ohio Valley to consider what could be done for flood control in the area. The program of the Congress and the important part it has played in promoting a national flood control policy are described by its executive secretary:[15]

At that time [1933] there was no law establishing a National policy of Flood Control for the United States.

The one outstanding Flood Control Project was the Miami Conservancy District, above Dayton, Ohio. The 1913 flood drowned 225 people and there was a property damage of $80,000,000 in the Miami Valley. The Miami Valley people created the Ohio Conservancy Law, allowing a conservancy district to be established and enabling them to prepare plans and let contracts for flood protection, and to assess the cost against the property that was damaged by previous floods that would be protected from future floods, but not more than the benefits derived.

The Miami Conservancy District built five reservoir dams between 1914 and 1918 at a cost of $33,000,000 and assessed the entire cost on property benefited. In 1937 there was more rainfall in the Miami Valley than there was in 1913 but there was no loss of life or property damage. The whole program was designed and executed by Mr. Arthur Morgan.

In 1930 the Muskingum Conservancy District above Zanesville, Ohio engaged Arthur Morgan to prepare plans for their valley. He did so, but when it was estimated that the project would cost $50,000,000 the undertaking was dropped.

The Muskingum people helped to organize our Congress and suggested, that as they had a survey project completed, we cooperate with them and help get a Public Works Authority appropriation.

In 1933 a group from the Muskingum Valley with Arthur Morgan and myself appeared before the President of the United States and later before Director Harold Ickes. We secured the first P.W.A. appropriation, money appropriated to the Army Engineers to build the reservoir dams, providing the local people would supply free of cost to the U. S. Government, the lands, easements, and rights-of-way, and hold the Government free from damages during construction, and maintain and operate same after completion . . .

Therefore, having established a precedent in flood control with the Muskingum Valley Project, our Congress with others in 1936, induced Senator Royal S. Copeland to introduce the first Flood Control Act, establishing a National Flood Control Policy. This act carried the same principles as the Muskingum Project, that is, the Government to build the dams for reservoirs, when the local people had provided the lands, easements, and rights-of-way.

We thought we had accomplished something, but found that the states of New York, Pennsylvania, West Virginia, Kentucky, Indiana, and Illinois had no laws allowing either the local people or the state to acquire the lands, easements, and rights-of-way . . .

In 1938 officials of our Congress appeared before Senator Alben Barkley stating that if National Flood Control was to be accomplished, that

ADJUSTMENT OF GROUP INTERESTS 45

the United States Government would have to acquire the lands, easements, and rights-of-way. He introduced an amendment to the 1936 Flood Control Act authorizing the U. S. Government to acquire the lands, easements, and rights-of-way for reservoirs.

Although Mr. Jordan, the executive secretary of the Flood Control Congress, tends to point up the central importance of his organization to the exclusion of other interests (for example, those in New England and in upper New York State) in the legislative history of the Flood Control Acts of 1936 and 1938, it is true that the Ohio Valley group worked very closely with the Corps of Engineers and the Congress in the formative period of national flood control policy. As for its more recent activities, the executive secretary reports: "Our Flood Control Congress works with the United States Army Engineers to get projects approved by them, with the Flood Control Committees of the House and the Senate for authorization, then with the Bureau of the Budget, then with the Appropriation Committees of the House and Senate, then with individual members of the House and Senate."

In addition to the regional interest groups which devote most of their efforts to promoting water and related developments, there are several large and important national groups.

The National Reclamation Association, with headquarters at Denver, represents irrigation interests. This organization, though it has frequent contacts with the Army Engineers, deals primarily with the Bureau of Reclamation, and for this reason is not considered in any detail here.

The National Rivers and Harbors Congress is perhaps the most important and most effective of the water development interest groups.[16] Organized originally in the year 1901, the Congress in its own words "was a pioneer in the struggle for the protection of our national resources and has taken a leading and active part in this fight for nearly four decades. The National Rivers and Harbors Congress . . . representing as it does the entire country affords a means for securing coordinated and united action by all the interests concerned with the various phases of water development." [17]

This comprehensive pressure group counts in its membership the "local interests" (state and local officials, local industrial and trade organizations, contractors); the United States Congress (Representatives and Senators are honorary members); and the Corps of Engineers (Officers of the Corps engaged in rivers and harbors work are all ex officio members). The honorary members, Members of Congress, take a very active part in the Rivers Congress, though they are in a real sense the lobbied. In 1949, for example, the President was Senator John McClellan of Arkansas, a member of the Public Works Committee, of the subcommittee of the Committee on Appropriations which handles Engineer Corps funds, and chairman of the Committee on Expenditures in the Executive Departments — to which the Hoover Commission recommendations proposing reorganization of the USED had been referred. McClellan, as a member of the Hoover Commission, had dissented from those recommendations which would divest the Army of rivers and harbors functions.[18] The national vice-presidents of the pressure group were Senator Wherry of Nebraska, Republican floor leader and a member of the Appropriations subcommittee on Engineer Corps funds; Representative Whittington of Mississippi, for a long time chairman of the House Committee on Flood Control and then chairman of the reorganized Committee on Public Works; and Representative Case of South Dakota, a member of the House subcommittee which considers appropriations for the Corps. The chairman of the board, until his recent death, was Senator Overton of Louisiana, long a senior member of the Senate committee which handles rivers and harbors legislation. The chairman of the powerful Projects Committee of the organization was Representative Sid Simpson of Illinois, a former member of the Committee on Rivers and Harbors.

In the past the ex officio members, officers of the Corps, also have taken part in the proceedings of the pressure group, and the relations between the Rivers and Harbors Congress and the Engineers have always been cordial. In addressing the convention of the Congress in 1940, Maj. Gen. Julian Schley, Chief of Engineers, said, "I feel that I am among old friends whose interests coincide with those of the Department I represent."[19] The feeling of coincidence of interests appears to be mutual, as evidenced by the resolutions concerning the Corps of Engineers regularly approved at conventions of the Congress. The following resolution, passed at the convention in 1947, is illustrative:

> We affirm our conviction that all planning and execution of public improvements of our water resources for navigation, flood control, and allied purposes, including beach and shore protection, continue as in the past

ADJUSTMENT OF GROUP INTERESTS

to be under the jurisdiction of the War Department as a function of the Corps of Engineers. We reaffirm our faith and confidence in the Corps of Engineers whose devotion to this Nation and loyalty to the Chief Executive have made possible the orderly and efficient development of the greatest waterway and flood control projects on earth. In their many years of experience, during peace and war, they have met many emergencies and have never failed to accomplish the greatest good for the greatest number of people in a manner most advantageous to the Government and to the people. Furthermore we believe that only through the plans developed by the Corps of Engineers can we obtain a consistent and coordinated improvement of our water resources.[20]

Perhaps the most interesting and important aspect of the Rivers and Harbors Congress is the work of the Projects Committee. When the National Congress was formed in 1901, its slogan was "a policy, not a project." The purpose was not to urge any specific waterway improvements but primarily to interest the public and the Federal Congress in the development of waterways in general. In 1935, however, the Congress reversed its policy, agreed to promote certain waterway improvements actively, and for that purpose organized a Projects Committee. The Committee consists of a chairman and twelve members, each representing, generally, the area covered by a Corps Division Office. If any sponsor of a waterway improvement is interested in having his project approved by the Projects Committee, he must submit on specified forms an application for endorsement. The Committee meets once a year for several days preceding the annual convention to act upon all applications. It holds hearings on each project; votes, by ballot, to classify it in one of several orders of priority; and presents its recommendations on all projects to the convention of the Rivers Congress for formal adoption.

The Committee will not take action on any application until the applicant or an authorized representative has appeared before it to justify the promotion of the project by the whole Congress. Senators and Congressmen sponsoring or interested in waterway improvements in their districts often appear before the Committee to obtain favorable recommendations for their projects. In these cases, Senators and Representatives request that the pressure group give approval to their individual projects so that these projects may have a better chance of being approved in turn by the United States Congress of which they are members. The following excerpts, in the

April, 1940, issue of the *National Rivers and Harbors News,* are from a report of the annual meeting of the Projects Committee:

Congressman Joe Hendricks of Florida presented testimony on the Cape Canaveral Harbor, which he stated will serve the $5,000,000 citrus fruit belt, which is now without proper harbor facilities.

Congressman John Jennings, Jr., of Tennessee, urged approval of the project for the construction of dams in the vicinity of Oakdale and Harriman, Tennessee.

Representative Frank C. Osmers, Jr., testified on behalf of the Hackensack River improvement project, which is now being surveyed by the Army engineers. 27,000 acres of meadow land will be reclaimed under the project and will be suitable for aviation fields and other defense purposes, he said. Congressman Osmers pointed out that this area is the key to defense of Metropolitan New York.

Improvement of the Charleston, South Carolina harbor to enable it to accommodate a larger fleet was urged by Congresswoman Clara G. McMillan.

Congressman Harry R. Sheppard, of California, testified on damage caused by floods in his State in recent years and urged approval of a project calling for a $15,000,000 expenditure over a period of ten years to halt such devastating deluges.

Representative Edith Nourse Rogers, of Massachusetts, asked approval of the Merrimack River project. The project will help protect the City of Lowell, Massachusetts, from disastrous floods, as well as the rest of that area, she said.

Representatives A. Leonard Allen and John K. Griffith, of Louisiana, urged approval of the Red River project to serve Arkansas, Texas, and Louisiana. The project involves flood control, navigation, irrigation, sanitation, and drainage.[21]

The Members of Congress whose projects the Rivers and Harbors Congress endorses are grateful to the group for the support received. For example, Representative Lex Green of Florida, in speaking to the 1939 convention of the Congress about the Florida Ship Canal, said: "I can't go further into this, but I did want you to know that we appreciate the force which your organization has given to bring this matter to the favorable attention of those who are now on the Rivers and Harbors Committee of the House and the Commerce

ADJUSTMENT OF GROUP INTERESTS

Committee of the Senate. Your continued cooperation in this, the greatest of all waterway developments in our land, will be appreciated and, with your continued cooperation, work will begin on it within the next year or year and a half." [22]

Furthermore, officers of the Rivers and Harbors Congress receive excellent treatment before Congressional committees. In testifying in support of certain endorsed projects these officers emphasize the fact that the projects are the very ones which have been so ably justified and defended in the Projects Committee of their organization by certain Senators and Representatives.

In addition to Federal legislators, the advocates who appear before the Projects Committee include representatives of State and municipal governments, flood control and water conservation associations and districts, regional and local interest groups, and, indeed, the Corps of Engineers. At the same Projects Committee meeting in March 1940, for example: "Captain J. W. Moreland, United States Army Engineer corps and District Engineer in the St. Paul office, gave the committee further information on projects in that area. There is a drastic shortage of water in Minnesota, he declared. Among the projects on which Captain Moreland spoke were the Lac Qui Parle project, the Rousseau River project and the Red River flood control project." [23]

As a general rule, the Projects Committee will not place in the endorsed class any project which does not have a favorable, or at best a noncommittal, report from the Army Engineers. An official publication of the Congress states that "it is generally the policy of the organization to follow the recommendations of the United States Army Engineers . . . in advocating projects . . ." [24]

In addition to supporting endorsed projects and generally increased appropriations for water resources development, the Congress has consistently opposed valley authorities, any executive reorganization which might affect the USED, and the assumption by the United States of any jurisdiction over the tidelands. It has given a very limited approval to Federal hydroelectric installations and opposes all Federal steam plants.[25]

It is difficult to evaluate the general effectiveness of the Rivers and Harbors Congress because it serves as a clearinghouse for uniting and coördinating the activities of many local and sectional interests. The Congress itself puts forth bold claims as to its influence:

"The influence of the National Rivers and Harbors Congress has been perhaps a more controlling force on legislation approved than that of any other organization . . . Thus far there has been no adverse criticism of any of the recommendations made by the Congress in its resolutions and reports, and virtually every bill passed by the federal Congress for the improvement of harbors and waterways has been composed almost in toto of projects previously investigated and recommended by the National Rivers and Harbors Congress."[26]

"The [Rivers and Harbors] Congress is the country's oldest and largest water organization and *occupies semi-official status* by reason of its close liaison with the governmental agencies, legislative and executive, responsible for public works . . ."[27]

Though the group may be correct in making these claims, we shall be content to accredit it with being one of the most effective lobbies in Washington today.

In 1944–1945 when Senator Murray of Montana began to press hard for passage of his bill to establish a Missouri Valley Authority,[28] two national pressure groups were organized for the specific purpose of opposing the bill and all similar proposals to establish regional authorities and for the purpose of promoting states' rights in water legislation. One of these, the National and Regional Land and Water Organizations' Coordinating Committee, represents thirty-three water organizations varying in size from the National Rivers and Harbors Congress to the Propeller Club of the United States. Its secretariat is the same as that of the Rivers and Harbors Congress.[29] The National Water Conservation Conference represents an equally varied group of national and local units. Its main focus is "the preservation of the rights and interests of the several states" in water development.[30] The pattern of relations between these organizations and the Corps of Engineers is not established sufficiently to allow careful analysis; but no discussion of types of interest groups in the water field would be complete without mentioning them.

With these additional facts concerning the group interests with which the Engineer Department coöperates and the nature of this coöperation, what conclusions may be drawn concerning the responsibility of the executive agency to the people organized as interest groups?

It has already been pointed out that the Corps of Engineers has recognized the nature of the responsibility delegated to it by Congress to adjust group interests in planning for water development projects, and has conducted its organization and operations in accordance therewith. Through a planning procedure which involves a decentralization of organization and administration, the Engineers have encouraged participation by local interests for the purposes of (1) protecting and safeguarding the respective interests; (2) obtaining information desired and necessary for the planning of projects; and (3) making possible an adjustment of diverse viewpoints and the winning of consent for proposed action based on such an adjustment.

As for the techniques of interest group adjustment, the Corps of Engineers has formalized the participation of group interests in the planning process so as to avoid the dangers of irresponsible action resulting from informal pressure on an administrative agency. For the most part, techniques of consultation, rather than those of shared participation, with interest groups have been used so that an incentive is placed upon the Engineers to win assent, and the interest groups are free to criticize. In this connection the cordial relations between the National Rivers and Harbors Congress and the Corps of Engineers should be mentioned. Many would question that the Engineers, as employees of a Government department, should be members and participate in the activities of a large pressure group. Although the USED–Rivers Congress tie-up is not a clear instance of shared participation in administration, it does involve more than executive consultation with a pressure group. Only insofar as consultation alone is involved does it meet the established criteria for administrative responsibility.

We have said that the Engineers encourage local participation for the purpose of protecting and safeguarding the respective interests. In order to really succeed in this purpose, the Corps must make certain that the groups whose interests it seeks to adjust represent all those likely to be affected by the proposed developments. Unfortunately, this is seldom the case; and it cannot be said that opportunities for interest representation are in fact equalized. This is because the Corps has traditionally emphasized the highly local aspects of water developments. The survey planning procedure is so oriented that each individual project is considered almost exclusively in the light of effects on the area immediately adjacent to the improvement; so that insufficient attention is paid to the interests of those in the wider area where the effects may be of even greater long-run significance. This local emphasis begins with the requirement that all surveys be authorized by Congress. The Members of Congress who propose survey items for inclusion in omnibus navigation and flood control bills usually do so in response to requests of local interests in their districts. These interests often have neither the desires nor abilities to visualize the relationships of the improvements they seek to basin-wide developments. As indicated, the local emphasis is accentuated by the Corps of Engineers. It seeks to limit the scope of investigations to what was intended by the Congressmen responsible for the particular authorizations. And it has developed procedures designed to obtain the views of interest groups where they are most articulate, and this is most often at the limited local level.

Local emphasis, though it may jeopardize the extent to which the USED protects respective interests, has led to the winning of consent by the Corps for the reason that those groups best organized for any development are usually the local groups which have initiated the proposal and would benefit most immediately and directly by its adoption. These groups often want the project considered in the light of local effects. Thus, for example, if the benefits from dredging a harbor channel at an east coast Florida port are measured in terms of additional traffic and business for the localized port area, the project will be easier to justify economically than if the benefits were measured in terms of the general effects of the new project on all east coast ports in the vicinity; some of these ports might lose traffic to the newly developed one.[31]

However, where large and important group interests with which the Engineers deal regularly take definitely opposite views on a project, the Engineers will often avoid meticulously any commitments as to their own preferences and will submit the matter to Congress for adjustment. This procedure, though it does not constitute winning of consent for any one program of action with respect to the project in question, nonetheless appears to have contributed to the satisfaction with which interest groups view the conduct of the agency. A classic example of this attitude on the part of the Engineers is found in the 1941 review report on the Mississippi River flood control project.[32] For the middle section of the Mississippi River, that section between the Arkansas River and the Red River, the authorized project, adopted in 1928 and amended in 1936, 1937, and 1938, called for

ADJUSTMENT OF GROUP INTERESTS

levees on both sides of the river and for a floodway on the west side discharging overland into the Red River backwater. The Eudora floodway, as it was known, was to include 737,000 acres (70,000 in Arkansas and 667,000 in Louisiana) and was to be used only in times of great floods, when it might carry as much as one-third of the peak discharge of the Mississippi at that point. Although the Engineer Department was authorized to procure flowage easements by purchase or condemnation within the floodway, the opposition of local interests to the use of the area as a floodway was such that the Department negotiated few easements and commenced no important construction on this feature.

The House Committee on Flood Control in 1939 and the Senate Committee on Commerce in 1940 requested the Chief of Engineers to review the entire project for flood control of the Mississippi River with a view to recommending any modifications that might be desirable. The Chief of Engineers assigned the review report to the Mississippi River Commission. With respect to the middle section of the Mississippi, the Commission found that, due to changes in the river channel which had been brought about since authorization of the Eudora floodway and which had increased the capacity of the main river leveed channel, "there are three physically feasible alternatives to the adopted plan which will afford protection equal to that contemplated by the existing project when it was adopted and a fourth which will give protection equal to that afforded by levee and flood-wall projects on other rivers."

The five plans are as follows:

(1) Existing authorized project (described above).

(2) Narrow Eudora floodway. This plan would utilize a floodway roughly one-half the area of the authorized project. It was not acceptable, however, to local interests on the west side of the river, where the States of Arkansas and Louisiana and the levee boards and other local interests urged that the floodway idea be abandoned in its entirety and that levees on both sides be brought to parity at a grade which would protect against the project flood.[33]

(3) Eudora floodway extension only. This plan would utilize a floodway of only 190,000 acres north of the Eudora floodway and entirely within Arkansas. The plan would increase considerably, however, the area which would be flooded at crest of project flood north of the mouth of the Yazoo River, which enters the east side

of the Mississippi, north of Vicksburg, Mississippi. This plan was not acceptable to local interests on either the east or west sides of the river. It was opposed by Arkansas interests for the same reason that they opposed plans 1 and 2. It was also opposed, however, by local interests in Mississippi who desired that as much protection as possible be given the Yazoo backwater area, and that maximum flood heights in the main leveed channel be not increased by greater flood confinement than provided in the authorized project.

(4) Levee plan — project flood. This plan would eliminate the Eudora floodway and its northern extension and would confine floods between levees of equal grades on both banks, with net levee grades set one foot above the crest flow line of the project flood. This plan was advocated by local interests on the west side of the river. It was not acceptable to those in Mississippi because it would (1) inundate an added 247,000 acres of lower Yazoo basin and (2) wipe out the levee superiority of three feet accorded the east bank under the plan of the authorized project and thus expose both sides equally to inundation by a flood exceeding in volume the project flood. This the east bank interests considered improper because of the higher and older development of east bank lands.

(5) Levee plan based on 1927 flood. This plan was based on giving the east bank complete protection and the west bank increased protection at once, deferring the question as to whether a west side overland floodway should be built and what should be its location and dimensions until requirements were more definitely determined on the basis of future floods. The plan would build west side levees to a grade three feet above the flow line of a confined 1927 flood, but three feet under the flow line of a confined project flood and three feet under the grade of the east side levees. This interim plan would require the west bank to defer for the time being final and complete protection against the hypothetical project flood in order to eliminate the floodway. It would afford the east bank interests the grade superiority desired, though it would require them to concede some added flooding of the lower end of the Yazoo Basin in event a flood in excess of that of 1927 did occur.

Having carefully analyzed the alternatives to the adopted project, the Mississippi River Commission then proceeded to make no recommendation with respect to them. The section of their report headed

"Mr. Allen. In other words you do not want anything you have said to be construed as a recommendation of plan 5 over any other plan?

"General Tyler. No." [35]

The Engineers apparently preferred this procedure to making any recommendation that might alienate a significant group of local interests and Members of Congress with whom they must work.[36] And the Engineers must have recognized that, with no recommendation from the Engineer Department to guide them, the legislators might well select a "feasible" project which did not represent the best program for the development of the water resources of the nation's most important river.

The project finally adopted in the Flood Control Act of 1941 was a modification of plan 4 which provides for complete confinement of the project flood within the leveed channel, except that the differential in favor of levees on the east bank is to be maintained by building them up so that there is an additional three-foot freeboard over and above the project flood. Thus, the project will protect both banks against the project flood, but in case of a superflood, one of greater magnitude than the project flood, the east bank will preserve its present superiority and the flood waters will top the west bank levees and flow through Arkansas and Louisiana. This modified project represents a compromise worked out between Representatives Whittington (Miss.), Norrell (Ark.), and Allen (La.) of the House Flood Control Committee and Senator Overton (La.) of the Senate Committee on Commerce. It is not believed that this compromise proved particularly desirable to the Engineer Department, but the Department did not raise its voice in opposition before the Senate Committee on Commerce when the bill reached that Committee and Generals Schley and Tyler were requested to testify. Providing the compromise were "physically feasible," and it appears to be so, the Department could not very well raise its voice in opposition, since it had failed to make any recommendations in the first instance.

The procedure followed by the Engineers in this case appears to have won for them general commendation from all sides. Representative Norrell (Ark.) told the House of Representatives, "I very greatly appreciate the fine cooperation I have had from General Tyler, Major Reber, and other engineers from the War Department." [37] Other members of Congress from the west bank of the river expressed simi-

ADJUSTMENT OF GROUP INTERESTS

"Recommendations" contained no mention of any of the alternatives. The previous section, headed "Conclusions," after summarizing the alternatives, stated: "The Commission has laid down four alternatives to the existing plan of the adopted project for the middle section of the river. Any one of the five plans can be executed if and when local interests compose their differences. As the difficulties confronting the Department are not of an engineering nature, the Commission believes that Congress alone can fix the policy to be followed."

In reviewing the report of the Commission, the Chief of Engineers made no recommendation with regard to the alternatives. He merely restated the position of the Commission. "Since . . . feasible engineering plans for the middle section have been adopted . . . by the Congress but have been found impracticable of execution on account of nonengineering reasons, the Commission feels that any further modification, to be successful, must be based on considerations additional to those of engineering adequacy . . . Hence it has seemed proper to the Commission to explore and define avenues of modification that appear to be unobjectionable from the standpoint of engineering, leaving to the wisdom of the Congress the decision as to whether and to what extent the present project is inequitable and requires modification on that ground."

It is indeed hard to believe that the Engineers had no preference as between the adopted project and each of the four alternatives. As a matter of fact, a careful reading of their report and of their testimony before the House Committee on Flood Control reveals a preference for the interim plan (plan 5).[34] And yet the Engineers made no recommendations; they reported all alternatives "physically feasible." In the hearings before the House Committee on Flood Control, General Schley, Chief of Engineers, and General Tyler, President of the Mississippi River Commission, both insisted that the Engineers were not recommending any one plan. When asked specifically whether the Engineer Department favored plan 5 over plan 4, General Tyler replied in the negative; the Department had no preference.

"Mr. Allen (La.). General, I believe you stated repeatedly that the Board of Engineers is not recommending any one of these plans over any other plan?

"General Tyler. That is correct.

lar satisfaction, and Representative Whittington, in particular, from the east bank, reasserted his confidence in the Engineer Department.

With respect to adjustment of group interests, it can be debated whether or not the USED action in this case meets the criteria for responsible conduct. On the one hand, it contributed to the satisfaction with which interest groups viewed the agency. On the other hand, the Engineers did not themselves successfully balance group interests so as to win consent for any one program of action. With respect to other aspects of administrative responsibility discussed in more detail in later chapters, the action of the Engineer Department can be viewed as a shirking of responsibility. As the professional organization of government having primary interest in the development of rivers for flood protection, the Corps of Engineers was unwilling to inform Congress of that plan of improvement which would result in the most economic and beneficial development of the nation's greatest waterway. In order not to alienate any significant group of local interests, it was satisfied to avoid its responsibility for recommending professional policy and to report on all "feasible" plans of improvement.[38]

The pattern whereby the Engineer Department wins consent for its own actions by transferring to others responsibility for making decisions which may prove unpopular with interest groups is found in a more general form in the appropriation process. The Engineers will satisfy the interest groups with which they must deal by recommending the inclusion in the annual Budget of tremendous sums for river and harbor works. Upon the President, then, and not upon them, will rest the onus of having slashed these requests so as to fit them into the national budgetary picture.

It is an established rule of the Executive Office of the President — a rule inherent in the effective operation of an executive budget — that all representatives of executive agencies, in appearing before Congressional committees, must support and justify the Budget estimates, may not request additional funds, and may not state the amount requested of the Budget Bureau by the agency unless in reply to a direct inquiry from a Member of Congress. The Engineer Corps has circumvented this regulation through a long-standing administrative practice. The Chief of Engineers, in his *Annual Report*, publishes a detailed statement of the amount that can be profitably expended in the next succeeding fiscal year for new work on all projects.[39] This statement appears in November or December, about a month or so before publication of the President's annual Budget, and is given wide distribution throughout the nation. In his tables of justification for the Appropriations Committees of Congress, the Chief of Engineers has in the past submitted these schedules of amounts that can be profitably expended for new work, as excerpts from his annual report, and has thereby violated the intention of the President's ruling.[40] The amounts which the Chief of Engineers can profitably expend are greatly in excess of the Budget allowances. For example, for the fiscal year 1947:[41]

Item	Budget appropriation request	Budget expenditure estimate	Engineer Department estimate
Rivers and harbors	$101,944,000	$133,844,000	$360,114,000
Flood control	188,356,100	252,185,000	632,342,095
Total	$290,300,100	$386,029,000	992,456,095

The following testimony of Mr. William Driver, president of the National Rivers and Harbors Congress, before the House Committee on Appropriations indicates the significance of the Engineer Department procedure.

Mr. Driver. For instance the engineers said to the Budget Bureau in their report that they are geared to expend $248,279,900 on the adopted projects.

Mr. Snyder (Pa., chairman, subcommittee). Under the authorization?

Mr. Driver. Under the authorization, yes. These are adopted projects.

Mr. Powers (N. J.). Did you say they requested $247,000,000?

Mr. Driver. $248,279,900. What they mean by that is that they are in a position to advertise for bids and secure the necessary material with which to complete this work.

Mr. Powers. You say that the Army engineers told the Budget Bureau that they were geared to spend that amount of money in the coming year.

Mr. Driver. They could, yes.

Mr. Powers. Did they ask for that amount?

Mr. Driver. They did not ask it, but they merely made their recommendation.

Mr. Powers. I want to know whether they recommended that amount to the Budget Bureau.

Mr. Driver. Yes; I am dealing with Budget figures. By that I mean the Army engineers' Budget figures.

Mr. Powers. Did they ask the Budget Bureau for $248,000,000?

Mr. Driver. I hesitate to say that they asked for it, but they did state to the Budget Bureau that they were prepared to economically expend that amount of money.

Mr. Powers. But you have no information to indicate that they definitely asked for that amount.

Mr. Driver. They never do that. That is in keeping with the usual practice of the different departments with regard to the Budget Bureau. You who are posted on the matter would not construe that to mean that they made a recommendation. I doubt that the engineers would say that was a recommendation, but I will say to the committee that they explained to the Budget Bureau that they were prepared to expend economically on adopted projects the sum of $248,000,000.

Mr. Powers. What I mean is this: When the War Department goes to the Budget Bureau, they ask for a definite amount of money, and the Budget Bureau either gives it or does not give it. What I want to know is whether the Army engineers actually asked for $248,000,000.

Mr. Driver. As I have said to you, I am not prepared to say that they recommended it or asked it, but they did make the statement that they were prepared to use that money in an economical way.

Mr. Powers. I understand.[42]

Senator Bailey, then chairman of the Senate Committee on Commerce which handled all rivers and harbors legislation, in speaking before the National Rivers and Harbors Congress, used this administrative practice as a means of putting the bee on the President and exonerating the Engineers for reduced appropriation requests.

I can present to you very briefly the situation with respect to the rivers and harbors and the flood control [sic]. The budget for which the President is responsible and which he has warned us not to go beyond, not to raise unless we are willing to levy taxes sufficient to meet the raise, provides for flood control $110,000,000, for rivers and harbors $71,000,-000, and then for flood control in the Lower Mississippi $38,000,000, a sum total of $219,000,000. The Engineers of the War Department have reported that they could economically and wisely spend $195,000,000 for flood control, $152,000,000 for rivers and harbors, and $50,000,000 for flood control in the Lower Mississippi. That is to say, the President's budget allows for the expenditure of $219,000,000 by the present Congress at the present session; the engineers would approve $397,000,000. There is a difference of $178,000,000.[43]

As for attaining the public interest in the process of interest group adjustment, no definite conclusions can be stated at this point. If, as seems to be the case, the Engineer procedure requires or allows a continued emphasis on the localized aspects of individual water projects, an avoidance of responsibility on controversial projects, and a shifting of responsibility to others where its assumption might mean loss of some support, then it would appear that the public interest is not attained by the Corps. However, the determination of public interest depends upon a complexity of factors — among them legislative standards, the nature of professional responsibility, the extent of interagency coöperation and coördination. After these have been examined in succeeding chapters, the issue of public interest can be determined.

THREE

Responsibility to the Executive and Legislative Establishments

"It has always seemed to me that projects should be examined and authorized primarily on the basis of the greatest good to the greatest number of people. I understand the urge to get Federal money for expenditure in every congressional district in the United States but I believe, as I have often recommended to the Congress, that instead of taking a bite here and a bite there, there should be a well-considered and well-rounded plan for projects to be undertaken in a definite order of human and national preference and desirability instead of putting them only on a local geographical basis" — F.D.R.[1]

THE ENGINEER CORPS PROCEDURE FOR PLANNING water resource development projects has been examined in the light of responsibility to the public organized as interest groups. Next, this process must be analyzed in terms of responsibility to the executive and legislative branches of government. It has already been established that clearly responsible government can be attained with more certainty in the modern democratic state if the administrative agency is held directly responsible to the chief executive and indirectly responsible to the legislature. Such a system of responsibility permits a better consideration of the *public* interest and the *general* welfare by encouraging the coördination of related government programs, by requiring the focusing of responsibility, and by allowing a more effective conduct of legislative business in insuring that balanced programs are responsibly placed before the legislature and in relieving the legislative body of the task of holding individual officers and agencies to a detailed accountability.

The means by which the administrative agency should exercise its responsibility to both legislative and executive establishments have been discussed in broad outline. How does the Corps of Engineers meet the requirements established? To what extent, for example, does the Engineer Department present to the legislature, through the chief executive, the broad policy issues which necessitate legislative determination, and play down administrative details generally unworthy of legislative consideration? How does the Engineer Department assist in the drafting of definite legislative standards by presenting to congressional committees, after clearance through the chief executive, competent professional recommendations and advice? What is the extent and genuine sincerity of agency coöperation with the Executive Office of the President and interdepartmental committees to insure conformity of programs and activities with those of the chief executive and of other administrative agencies?

To answer these and other questions relating to the responsibility of the Corps of Engineers to the legislature and to the chief executive, it is desirable to examine the development of the agency's procedures and policies in these respects since 1934.

The Situation in 1934

As of 1934 the Corps of Engineers did not fall into the desired pattern of direct responsibility to the chief executive and indirect responsibility to the legislature. The Corps reported directly to the Congress, made little effort to clear its plans and programs with other executive agencies, and, in a sense, took its orders directly from the Congress.

As might be expected, Congress as a whole was not equipped to exercise direct control over the conduct of Engineer Corps civil functions. It was, rather, certain congressional committees — those with competence over navigation and flood control matters — that attempted to hold the Corps accountable. Witness the review resolution procedure in which Congress in effect allowed certain committees to legislate for it. Resolutions passed by these committees had the binding effect of law in directing an executive agency to carry out particular duties. The chief executive was denied the right of veto; he could not intervene between the committees of Congress and one of his executive bureaus.

In respect not only to the review resolution, however, but to the general conduct of Engineer Corps civil functions, the chief executive in 1934 had devised few means for interposing his authority in the direct relationship between the USED and the committees of Congress. And through this relationship, the committees and the Corps had developed a very close identity of interests. The House Committees on Rivers and Harbors and on Flood Control and the

Senate Committee on Commerce felt a proprietary interest in the Corps of Engineers and in the direct relations which prevailed.

In some respects the Engineer Department was more nearly responsible to individual Members of Congress directly than to Congress as a whole or to certain congressional committees. Senators and Representatives, knowing that the projects they sponsored could not as a rule be undertaken without favorable Engineer survey reports and support from the USED for congressional authorizations and appropriations, attempted to pressure the executive agency into approving those projects.

Close contact between individual Members of Congress and the Engineer Department in the conduct of surveys and reviews has been pointed out. It was the Member of Congress who initiated the legislative proposal for survey; he was first contacted by the District Engineer to determine the scope of the desired improvement and the interested parties; he was first to be informed of any change in the status of the investigation; he appeared before officers of the Corps in support of the proposed improvement. The procedure for congressional committee action on review resolutions was such as to encourage their adoption and, in this way, to encourage the individual Member of Congress in his attempts to secure a favorable report from the Engineer Department.

The nature of the authorization process — the enactment of omnibus rivers and harbors and flood control bills — was such as to further encourage direct responsibility to individual Members of Congress. When hearings were held by congressional committees on favorably reported projects to be included in omnibus bills, the testimony of the Members of Congress from the districts in which the projects were located was usually corroborated and supplemented by the Army Engineer present at the hearing.

In 1934, then, the Corps of Engineers exercised a direct responsibility to the legislature as a body, and more particularly to certain legislative committees and to individual members of the legislature. There was little, if any, coöperation with other executive agencies, as revealed by an examination of the *Orders and Regulations* in effect at that time. What were some of the consequences of this 1934 situation?

It has been noted that the Engineer Corps procedure for obtaining the views of interested groups was such as to encourage the traditional inclination of the Department to consider individual water development projects *in vacuo*, that is, almost exclusively in the light of benefits to be derived by the localized areas whose representatives initiated the requests for the particular projects. Direct responsibility to the legislature and lack of coördination with other executive plans and programs further emphasized this tendency. Omnibus authorization bills represented more nearly a sum of the individual projects desired by individual Congressmen, and on which the Engineer Department had submitted individual favorable reports, than they represented any rational national water development policy.

In this connection, another effect of direct responsibility to the legislature, apart from the consideration of individual projects, was a notable failure on the part of the Corps of Engineers to formulate any national water policy. The development of policies and programs was regarded by the Engineer Department as the duty of Congress; and Congress, they said, never specifically directed them to formulate either. The Department looked upon itself merely as an executing agent to carry out orders given to it. In reporting to Congress the Corps made no special effort to point up the broad policy questions, to recommend or encourage the enactment of laws containing a careful definition of national policy in the water field. This is brought out by the testimony of former Secretary of War, Henry Stimson, before a congressional committee in 1919. He said:

> When I was Secretary of War I found this situation, and I found that the reports of the Chief of Engineers which came to me were not "Is this an improvement which should be made in view of our particular funds this year — our particular budget this year — and in view of all the improvements in the United States taken at the same?" but simply and solely "Is this an improvement of a waterway which should be made?" And the Chief of Engineers said he was directed by Congress to report in that way, and this was the way he was going to interpret that, not in comparison with other projects, but simply whether in the milennium it would be a good thing for the country to have that waterway improved. When I said "That does not suit me at all. You come in here with a lot of propositions which you have approved, and you want me to approve, to improve the navigation of such and such a river and such and such a creek and such and such a harbor, I want to know how does that compare with the situation of the whole?" He said, "I have nothing to do with that. I cannot have anything to do with it. Congress will not listen to me on that. They reserve the judgment to do that themselves." [2]

A third effect of direct responsibility to the legislature stemmed from the congressional committees' proprietary interest in the Corps and in the direct relations between themselves and the Engineers. These committees and the Congress as a whole supported the Engineer Department in the fight to prevent control over its planning functions by any other executive agency, including the President's office. Prior to 1934 there had been three notable, and several less important, attempts to revise the procedure for planning river and harbor projects. All failed.

President Theodore Roosevelt appointed an Inland Waterways Commission in 1907 to investigate and report on the development and regulation of inland waterways. The preliminary report of the Commission, signed by all members except the Chief of Engineers, was submitted to Congress and the President in 1908. In his message of transmittal, President Roosevelt challenged the existing Federal policy of regarding navigation as of paramount importance in river development and pleaded for a comprehensive use of water resources. For this purpose he emphasized the need for creating a single Federal water agency. He said in part:

> The various uses of waterways are now dealt with by bureaus scattered through four Federal departments. At present, therefore, it is not possible to deal with a river system as a single problem, but the Commission here recommends a policy under which all of the commercial and industrial uses of the waterways may be developed at the same time . . . To that end Congress should provide some administrative machinery for coordinating the work of the various departments as far as it relates to waterways. Otherwise there will not only be delay, but the people as a whole will fail to get from our streams the benefits to which they are justly entitled . . .
> We shall not succeed until the responsibility for administering the policy and executing and extending the plan [for waterways improvement] is definitely laid on one group of men who can be held accountable. Every portion of the general plan should consider and so far as practical secure to the people the use of water for power, irrigation, and domestic supply as well as for navigation.[3]

The Commission report urged that Congress make provision for handling water resources on a businesslike basis, and that expert assistance be utilized in framing a national policy and prosecuting a national works program. For this purpose the Commission recommended setting up a water resources authority with power to plan and coördinate the work of the several bureaus whose functions related to inland waterways. The Chief of Engineers, General Alexander Mackenzie, in a separate statement pleaded for continuation of the *status quo* on the ground that "so radical a departure in the method of planning and executing the improvements of waterways as that proposed, the establishment of a permanent commission, is at least premature," if not "impracticable."

The Inland Waterways Commission was succeeded a year later by a National Waterways Commission, dominated by the House Committee on Rivers and Harbors and the Senate Committee on Commerce. So far as Federal policy and administration were concerned, results were slight, being confined primarily to a limited expansion of the scope of Engineer Department surveys. The Rivers and Harbors Act of 1910 required that surveys of navigable streams made in future include "a proper consideration of all uses of the stream affecting navigation." [4] Legislation designed to effectuate the recommendations of President Roosevelt and the Commission failed to get out of committee in the Congress.[5]

Although the recommendations of the Waterways Commission were not adopted by Congress, Senator Newlands of Nevada, a member of the Commission, persisted in efforts to obtain approval for a commission to plan the development of water resources for all purposes.[6] Presidents Roosevelt, Taft, and Wilson supported the Senator, Wilson having appointed a cabinet committee which again reported for a national waterways commission. But the interested congressional committees insisted upon their satisfaction with the manner in which the Engineers were planning water developments. "Senators looked to local matters first, called Newlands impractical, or thought he was 'out to get' the Army Engineers." [7]

Finally, in 1917, Newlands manged to obtain approval for the creation of a Waterways Commission "to formulate and report to Congress as early as practicable a comprehensive plan or plans for the development of the water resources of the United States . . . for every useful purpose." [8] The Commission was "to bring into coordination and cooperation the engineering, scientific, and constructive services . . . of the several governmental departments . . . that relate to study, development, or control of . . . water resources."

The Waterways Commission, however, was never appointed. Attention was diverted by the War; and in 1920 the Newlands amendment was repealed and in part superseded by Section 29 of the Water Power Act, which authorized the newly established Federal Power Commission to make investigations of the water resources of any region.[9] The Power Commission did very little under this authority, and the planning procedure of the Corps of Engineers was not modified at all.

The third important attempt prior to 1934 to revise procedure for conduct of Engineer Corps civil functions was made by President Herbert Hoover.[10] Under the Economy Act of 1932, the President was authorized to draw up executive orders for the transfer and consolidation of government agencies and functions. These orders were to be submitted to Congress and were not to become effective until sixty days after transmittal, during which time either House could veto an order by passing a resolution of disapproval. President Hoover, under this authority, drew up a series of executive orders proposing a large number of transfers, the most important of which involved a transfer of the nonmilitary activities of the Corps of Engineers, along with certain public works functions of other agencies, to the Department of Interior.

Hearings were held before the House Committee on Expenditures in the Executive Departments on the proposed transfers and consolidations. The hearings turned largely on two points: first, the fact that a new President had been elected and a retiring President should not tie the hands of the President-designate with hastily conceived executive consolidation plans; second, opposition to that provision which would affect the Corps of Engineers. Representative Whittington, a member of the Committee on Expenditures and later to become chairman of the House Committee on Flood Control, stated his opposition in no uncertain terms. Representative Mansfield, chairman of the House Committee on Rivers and Harbors, speaking at the *unanimous* request of his committee, appeared to urge defeat of the plans affecting river and harbor projects, as did many others.

The Expenditures Committee reported unfavorably on the plans, and a motion to disapprove was adopted by the House of Representatives on 19 January 1933. It may well be that the primary reason for disapproving the plans was the election of a new President, and the report of the Committee so stated. However, opposition to the transfer of the civil functions of the Corps of Engineers was significant; and it is felt that, regardless of the changing political situation, no plan for such a transfer could have won approval from the Congress. Republican Congressmen who might have been expected to support the Hoover plans (for example, Fred M. Davenport of New York) stated on the floor of the House their opposition to any change in the conduct of Engineer Corps civil functions.

To sum up the situation as of 1934, it may be said, then, that the Engineer Department was not responsible directly to the chief executive and indirectly to the legislature. Rather was it responsible to the legislature directly and hardly responsible to the chief executive at all. In its direct responsibility to the legislature, the Engineer Department did not aid in developing legislative standards by recommending any national water policy. It regarded the development of policy as the sole duty of Congress and regarded itself as no more than an executing agent of specific congressional directives. Finally, this very pattern of legislative responsibility helped win for the Engineer Department an unusual degree of congressional support.

The Years 1934–1949: A Changing Situation?

The history of the development of procedures for planning water resource projects between 1934 and 1949 is largely the history of attempts to break down this pattern of direct USED responsibility to the legislature. Those most active in working to bring about the change were the President; his Executive Office, including the National Resources Planning Board and its predecessor agencies and the Bureau of the Budget; and other Federal agencies, particularly the Bureau of Reclamation, which did not enjoy equally effective legislative support and whose functions and projects often came in conflict with those of the Engineer Department. Those most active in working to prevent a change — to maintain the *status quo* — were the Corps of Engineers and the Congress, more particularly the congressional committees and individual Members of Congress to whom the Engineer Department was in fact directly accountable.

Those who would change the pattern of administrative responsibility have been interested primarily in the development of a comprehensive national water program by the executive branch. They

RESPONSIBILITY TO EXECUTIVE AND LEGISLATURE

have attempted to achieve such a program by promoting a procedure and organization for coördinated planning.

A PROCEDURE FOR COÖRDINATED PLANNING

An analysis of the many proposals designed to achieve coördination of water plans within the executive branch reveals the broad pattern of initial preparation of basin-wide comprehensive plans and the subsequent translation of these plans into projects and proposals properly related to the best use and control of water in the basins.[11] It is desirable to mark out this pattern in more detail before proceeding with Engineer Corps policies.

In the preparation of basin-wide plans, emphasis is put upon the drainage basin as a whole — upon the concept of one river, one problem — with the objective of attaining a unified regulation and development of the river and its drainage basin for all beneficial purposes in effective combination. Six steps are necessary to assure preparation of sound basin and project plans:

(1) Identification of water and related problems and of the possibilities of resources development which are the most urgent in the basin; and adoption of a continuing program leading to the clarification of the problems, and to decisions with respect to the feasibility and propriety of development possibilities. A general investigation of the basin should be made as the first step in the identification of resources problems. The natures of the several problems and the areas which they affect most seriously should be determined, along with relations between the areas. From that general identification should follow a series of specific studies to obtain data which will establish the relative magnitude and urgency of each of the individual problems and its relative effects upon the social and economic structures of the basin.

(2) Determination of objectives of a basin plan. The objectives of the plan should indicate clearly the functions to be performed in each area in the basin. For example, if the dominant problems in a basin are need for hydroelectric power, flood control for known reaches of the main stream, and soil improvement practices on range lands; and if the resources of the basin are such that facilities for providing them appear practicable, then it is possible to determine the most suitable facilities together with the most favorable types of

regulation to meet all demands. The statement of the objectives, with a real and quantitative definition, forms the first general outline of the drainage basin plan. While at this stage certain parts of the plan may necessarily need further clarification, it will provide a general framework within which later and fuller information may be fitted. It will provide a basis for judging the relative weights to be given to the different resource needs and to the possibilities of alternative uses of the resources and the extent to which any two or more uses may be inconsistent.

(3) Interpretation of basic data, and the conduct of investigations which are considered preëssential to conclusions with respect to the development plan for the basin. The collection of data which are needed in specific cases must be founded upon concepts at least as broad as the objectives of the plan itself. It is not meant to imply that collection of basic data should begin at this point; data must be accumulated over a great number of years. At this stage interpretation of available data in terms of basin objectives should be made.

(4) Formulation in broad outlines of the development plan. The formulation of the basin plan follows from the general statement of objectives. The agencies concerned in the preparation of the plan should bring their expert judgments and facilities to bear on drafting the separate elements of the plan, on combining these elements into a single plan for the unified regulation and development of the drainage basin, and on fitting that plan into the regional and national pattern of resources development. The drainage basin plan should be revised from time to time on the basis of new information and data or on the basis of new needs for the control or use of the resources involved.

(5) Translation of basin plans into specific projects. Care must be taken to insure that the project plans conform in all respects to the drainage basin plans and to national and regional policies.

(6) Development of a construction program of approved projects. Since all approved projects in the many basin-wide plans cannot be built at one time, an orderly program involving priorities is necessary. Six-year programs of development projects should be prepared, reviewed, and revised annually. In formulating these programs applicable criteria for rating and timing should be developed.[12] The preparation of long-term programs in accordance with a definite

order of project priorities is a requirement for intelligent budgeting. In this connection, budgeting is the process of selecting top priority projects from a program in the light of the finances available, with due regard to the future financial commitments that the construction of such projects will involve. The selection of projects from long-range programs can be accelerated during periods of business depression as an aid to stabilization of employment and in times of danger as an aid to defense and war, and they can be decelerated during periods of inflation as a means of relieving pressure on critical materials and labor.

The preparation of basin and project plans in accordance with this procedure requires coöperation from the very beginning of the planning process among all agencies of all levels of government concerned with water resources development.

At their initiation, investigations should be organized so as to use the services of agencies best suited to handle all of the problems that are involved. Integration of investigations is effective if undertaken at the initiation of project studies, but is largely and necessarily perfunctory if delayed until the basic conclusions have been reached independently by those concerned. Unless field and office studies are carried on jointly by the interested groups before the findings are crystallized, the resulting plans will always be disjointed ones.

To this end, each important investigation contemplated by a Federal agency should be thoroughly analyzed *before* detailed work is initiated in order to determine its relation to the proposed work of other Federal agencies and of State agencies, and in order to insure that full use will be made of the experts available in the several units concerned with resources development. The agencies participating in the preparation of plans should submit joint or, at the very least, concurrent reports.

Near the completion of investigations and surveys in the field and in Washington, the tentative reports should be reviewed to make certain that the recommendations are not needlessly in conflict with those of other surveys, to assure compliance with national policies, and to afford final opportunity for relevant comments by all interested agencies.[13] Because important water resources developments affect all aspects of a basin's economy, they relate to the activities of a great many Federal agencies, as well as those of State and local units of government. For this reason, the reviews can be conducted best by a unit under the direction of the chief executive and representative of various resources interests.

AN ORGANIZATION FOR COÖRDINATED PLANNING

In order to achieve this desired procedure for water resources planning, it is necessary that one Federal agency have coördinating authority. But all efforts to establish a coördinating agency or to assign to an existing agency important functions in promoting the coördinated planning of water resources have been fought actively by the Corps of Engineers. A history of the conflict between the Engineers and those attempting to bring about the desired pattern is necessary for any evaluation of planning progress in the years 1934–1949.

President's Committee on Waterflow, 1934.[14] In February 1934, Congress, by resolution, requested the President to report on "a comprehensive plan for the improvement and development of the rivers of the United States; with a view to giving the Congress information for the guidance of legislation which will provide for the maximum of flood control, navigation, irrigation, and development of hydroelectric power." The resolution was sponsored by Senator Norris (Neb.) and was the outcome of a number of bills which had been introduced into Congress calling for the multiple purpose development of several watersheds.

The President appointed a Committee on Waterflow, consisting of the Secretaries of Interior, War, Agriculture, and Labor, to prepare the report. He requested this Committee, in coöperation with the Federal Power Commission and the National Planning Board, to prepare a preliminary report recommending the ten most desirable river basin development plans. After the preliminary report had been completed, the question of more detailed study would be considered by the President and the Cabinet committee.

The Committee submitted its report to the President on 17 April 1934, and the President submitted the report to the Congress some six weeks later. In his letter of transmittal, the President emphasized the tentative and preliminary nature of the report:

> In view of the above, I therefore, suggest that the Congress regard this message and the accompanying documents as merely a preliminary study and allow me, between now and the assembling of the next Congress, to

complete these studies and to outline to the next Congress a comprehensive plan to be pursued over a long period of years. Further legislative action on this subject at this session of the Congress seems to me, therefore, unnecessary.

The Secretary of War, Mr. Dern, signed the report "with strong mental reservations" and submitted a supplemental letter, addressed to the President. In this letter the Secretary protested that the Corps of Engineers was in a position to prepare a comprehensive plan and implied that a Cabinet coördinating committee or a planning agency was neither necessary nor desirable. He said:

> It [the report] ignores the fact that the data are available right now for the preparation of a comprehensive plan in full compliance with the request of Congress . . . If you now wish to expand the study beyond the scope prescribed by Congress the War Department will cheerfully and wholeheartedly cooperate with such other Departments as may be able to make a contribution to the study. It would, however, be wasteful not to make the fullest possible use of the painstaking and intelligent work performed during the past seven years. The Army engineers have a familiarity with water-use problems that could not be acquired by any new group without years of intensive and continuous study. To supersede them now instead of seeking their cooperation would be an inefficient procedure . . .
> National planning for putting the waters of the United States to the highest beneficial use is therefore well under way, so far as assembling the basic data is concerned . . . The Secretary of War and the Chief of Engineers can, within a very short time, prepare for you a comprehensive plan such as Congress has requested.

The Secretary further indicated doubt as to the desirability of fully comprehensive planning of the many land and water uses of river basins. He said:

> I have been trying to make up my mind whether all elements of a program of national planning should be combined in one plan. I do not think it is necessary to do so.
> For example, putting an end to stream pollution seems to have little or no connection with improving the streams for navigation, flood control, power, or irrigation, because it is chiefly a matter of the construction of sewage-disposal plants, which so far has been a municipal question.
> Soil erosion, except along the banks of the streams, would appear to be more closely allied with reforestation and restoration of plant cover

than with stream improvement. In some cases, however, soil-erosion work will involve the construction of dams.

Reforestation plays an important part in flood control and soil erosion but it may be carried on quite independently of river-improvement works.

And so it goes. Each of these activities is a special problem, to be handled by a special group of experts if satisfactory results are to be obtained. Here is a place where too much coordination, or the coordination of unrelated activities, might prove harmful instead of beneficial.

And finally, the Secretary appears to have protested against attempts by the President to interfere in the direct relations between the Engineer Department and the legislature on water resources matters. He said in this connection:

> The compilation of these data has been one of the most noteworthy and praiseworthy achievements of the Corps of Engineers, acting in pursuance of law *as an agency of the legislative branch* . . .
>
> It [national planning for water use] was initiated by Congress, which constituted the Secretary of War and the Chief of Engineers as its agents in finding the facts upon which it might act. They are required by law to report their findings to Congress, but this provision does not make it inconsistent for them to supply the information to you, so as to enable you to comply with Senate Resolution 164.

Reference by a member of the President's own Cabinet to an agency under his administration as "an agency of the legislative branch" and the implied reluctance to report to the President give further support to the pattern of responsibility outlined above and augur ill for future efforts by the President and his staff to change that pattern.

Water Planning Report, January 1935. In June 1934, the National Resources Board was appointed by the President with instructions to prepare a report on water resources in time for consideration at the next session of Congress.[15] For this purpose the Board set up a Water Planning Committee consisting of a representative of the Corps of Engineers and seven consultants from outside the Federal establishment. The report of the Water Planning Committee and of the Board, accompanied by the report of the Mississippi Valley Committee, was transmitted to the Congress in January 1935, in accordance with the promise made to the Congress by the President in connection with the preliminary report of the Committee on Waterflow.[16]

Among other recommendations, these reports emphasized the need for comprehensive planning of drainage basins for multiple use of their resources and the need for a planning agency to coöperate with and use the facilities of existing Federal and State agencies in coordinating water resource programs.

Major General Markham, the Chief of Engineers, signed both the Mississippi Valley and Water Planning Committee reports without reservations. When it came to approval of the Water Committee report by the Cabinet Resources Board, however, and to submission of the report to the President, the Corps of Engineers apparently had a noticeable change of heart. In a letter dated 28 September 1934 to Secretary Ickes, chairman of the National Resources Board, Secretary Dern stated:

I note the proposed plans and policies for the various sections of the report with much interest. The outline of the report to be submitted by the Committee indicates that it will have such a broad scope that the attainment of practical results will require a separate and distinct program for the improvement of the rivers and harbors of the country for flood control, navigation, power, and irrigation.

The War Department has been charged with the major activities of the Government in connection with the improvement of its rivers and harbors for many years, and as a result has accumulated a vast amount of data which is of course available to our Board. It is suggested that the War Department is most familiar with this problem, and it therefore should prepare for the consideration of the Board a definite program for the improvement of rivers and harbors of the country. Whatever coordination with respect to irrigation is necessary can be secured by cooperation with the Reclamation Service.[17]

Chairman Ickes chose to interpret the Secretary of War's letter as an expression of a genuine desire to coöperate with and support the Resources Board. In replying to the Secretary, he was careful to point out the extent to which the Corps of Engineers had already participated in the activities of the Water Planning Committee.

I appreciate greatly the spirit of cooperation expressed in your letter of September 28 concerning the work of the National Resources Board.

The planning organization which has been set up by the Board to deal with water problems seems well suited for the purpose. The members of the Advisory Committee of the Water Resources Section have worked together effectively for a year as the Mississippi Valley Committee of the

Public Works Administration. General Markham, as a member of the group, has at all times made fully available the rich store of relevant information, unpublished as well as published, possessed by the War Department. Of course, if you have something special or additional in mind, we should be very glad to have it.

The diversified professional experience of this Water Resources group has facilitated the coordination of water problems and their articulation with inseparable cultural and economic problems. The work within and beyond the Mississippi Basin has advanced to a stage comparable to that reflected in the report of the Mississippi Valley Committee, a somewhat cursory examination of which reflects not only a practical approach to water problems but an approach considerably broader than has been current practice.

It is gratifying to know that we can depend upon the continued support of the War Department.[18]

Ten days later, by which time the Secretary of War had been requested to review for final approval and submission to the President the full report of the Board and its technical subcommittees, the Secretary expressed an unwillingness either to approve the report or to discuss any reasons for not approving. He said, "I am not prepared to approve it in its entirety nor to discuss in detail at this time some of the items which appear to me to be of questionable merit." [19] This, despite the fact that the Chief of Engineers had previously signed the water section of the report without qualification.

Engineer Department participation in, and approval of, work of the technical subcommittees of a planning agency, and subsequent opposition to the finished product on a higher level became a familiar pattern, as we shall observe. All evidence indicates that the views of the Secretary of War were those of the office of Chief of Engineers. It will be remembered that the Secretary exercises little or no supervision over Engineer Corps civil functions.

In transmitting these water reports to the Congress, the President stated that "for the first time in our national history we have made an inventory of our national assets and the problems relating to them. For the first time we have drawn together the foresight of the various planning agencies of the Federal Government and suggested a method and a policy for the future." The President recommended that "we should be looking forward . . . toward the establishment of a permanent National Resources Board." [20]

Legislation for a permanent planning board, 1935–1936. Pursuant to the recommendations contained in the Board report and to the message of the President transmitting it to the Congress, Senator Copeland (N. Y.) in May 1935 introduced a bill to establish a permanent national planning board.[21] This bill had been cleared and approved by the President in a conference with officers of the Board in the preceding week.

Hearings on the bill were held before the Senate Committee on Commerce in June 1935. The only witnesses were Secretary Ickes, chairman of the NRB, Mr. Frederic A. Delano, vice-chairman, and Messrs. Merriam and Mitchell, members of the advisory committee. There were no communications from any Federal agencies, and the hearings reveal no opposition to the bill. Within two weeks the bill was reported favorably by the Committee but failed to come up for a vote before the adjournment of the Congress in August.[22]

With the convening of Congress in January 1936, new attempts were made to obtain passage of legislation for a permanent resources board. On 16 January, Representative Maverick (Tex.) introduced a bill for this purpose and a month later Representative Walter (Pa.) introduced a similar measure.[23] The House Public Lands Committee conducted hearings on these two bills in February and March. Letters of support for the legislation were submitted by the President, by the Bureau of the Budget, the Secretaries of Agriculture, Interior, Commerce, and Labor. Significantly, the Secretary of War submitted no expression of approval or support although he was a member of the National Resources Committee (the Board had been reorganized by Executive Order), had been requested by the executive officer of the Committee to prepare a letter, and was aware that the President had indicated in no uncertain terms that the bill was an Administration measure.[24] The President had said:

> THE WHITE HOUSE
> *Washington*
> *February 12, 1936*
>
> My dear Mr. Maverick,
> I entirely approve the establishment of a National Resources Board.
> As I stated in my Message to the Congress in transmitting the report of the National Resources Board on January 24, 1935, "a permanent National Resources Board, toward the establishment of which we should be looking forward, would recommend yearly to the President and to the Congress a priority of projects in the national plan."

Definite legislation would provide for the continuance of the effective work already done by the National Resources Committee and its predecessors.

Very sincerely yours,
/s/ Franklin D. Roosevelt

Testimony before the Committee was given by members and officers of the NRC, the sponsors of the two bills, and several representatives of nonpublic and State planning organizations. On 3 March 1936 the Committee completed the hearings and, after some discussion in executive session, tabled the bill.[25] The NRC made unsuccessful efforts to have the bill reported out. They were not supported in these efforts by one member of their Committee — the Secretary of War. The subject of the legislation was included on the agenda for a meeting of the Resources Committee scheduled for 11 April 1936. The Secretary of War did not expect to attend the meeting and, therefore, prepared a written report for the chairman, Secretary Ickes. The section of this report devoted to the subject of planning legislation is considered so unusual in the light of the views of the President and other Cabinet members that it is quoted in full:

The proposed legislation for the establishment of the National Resources Committee as a permanent Governmental agency is open to several objectionable features, some of which are as follows:

(a) The permanent addition of a new, independent, executive establishment is undesirable.

(b) No executive agency should be established by statute with fixed authority which interposes between the President and his Cabinet, even if some of the members are also members of the Cabinet.

(c) Such a committee, composed in part of full time members and in part of Cabinet members only to devote only part time would in effect relegate the Cabinet officers to the position of consultants to the full time members. The placing of the non-Cabinet members on a per diem basis of employment for so many days per month would not alter this fundamental objection.

(d) The proposed legislation confers upon the Committee very broad, but not clearly defined authorities and responsibilities, which are evidently intended to cover the direction of all Governmental activity in the development of national resources, a subject with which every Executive Department is deeply concerned. It would, therefore, add another independent agency to the Government organization, with functions overlapping those of the existing agencies.

(e) The proposed legislation is founded on the theory that planning should be disassociated from the execution of plans; that it is an end in itself; that there are professional national planners to whom all planning should be intrusted; that planning has not heretofore been carried on by Government agencies; and that existing agencies are incapable of planning efficiently the operations which they may safely be intrusted to execute. None of these theories is sound or proved by the test of time.

(f) There is no need to perpetuate the National Resources Committee with the inflexibility of permanent law. The definite accomplishments of the present Committee and its predecessors during the past two years, appear to be limited to the stimulation of interest in planning. Very large sums of money have been expended during this period, and volumes of literature have been issued in the form of reports, press releases, and similar publications. The Committee itself should be furnished with a detailed schedule of expenditures to date, including salaries and services performed by the higher paid personnel.

(g) Further experimentation along the lines of national planning, if desirable, can be provided without permanent legislation. The President now has ample authority to create, or to continue, interdepartmental boards of such composition as he may desire, to prescribe their duties, and to change their membership and functions as circumstances may prescribe. Permanent legislation would circumscribe his authority in these respects. The existing Departments and independent agencies can perform in their several fields of specialization every legitimate planning function of the National Government. A coordinating board, if needed, can be best provided by a Committee of Cabinet Members, having as their deputies the heads of the various agencies directly concerned with the execution of the work. Such a board would insure continuity of effort, full availability of the detailed information assembled by the said agencies, and definite coordination of activities. The support of State, regional, or local planning boards in whole or in part at Federal expense is of doubtful wisdom and legality. Cooperation between Federal and State agencies is commendable, but their commingling is not of manifest propriety. It is doubtful if State planning agencies can be so formed as not to have as the basis for their enthusiastic cooperation their desire to secure Federal expenditures in their respective States.

(h) The all-embracing title of the proposed committee — National Resources Board — may be accepted as referring to "nature resources" only; nevertheless, the scope of such a committee would be virtually unbounded. Its authorities and recommendations would undoubtedly supersede those of the Departmental heads. It is impossible to forecast the ultimate effects of permanently delegating the control and direction of the development of the national resources of the country to any single agency, with the drastic reductions which would necessarily follow in Departmental authorities and responsibilities. The purposes of the legislation would appear to embody in a single agency the major responsibilities and duties of the entire National Administration.[26]

One cannot say precisely to what extent Engineer Department failure to support the bill contributed to the inaction of the House Committee. On the one hand, it is true that several members of the Committee expressed concern as to the proposed agency's encroaching upon the rivers and harbors functions of the Corps of Engineers.[27] On the other hand, the Committee on Public Lands has never been as favorably disposed to the Corps of Engineers as the Committees on Rivers and Harbors and Flood Control; and other factors — opposition to the establishment of a new independent agency; controversy over Secretary Ickes (some feared the bill would conflict with his proposal for a Conservation Department, though the Secretary denied this; others feared the bill would place too much authority in the Secretary of Interior) — seemed to have had more direct bearing. However, the action, or failure to act, of the Engineer Department is significant with respect to later developments.

On the Senate side of the Capitol, the planning board bill, which had been reported favorably at the last session, was making little headway. In May, Senators Hayden (Ariz.) and Copeland (N. Y.), both of whom were guiding through the Senate the 1936 Flood Control Bill, attempted to add the planning legislation to that bill. When their proposed amendment came up for debate in the Senate, it and the original planning bill, S. 2825, were both recommitted to the Committee on Public Lands on the motion of Senator O'Mahoney (Wyo.).[28] The speeches of Senators O'Mahoney and Pitman (Nev.) indicated that the Public Lands Committee had passed a unanimous vote that morning requesting such reference. It was stated that setting up a separate board would be an insult to Secretary Ickes and would be inconsistent with the recent action of the Senate in voting to change the name of the Department of Interior to Department of Conservation; and it was implied that the existing NRC, with Cabinet members, was opposed to the bill. The latter implication was true only with regard to one Cabinet member, the Secretary of War. Why the former idea persisted in the face of active support of the planning board bill by the Secretary of Interior is not known. Commenting on this Senate action, the executive officer of the NRC complained, "Thus through the action of 'supporters' of Secretary Ickes, and through the 'fine' hand of the Corps of Engineers we must start all over again with another Senate Committee." [29] Although Senator O'Mahoney did offer a proposal, completely rewriting the planning bill, the rush at the end of the session prevented any action by the Public Lands Committee.[30]

Flood Control Bill, 1936. A serious conflict between the views of the Corps of Engineers and the National Resources Committee developed with respect to the Flood Control Bill of 1936. Variant opinions on the policies and projects in this important law, the first to establish a Federal flood control policy for the United States as a whole, are discussed more fully in Chapter IV. The controversy over the bill, however, affected proposals for planning organization, and as such calls for attention here.

With the disastrous spring floods in the eastern United States in 1936, interest in general flood control legislation quickened on several fronts. In the first place, there was a concerted effort to initiate large-scale flood damage studies. At least one resolution was introduced in the Congress calling for a study of conditions resulting from the recent floods and for recommendation of measures for reconstruction and flood prevention.[31] The Water Resources Committee on 2 April 1936, with the written concurrence of Lt. Col. Edgerton of the Engineer Department, recommended to the NRC a procedure and program for flood control studies.[32] This program called for (1) the immediate expansion by the Geological Survey, Engineer Department, and WRC of scientific investigations designed to improve hydrologic data; (2) the undertaking by Federal agencies of special coöperative research on two highly controversial problems associated with flood control — effects of soil erosion on flood peaks and means for estimating benefits and costs of flood control projects; (3) intensive studies of floods and flood control measures in the major basins which had experienced recent flooding; (4) "that because there is a danger that many new flood studies of the type suggested under (1) and (2) may be undertaken without reference to each other by Federal and State agencies in the near future, and because of the desirability of correlating the new flood control investigations with the current nation-wide water resource program now in preparation by the Water Resources Committee, the National Resources Committee be authorized to act as a clearing house of information and opinion concerning flood investigations . . . It would correlate programs and promote cooperative attack on problems which too frequently in the past have been viewed from a narrow viewpoint. It would bring the State agencies into the Federal program. It would insure consideration of land misuse as well as engineering construction, and of water uses as well as flood control alone."

In the meantime the President, from Hyde Park, had radioed the White House and the Secretaries of War, Interior, and Agriculture on 27 and 29 March that he had no objection to the appropriation of five million dollars for study of flood control, "but that this [is] only one phase of the subject and that it is inextricably tied in with other projects and cannot be separated from them from the point of view of Federal planning and Congressional appropriations. The preamble and purpose of legislation should include all forms of land misuse covering erosion, reforestation, afforestation, water storage, irrigation, and drainage . . .

"Because the National Resources Committee includes representatives of all necessary agencies it occurs to me on further consideration that this committee could well be the primary agent in correlating the flood investigation work. Please consider this together and take up with the Congress."

The Secretaries did consider this matter together at the next meeting of the NRC on 11 April. Despite the facts that the Engineer Department representative on the Water Resources Committee had signed the memorandum on flood control studies, and, more important, that the President had indicated to the Secretary of War his approval of a five million dollar flood control study with the NRC acting as primary agent, the Secretary of War vigorously opposed approval of the WRC program. In the same letter in which he opposed permanent resources board legislation he stated:

> The program in its entirety would appear to largely represent duplication of work now under way. The War Department has completed studies of the major stream basins throughout the United States, and has been

authorized by general legislation to keep these studies up to date. In addition, the appropriate committees of Congress, with legislative authority for such authorization, have already called on the Department for a review of previous studies on the streams suffering major flood losses during the recent severe floods. A large number of field parties are now actively engaged in the field in accumulating this data, in determining the economics of remedial measures, and in preparing reports for submission to Congress. Since these reports will be full and complete, the abstracting of data for consolidation in a single report would certainly be duplication. It is understood that the Geological Survey is already engaged in run-off studies, and that the Soil Conservation Service and Forestry Service are likewise investigating their particular relationships to flood conditions. My own Department is cooperating closely with the Department of Agriculture and is prepared to cooperate even further in these investigations. The situation from an investigation standpoint would appear well in hand, and it is difficult to see where the contemplated expenditure would not represent almost entirely duplication of both effort and funds.[33]

With Secretary Dern alone voting in the negative, the National Resources Committee agreed to recommend to the President (1) the issuance of an executive order designating the Committee as a clearinghouse of information on flood studies, and (2) the appropriation or allocation of additional funds in the amount of $500,000 for proposed flood investigations to be conducted by the Water Committee, utilizing appropriate bureaus of the Federal or State governments. The first recommendation was effectuated by Budget Circular No. 338 of 14 May 1936. Action was never taken on the second recommendation; attention became focused elsewhere — on the general Flood Control Bill which by this time had been reported to the Senate by its Commerce Committee.

Before turning to that legislation, however, it might be well to point out in the action of the Army Engineers on the flood study proposals a repetition of the maneuver, "about face," already found in their action on the 1935 National Planning Board report and to be found yet again in the 1936 flood control controversy. The Corps representative on the technical committee of the planning agency approved proposals for coördination; this approval was reversed at a higher level.

A national flood control bill, authorizing projects approved by the Corps of Engineers, in the amount of $400 million, passed the House of Representatives in August 1935.[34] This bill was drawn up by the

Flood Control Committee of the House as an "emergency measure," designed primarily to insure that flood control projects would receive a large allocation under the $4.8 billion emergency relief appropriation then under consideration by the Congress. It was not considered a vehicle for determining important policy in resources development. When the bill emerged from the Senate Commerce Committee, however, it had been expanded in scope to expound new national policy in river development for flood protection.[35] In deriving this policy, the Commerce Committee had worked almost entirely with the Army Engineers; and the Committee reported that "the bill . . . has the approval of the Department of War." No mention was made of the President nor of other agencies of Government; for, indeed, it appears that they had not been consulted and did not approve the bill as reported.

The legislation was amended on the floor of the Senate to meet some of the objections of the President, the National Resources Committee, and the Department of Agriculture arising from failure to give consideration to agricultural plans for flood abatement; but these amendments were not considered adequate by the NRC.[36] On 3 June 1936 the Director of the Budget requested the Resources Committee to submit a statement of its views on the enrolled Flood Control Bill within twenty-four hours.[37] The speed was necessitated by the President's impending departure on a southwestern trip. As there was not sufficient time to convene a meeting of the full NRC, the chairman of the advisory committee forwarded to the Budget, through Chairman Ickes, and with the personal approval of himself and Ickes, a memorandum prepared by the chairman of the subcommittee on flood studies of the WRC. The subcommittee on flood studies (consisting of Abel Wolman, chairman, also chairman of the WRC; Lt. Col. Edgerton, USED; Thorndike Saville, New York University; and Thomas R. Tate, Federal Power Commission) at a meeting on 29 May 1936 had passed the following motion unanimously:

"That the Chairman is requested and authorized to prepare a statement setting forth the four deficiencies of the Flood Control Bill pointed out by him, and to be followed by a statement that in the light of these comments the Bill should not be approved."

The four deficiencies of the bill, stated in the memorandum of the subcommittee chairman which was forwarded to the Budget, were in brief as follows: (1) the bill ignores in large measure the close and delicate interrelations among land use and waterflow, and those other uses and controls of water such as irrigation, hydroelectric power, pollution control, and water supply; (2) the policy of allocation of costs proposed by the bill is inequitable and in the long run will tend to foster abuses of sound conservation principles; (3) numerous flood control projects are authorized for areas where other conservation problems are no less urgent or where combinations of flood control and other types of work might be practicable; (4) the list of specific construction projects is premature, containing many projects still under study.

On 6 June the chairman of the advisory committee received a joint letter from Lt. Col. Edgerton and Mr. Tate stating that it was their understanding of the action taken on 29 May that the statement of the subcommittee chairman, when drafted, "would be submitted to the members for their consideration and further comment"; that they "believe that the memorandum unduly emphasizes theoretical imperfections in the bill and expresses unwarranted apprehension concerning the practical results of this enactment"; and that they recommend that the bill be approved.

The chairman of the advisory committee forwarded this letter to the Budget, pointing out the misunderstanding with respect to procedure and further pointing out that Lt. Col. Edgerton and Mr. Tate "had subsequently reconsidered their opinion concerning the merits of the Bill and have . . . recommended that the Bill be approved." And indeed the Army Engineers had about-faced again in its work with the WRC on flood control policy; for, although there was apparently a misunderstanding with respect to submittal of the drafted statement to subcommittee members for review, the Engineer representative did not challenge the fact that the chairman had been instructed by a unanimous vote of the subcommittee to prepare a statement recommending that the bill be vetoed. At a later date, the USED representative agreed that he had voted for the motion to request veto of the bill and then changed his mind.[38]

The President signed the bill on 22 June and immediately attempted to rectify some of its deficiencies by designating the National Resources Committee as coördinating agency in the selection of those projects to be undertaken immediately with work relief appropriations in certain eastern river basins which had been subjected to disastrous spring floods. These efforts at rectification were unsuccessful in the long run. The procedure and organization for project planning set forth in this first national flood control law came to be repeated in subsequent laws, though they continued to meet with Presidential opposition. Thus, for example, in approving the Flood Control Law of 1938, President Roosevelt said:

I have approved this bill with some reluctance . . . It is not a step in the right direction in the set-up provided for general government planning.

I am in doubt as to the value of some of the projects provided for and it is unwise to place recommendations to the Congress solely in the hands of the Engineer Corps of the Army in some cases and of the Department of Agriculture in other cases.

Coordination of all such public works involves a wider survey and the examination of more national problems than any one bureau or department is qualified for.

In these respects future legislation will be vitally important, in order to give to the Congress and to the country a complete picture which takes all factors into consideration.

For the coming year, however, I shall try to obtain this coordination by asking for complete consultation between all groups and government agencies affected. In this way the whole of the problem can be made more clear. I have, however, approved the bill because it accomplishes a number of good things, with, however, the reservation that its deficiencies should be corrected as early as possible.[39]

The deficiencies were not corrected. The Corps and its supporters were opposed to a coördinating agency; and the controversy between the Planning Board and the USED, despite some interludes of harmonious coöperation, continued until the coördinating board was abolished by Congress.

Public Works and Drainage Basin Reports, December 1936. One interlude of harmony occurred with reference to the report on *Public Works Planning,* submitted to the President by the NRC in December 1936.[40] In this report the Committee recommended unanimously "the permanent establishment of an advisory planning board . . . for (a) correlation of planning within the Federal Government; (b) correlation of planning among Federal, State, and local jurisdictions; (c) stimulation and assistance to the planning agencies within the Federal Government and in regions, States and localities; and (d) fundamental research directed toward the development of basic national policies and programs." Part II of the public works report consisted of a report of the WRC on *Drainage Basin Problems and Programs*. The National Resources Committee said of this latter report that it represents the first coördinated attempt to formulate a nation-wide water plan and program through the joint efforts of Federal, State, and local agencies, official and nonofficial. The WRC, in its unanimous report, made no specific recommendations concerning a planning agency. It did emphasize, however, the need for a coördinated national water plan.

"Too often, also, specific water problems have been treated solely in terms of particular localities, urban or rural, with resultant injury to other localities on the same river system. Water development in general has been haphazard . . . Without discussion of the merits or demerits of existing policy, it may be affirmed with confidence that a *coordinated* Federal water policy is now needed, not a collection of *unrelated* policies applicable respectively to individual types of water problems."

This admirable self-criticism on the part of the Engineer Department (Gen. Markham signed the report) is unfortunately inconsistent with the attitude of the Department towards planning legislation and all efforts to clarify national water policy.

Senate Joint Resolution 57, 1937. In January 1937, Representative McClellan (Ark.) and Senator Caraway (Ark.) introduced companion joint resolutions to authorize the Chief of Engineers, through the Secretary of War, to submit to Congress a full report or a series of reports embodying a comprehensive national program and plan for the control of floods of all major rivers of the United States and their tributaries.[41] Although the House Committee on Flood Control held no hearings on the resolution, it did request advice from the Secretary of War, who endorsed the legislation, stating in part:

"The surveys undertaken by the War Department under the provisions of House Document 308, 69th Congress, first session, have made much of the basic data necessary for the formulation of this plan available, and the extension of this data as required could be undertaken over a period of time with funds previously or hereafter authorized for flood control purposes to permit considered up to date plans being submitted for the consideration of Congress where acute flood conditions exist."[42]

The Secretary of War had cleared his endorsement through the Budget Bureau, as required, and had been informed by the Director of the Budget "that there is no objection to the submission of this report." Resources Committee files reveal that the Budget failed to consult the Committee on this matter, and this was to prove somewhat embarrassing for the Budget within a few months.

The House Flood Control Committee amended the resolution so as to (1) extend the authorization to include "provisions for . . . utilization of water resources through the building of power dams or a combination of power, reclamation, conservation, and flood control dams, and all works necessary for an effective soil and water conservation," and (2) authorize the Secretary of Agriculture to make reports on run-off and waterflow retardation and soil erosion prevention. In its report, the Committee said that "the enactment of this resolution will result in the highest and most competent authorities [War and Agriculture Departments] submitting to Congress a plan, in the nature of a blueprint, so to speak, of projects recommended for construction to effectuate the results desired."

Debate on the resolution in the House reveals that it was drafted and supported with the intention of requiring that the Engineer Department report directly to Congress, thus protecting the Department against any interference by the planning agency, and of insuring that the water development functions of the USED be protected against any legislation authorizing additional valley authorities.

Concerning the first point, reporting directly to Congress, the Engineer Department and many Members of Congress were highly displeased with recent action of the NRC and the President in regard to the Engineers' comprehensive survey of the Ohio and Lower Mississippi Valleys. In a letter of 3 April 1937 to the Secretary of War, the President had requested that the pending report of the Chief of Engineers on these valleys be submitted to him *prior* to submission to the Congress. The Secretary of War complied five days later. His letter of transmittal demonstrates well the resistance of the Engineer Department to any interference with its direct responsibility to the legislature.

I submit herewith, in compliance with the instructions contained in your letter of April 3, 1937, the report of the Chief of Engineers containing a comprehensive flood control plan for the Ohio and Lower Mississippi

RESPONSIBILITY TO EXECUTIVE AND LEGISLATURE

Valleys called for by Resolution of the Committee on Flood Control of the House of Representatives.

Under former procedure this report would be submitted direct to the Chairman of the Committee on Flood Control. The Department has been of the view that the scope of the project makes it of such significance in the national program as to warrant deviation from the established procedure. Accordingly, the report was prepared prior to receipt of your letter of April 3, with a view to its transmission to Congress with an appropriate message from you. A draft of such a message is also transmitted herewith.[43]

The letter contains a definite implication that only under certain special conditions would the Engineers be justified in deviating from the established procedure of reporting directly to the committee of Congress; and that the USED is the judge of such conditions in each case.

The President, after obtaining a hurried review of the report by the WRC, and after discussing the matter with members of the staff of the NRC, submitted the Engineer Department report to the Committee on Flood Control, accompanied by the views of the NRC Advisory and Water Resources Committees and by a letter to Representative Whittington. In this letter the President said:

The report of the Chief of Engineers considers, of course, only one phase of the very large interlocking problem. For this reason it may be considered neither truly comprehensive nor effectively integrated. No opportunity has been possible, in this short space of time, to consider the report in relation to other Federal agencies, such as the Soil Conservation Service, the Forestry Service, the TVA, the U. S. Public Health Service, the Federal Power Commission and others.

For example, the report apparently does not consider the flood regulation work now under construction or planned by the TVA, which system is expected to reduce crest floods at Paducah and Cairo by 200,000 second feet.

No serious delay can come if the present Session of the Congress appropriates funds to undertake and continue some of the projects already authorized by previous Congresses for the Ohio and Mississippi Rivers. The amount of these appropriations should, of course, be viewed in the light of the budgetary necessities of the Government.

In the light of all the circumstances attaching to this report, I am requesting that a further and complete study be made by all of the Government agencies involved, sitting together as a group to make recommendations for a complete picture. This report should be available to the Congress by next January.[44]

The joint resolution, then, was intended in part to prevent similar interference by any planning agency in the direct submittal to Congress of other Engineer Corps comprehensive surveys. Representative Whittington, for example, said on the floor of the House:

We hear much about planning and planning agencies. Much of the planning and many of the agencies would be duplications. I can understand that the Chief Executive would like to be fully advised respecting the conflicting recommendations submitted by the various departments of the Government but in national flood control we have adequate plans. The Corps of Engineers are the best equipped flood control engineers in the world. They are efficient; they are dependable; they have utilized the services of the best available civilian engineers in the preparation of reports. The establishment of additional agencies for flood control would result in delay. It would be difficult to improve on the set-up in the Corps of Engineers.[45]

Representative Englebright (Calif.), the ranking minority member of the Flood Control Committee said: "This bill . . . places the coordination, the working out of proper flood control measures on all of the major streams of the United States in the hands of the Board of Engineers of the United States Army. That is where the problem should rest." [46]

The joint resolution was further supported as a means of warding off the passage of the Norris-Rankin valley authority bills. On 3 June, the President had submitted to the Congress his now famous message advocating seven additional TVA's.[47] The Norris-Rankin bills were designed to implement this message; neither, however, had made much progress in the legislative mill. With respect to protecting the Engineer Department against such new legislation, Representative McLean (N. J.) said:

The resolution contemplates a comprehensive study of the Corps of Engineers. That is wise. There is no need to create new agencies. The Army engineers have proven their ability to guide and direct the conservation of our natural resources. The Corps of Engineers has the confidence of the American people. It has been studying the conservation of our natural resources since the beginning of the Government. It has always been called upon when any great public work has been contemplated by the Government.[48]

With the addition of an amendment providing that "any plans or reports which include or recommend projects for reclamation . . . be prepared in conjunction with the Department of the Interior," the resolution passed both the House and Senate with no opposition.[49]

The National Resources Committee was very much opposed to the joint resolution for reasons which are so well presented in a memorandum on the subject that the document is quoted at length:

The resolution, as passed by the Senate originally was intended to provide Congress with a comprehensive statement on flood control projects in major drainage areas. Such a statement is needed as an aid in the consideration of individual projects. However, as the recent experience with the Ohio-Lower Mississippi comprehensive flood control plan has shown so forcefully, strictly flood control plans are of little value unless integrated with larger programs for use and control of water for other purposes. The House amendments extended the authority to include "provisions for . . . utilization of water resources through the building of power dams or a combination of power, reclamation, conservation, and flood control dams, and all works necessary for an effective soil and water conservation." The amendments are in the right direction, but provide procedures unsatisfactory for the the following reasons:

(1) The planning of the use and control of water resources and related land resources is distributed by law among numerous agencies not included in the resolution. The Federal Power Commission, the U. S. Public Health Service, the International Boundary Commission, and the TVA are among the more important ones omitted. Moreover, several bureaus within the Department of Agriculture are concerned with water utilization from standpoints other than run-off retardation and erosion control. Although all of the agencies are actively engaged in water planning work, under the joint resolution they are not authorized to a formal part in preparing plans. The current controversy between the War Department and the Federal Power Commission over hydroelectric and flood control development on the Connecticut and Merrimac Rivers illustrates the difficulties to be expected to result from the procedure outlined in the resolution. The resolution does not indicate clearly whether or not the War Department and the Department of Agriculture reports are integrated. Under the Flood Control Act of 1936 the two sets of reports need not be integrated, and the present plan seems to be to submit them to Congress independently.

(2) In preparing the report on *Drainage Basin Problems and Programs* [the national water plan] at the direction of the President last year, all

interested State as well as Federal agencies participated in the program. For example, State sanitary engineers and conservation commissioners submitted proposals through the State planning boards. Water planning activities were initiated in most States as a result of the first national survey. Arkansas is drawing up its own water plan; North Dakota, South Dakota, and Minnesota have prepared and approved a tri-state plan for the Red River of the North drainage area; and Oregon has worked out a tentative program for the Willamette Valley. Continued cooperation with those State and local groups in the planning of developments which affect those groups primarily is vital. Such cooperation is not authorized or directed in the joint resolution.

(3) In his message of June 3, 1937 the President outlined a program of planning of natural resources on a regional basis. A group of regional planning bodies to be integrated through a national planning board and the Budget Bureau were the essential features of this program. If the present joint resolution were to be approved, the authority for such planning would in effect be delegated to the Secretary of War. He would report directly to Congress. The planning would not be organized on a regional basis. It would not "start at the bottom" with the State and local groups as suggested by the President. The results would not necessarily be coordinated with the work of other agencies. There would be no provision for revising and checking the program in the light of national budgetary considerations and of national planning policies. This would render unnecessary and ineffective the regional organization proposed by the President.

(4) A comprehensive program has been prepared, and the machinery to improve it is in operation. The Water Resources Committee of the National Resources Committee now is carrying forward its first report on *Drainage Basin Problems and Programs*. The majority of the States have submitted proposed improvements to the plan; several regional conferences on the subject have been arranged. All Federal agencies are preparing to make improvements in the broad program or in the specific projects. The War Department, the Department of Agriculture, the Department of the Interior, the Treasury Department, the Federal Power Commission, the TVA, two representatives of State engineers, and two university men are represented on the Committee. A first tentative plan is being advanced and a second report will be ready during the next regular session of the Congress.

(5) By the resolution, the Secretary of War becomes the National water planning agency and the Public Works agency in the water field, of the Federal government. He reports directly to Congress instead of to the Chief Executive and, in addition, reports for coordinate Federal agencies hitherto of equal responsibility in water resources work.

The joint resolution substitutes a new water planning structure for that which was developed during 1935. In so doing, it ignores certain Federal agencies, it interrupts the present joint State-Federal planning relationships, and it establishes an organization contrary to that proposed by the President in his message on regional planning.

In view of these considerations, the joint resolution should not be approved by the President.[50]

The chairman of the advisory committee, Mr. Delano, was of the erroneous opinion that the joint resolution could not be vetoed by the President and he wrote of his concern in this respect to the President's son and secretary, James. The President replied:[51]

THE WHITE HOUSE
Washington
August 12, 1937

Dear Uncle Fred:

Jimmy has shown me your letter. It is a Joint Resolution; it is on my desk, and I am going to veto it!

You will hear from me in a day or so in regard to a committee to be formed to bring in a comprehensive plan by January.

Affectionately,
/s/ F.D.R.

The President in his veto message stated that he proposed "to present to the Congress in January a comprehensive national plan for flood control and prevention and the development of water and soil conservation, such a plan to be prepared by all of the many Government agencies concerned."[52] To implement this proposal, the President on 20 August requested the NRC to proceed with its review and revision of the report on *Drainage Basin Problems and Programs* and, through this means, to present to him in January 1938 a comprehensive plan for submission to the Congress.[53] The report prepared in response to this request, and published as *Drainage Basin Problems and Programs, 1937 revision,* contains improvements in the 1936 statements of the principal water and land problems in the various drainage areas; alterations in the earlier plans for the solution of regional problems; adjustments of the six-year project priorities in terms of the plans as revised; and some additional contributions to a consideration of Federal policy as it affects a national water plan.

Except for a foreword by the NRC, the report is the work of the

Water Resources Committee. The Secretary of War signed the NRC letter of transmittal to the President, and the Chief of Engineers signed the WRC letter of transmittal to the full Committee. With respect to the latter, however, the following sentence in the letter is significant: "As might be expected, each member of a Committee of this size cannot concur with each and every part of a report of this scope and character, but the report represents the consensus of opinion of the Committee." And, indeed, the Engineers did not concur with that section of the report dealing with Ohio-Lower Mississippi River regulation. This section was designed as a progress report of the special committee set up by the President, in accordance with his letter to Representative Whittington, to review the Engineer Department comprehensive survey of these two rivers.[54] The special committee, in effect, recommended that the Congress not authorize any additional flood control plan based on the survey submitted by the Engineer Department, and that certain comprehensive studies be inaugurated at an early date. "The interlocking problems presented by the Ohio and Mississippi Rivers . . . are so complex in character, so broad in scope, so inadequately explored as yet, and so far reaching in their relationships to various unsolved problems of national policy that it would be most unwise for the Congress to authorize at this time any additional general flood control plan for them." [55]

Administrative reorganization. In January 1937, the President had transmitted to Congress with his full endorsement and support the report of his Committee on Administrative Management.[56] This Committee recommended that a permanent National Resources Board be set up as the planning arm of the President. Such a Board "should serve . . . as a general staff for gathering and analyzing relevant facts, observing the interrelation and administration of broad policies, proposing from time to time lines of national procedure in the husbanding of our national resources, based upon thorough inquiry and mature consideration; constantly preparing and presenting to the Executive its findings, interpretations, conclusions, and recommendations for such final disposition as those intrusted with governmental responsibility may deem appropriate." The Board should not make final decisions upon broad questions of national policy — "a responsibility which rests and should rest firmly upon the elected representatives of the people of the United States"; nor should the Board be involved in "special administrative responsibilities which properly devolve upon the appropriate departments of the Government set up for that purpose." To carry out its duties, the Board should "work through various technical committees, consisting partly of Government personnel and partly of other qualified persons [such as] the present . . . Water Resources Committee."

The administrative reorganization bills designed to carry out the proposals of the President's Committee became the subject and object of one of the most bitter controversies between the Congress and the President to occur at any time during the full tenure of Franklin D. Roosevelt. It is not within the scope of this study to analyze this controversy. Suffice it to say that the highly watered-down reorganization bill finally adopted in 1939 contained no provision for a planning board, despite a special appeal by the President to Senator Byrnes (S. C.) and Representative Cochran (Mo.), chairmen of the Senate and House Select Committees on Government Organization.[57]

Supporters of the Corps of Engineers were the chief source of opposition to planning board legislation in the Congress. The following letter of Representative Cochran to a planning agency proponent in Iowa points this out in certain terms:

> Personally, I am strongly in favor of the National Resources Committee. There is a bloc in the House known as the River and Harbor bloc which interests itself in the improvement of our Rivers and Harbors for navigation purposes, as well as flood control. This is a very strong bloc, but although I reside in the Mississippi Valley I am not a member of the bloc or of any bloc. This bloc is very powerful and I have been advised that the leaders of the bloc are almost unanimous in opposition to the National Resources Committee.
>
> I am very sorry to hear this, because I fully agree with you in reference to the value of this Committee. Personally, I tried to get it in the Reorganization Bill and I will make the suggestion again if the Committee is continued, which I expect it to be.[58]

Equally frank is a statement of Representative Driver (Ark.): "In that recommendation for a reorganization I found one suggestion that stopped me absolutely from supporting it, and that was the creation of a Water Resources Board, an agency of your Government that would stand on an equal plane with your great organization of Army Engineers. I will not stand for its displacement by any body of people that may be drawn together. They have proven their loyalty and worth to your Nation during the more than 100 years in which they have operated on your behalf and I am unwilling to supplant them with a board of theorists. (Applause)." [59]

Though planning agency authorization failed of acceptance in reorganization legislation, special provisions protecting the status of the Corps of Engineers were enacted. From the very first moment that any proposed reorganization legislation was reported by committee to either the Senate or the House, that legislation contained a provision exempting the USED and its rivers and harbors functions from all provisions of the bill, thus insuring that, under his authority to reorganize and consolidate government agencies and functions, the President might not transfer Engineer Corps functions to any other agency, and further insuring that a planning agency would not have authority to assume any Engineer Corps functions. This exemption is noteworthy because, with respect to the reorganization bill which passed the Senate in 1938, the Engineer Department was the only "regular" agency of Government so favored and, with respect to the reorganization bill as finally passed in 1939, the Engineer Department was one of the relatively few "regular" agencies exempted.[60]

In the House report on the final reorganization bill of 1939, a detailed explanation of the all-inclusiveness of the Engineer Corps exemption was given in order to allay any suspicions as to preferred status of that agency.

The Engineer Corps of the Army . . . have the function of prosecuting civil works for river and harbor improvement and flood control. The Engineer Corps, under this subsection, cannot be transferred to the jurisdiction of any other agency, nor can such functions be transferred. Further, the head of the agency, the Chief of Engineers, and his office cannot be transferred to any other agency nor can his functions be transferred, nor can the Engineer Corps or the Office of Chief of Engineers or any office in them be abolished or its functions abolished. No consolidation within the Engineer Corps or the Office of Chief of Engineers can be effected. But a reorganization plan can provide for the transfer to the Chief of Engineers or the Engineer Corps of any function or any agency, subject only to the exception that no transfer to the Engineer Corps or the Chief of Engineers of any of the enumerated agencies, or their heads or functions, may be made.[61]

By statutory limitation the Reorganization Act of 1939 expired in 1941. But immediately after the War in 1945 President Truman requested Congress to reënact reorganization legislation. He asked specifically that no agencies be exempted from its provisions.[62] The Reorganization Act of 1945, enacted in response to this request, contained relatively few exceptions, and most of them were independent regulatory commissions. However, the civil functions of the Corps of Engineers were given special treatment. The Act established three categories of exempted agencies, and the Corps of Engineers was the only agency in the most protected category — that for which Congress prohibited any reorganization whatsoever.[63] The favored treatment accorded the Corps of Engineers throughout gives further testimony to the strength of the direct ties between the USED and the legislature, and to the congressional support enjoyed by the Engineer Department in its resistance to any coördination imposed from above.

The Engineer Department supporters were not satisfied, however, with the specific exemptions obtained in the reorganization legislation. First in the Rivers and Harbors Act of 1938, then, more positively, in the Flood Control Act of 1939, and later in subsequent rivers and harbors and flood control legislation, they included provisions designed to "contribute materially to the clarification of the limitation of the reorganization power of the President of the United States." The Flood Control Act of 1939 provided that "the surveys authorized to be performed under the direction of the Secretary of War as well as all duties performed by the Chief of Engineers under the direction of the Secretary of War shall be functions of the Engineer Corps U. S. Army, and its head, to be administered under the direction of the Secretary of War and the supervision of the Chief of Engineers except as otherwise *specifically* provided by Congress." [64]

Regional conservation legislation, 1937. While the reorganization legislation was under consideration, the President sent to Congress his message on regional authorities in which he proposed the division of the nation into eight areas for the purpose of planning and, in some cases, management of natural resources conservation and use. The President said:

Apart from the Tennessee Valley Authority, the Columbia Valley Authority, and the Mississippi River Commission, the work of these regional bodies, at least in their early years, would consist chiefly in developing integrated plans to conserve and safeguard the prudent use of waters, water power, soils, forests, and other resources of the areas entrusted to their charge . . . When the National Planning Board is established [on a permanent basis], I should expect to use that agency to coordinate the development of regional planning to insure conformity to national policy, but not to give the proposed National Planning Board any executive authority over the construction of public works or over management of completed works.[65]

In this way, legislation to authorize a permanent planning board became tied up with another highly controversial measure. Bills to effectuate the President's proposal were introduced in both Houses of Congress and hearings were held by the Senate Committee on Agriculture and Forestry and by the House Committee on Rivers and Harbors.[66] Despite a further Presidential message urging legislative action on his proposals, the Senate bill was never reported out of committee and the House bill, though reported in an amended form, was never considered by the House.[67]

The hearings revealed that almost all opponents of the bills, no matter whether their hostility to the legislation was inspired principally by opposition to hydroelectric power, by fear that the favored position of navigation interests in river development might be adversely affected, or by other causes, expressed complete confidence in the Engineer Department, and an unwillingness to see any tampering with its duties in regard to rivers and harbors and flood control.

In testifying before the House Committee on Rivers and Harbors the Chief of Engineers stated under questioning that the Engineer Department had prepared, in response to a Committee request, an unfavorable report on the legislation, but that this report had failed to clear the Budget Bureau. On request, he agreed to provide the Committee with a copy of the report. Although General Schley did not state his categorical opposition to the legislation, the following testimony[68] indicates opposition and, what is more important, reveals the continued restricted concept of planning held by the Engineer Department, the continued orientation of the Department to thinking in terms of single projects and single water uses, and the continued importance which the Engineer Department attached to its direct responsibility to the Congress and to congressional committees:

General Schley. In governmental or business affairs of great magnitude, planning is essential to wise development and efficient management. In a form of government such as ours, however, planning is necessarily restricted to the extent to which the prescription of general policies has been delegated by the Congress.

In a country as extensive as the United States, embracing such a variety of topography and diversity of needs, complete integration of planning by a central agency is difficult. To deal with this problem the Engineer Department is organized into districts which are effective regional planning agencies for definite watersheds. Correlating the efforts of these regional agencies are larger territorial agencies, known as divisions, which integrate the plans of the districts where these plans have geographical unity. Over all, is the coordinating authority of the Chief of Engineers, which standardizes the efforts of the subordinate planning and correlating agencies.

Generally speaking, there are but two kinds of planning: (1) Technical or departmental. This includes the test of economic justification. (2) Fiscal or budgetary. This deals with the years within which or the rate at which plans can be or should be prosecuted. It seems to me to be important that the two kinds of planning be not confused.

The Government being divided functionally into departments, presumably these departments contain technical personnel capable of planning as well as execution. In point of fact, many of the ablest specialists in the several branches of endeavor are to be found in the appropriate departments of our Government.

Concerning budgetary planning, a Bureau of the Budget, properly organized and efficiently manned, can be depended on to break down the total planned expenditures into component items for each activity of the Government (and for each region of the country if necessary), in a manner to conform to the policies of the Executive, extending as many years into the future as is wise or practicable . . .

In its planning, in compliance with the directives of Congress, the Corps of Engineers has followed the procedure laid down in the statutes. In my judgment it is completely in accord with our representative form of Government. It is democratic because the initiative is in the people and is effected through the action of their duly elected representatives in Congress. All State, municipal, and other local governing bodies and all individuals having any real or imaginary interests are given full opportunity to be heard in open hearings, to have their statements recorded, and to submit written arguments and briefs. The Congress and its appropriate committees have control at the outset and retain it throughout the procedure . . . The system of planning is regional, workmanlike, thorough, and economical.

I have spoken of the effectiveness of planning when directed at a specific objective. When the Congress wants plans for a canal, plans are made for a practical canal at least cost which will meet the requirements, but which will not block some other more important project of some other kind which is foreseen as reasonably prospective. When Congress wants plans for a flood control project, then the plans are made to present the most practical, economical, and effective flood control program which will not sacrifice or prevent the development of more valuable navigation, hydroelectric power, irrigation, or other uses of land or water . . . I have no feeling at all that we are failing to obtain all the desirable factors of planning . . .

Mr. Dondero (Mich.). General Schley, do you see any justification for the setting up of regional planning agencies to supersede your own Corps of Army Engineers as proposed in this legislation?

General Schley. I think I can best answer that, sir, as I answered a question similar to that a moment ago. I do not myself feel the absence of full planning in the work which the Corps of Engineers does or its relationship to work closely connected with it. My own specific thought on the subject along that line is that if Congress sees fit to create such agencies as you refer to, I trust that it will not disturb some very close relationships and possibilities of cooperation which we now enjoy in our work. And those I might group into three classes. One is our contact with the local interests and the local government representatives of the areas within which a project is to be done. That is the first.

The second is our contact with Congress, and particularly the three committees that I referred to, this committee, the Committee on Flood Control of the House, and the Committee on Commerce of the Senate, as well as the appropriation committees, with which we have very close relationships and which I think should not be disturbed.

The other is the cooperation which we now enjoy between our own Corps and those bureaus of the two departments I referred to which have so much work which comes closely to us. Those are in the Department of the Interior, the Bureau of Reclamation, the U. S. Geological Survey, and in the Department of Agriculture the Forestry Bureau, Soil Conservation Bureau, and Weather Bureau.

If this statement by the Army Engineers is compared with the memorandum of the Resources Committee recommending veto of Senate Joint Resolution 57, the very fundamental nature of the conflicting points of view of the two agencies is highlighted. Since the Resources Committee view was that held by the President and the Engineer Corps view that apparently held by the Congress; and since the Engineer Corps, though a purely executive agency, continued to report directly to the Congress, the inevitability of constant conflict in bureau-department-chief executive relations and in executive-legislative relations is seen.

An effort at revising planning procedure, 1939–1940. In the years 1939 and 1940 the President and his newly organized Executive Office (consisting primarily of the Bureau of the Budget and the National Resources Planning Board)[69] made a serious effort to improve water planning procedures within the limitations of the laws they had been unable to revise.

First, in order to provide agency coöperation in the preparation of reports on multiple-purpose projects, the President and the Planning Board secured the adoption of a written agreement, known as the Tripartite Agreement, between the Corps of Engineers, the Bureau of Reclamation, and the Bureau of Agricultural Economics.[70] This agreement authorized free interchange of information between the three agencies in the field in the preparation of reports, and joint consultation in the field and in Washington. As we shall see later, the Tripartite Agreement did not eliminate conflicts and divergencies in resulting reports, atlhough it did contribute to some improvement in field coöperation.

Second, the NRPB and the Bureau of the Budget drew up an executive order providing that Federal construction agencies (1) continuously report all surveys and investigations to the Executive Office of the President to enable the NRPB to study and report on the projects proposed thereby from the standpoint of any related national, regional, or local development plans; (2) clear with the Executive Office all survey and investigation reports before such reports are sent to Congress, so that statements may be included in the agencies' reports as to the relationship of all proposed developments to the program of the President; (3) at the same time that they submit their budget estimates to the Executive Office, submit six-year programs of public works construction, with projects arranged according to priorities.[71]

The significance of this order is indicated by the enumeration of its provisions. With respect to the Engineer Corps, it represents a bold attempt on the part of the President's office to break up the pattern of direct responsibility to the legislature, to require the Corps to report first to the President. The results of this attempt will be analyzed elsewhere.[72] Suffice it to say that they have been largely unsuccessful and disappointing.

An effort at developing a national water policy, 1939–1941. Despite some five years of attempted policy coördination, the nation in 1939 had no program which could be dignified by the name "national water policy." Realizing this, the NRPB in October 1939 organized a subcommittee on national water policy of the Water Resources Committee "to develop and recommend a comprehensive Federal policy for control, development, and utilization of water resources." [73] Great importance was attached to the study by the members and staff of the WRC.

Throughout the work of the subcommittee and the preparation of its final report, there appears a lack of genuine and sincere coöperation on the part of the Corps of Engineers and a constant effort to protect its own interests from any recommendations for change. In its preparatory work, for example, the chairman asked for comments from each member on the double question, "Do the members of the subcommittee accept the need and the principle of better coördination and will they work wholeheartedly for it?"

"General Robins replied affirmatively to both parts of the question, *in principle,* but emphasized the ideas of cooperation as well as coordination and remarked that each member of the subcommittee should properly reserve the right to protect the specific interests for which he has been made responsible." [74]

In reviewing the text of the preliminary draft report, "General Robins doubted the need for a coordinating agency with the broad powers and possibly cumbersome duties recommended in the report . . . On the whole he considered it [the report] too idealistic and far-reaching to be of practical use." [75]

General Robins dissented from the final report transmitted by the subcommittee to the WRC. He wrote to the subcommittee chairman: "I am unable to concur in this report sufficiently to recommend adoption in its entirety by the Water Resources Committee. Some of the recommendations in the report have merit in furthering comprehensive planning for water projects, but others seem to me unnecessarily complicated, time-comsuming and not in the interests of efficiency and economy. The report has been made in a worthy cause and the necessity for withholding my concurrence is regretted." [76]

In the meeting of the full WRC which considered the report presented by its subcommittee, the chairman of the full committee "inquired of General Schley [Chief of Engineers] whether, after considering the report in detail, he would feel that he could sign the report, *with specific reservations,* or could furnish the committee with an appropriate statement indicating his *specific objections*. General Schley replied that he would be glad to attempt the latter . . . Mr. Barrows [chairman of the subcommittee and also a member of the WRC] said he was gratified that General Schley found practical this suggestion by Mr. Wolman [chairman, WRC] to make a statement of favorable and unfavorable parts of the report, his gratification was not only in behalf of the consideration of the report, but also to indicate the position of the Corps of Engineers in the matter of national water policy." [77]

The Chief of Engineers was unsuccessful in his attempt to state specific objections, as the following letter to the WRC chairman indicates:

During the meeting of the Water Resources Committee on November 8, 1940, you requested that I submit comments on the second draft report of the subcommittee on national water policy dated October 31, 1940.

I agree in general with the idea that Congress would do well to give consideration to existing laws on the development of rivers with a view to simplifying, specifying and standarizing principles, policies and practices, and with a view to requiring appropriate action by States or other local governments to undertake to protect Federal waterway improvements against destructive practices. However, Congress has done this from time to time in the past and the description of conditions today in these regards in the draft report is overstated in my opinion.

While I favor coordination, of course, the duties of the coordinating agency proposed to be established are unnecessarily extensive and, in fact, duplicating in nature. Excellent cooperation is now experienced among the Federal agencies engaged in the planning for a development of water resources. Also the duties of the proposed agency go far beyond coordination.

I realize the good cause which prompted this report, and I recognize the value of some of its recommendations, but in view of my disagreement with a considerable portion of it which goes to the substance rather than to details or to its form, I regret that I cannot concur in it as a whole.[78]

This letter is notable in at least three respects: (1) It indicates the continued general satisfaction of the Engineers with the *status quo*. (2) It indicates a continued positive opposition to any coördinating agency. (3) It indicates a continued unwillingness on the part of the Engineers to recommend policies to Congress; Congress has made changes from time to time in the past on its own initiative and can do so in the future.

Thus, the report on national water policy — a report to which the WRC attached such great importance and in the successful completion of which it placed great hopes — went to press with a double dissent from the Corps of Engineers.[79]

Planning Board legislation, 1938 to finale. Though it became apparent in 1938 that Congress was not disposed to grant permanent authorization for a National Planning Board in reorganization, regional authority, or other legislation, President Roosevelt, in order to continue the planning agency at least on a temporary basis, requested annual appropriations of Congress on the basis of work relief and other less permanent authorities. In the face of considerable opposition, appropriations were made in 1938 and 1939.[80] In early 1940, however, an all-out effort, supported largely by friends of the Corps of Engineers in the Congress, was made to deny all appropriations to the Board for the next fiscal year. Only personal appeals by the President to strategic members of Congress stating that a continuance of the Board and its work was essential to the conduct of his own executive office saved the day for the agency.

The President had recommended an appropriation of about one million dollars for the Board for fiscal year 1941.[81] The House Appropriations Committee failed to include any estimate, "due to the fact that an investigation of the legislative history of the Board fails to disclose any basic law authorizing its existence." The House of Representatives, thereby, was not called upon to vote on any aspect of the Board's appropriation or legislation when the money bill passed the House. Those who had blocked permanent planning board legislation were set to reap the harvest of their efforts.

Nation-wide publicity was given to the action of the House and to the President's indication, at two press conferences, of his personal interest in the situation. The Senate Appropriations Committee reinstated the Board's appropriation to the extent of $710,000; and the Senate upheld this amount, with a proviso designed to limit somewhat the functions of the Board, after a test vote to reduce the appropriation to $100,000 had been beaten by a single vote, 34 to 35. Senator Overton (La.), one of the most ardent supporters of the Army, chairman of the board of directors of the National Rivers and Harbors Congress, and chairman of the subcommittee on rivers and harbors and flood control of the Senate Committee on Commerce, offered the amendment to all but wipe out the Board. Senator Byrnes, who led the fight for the NRPB, recognized the opposition of friends of the Army Engineers and attempted to allay it by stating:

The statement has been made that it [NRPB] conflicted with the action of the Army Engineers. I have in my hand a statement from the Chief of Engineers, dated January 23 [about two weeks earlier], in which he says:
"This Corps has always adhered steadfastly to the view that it is in no sense a policy-making branch of the Government, but solely an executive agency to carry out the functions required by law. *Pursuant to this general policy* there has been complete cooperation between the Corps of Engineers and the National Resources Planning Board in carrying out its purposes. This cooperation has not only extended to the Chief of Engineers and his staff in Washington but also to the field offices of the Corps."

The Majority Leader, Senator Barkley, also recognized the significance of the opposition engendered by friends of the Army and, in his final appeal to the Senate to uphold the Board, said:

There should not be any jealousy or controversy between the National Resources Planning Board and the Corps of Army Engineers. I have always been a defender of the Corps of Army Engineers, and I am now. I think they constitute probably as expert a body of men as there are employed by the Government of the United States. There is no real controversy between these two bodies. They have up to now worked together; they have coordinated their functions and activities; they have advised with one another; and there has been no real cause for any controversy between the National Resources Planning Board and the Corps of Army Engineers with respect to the development of our national resources. There may be less cause for friction in the future . . .

The coöperation between the Corps of Engineers and the National Resources Planning Board, pictured by Senators Byrnes and Barkley and by the quoted statement of the Chief of Engineers, unfortunately did not exist, and Senator Barkley's prediction of less cause for future friction did not materialize. We have already cited, for example, the work of the Water Resources Committee on national water policy.

It was with respect to obtaining House concurrence with the Senate action, however, that the greatest Administration effort was made. The President was aware of the "well known opposition from the group which is interested in rivers and harbors and flood control projects," and it is reported that "Judge Mansfield [chairman of the Committee on Rivers and Harbors] received some word from the President concerning the bill," as well as the Speaker, the Majority Leader, and Representative Woodrum (Va.), the leader of the House conferees. The conference committee reported in disagreement on the Senate amendment; and Representative Woodrum on the House floor moved that the House recede and concur with the Senate. He read to the House the following personal letter from the President and commented, "Now, Mr. Speaker, I do not see how the legislative branch of the Government can turn a deaf ear to this President or to any President when he comes to the legislative branch of the Government and says he needs a reasonable facility to help him to secure information and to coordinate information, to analyze reports of the vast and multitudinous operations of this complex Government."

THE WHITE HOUSE
Washington, February 14, 1940

My dear Mr. Woodrum: I am dictating this just as I leave to go on a little holiday to take the place of the one I missed last summer.

It relates to the appropriation to continue the National Resources Planning Board for the coming fiscal year.

As you know, the reorganization plan last spring placed the National Resources Planning Board under the office of the President. This was done because the President — any President — really needs some kind of coordination and research staff; in other words, expert assistants to study many problems which relate to different phases of government. So many questions continue to arise — many of them in response to policy problems on which Members of Congress and the committees of Congress query the President — that he has to have some kind of machinery for his own information and that of the Congress.

I have found the National Resources Planning Board of very great assistance in this.

Because the President is, under the Constitution, the responsible head of the whole executive branch of the Government, I must earnestly plead for the continuation of the National Resources Planning Board. I am sure that this need applies not to me personally as President but also to any President in the future . . .

That is why I am appealing to you and to other Members of the House to help me . . .

With my sincere regards,

Faithfully yours,

/s/ F.D.R.

The House debate turned largely on the nature of the President's personal request and on the conflict between the Corps of Engineers and the Board. The Majority Leader, Representative Rayburn, concluded the debate with a stirring appeal to Democrats "to stand by this recommendation, this request, this urging upon us by our Democratic President. (Applause)." By a partisan vote of 184 to 130, the House upheld the Board.

The long fight of the Planning Board to obtain permanent status ended in June 1943 when the Congress abolished the agency, consigned its records to the National Archives, and provided that its functions not be transferred to, nor performed by, any other agency.[82] This decisive Congressional action, taken in the face of a personal appeal from a wartime President to retain the agency for postwar planning, was a final victory for the Congressional rivers and harbors bloc.[83] The victory was won with the aid of a strong and cohesive Republican minority, which was joined by a group of recalcitrant Democrats. They opposed the appropriation for the Board not only because of the Board's conflicts with the Corps of Engineers, but also because such opposition represented: (1) a chance to hit the President on an issue not too closely connected with the war (hence the recurring emphasis on "the President's Uncle," in referring to Mr. Delano, the chairman of the Board); (2) a desire on the part of Congress to take the lead in "policy" matters, and opposition to "bureaucrats" generally; (3) a belief that the Board's policies tended leftward instead of "back to normalcy" (hence the outcry against the Board's work in planning for human resources and the labeling of the Board's social security report as an un-American socialist cradle-to-grave scheme; and the outcry against the Board's work in planning fiscal policy and against Harvard's Alvin Hansen).[84]

As for the opposition engendered specifically by friends of the Engineer Corps, the following statement by Representative Case (S. D.) on the floor of the House represents a guarded estimate of the situation:

> But the difficulties that have developed for the National Resources Planning Board rest upon a feeling in some quarters that it has become too much of a superreview board, setting up a superengineering agency, setting up a superplanning organization, with veto power over the responsibilities of the regularly created executive departments.
>
> It has never seemed to me that when the Corps of Engineers, for example, passes upon the engineering features of a particular improvement project, it should be necessary for the National Resources Planning Board to have a superengineering body to give superengineering review to that which has been passed upon by the Corps of Engineers.[85]

In the Senate, Senator Overton spoke for the Engineer Corps supporters when he contended that, since the committees of Congress pay no heed to the Planning Board, the Board might just as well be eliminated:

> I am familiar, for example, with the work done by the Army engineers with reference to rivers and harbors, flood control, and various other projects. They make their recommendations made by the Chief of Engineers with respect to these projects. However, I understand — I may be in error — that there was an executive order that all the projects approved by the Board of Engineers for Rivers and Harbors should be submitted to the National Resources Planning Board before any report thereon was made by the Chief of Engineers. Nevertheless the Commerce Committee of the Senate and the Rivers and Harbors Committee of the House act upon the recommendations of the Chief of Engineers. We do not wait for any recommendation to be made by the National Resources Planning Board in respect to any such projects.[86]

USED v. Budget Bureau, 1943 to date. With the abolition of the NRPB, all significant coördination of the planning of water resource development projects came to an abrupt end. The two important advances in planning organization and coördination, effected in 1939 and 1940, were reversed, at least temporarily. The Corps of Engineers refused to continue the Tripartite Agreement; and the executive order, administered jointly by the Budget Bureau and the

Planning Board, requiring public works agencies to clear through the Executive Office of the President all reports to Congress and to submit six-year public works programs, became no longer appropriate.

The Bureau of the Budget, however, in October 1943 attempted to fill the vacuum and assumed certain public works coördination responsibilities. At its suggestion, the President issued a new executive order which required public works agencies to submit with their budget estimates advanced public works programs and estimates of required planning funds, and to continue to clear all project reports to Congress through the Executive Office of the President in order to determine their relationship to the program of the President.[87]

Immediately upon this assumption of responsibility by the Budget Bureau, the Corps of Engineers took action. Having refused to continue the Tripartite Agreement in June, they, in December, announced the reconstitution of this arrangement as a Quadrupartite Agreement among the Corps of Engineers, Bureau of Reclamation, Department of Agriculture, and Federal Power Commission.[88] Unlike the old agreement, this new one provided for no coördinating agency representing the Executive Office; it was under the sponsorship of the Corps of Engineers. The new agreement, like the old, authorized the interchange of information among the participating agencies in the field in the preparation of reports on multiple-purpose projects, and joint consultation in the field and in Washington on these reports.

This agreement was used successfully by the Corps of Engineers to thwart efforts of the Budget Bureau to obtain funds to administer its newly assumed public works coördination responsibilities. The Bureau requested $200,000 for this purpose in its appropriation for fiscal year 1945.[89] In supporting this request before the House Appropriations subcommittee on 13 December 1943, the Director of the Budget was questioned closely by Representative Case concerning an "executive order" which required the Chief of Engineers to submit all flood control project reports to the Bureau of Reclamation, Department of Agriculture, and Federal Power Commission and to take cognizance of the comments of these agencies in his final report to the Congress. The implication was that the existence of such an order made unnecessary the proposed public works programming activities of the Budget Bureau. The Director was confused; he obviously had no knowledge of such an order; he was unable to reply fully to the Congressman's inquiry. Apparently Representative Case was referring to the Quadrupartite Agreement, of which he had advance knowledge and the Budget Bureau no knowledge; for the agreement was not issued until 29 December.

The Appropriations Committee eliminated the entire estimate, reporting no reason therefor. When, in considering the bill, the House came to the section on the Executive Office of the President, Representative Case arose and inserted a copy of the agreement in the *Record* "as evidence of the coordination that can be accomplished and is being accomplished in the planning of public works." Here again, without openly saying so, since there was no debate on the item, Representative Case was apparently implying that coördination of planning could be achieved without the necessity of Budget Bureau participation. To the present time, the Budget Bureau has not obtained sufficient funds to employ more than a very few professional employees to conduct the entire resources and public works coördination function.

Consultation in Washington among the participants in the Quadrupartite Agreement has been conducted through a new interagency committee, the Federal Inter-Agency River Basin Committee, established and managed in its early days largely under the leadership of the Corps of Engineers. As we shall see, this agreement, similar to the Tripartite Agreement, has encouraged greater coöperation in the field by the participating agencies and some standardization of technical factors, such as hydrologic data, basic to the planning of water resources projects. However, with respect to top-level coöperation on policy matters and the reconciliation of conflicts in investigation and survey reports, the Committee has accomplished little.[90]

In March 1945 and in February 1946, the Federal Inter-Agency Committee established subcommittees for the Missouri and Columbia Rivers, respectively.[91] These subcommittees consist of field representatives of the Federal agencies represented on the Washington committee and of Governors of the affected States. Governors of five of the ten Missouri Basin States are members of the Missouri Basin Inter-Agency Committee; Governors of all seven of the Columbia Basin States, of the Inter-Agency Committee for that area. The committees are intended to provide a means through which the representatives of the participating Federal agencies may interchange information effectively and coördinate their activities among themselves and with those of the States in the preparation of reports and in the planning and execution of resource developments. The committees can take action on those matters in which there is unanimous agreement. Questions that cannot be resolved by the committees are referred by the Federal members to their respective chiefs in Washington. The effectiveness of the subcommittees, along with that of the parent Federal Committee, will be evaluated later. In brief, their successes have been in the areas of physical plans and technical considerations; no important policy matters have been settled.

As the result of a serious conflict of interests which developed during consideration of the 1944 Flood Control Act between the irrigation and navigation uses of the water of the Missouri River, Senator O'Mahoney, representing the former, succeeded in obtaining acceptance of a new Congressional declaration of policy designed to limit navigation works to economic projects that do not conflict with other uses of water and to recognize the rights and interests of the States in the Federal development of water resources.[92] To accomplish this policy in part, the so-called O'Mahoney amendment established a procedure for review of reports of the Chief of Engineers and the Secretary of Interior by the States, and for including the comments of the States in the completed reports as submitted to the Congress. It also provided that all reports of the Chief of Engineers on rivers rising west of the ninety-seventh meridian be referred to the Secretary of Interior for his views; and similarly that all such reports of Interior be referred to the Army. This first statutory requirement for formal clearance of reports was obtained, it should be noted, by those primarily interested in protecting a particular use of water. Whatever its source, the provision represented an advance in water resources planning and complemented the informal procedure of the Inter-Agency River Basin Committee.

The Corps of Engineers, then, has in the past thwarted efforts of the Bureau of the Budget to assume for the Executive Office of the President the water resources planning functions formerly exercised for that Office by the National Resources Planning Board. At the same time, the friends of the Engineers in Congress have attempted to enact insurance against any tinkering by the executive branch of Government with the civil functions of the Engineer Department.

Hoover Report.[93] In early 1949 the Hoover Commission on Organization of the Executive Branch of Government reported to the Congress and the nation. Its recommendations on organization for water and other natural resources were derived largely from the proposals of the Commission's Task Force on Natural Resources.[94] The Task Force recommended a review and coördinating board for natural resources projects within the Executive Office of the President. (A majority of the Commission preferred to call the proposed organization a Board of Impartial Analysis.) The procedures and functions of this board, defined in some detail in a published appendix to the Task Force report, accord very nearly with the desired procedure for coördinated planning set out earlier in this chapter.[95] The board would insure that basin and project plans were developed from the start with a view to the best use of the several resources available in the area, and that the completed plans represented the best combined judgment of the Executive Branch and of State and local agencies for the improvement of the area. In addition to plan preparation, the board would be made responsibile for the programming of water development projects by review and evaluation of agency six-year construction programs, and for the formulation of broad administrative and legislative policies for water resources development.

The Commission and the Task Force recommended that the review board be placed in the Executive Office of the President. In this connection the Task Force said: "Where so many types of governmental activity are involved, affecting significantly such a broad range of governmental policies, there is no point below the Executive Office where an objective review can be obtained of project programming, determinations of project feasibility, and broad administrative development policies." [96]

Two members of the Commission, Senator McClellan (Ark.) and Congressman Manasco (Ala.), objected to giving the review board any authority or jurisdiction over the activities of the USED and dissented from the Commission report in this regard.[97] McClellan had long been an active supporter of the Engineers in Congress. He was at the time President of the National Rivers and Harbors

Congress and, it will be remembered, had sponsored in 1937, as a Congressman, Senate Joint Resolution 57. It is interesting to observe that even as late as 1949, when the necessity of building up the President's office to allow effective coördination and direction of executive functions came to be accepted widely, the supporters of the Army Engineers continued to object to interposing any executive authority between the Corps and the committees of Congress.

The Hoover Commission and the Task Force on Natural Resources were both convinced, however, that a coördinating agency alone would not suffice to rationalize national organization for water development.[98] They both proposed that the water resources functions of the Corps of Engineers and the Bureau of Reclamation, the power functions of the Interior Department, and certain functions of the Federal Power Commission be consolidated in a Water Development Service. The Task Force and a minority of three members of the Commission proposed that this Service be organized within a new Department of Natural Resources, which would include, in addition, most of the current functions of the Department of Interior and those of the Forest Service of the Department of Agriculture. The Department of Interior would be abolished. The Commission majority preferred to retain the existing Department of Interior, place the Water Development Service therein, but leave the Forest Service in the Department of Agriculture and transfer to it certain land management functions of Interior.

But these differences do not concern us here. The significant fact is that the Task Force unanimously, and the Commission with but two members dissenting,[99] recommended that the Army be divested of its water functions which should be consolidated with those of the Interior Department. And one of the most compelling reasons for this recommendation was the refusal of the Corps to coöperate wholeheartedly in executive coördinating procedures and the resulting failure of these procedures and the agencies which administered them to bring about economic and adequate development of the nation's water resources.

With respect to the Federal Inter-Agency River Basin Committee and its two subcommittees, the Commission quoted the Task Force report in part as follows:

. . . no effective method has been found for reconciling conflicting opinions and programs . . . The committees have failed to solve any important aspects of the problem . . . because the dominant members, the Corps and the Bureau [of Reclamation], have been unwilling to permit inter-agency committees to settle their differences. The result has been neglect or avoidance by the committees of virtually all major areas of inter-agency conflict, and concentration instead on technical studies and publicity . . .[100]

With respect to Budget Bureau review of Corps project reports, the Task Force found on investigation that the "clearance procedure has not been as effective as it ought to be." One important reason is that "the Corps of Engineers generally makes no effort to change a completed report when informed by the Budget Bureau that the report is not in accord with the President's program. The Corps submits the report to Congress with its favorable recommendation, but accompanied by a statement as to the advice received from the Budget Bureau." [101]

As a consequence the Task Force and Commission concluded: "There is simply no escaping the fact that so long as the present overlapping of functions exists with respect to the Corps of Engineers, the Bureau of Reclamation, and the Federal Power Commission, costly duplication, confusion, and competition are bound to result. It has been demonstrated time and again that neither by voluntary cooperation nor by executive coordination can the major conflicts be ironed out . . ." [102]

The Resources Task Force was well aware of the reception its proposals would receive:

Perhaps the most imposing argument against transferring the civil functions of the Corps of Engineers to another agency is found in the intense opposition with which any such proposal is likely to be met. There is no need to emphasize the powerful local and congressional support for the Corps . . . The history of past reorganization efforts reveals the difficulties encountered when measures have been proposed involving any change whatsoever in the civil functions of the Army Engineers. As one writer[103] has said, "the civil functions of the Army Corps of Engineers constitute a veritable Rock of Gibraltar against all executive attempts to introduce any organizational integration of flood control and river development with the land-use, irrigation, and electric-power activities of other Federal agencies." [104]

Commissioners McClellan and Manasco entered a vigorous dissent to the majority proposals. And as we shall see presently, Commissioner McClellan, as chairman of the Senate Committee on Expenditures to which the Hoover report was referred, has done his best to insure Congressional adoption of his minority views.

To provide a means for implementing many proposals of the Commission, including that for transfer of Engineer Corps civil functions, President Truman and former President Hoover urged Congress in 1949 to enact a general reorganization bill. The legislation was to be similar to early reorganization bills in that plans submitted by the President would become law unless vetoed by both Houses of Congress within sixty days. It was to differ from earlier legislation in that both Truman and Hoover insisted on a "clean bill" — no exceptions — and on a permanent bill — not one that expired within a few years.[105]

The supporters of the Corps of Engineers, both in and out of Congress, raised the most voluble and the only serious opposition to the legislation. The supporters in Congress were led by Representative Whittington, chairman of the Committee on Public Works, and Senator McClellan; those out of Congress, by the National Rivers and Harbors Congress, the Mississippi Valley Association, and various contractors' organizations. Herbert Hoover lashed out at these supporters and their demands for exemption for the Corps. For example, in testifying before Senator McClellan's committee he confirmed his conviction that water functions should be consolidated and then said:

> Of course, when a bureau makes up its mind that it is going to fight something in Congress, there is no limit to the stories which will be spread . . . I have had some experience for over 25 years with this problem of bureau obstruction. I have witnessed their ingenuity and capacity to invoke enormous drives. You are in the presence of one. I think it is one you must resist if you are ever going to reorganize the Government. Success in this drive will result in every other quarter of the Government putting on similar campaigns. We will get nowhere.[106]

And in a special press conference on the pending legislation, Hoover stated that if Congress yields to this "type of grasshopper bite that will destroy reorganization we may as well as quit tomorrow. If the Army Engineers can succeed it is evidence to every other agency that they can get away with it." [107]

Senator Lodge (Mass.) several times on the Senate floor accused the Engineers of lobbying activities and asked for a Congressional investigation. At one point he said, "When officers of the Army Engineers undertake to stir up agitation against the report of the eminent, distinguished and patriotic Commission on the Organization of the Executive Branch, the time has come to call a halt." [108]

As a result of the wide publicity given to the statements of Hoover, Lodge, and many others on the campaign to obtain exemption for the USED in the reorganization bill, the Secretary of the Army on 19 February 1949 issued special instructions that officers of the Corps were not to engage in any political activities whatsoever in connection with the Hoover Commission reports. And one month later he issued similar instructions for civilian employees of the Corps.[109] The fact that the Secretary of the Army felt compelled to issue these instructions is indicative of the national importance which was attached to the efforts of the Corps' supporters. It will be remembered that as a general rule the Secretary of the Army has nothing to do with Engineer Corps civil functions.

Despite considerable opposition from the rivers and harbors bloc, the House passed the reorganization bill with no outright exemptions. The Senate, too, passed a "clean bill" with no exemptions. But the Senate bill had a joker, providing that any reorganization plan submitted by the President should become law unless vetoed by *one* House. This constituted a major reverse for administrative reorganization; the bills of 1939 and 1945 had required veto by both Houses. Why did the Senate insist on this change? Because the Congressional supporters of the Corps of Engineers announced that they would forego outright exemption for the Corps *only* if Congress would agree to a one-House veto.

They were sure that any proposed transfer of the Corps could not get through Congress under these conditions; and to make sure that future changes in the complexion of Congress might not alter this situation, they provided that the bill expire at the end of Truman's term of office. The report of the Senate Committee on Expenditures contained the following:

> By far the largest number of witnesses appeared in behalf of the exemption of the civil functions of the Corps of Engineers, including representatives of valley improvement, flood control and development associations, chambers of commerce, and other State and civic organizations: 17 of the 25 witnesses appearing at the hearings, and 14 of the 23 resolutions and communications submitted for the record, were in support

of such exemption. In addition, hundreds of telegrams and letters from 44 States and the District of Columbia were received by the committee, expressing opposition to granting any reorganization authority to the President which would permit the transfer of the civil functions of the Corps of Engineers to any other department or agency . . .

An amendment to exempt the civil functions of the Corps of Engineers, offered by the chairman [Senator McClellan], was defeated by a vote of 5 to 4. Several members of the committee indicated, however, that in voting against this exemption they reserved the right to favor such exemption should the Senate not approve the amendment providing for disapproval of reorganization plans by either the House of Representatives or the Senate.[110]

For one month the Senate-House conference committee remained deadlocked over the bill. The House conferees refused to agree to the Senate's one-House veto; the Senate conferees took a stand on this or nothing at all, and their reason — the Army Engineers. When supporters of the Hoover Commission grew impatient and demanded action by Congress, Representative McCormack, Majority Leader and member of the conference committee, reported on the House floor that differences between the two versions of the legislation "would have been settled in five minutes if it were not for the Army Engineers." He said:

> But now the Army Engineers are the key. The Army Engineers are afraid. I am friendly to the Army Engineers, but all I can say is that some of the friends of the Army Engineers are doing them irreparable harm because they are putting the Army Engineers in a position of being more powerful than Congress, more powerful than the President, more powerful than everybody, more powerful than the Government itself.[111]

Finally, the House conferees gave in; the only concession they were able to extract from the Senate was an agreement that the resolution of veto passed by either House must be approved by a constitutional or absolute majority of all members rather than a simple majority of those present and voting. The ease with which Congress, under this scheme, can defeat reorganization plans of the President has been demonstrated since with grim reality.

This fight over reorganization legislation illustrates again the peculiar strength of that direct agency-legislative relationship which has developed between the Engineers and Congress. In this instance, the demand for "clean" reorganization legislation was strictly nonpartisan, supported equally by Truman and Hoover. Through the excellent press given the Hoover reports and through the efforts of the newly organized Citizens' Committee for the Hoover Report, the public was aroused as perhaps it had never been before to the need for good reorganization legislation.[112] Despite this, the Congress enacted assurances that the Engineers would not be touched. As a matter of fact, it may well be that an outright exemption of the Corps would have proved very unpopular, whereas the device adopted was of such a technical nature that its real significance was not readily understood by citizens interested in government reform.

EFFECTUATION OF DESIRED PATTERN FOR COÖRDINATED PLANNING

In the light of this fifteen-year history of conflict between the Engineers and those interested in the development by the executive branch of a comprehensive national water program, we can evaluate success in bringing about the desired procedure for integrated planning.

Basin-wide plans. Some progress has been made toward the coöperative planning of drainage basins as units. A step in this direction was taken by the President's Committee on Waterflow in 1934. The report of the Committee relied very heavily on Engineer Department "308" reports which had been prepared recently. In the same year a pioneer demonstration of drainage basin planning was made by the Mississippi Valley Committee. In 1936 this technique was applied to the entire country by the Water Resources Committee in its report on *Drainage Basin Problems and Programs,* which was revised in 1937.[113]

The organization of the drainage basin studies was designed to secure joint planning by State and Federal agencies. Each of the forty-five drainage basin committees which participated in the 1937 revision was composed of field representatives of Federal and State agencies most concerned with the particular water problems of the basin. The distinctive function of the drainage basin committees was to bring together and unify the local, State, and Federal points of view on these water problems. They were not organized to perfect plans in detail — a function of construction agencies — but rather to discover possibilities, to stimulate investigations necessary to the formulation of general plans and programs, and to formulate for each basin a systematic plan for the best use and control of surface and underground waters.[114]

With the abolition of the Planning Board, active organization and support for joint basin planning expired largely by default. The Budget Bureau has had no staff for this purpose; the Federal Inter-Agency River Basin Committee and its subcommittees, the Missouri and Columbia River Basin Committees, have not concerned themselves with organizing or preparing joint basin plans.

Take the Columbia River for example. When the disastrous floods occurred in late May 1948, both the Bureau of Reclamation and the Corps of Engineers were at work on separate comprehensive plans for this great basin. On 1 June, and later on 16 September, the President wrote the Secretaries of Army and Interior to correlate and expedite these plans.[115] Although the President did not actually direct a single report combining the views and recommendations of all agencies (possibly because the Corps has always insisted it has an obligation to present its own report directly to the Congressional committee which has authorized it), he certainly indicated that one might be prepared and at the very minimum required that separate reports be in full agreement. He said to the Secretary of the Army:

"I suggest that the field studies and recommendations of the Corps of Engineers . . . be closely coordinated with other affected departments and agencies, possibly through the Columbia Basin Inter-Agency Committee, with the objective of attaining the fullest possible agreement on *a comprehensive plan for the basin.*" [Emphasis added.]

The President's desires in this regard were not realized. The Corps of Engineers and the Bureau of Reclamation presented separate reports to the President. The Columbia Inter-Agency Committee was not used as a means for achieving real coördination. Instead, the Secretaries of Army and Interior entered into a bilateral agreement, reached *after* the uncoördinated reports of the two agencies had been submitted to Washington, and accomplishing little other than dividing up the construction job between the Corps and the Bureau.

As for Interior's Columbia River Basin Report, records reveal that it was first presented to the CBIAC after it had reached a well crystallized or nearly final form, and that the Committee did not comment upon it. The Secretary of Interior in his letter of transmittal to the President has stated that he considers the report an "inventory" and not a fully effective plan "for accomplishing and administering a comprehensive program of resources development."

Like the Interior report, the separate report of the Corps of Engineers was not given any real consideration by the CBIAC. The Committee did not participate at all in the preparation of the report. It received progress reports from time to time, but on no occasion was there a discussion of definite points of view or policy matters having to do with the coördination of the plans contained in the report. The Secretary of Interior found the same limitations in the Corps' report as he had found in that prepared by his own Department.

The Army-Interior Agreement has very serious limitations and cannot be said to meet the requirements for coördination set out by the President in 1948. Nor can a bilateral agreement of this sort be considered an effective substitute for the Inter-Agency Committee consideration suggested by the President. In testimony before the Senate Committee on Public Works, Secretary of Interior Krug said of the Agreement: "There are certain essential things that the Army-Interior agreement does not or cannot provide. First of all, the agreement does not cover the full Federal responsibilities for development in the region and, therefore, is not a single unified plan . . ."

It is discouraging, but instructive, that the CBIAC failed in this important task. The Columbia Basin Committee was set up in May 1946 and was an operating unit at the time the agencies were making their early investigations and preparing their original reports — the very time when maximum effective coördination is both possible and feasible. If it had taken fullest advantage of the situation, there would have been one, not two, comprehensive reports. But measuring its success by standards much less exacting than this one, failure still results. The most that can be said is that the Committee was informed of the preparation of the reports and of the preparation of plans for specific projects included in the reports. It did not examine these in any detail, nor discuss their interrelations. Negotiations on the plans in the field were carried on between the Corps and the Bureau and largely outside the CBIAC. Similarly, when final agreement was reached at the Washington level, the two agencies *in-*

formed the Federal Inter-Agency Committee. Keeping informed about the reports can hardly be said to constitute effective coördination. One of the most significant reasons for failure to prepare a single comprehensive report and for failure in coördination was the attitude of the Corps of Engineers. The Department of Interior, prior to 1947, made tentative proposals for a joint investigation of unified development of the Columbia River Basin, but these proposals were rejected by the Corps.

The Central Valley of California provides another example of failure to prepare fully integrated and comprehensive basin plans.[116] In 1945 both the Corps of Engineers and the Bureau of Reclamation submitted to the President advance copies of comprehensive reports on this basin. (In this case, too, it is somewhat anomalous, to say the least, that the Federal Government should sponsor the preparation of two separate comprehensive reports.) As the reports were obviously in conflict, the President returned them to the originating agencies for reconciliation of differences — such reconciliation to be accomplished, it was hoped, through the Federal Inter-Agency River Basin Committee. For this purpose the Committee set up a special subcommittee. The subcommittee, however, and its parent body were unable to come to any agreement on settling differences. Not only that, but the committees were unable even to come to any agreement on a statement of the differences between the two reports — a striking example of the difficulties of coördination where one or more of the participants has no sense of the broad advantages to be gained thereby. The result was that in July 1948, almost three years after the President had requested a reconciliation of reports, there were submitted to the Executive Office of the President four separate reports — the final comprehensive reports of the Chief of Engineers and the Secretary of Interior, and the two separate statements of differences in these reports.

Finally, in August 1949, the President's Office completed review of these documents. The President concluded that the content of the reports of neither the Corps nor the Bureau justified the approval of either as a comprehensive valley plan; but he authorized the agencies to submit their reports to Congress along with a statement of his proposed reconciliation of their differences.

Thus, today, really comprehensive basin plans are not available, and in most instances our river basins are being developed in the absence of such plans. However, we have seen that the Corps has given more and more attention in recent years to water planning for entire river basins, and this represents a considerable improvement over the situation in 1934. The greatest emphasis on basin planning is to be found in the West, and here the broader view on the part of the Engineers is inspired no doubt by competition with the Bureau of Reclamation which has traditionally used the multiple-purpose basin-wide approach. But elsewhere in the nation the Corps has given greater emphasis to the preparation or revision of "308" reports, and Congress has approved a large number of USED basin plans for flood control, power, and navigation.

As late as 1945, however, President Roosevelt was not satisfied that the Corps of Engineers was making adequate use of its authority to prepare basin plans. In a letter to the Secretary of War he said:

> I think that all of us concerned with rivers and harbors and conservation of water resources recognize that one river is one problem. No longer can we make a practice of treating each consideration as an isolated problem. Rather, the whole must be considered. I think that your Department has had for some years now full authority to make continuing surveys for flood control, navigation, and hydroelectric power development on practically all of the major streams of the Nation, and it seems to me that these individual flood control surveys might well be consolidated in comprehensive basin studies.[117]

Only recently President Truman reiterated this complaint in a message to Congress:

> I urge the Congress to develop more satisfactory procedures for considering and authorizing basin-wide development programs. We are a long way still, both in the executive and legislative branches, from the kind of comprehensive planning and action that is required if we are able to conserve, develop and use our natural resources so that they will be increasingly useful as the years go by. We need to make sure that each legislative authorization, and each administrative action, takes us toward — and not away from — this goal.[118]

Translation of basin plans into projects. With respect to project plans, the situation is somewhat similar to that found for drainage basin plans. The President and his Executive Office have urged joint planning, largely unsuccessfully; and the Corps and the Congress have resisted. While Congress was considering the important

1936 Flood Control Act, the President, the National Resources Committee, and the Departments of Agriculture and Interior sought provision for fully coöperative project investigations. They obtained from Congress only an authorization for the Department of Agriculture to investigate upstream watershed protection. Because of failure to provide for coöperative investigations in the 1938 Flood Control Act, the President approved the legislation "with some reluctance." With respect to project planning, he found the Act "not a step in the right direction." While the Flood Control Act of 1941 was under consideration by Congress, the President in a letter to the Speaker of the House asked again that "provision be made . . . for the active participation of other Federal agencies concerned with multiple-purpose aspects of the surveys," and submitted a draft amendment to accomplish this.[119] But Congress turned a deaf ear on the President's request in 1941 and failed to respond to his desire for the provision in the Flood Control Act of 1944 and the Rivers and Harbors Act of 1945.[120]

Congress, then, has refused to direct the Corps of Engineers to conduct coöperative project investigations, and the President and his Executive Office have been unable to obtain from the USED any general agreement to do so or to submit joint reports. The Tripartite Agreement was the product of direct Presidential intervention in a feud between the Corps of Engineers and the Bureau of Reclamation over several project reports.[121] The President, at a conference in his office, requested the agencies to coöperate in developing a system of joint investigations and joint reporting of multiple-purpose projects. But the resulting agreement, though it did contribute to some improvement in field coöperation, failed to inaugurate any procedure for joint investigations (other than occasional joint public hearings in the field) or for joint reporting. Similarly the Quadrupartite Agreement and the agency set up to administer it, the FIARBC, have not brought about coöperative planning and joint reports.

The inadequate planning which results can be seen most clearly in the seventeen Western States where both the Corps and the Bureau of Reclamation seek to construct multiple-purpose projects. A survey of current water development activities in these States reveals that within every large drainage basin there is at least one major unresolved conflict between the project proposals of the Corps and those of Reclamation or of the Department of Agriculture. The most obvious cases of duplication and conflict occur where both the Corps and the Bureau have prepared project reports on the very same developments. In 1939 each agency completed survey reports on the Kings River in California. These reports were in sharp conflict on matters of policy relating to distribution of project benefits; and the issues raised then because of separate, rather than joint and coöperative, planning were not fully settled ten years later, in 1949.[122] Separate and conflicting reports or plans have been prepared for Hell's Canyon on the Snake River between Idaho and Oregon, Jamestown Reservoir in the Missouri Basin in North Dakota, the San Luis Valley project in Colorado, and elsewhere.[123]

In addition to these cases of duplicate planning, there are a great number of Corps reports on multiple-purpose projects which conflict with the views of the Department of Interior and other agencies having special interest in one or more of the purposes for which the projects are to be built. The Grand Prairie-Bayou Meto development in Arkansas provides a good example.[124] Here the Corps proposes to construct a drainage, irrigation, and flood control project. The Interior Department objects to the proposals on the grounds that they undermine the basic principles of Reclamation law under which all Federal irrigation development in the West has taken place. Interior had offered to assist in the investigation of the Grand Prairie region; but its offers were rejected by the Corps, which held that the Bureau of Reclamation had no authority to operate outside of the seventeen Western States. Numerous other examples could be cited: survey reports on the Russian River in California, the Humboldt River in Nevada, the Neches Waterway in Texas, among others.[125]

It is not meant to imply that no progress has been made since 1934. A comparison of the *Orders and Regulations* of the Corps of Engineers for 1949 with those for 1934 reveals several new and specific provisions for coöperation with other agencies in the conduct of investigations; but these provisions are sufficient neither in number nor in content to meet the requirements of the desired planning procedure.

Review of basin and project plans. Top level review of water plans to insure compliance with national policies and to eliminate conflicts with other development plans was initiated in the middle thirties for projects undertaken with public works and relief funds. In September 1935 the President instructed Federal agencies concerned with allotments for water use in the Upper Rio Grande Basin to secure prior review of all proposed projects from the National Resources Committee. The Water Resources Committee soon thereafter entered into a formal agreement with the Public Works Administration for the review of all water resource project applications. In July 1936 the WRC, on request of the President, also reviewed emergency flood control projects proposed for construction by the Corps of Engineers with funds allocated by the WPA and CCC.[126]

Review and evaluation of a great number of projects proposed by State, local, and Federal agencies was accomplished by the NRC in preparation of the 1936 and 1937 drainage basin reports. However, systematic review of regular Engineer survey reports prior to their submittal to Congress was not initiated in any form until April 1937, when the President requested the Secretary of War to submit to him the Corps' comprehensive report on the Ohio and lower Mississippi Rivers. On that day the President informed the nation that a new procedure for submitting flood control proposals to Congress was being developed:

> Under the new system all such recommendations will be taken by the Secretary whose department is asked for the recommendation to the President, who will then send it to the other departments and to some review board, possibly the National Resources Committee. It will then go back to the President who may make some comment himself and send the project to the committees of Congress . . . The policy was adopted, the President said, in an effort to produce some order out of the present system, whereby congressional requests for recommendations on flood control projects go directly to and from bureaus and departments, and are not coordinated with the work of other agencies in this field.[127]

It took over three years to implement the new procedure. In the meantime the NRC did review for the President some thirteen important Engineer Department surveys, but a great many reports went direct to the Congress without review.[128] The fully implemented procedure called for (1) consultation among the agencies of major interest when tentative drafts of reports are prepared, so as to permit discussion of them prior to their submission in final form; and (2) formal submission of all final reports to the Executive Office of the President where they could be reviewed to determine their relationship to the program of the President.

Consultation among agencies of major interest was provided for originally in the Tripartite Agreement of 1939. As we have noted previously, this agreement did not operate to eliminate conflicts and divergencies in final reports, just as it did not encourage the conduct and preparation of joint investigations and reports. Similarly, under the Quadrupartite Agreement, the Federal Inter-Agency River Basin Committee has accomplished little by way of reconciliation of conflicts in investigation and survey reports. An analysis of the minutes of the FIARBC shows that the Committee has not discussed the issues and conflicts presented by important reports. Indeed, there appears to be a disposition on the part of the Committee to avoid precipitating controversial issues at its meetings; and in some cases the Corps of Engineers has submitted multiple-purpose project reports to the Congress without even referring them first to the Inter-Agency Committee.[129]

Formal clearance of investigation and survey reports with the Executive Office of the President, in the manner that departmental reports on legislation had been cleared for a number of years, was originally provided for in Executive Order 8455 of June 1940. The procedure developed thereunder required the reporting agencies to submit their proposed reports to the Budget Bureau. The Budget then requested the NRPB to review them in the light of national policies and possible conflicts with other existing or proposed developments. The WRC set up an evaluation subcommittee, with representatives from the Corps of Engineers, Department of Agriculture, Federal Power Commission, and Bureau of Reclamation, to study the projects and rate them in accordance with an approved evaluation scale.[130] The evaluations were reviewed by the full WRC and, on occasion, by the full Planning Board and were communicated to the Budget Bureau. The Budget, then, on the basis of the evaluations and of additional budgetary considerations, informed the reporting agencies of the relationship of their reports to the program of the President. If a report was not in accord with that program, the agency could either transmit the report to Congress with a statement to that effect, or it could choose to hold the report, attempt to reconcile it with the President's plans, and resubmit it to the Budget Bureau and the Planning Board.

When the Planning Board was abolished, the Bureau of the Budget continued to require the formal clearance of reports under a new Executive Order, No. 9384. However — and this is quite important — the Budget did not continue the evaluation subcommittee of the Board nor did it establish any substitute therefor. The Congress denied appropriations for that purpose. So that today the Budget is in no position to give either the careful review or the positive assistance in the reconciliation of conflicting reports afforded by the Planning Board procedure. The provisions of the Flood Control Act of 1944, requiring submission of reports for comment to the Governors of affected States and, in certain cases, to the Secretary of the Interior, are important; they represent an advance in water planning; but they do not serve as a substitute for an effective top-level clearance procedure.

A final test of the effectiveness of water plan review can come only from an examination of Engineer Department reports submitted to the Executive Office of the President and to the Congress since 1940 to determine, first, whether the Engineer Department makes a serious effort to reconcile its reports with the program of the President and is reluctant to submit to Congress reports which the President's office has found not in accord with his program; and second, whether the Congress is reluctant to authorize projects recommended by the Engineer Department in reports which are not in accord with the President's program, but have nonetheless been submitted to Congress by the USED.

Taking the period from January 1941 to August 1948, the Executive Office of the President cleared 914 Engineer Department reports.[131] Of these reports, 478 recommended no Federal improvements and were cleared by the EOP with no objection. (To date all reports recommending against Federal improvement have been in accord with the President's program.) Of the remaining 436 reports favorable to construction, 360 were cleared with no objection to authorization, and 76 reports were (a) held to be wholly or partially not in accord with the President's program (44 reports) or (b) were the subject of specific reservations stated in special comments by the Budget Bureau (32 reports). The following tabulation shows the breakdown of these reports.

Unfavorable Reports	River and Harbor	277
	Flood Control	187
Beach Erosion (no Federal cost)		15
Favorable Reports (EOP action)		
No objection	River and Harbor	239
	Flood Control	120
Not in accord	River and Harbor	22
	Flood Control	20
Reservation or comments	River and Harbor	15
	Flood Control	19
Total		914

With regard to the 42 projects held not in accord with the President's program, the Corps of Engineers had transmitted reports on *all* of these projects to Congress with its own favorable recommendations. Congress, at the time this compilation was made (August 1948), had authorized 36 projects, of which 21 were for flood control and 15 for navigation. Of the total of 76 projects on which the Budget Bureau has made some reservations and comments, Congress had authorized 62, 7 had either been abandoned, or considered by Congress and rejected, while 7 projects had not been formally considered by Congress.

From the above analysis it can be seen that the Executive Office of the President has not been effective in convincing either the Corps of Engineers or the Congress to consider its views on these projects. With respect to the Engineer Department, it chose to transmit to Congress all of the reports not in accord with the program of the President and, in addition, to transmit informally one report which had been returned for restudy.

With respect to Congress, it abandoned one project to which the President's Office had objected; failed to authorize 6 after considering them; and authorized 62 projects which they knew were not in accord with the program of the President for any one of several reasons. The projects so authorized have a total estimated cost in excess of two billion dollars; those rejected, about one-half billion dollars.

Senator Overton, for many years chairman of the subcommittee which handled Corps projects, said that his committee and the Congress paid little or no attention to the recommendations and evaluations of the NRPB, even though these were the views of the

President. Congress based its decisions directly on the recommendations of the Chief of Engineers.[132] The Senator's frank statement appears to hold equally for evaluations of the Budget Bureau made after the Planning Board was abolished. The Corps and the Congress seem to be in full agreement on their mutual relations — the officers of the Corps are "the engineer consultants to, and contractors for, the Congress of the United States."

Construction programs. First steps toward development of an orderly construction program were taken early in 1935, when the National Planning Board, in coöperation with the Public Works Administration, undertook a nation-wide inventory and priority rating of water projects. This was done to provide a more rational basis for the allocation of emergency public works and relief funds to such projects and to plan future appropriation requirements for this purpose.[133] The more than two-thousand projects in the inventory were classified as worthy of immediate action, worthy of action within ten years, or twenty-five years, or unsuitable for use. The projects were also arranged in order of priority within each classification, and each was analyzed in regard to the amount of employment which it would offer. This hastily compiled inventory was reviewed and revised in the light of the problems and programs of 115 separate drainage basins, when the drainage basin reports of 1936 and 1937 were undertaken.

Expenditures for water projects must, of course, be geared to a long-range program for all public works. In this connection, the President in 1936 requested the National Resources Committee, in coöperation with the Projects Division of the PWA, to prepare and revise annually a Federal six-year program of public works.[134] Between 1936 and 1938 three revisions of this program were transmitted by the NRC to the President and the Bureau of the Budget for use in administering relief and public works funds. These programs, though valuable for emergency expenditure purposes, were not related sufficiently to the regular budgetary operation. A more orderly process was needed, and such was evolved when the Budget Bureau and the National Resources Planning Board were both placed within the President's office. By Executive Order 8455 and the procedures developed thereunder in 1940, Federal construction agencies were required to prepare and keep up to date six-year programs of public works construction and to submit such programs to the

Executive Office of the President at the time they submitted their budget estimates.

The six-year programs as a whole and the individual projects were reviewed by the Planning Board; water projects, by an evaluation subcommittee of the Water Resources Committee, which developed suitable criteria for programming purposes.[135]

On the basis of the Planning Board review and of other budgetary considerations, the Bureau of the Budget and the President determined the executive budget for resources development and public works for the ensuing fiscal year which then became the revised first year of the six-year program. The Planning Board, in coöperation with the development agencies, adjusted the six-year programs to fit the revised first year; and the President, shortly after he sent his annual Budget to the Congress, submitted the long-range program of resources development. In transmitting the first program report to Congress, the President said: "The Budget contains the recommendations of the Chief Executive for the financial outlays to carry on a public works program during the next fiscal year. This report [the Planning Board report] places these recommendations within the framework of a long-range policy of intelligent planning for the future. It contains a six-year program of public construction and a statement of related future policies and plans of the Federal Government." [136]

Three annual reports were prepared by the NRPB prior to its abolition. These reports, it must be noted, were deficient in one important respect. The recommended six-year program, as published, contained only a list of projects recommended for the ensuing fiscal year, with estimates for each project of expenditures proposed in the Budget and additional expenditures required thereafter to complete. These additional expenditures were not programmed over the succeeding five years nor were any projects included other than those for which expenditures were estimated in the Budget. As for expenditures on all programmed projects in all later years, the report gave only a single lump-sum estimate. In other words, the six-year program, as published, was not a six-year program at all. The blame for this must be laid squarely at the feet of the Bureau of the Budget. The Planning Board, in coöperation with the construction agencies, had prepared careful six-year programs. The Budget, however, feared the publication of any program for the future; it was unwilling to provide the Congress and the public with any indication of the amount of public works appropriations which might be expected in the budgets of later years for fear that such an indication might become embarrassingly binding. The Budget Bureau just was not ready for any real advanced public works programming although it was anxious to have such programs for restricted Executive Office use.[137]

For this latter reason the Budget Bureau, after the Planning Board was abolished, continued to require Federal construction agencies to submit six-year public works programs along with their budget estimates.[138] However, as in the case of review of reports, the Planning Board evaluation machinery was not continued, and the Bureau has not given these programs the careful review and consideration they deserve.

The Corps of Engineers has coöperated excellently with both the NRPB and the Budget in the preparation of construction programs of authorized projects for navigation and flood control. Its programs are carefully prepared in the Office of the Chief of Engineers on the basis of recommendations by District and Division Engineers. The Engineer Department, in fact, is more sympathetic to the programming concept than is the Bureau of the Budget. Whereas Budget has not developed an advance program for the Government as a whole, has not taken any action to approve or disapprove the agency programs submitted to it, and has not given Congress and the public any information on future public works expenditures, the Engineers have in the past informed Congress and the public of their six-year programs at the time of appropriation hearings.[139] However, this Corps procedure, similar to the procedure for publishing in the annual report estimates of funds which could be expended profitably in the future, is calculated to put the Engineer Department on record in favor of large appropriations and to place on the President and his Executive Office all responsibility and onus for reducing these.

One final aspect of the programming-budgeting operation should be mentioned. Where the President and the Executive Office have failed to insure the adoption of fully coördinated water project plans in authorizing legislation, they have attempted to obtain this result by budget control; first by refusing to submit budget estimates for authorized projects not fully coördinated, and second, where Congress nonetheless appropriates funds for such projects, by refusing to approve allotment or release of the appropriation. For example, the President in signing the Rivers and Harbors and Flood Control Acts of 1946 said:

> Furthermore there are many unanswered questions in connection with the projects authorized by the two bills I have just signed. These questions must be satisfactorily answered before the construction authorized is initiated. I do not intend to approve any requests for appropriations or allocations of funds for the construction of any of these projects until all the important questions concerning them have been satisfactorily resolved, and until all the Federal agencies directly concerned are substantially agreed upon the technical features involved.[140]

These budgetary techniques have not been successful. Congress often has provided funds where the President has refused to request them because the projects were not fully reconciled; and the Engineer Department has not opposed such Congressional action.[141] Similarly, Congress has opposed successfully attempts to place in reserve appropriations for Engineer Corps civil functions. "The members of Congress feel that they are better qualified than the Budget Bureau to judge the amount of funds needed for flood control purposes, and they bitterly resent, according to indications, the direct slap in the face which they feel they have received for daring to tinker with the budget estimate in the last regular session." [142]

CONCLUSION, 1950

Can we say in conclusion that the system of administrative responsibility of the Corps of Engineers is substantially different in 1950 than it had been in 1934? Does the 1950 system approach the desired standard as we have defined it — Engineer Department directly responsible to the President for recommending and executing water resources policies and programs; President directly responsible to Congress for these policies and programs; and Engineer Department responsible to Congress indirectly, i.e. through the President, for water policies?

Undoubtedly there have been notable advances toward this objective, as seen in the water planning process. The nature and timing of these advances have been discussed with some care. Many of them have escaped since the planning agency was abolished. A realistic appraisal of the situation in 1949, however, must lead to the conclusions that (1) the USED is still responsible directly to committees and to Members of Congress to a significant degree; (2) the USED is responsible to the chief executive to a much greater extent than in 1934, but not to a point which approaches the set standard; (3) the desired procedure for planning water developments has not been realized; (4) the USED has not assisted in developing legislative standards by recommending national water policies. The Corps still regards the development of policy as the sole duty of Congress and regards itself as no more than the executing agent of specific Congressional directives. Finally (5), this very pattern of legislative responsibility has continued to guarantee for the Army Corps of Engineers an unusual degree of Congressional support.

FOUR

Responsibility to Profession

A Seamless Web: The Unity of Land and Water and Men — David Lilienthal [1]

AN ADMINISTRATIVE AGENCY CAN BE HELD RESPONsible to technical knowledge, to the standards of craftsmanship and professionalism applicable to the function administered. As this study is concerned with the planning of water resources projects, not with their construction, the objective standards of professional performance to which the Engineer Department should be held accountable are those relating to national policies for water development.

But we have seen that the Engineer Department refuses to concern itself with policies, as a general rule. At the same time, however, we have held that failure of an administrative agency to recommend needed and proper policies constitutes a failure in the exercise of administrative responsibility, just as does recommending or acting on improper policies — policies not in accord with the substantial opinion of those considered highly competent in the professional field. Thus, an evaluation of Engineer Corps planning to determine responsibility to profession requires not only the examination of action taken and policies recommended to determine whether or not they are considered professionally responsible or irresponsible, but also the identification of policies which should have been recommended and action which should have been taken according to professional standards.

What are the professional standards? There is no professional organization of water resource planners which can provide an answer to this question. The planning of the nation's water resources for multiple-purpose use and control is a highly complex business as is revealed by a mere enumeration of the many uses to which the waters of a single stream can be put. There are conflicts between these uses; the professionally competent agency must attempt to harmonize these in the public interest. The professional standards, then, must represent a composite of the professionally competent views of those concerned with the many uses of water and with the relation of water use to the utilization of other natural resources in the national interest. Such a composite of professional views is found, for example, in the reports of the Water Resources Committee of the National Resources Planning Board and its predecessors. That Committee and its numerous policy subcommittees have contained the most technically competent representatives of numerous Federal and State water agencies and professionally renowned private consultants and university professors of water engineering.[2] The reports of the WRC, of its subcommittees, and other sources will be used to develop the professional standards of responsibility against which Engineer Corps planning can be measured.

Tests of a Sound Water Plan

The plans for any water development project should meet successfully certain tests, "abundantly confirmed by the experience of many agencies and repeatedly affirmed in essence by the Water Resources Committee," if the plans are to be practical and of maximum utility.[3] What are these tests and how do the plans of the Engineer Department meet them? The general tests will be stated first. Then Engineer Corps planning for flood control, navigation, hydroelectric power, and irrigation will be evaluated in the light of these general tests, applied specifically to each function.[4]

MULTIPLE PURPOSES

In planning any water development, an agency should consider it in relation to all useful purposes which can be attained, in the combination which will yield maximum total benefits at minimum total costs.

No matter what the originating purpose of a project, whether improvement of the navigability of a river channel, development of a power site, protection of a city from floods, or something else, every other reasonable purpose must be considered adequately in determining its final scope and character if the project plan be sound. Many projects, though inspired by a single need, afford practicable opportunities for combinations that would multiply benefits and in most cases reduce the costs of each of them below what it would be if the benefit were sought alone. Failure to recognize, appraise, and, insofar as feasible, develop the multiple potentialities that may be inherent in a project of magnitude is not only to invite waste but perhaps also to preclude later highly desirable development in the place involved. Unwise action today may prevent wise action tomorrow.

The multiple-purpose test requires not only that all purposes be considered in planning a water development, but more important, that they be considered *in balance.* Planning is too often in terms of *major purpose* (or dominant interest) and *secondary purposes* defined according to the basic legislation and orientation of the particular development agency involved. In other words, it is not sufficient for the Corps of Engineers to go into the lower Arkansas River, for example, with the established purpose of developing it primarily for navigation (a purpose of dominant interest to the Corps), and then to determine what secondary purposes can be included in order to make the development multiple-purpose. The true multiple-purpose concept will not give primary billing to any one or two purposes until the resources problems of the area have been investigated thoroughly. Furthermore, the final objective should not be merely to include as many purposes as possible. The inclusion of some may do great detriment to the realization of others. The objective should be the best, or most profitable and balanced total use of resources.

BASIN RELATIONSHIPS

In planning any water development, an agency should consider it in relation to all projects which the proposed development may affect or by which it may be affected within the river basin or in other river basins.

A large project cannot be planned wisely if considered, however fully, by and for itself alone. It may affect and be affected by other projects or opportunities for projects. Thus, water diverted from a stream for one locality has upon occasion reduced inequitably the supply available for localities farther downstream . . . Such interrelationships between projects in the same river basin result from the mobility of water and the unity of river systems. It follows that river systems cannot be divided satisfactorily for major water planning purposes. The upstream and downstream segments cannot well be treated separately. Plans for interstate rivers cannot stop at State lines. The mutual adjustment of related problems and purposes throughout each river system must be promoted if planning and plans are to have maximum effectiveness.

One river, one problem.

SHIFTING CONDITIONS

In planning any water development, an agency should consider it in relation to shifting conditions by which it may be affected in the future.

If plans for the control and use of water are to have full utility in the public interest, they must be dynamic to the greatest degree practicable, not static. The long view, no less than the broad view, is desirable, but it is limited and circumscribed by unforeseeable conditions. The future requirements for most areas for water will be influenced by unpredictable changes in population density, in land use, in business and industry, in social needs and conditions. Such changes will themselves be influenced by the supply of water . . . For these reasons, water plans will need revision indefinitely and water planning will be required indefinitely.

In designing individual structures as components of a unified plan, provisions should be made to meet new needs which may arise. In formulating or revising a plan for the development of a river, all projects with benefits greater than costs should be included, and no project under the plan should be approved because of a high short-term rate of return if it would prevent later development of a larger project of promise with a lower ratio of benefits to costs.

An appraisal of shifting conditions necessitates periodic resurveys of development programs in order to determine the uses to which they are in fact being put and the requirements to which they must yet be adapted. Whether or not resurveys are conducted is in itself an indication of the adequacy of planning.

BROADER PROBLEMS AND INTERESTS

In planning any water development, an agency should seek above all to promote *public interests* by considering the development in relation to broad regional and national problems and interests.

Water problems project themselves into every phase of earth economy. They merge into problems relating to the use of lands, minerals, and forests, into problems of business and industry, into problems of social welfare and national defense. Any sound water plan formulated and promoted by a public agency, Federal, State, or local, or through the cooperative efforts of such agencies, will seek, above all else, to promote *public interests*.

The broader interest for inland navigation, for example, is an integrated nation-wide transportation system; so that the feasibility of a navigation improvement must be examined in the light of its effect upon such a system. Similarly, with respect to flood control, the broader interest test requires that plans for flood protection works be considered in the light of the more general problems of land use and flood plain occupance.

ECONOMIC SOUNDNESS[5]

The test of economic soundness requires that all survey agencies adhere to the following principles:

(1) Total benefits greater than total costs. No development plan is sound unless it meets the test of economic desirability by showing total benefits greater than total costs.

All types of benefits and costs should be evaluated upon a *consistent and comparable basis.* The economic appraisal of any project should give due weight to less tangible social benefits as well as to tangible economic benefits (e.g., recreation as well as power). It should cover potential benefits (like improved use of land freed from flood risk) as well as actual benefits (reduced flood damage to existing property). It should consider general benefits accruing to entire communities (like city-wide flood protection) as well as special benefits attaching to particular individuals or groups. It should take account of secondary as well as primary benefits, e.g., over and above the value of the immediate products or services of a project (like wheat from an irrigated farm), it should include values resulting from subsequent processing (milling the wheat). On the cost side, similarly, the appraisal should consider associated, secondary, or consequential costs (such as those which may result from the displacement of people from reservoir lands), as well as primary and direct costs of project construction, maintenance, and operation.

In order that benefits and costs may be evaluated on a comparable basis, they must be measured in common terms. Among the desired measurement standards are the following:

(*a*) *Uniform interest rates.* Allowance for interest should always be included in the evaluation process, whatever the policy toward ultimate repayment of project costs.

The monetary values of benefits and costs that accrue at varying times are mutually comparable only if all are adjusted to a uniform time basis. Interest rates are a measure of the value attached to time differences, and hence, provide a means for converting estimates to a common time point. The interest rates used for this purpose should in general be the long-term borrowing rates applicable.

(*b*) *Uniform amortization.* The maximum period of amortization for economic analysis should be the expected economic life of the project or fifty years, whichever is shorter.

A number of economic and physical forces limit the life of any project. Physical depreciation, obsolescence, changing requirements for project services, and time discount and allowances for risk and uncertainty may limit the present value of future project services. The economic life of a project is determined by the point in time at which the effect of the foregoing factors is to cause the costs of continuing the project to exceed the additional benefits to be expected from continuation. As so used economic life is generally less than the physical life of a project, and never more than the estimated physical life.[6]

While economic life establishes an upper limit on the period of analysis, it is often convenient and desirable to use a period short of this limit. A shorter period provides additional means of allowing for risks and for the difficulties and uncertainty associated with estimating the value of very remote effects. Today a subcommittee of the Federal Inter-Agency River Basin Committee recommends that one hundred years be considered as the upper limit of economic life. The Water Resources Committee in 1941 recommended fifty years. Whatever period is used, the amortization charge should be sufficient to cover the capital investment during the period of analysis, calculated on a sinking fund basis using long-term interest rates.

(*c*) *Uniform price levels.* The economic analysis should be stated in terms of prices expected to prevail at the time when costs are incurred and benefits received.

For construction costs, prices expected during the construction period should be used. In calculating most types of benefits, the prices used should be the average prices estimated to prevail over the life of the project.

Despite these and other standards for uniform measurement, the complexity of the many factors involved and the difficulty experienced in measuring them dictates caution in the finality with which hard ratios of measured costs to measured benefits are used.

(*2*) *Incremental benefits and costs.* As far as possible, the scope of a development should be expanded in respect to any or all of its purposes, or provision made for expansion in the future, to the extent that the incremental benefits exceed or equal the incremental costs of expansion.

The most effective use of economic resources is made if the amount by which benefits exceed costs is at a maximum (rather than if a maximum benefit-cost ratio is produced). That condition is met if the development is extended to the point where the benefits added by the last increment of extension of scope are equal to the costs of adding that increment. (Separable segments or increments of size of a project are the smallest segments or increments on which there is a practical choice as to inclusion or omission from the project.)

The same principle applies for multiple-purpose developments in selecting the purposes or functions to be included. The addition of a function is justified if the benefits from the added function are equal to or greater than the separable costs incurred solely for that purpose.

(*3*) *Alternate means of serving a function.* The project and any separable segment selected to accomplish a given purpose should be more economical than any other actual or potential available means of accomplishing that specific purpose which would be displaced or precluded from development if the project is undertaken.

At various stages of project formulation, the program, project, or segment of a project under consideration must satisfy the criterion that it would be more economical than any other . . . means of accomplishing

RESPONSIBILITY TO PROFESSION

the specific purpose involved . . . It should not be undertaken if it would preclude development of any other means of accomplishing the same results at less cost. This limitation applies to alternative possibilities which would be displaced or economically precluded from development if the project is undertaken. Other means of obtaining similar benefits which would not be precluded from development are not limitations on project justification but are, in effect, additional projects which may be compared in an array to determine which should be given prior consideration from the standpoint of economic desirability.[7]

Thus, for multiple-purpose projects, alternative means of serving each function should be considered, and no function should be undertaken if its separable costs exceed the total costs of an alternative means of supply which would be precluded by construction of the project.[8]

REPAYMENT OF COSTS

As a general principle development costs should be repaid by the beneficiaries, with due consideration for the amounts of benefits received.

This general principle is developed more fully in the separate paragraphs which follow. However, it should be noted here that a number of water economists hold that repayment by beneficiaries should be controlled by their *ability to repay* rather than by *amounts of benefits received*. The relation between these two repayment concepts is controlled in part by the type of economic analysis used in the first place.

(1) Federal contributions. In accordance with the general repayment principle, Federal contributions should be limited to amounts proportionate to the estimated national benefits involved.

The key to this test is the definition of national benefits. They could be defined so narrowly in flood protection, for example, that only the benefits from protection of Federal property would be included. Or they could be defined quite broadly so as to include national defense or the new market for manufactured goods created by opening up new agricultural lands. It is believed that the most workable definition which accords with the general principle is one which would limit national benefits to those which cannot be identified with any other beneficiaries — individuals, organizations, or any levels of government below the Federal. If certain benefits cannot be identified with particular beneficiaries, then it follows that they are so broad in their incidence that the costs of providing them should be paid for generally by the nation's taxpayers.[9]

To this method of determining national contributions there will be two important qualifications in accordance with national policies adopted by Congress: provision for special Federal aid to economically distressed areas (which, of course, will vary); and provision for aid to depressed social groups.

(2) *Charges for vendible services.* Where benefits to both public and private beneficiaries are vendible, charges should be made with due regard for the volume of benefits.

The major products of water development which may be sold unit by unit are hydroelectric power; domestic, industrial, and irrigation water; and navigation facilities. In formulating rate policies for these and other vendible products, repayment of a fair share of the costs should not be the sole consideration, however. Two other factors should be weighed: (1) the most efficient areal distribution of agriculture and industry and the most efficient use of natural and human resources; and (2) wider policies applicable to particular services, such as the use of public competition as a regulatory device. As a general rule, "no group of project beneficiaries should be required to support more than a justifiable share of the costs because they consume a vendible service. At the same time, a maximum limit will be set to charges by the cost of an alternative means of supply, if such an alternative exists."

(3) *Charges for nonvendible services.* Where benefits to both public and private beneficiaries are nonvendible, suitable techniques should be devised for assessment.

For charging costs of nonvendible benefits, benefits from flood protection, for example, reliance should be placed upon the States. The Federal Government should avoid the impolitic consequences of contractual relations with individuals for property assessment purposes. And there are some who assert that the Federal Government is without authority to levy such assessments; that they are in essence direct taxes, and that the Federal Government may not levy direct taxes (other than income taxes) except in proportion to the entire population.

The fact, however, that the Federal Government should not make direct charges for nonvendible services should not serve to obscure the basic principle that beneficiaries should repay in proportion to benefits received. Suitable means should be found for assessing these beneficiaries. These means must include (1) collecting from individuals by an authority which has been granted the power to tax by the State; and (2) negotiating a contract between this taxing authority and the Federal Government whereby the Government requires as a condition of building the project that the authority contribute an amount in proportion to the nonvendible benefits. In this connection, fruitful experiments have been made by States and municipalities in assessments for sewage disposal and other special purposes. Similar techniques for flood control were applied successfully on a large scale by the Miami Conservancy District, as described briefly in Chapter II.

Repayment contracts should allow sufficient flexibility to care for economic fluctuations. "Where the incomes of beneficiaries are subject to marked fluctuations from causes beyond their control, the Federal investment will be safeguarded best by provision in repayment contracts for flexibility to make allowances for such fluctuations." One important type of flexibility can be obtained by allowing developmental periods immediately after a project is put into service, when amortization charges may be deferred in whole or in part.

ADVANCE OF CAPITAL

The Federal Government should be ready to advance capital for the construction of all developments in which a substantial national interest is involved.

Two analytically separate functions, often confused, should be distinguished carefully in considering the financing of water developments. One is the *advance of capital* for project construction in the first instance; the other is *repayment,* or the ultimate provision of project costs. Different standards apply for these separate functions, and the standard for advance of capital depends on the definition of "substantial national interest" for this function. According to the WRC:

Such a national interest presumably inheres in all projects toward which the Federal Government . . . will contribute part of the ultimate cost, and also in projects that are local in scope but represent furtherance of region wide or Nation wide policy . . . Ordinarily Federal credit will obtain a saving of one percent or more in the interest rate, a sizable amount where capital charges are a large share of the annual burden. The interstate character of most drainage basins and the benefits which accrue to the Nation as a whole from wise use of its water resources make it appropriate for the National Government to supply this banking service as its normal minimum contribution.

PREVENTING SPECULATION

Speculation in benefits derived from Federal developments should be avoided.

Speculation occurs usually where project benefits accrue to a few rather than the greatest number of beneficiaries and where vendible benefits pass through the hands of one or more intermediaries before reaching the ultimate consumer. The types of measures that may be adopted to avoid speculation are illustrated by the following in current use: for irrigation, limiting to one hundred and sixty acres lands in a single ownership to which project waters will be delivered, and requiring that excess lands be sold at a price which excludes value added by the Federal development; for hydroelectric power, providing priority to publicly owned systems in distribution of power produced at Federal developments, and for this purpose constructing power lines to load centers.

STATE REGULATORY MEASURES

The Federal Government should make contributions to water developments contingent upon enactment by the States to be benefited of legislation designed to insure the most effective and full use of the benefits.

The nature of the legislation will vary with that of the development and will depend in large part on policies adopted to implement the tests stated previously. For a development providing flood protection, for example, it may be essential that a State enact zoning legislation to control settlement in the flood plain; for one providing irrigation, legislation to prevent extension of the irrigated area beyond the limits of reliable water supply; for development of hydroelectric power, legislation to authorize formation of distribution cooperatives.

ESTABLISHED LEGAL RIGHTS AND RESPONSIBILITIES

In planning any water development, an agency should observe the legal rights of individuals, groups, and States, wherever they are involved.

"If such established rights are not in the public interest, they should be altered or withdrawn by due process of law; meanwhile, they should be recognized fully. (The words 'rights' and 'due process of law' are used in a realistic sense which recognizes the necessity for continuing changes in the conception of their meaning in the light of developing human needs.)"

The major concern for water rights arises in the Western States where scarcity of water and related environmental factors have brought about the development of a complex system of water law, including individual property rights to appropriated waters.

Flood Control

More than any other agency, the Corps of Engineers has been concerned with the development of rivers for the purposes of navigation and flood control. Thus a comparison of national navigation and flood control policies and Engineer Department policy proposals with professional standards in these fields should provide an indication of the professional responsibility of the Corps. The standards will be the general tests for water development applied specifically to the functions involved.

The very fact that the Engineers have been concerned primarily with the development of rivers for navigation and flood control and only secondarily for other purposes would appear to be a serious deviation from the true multiple-purpose test; and indeed it is. But even with a genuine multiple-purpose approach to water development, functional policies are needed. In the analysis which follows we shall concentrate on the policies first for flood control and then for navigation, and overlook for the time being the Corps' limited-purpose point of view.

"Floods are 'acts of God,' but flood losses are largely acts of man. Human encroachment upon the flood plains of rivers accounts for the high annual toll of flood loss." Dealing with floods, therefore, is a problem "of adjusting human occupance to the flood plain environment so as to utilize most effectively the natural resources of the plain, and, at the same time, of applying feasible and practicable measures for minimizing the detrimental impacts of floods." [10]

In the words of a distinguished geographer and water expert, Gilbert F. White, this is the only sound approach to the flood problem. In terms of general water planning, these words express the broader interest for flood control policy — i.e., plans for adjusting to the flood hazard should be considered in the light of the more general problems of land use and flood plain occupance. Thus, if the resources of flood plains are to be used in the public good so as to yield maximum returns to the nation with minimum possible social costs, action affecting their continued occupance must be based upon the following essentials:

First, all possible adjustments of occupance which might be made to the flood hazard should be taken into account. At least seven types of adjustments have been tried successfully.

(1) *Land elevation* provides a permanent means of escape from floods at relatively high construction costs. It is impracticable for densely settled areas, but may be suited to new urban developments, to strategic sections of highways and railways, and to isolated residential, commercial, and other occupance in sparsely settled flood plains.

(2) *Flood abatement* by means of erosion control, forest planting, and related methods of land improvement and management in areas upstream from a flood plain affords the possibility of reducing the magnitude of floods in a few sections. However, the principal effect on floods of land use and vegetative measures applied to the lands of a watershed is in the reduction of the small, but frequent floods on small but medium sized streams.[11] Such measures will produce only very slight reductions in the great floods that do so much damage to cities on the main stems of major rivers, because intense or prolonged rains produce so much water that even watersheds in the best of condition cannot hold the flood or storm runoff. Thus, the major benefits of land management measures accrue to the owners of the land on which the improvements are made.

(3) *Flood protection* by levees and floodwalls, channel improvements, diversions, and reservoirs is in many instances the most reliable means of reducing flood losses. Any sound evaluation of protective works, however, requires appraisal on a consistent basis of all possible costs, social as well as engineering, and all possible benefits.

(4) *Emergency measures,* such as emergency removal of populations and movable property, emergency levees and bulkheads, coating of immovable machinery parts with protective oil, may reduce greatly the impact of floods if there are accurate, timely forecasts of their occurrence and height, if efficient plans for emergency action have been prepared, and if the persons affected know the plans sufficiently to act promptly. "It is believed that in most urban areas the mean annual flood losses could be reduced by at least 15%, and, under favorable circumstances, as much as 50% by emergency measures. They have been adopted by only some of the public utilities and large manufacturers, and they are generally not practiced or even understood by small property owners and by occupants of upper flood zones."

(5) *Structural adjustments* may be used to prevent or reduce losses of valuable property, interruptions of essential public services, and scouring of farm land. Without attempting to provide protection for an entire area subject to floods, changes in building design, communication lines, street grades, and like measures, in conjunction with emergency measures, can minimize, or even eliminate, public utility interruptions in urban areas, and can reduce materially losses to buildings and lands in rural areas.

(6) *Land use readjustment* can prevent largely those losses in agricultural areas which accrue to property and crops that do not depend upon social advantages of flood plain location. It can also curb unsound urban occupance of undeveloped land. In this connection, zoning can be an effective means of preventing further undesirable human encroachment upon flood plains and of promoting improved land use therein.

(7) *Insurance* against flood losses has failed under private management in the United States. However, "it is a measure that probably would be practicable if national coverage and guarantees against catastrophic losses were to be provided during the early years of operation. Once in operation, it would allow systematic indemnification of losses, and an inspection service which would promote the adoption in unprotected areas of emergency measures and of structural and land-use readjustments."

Second, in comparing possible adjustments a sound approach to the flood problem should evaluate for each (a) the advantages and disadvantages of the site for the particular occupance in question;

and (b) the benefits and costs of making the adjustment. The relations of factors affecting the feasibility of a single adjustment can be written in this general form:

$$\text{Economic justification} = \frac{\text{Advantages of site + benefits from readjustment}}{\text{Disadvantages of site + costs of readjustment}}$$

This formula applies equally well to all types of adjustments. However, it has real significance only when used simultaneously for all possible adjustments in a flood plain. For example, a flood protective work for a utility may be justified if viewed alone, but it may be far less desirable if compared with a plan for structural change or for emergency measures.

This formula adopts a much broader view than is commonly applied. A formula for most estimates used in the past in determining the feasibility of flood protection would be written:

$$\text{Economic justification} = \frac{\text{Benefits from protection}}{\text{Costs of protection}}$$

Such a formula "ignores the question of whether or not a given location has real advantages for present or prospective uses. From the standpoint of the individual property owner concerned, that question may seem irrelevant because it may be argued that the only issue for him is whether or not he will prosper in his present location. From the broad standpoint of rational utilization of resources of the flood plain, the prosperity of the individual is not an entirely reliable index, inasmuch as it may be developed at the cost of public subsidy for relief and protection."

As can be seen, the recommended method for comparing adjustments takes into account both the broad approach to the flood problem and the principles for economic soundness. It requires that benefits exceed costs, that as nearly as practicable all benefits and all costs be counted, and that each possible adjustment be measured against alternative means.

A word of warning, however, about the use of a simple ratio as a final expression of the feasibility of a given adjustment. The components of any comparative evaluation are complex and often difficult to measure. Since there can seldom be assurance that all pertinent data have been evaluated properly, caution should be exercised in the use of ratios.

Third, any action should promote that occupance most likely to contribute to effective use of flood plain resources. To illustrate, there follow some considerations that might affect a choice in terms of this principle of action: All possible adjustments except those in land use and insurance tend to favor the preservation of existing land occupance; insurance and structural adjustments, by requiring a property owner to make some payment for the advantages of flood plain location which he enjoys, stimulate the abandonment of occupance that is not profitable; flood protection, by placing upon public agencies the major burden of losses, encourages the occupants of flood plains to seek this adjustment at public expense even though other adjustments at private expense might be less costly and more effective from the national standpoint.

ENGINEER DEPARTMENT POLICY FALLS SHORT OF THESE ESSENTIALS

To what extent does Engineer Department policy meet the requirements of a sound approach to the flood problem? It fails to take into account all possible adjustments which might be made to the flood hazard. Surveys of the flood problem are directed almost exclusively at engineering works for flood protection. The National Resources Planning Board and the Water Resources Committee have complained that "attention has been centered too much upon control of destructive flood waters, or upon protection against them by physical works, and too little upon control of the occupation and use of valley bottoms, which are natural floodways. Too often the habits of the rivers have been ignored." [12]

Present policy "deals solely with the regulation or control of flood waters through watershed protection, reservoirs, levees, floodwalls, channel improvements, and the like — ignoring the possibility of reducing flood damages through improved storm warnings, through well planned measures for temporary evacuation of threatened areas upon the approach of uncontrolled flood waters, and through control of hazards by zoning restrictions covering property subject to overflow. [Present policy] ignores the established natural habits of the rivers." [13]

In reporting to the President in July 1940 on the USED survey report on the Thames River in New England, the chairman of the Resources Board objected that "attention is focused almost wholly on engineering works as remedies for flood damage to the virtual exclusion of other types of remedies such as zoning, readjustments in structures and public utilities, temporary evacuation plans, and insurance. The other remedies may be cheaper and more effective, but without field study we are not in a position to state any conclusions." [14]

A good example of the failure of the Engineer Department to consider the possibility of reducing flood losses by land elevation is found in the report of the Chief of Engineers on New Creek, Staten Island, New York. By using the traditional cost-benefit formula for determining justification, the Corps of Engineers found a flood protection project justified for the New Creek area. The project was deferred, however, at the request of municipal authorities who planned instead to raise street levels and sidewalk levels in preparing the area for subdivision.[15]

The Congress has recognized the possibility of a change in land use as an alternative to local protective works by authorizing the Chief of Engineers, in lieu of constructing such works, to contribute equivalent funds to those municipalities that prefer to relocate on higher ground. However, in no instance has this authority been used to date. The reasons for the lack of application of the subsidy for relocation are not entirely clear, but are believed to be due in part to the attitude of the Engineer Department.[16]

It is true that measures for flood abatement are surveyed by the Department of Agriculture; but the failure of the two Departments to prepare joint reports, as has been pointed out, has resulted in an unfortunate separation of the planning for upstream and downstream water control.

Failing to take into account all possible adjustments which may be made to the flood hazard, the Engineer Department is unable, for any given area, to compare all factors affecting the success of the flood plain occupance which is possible under the various adjustments, and to evaluate upon any consistent basis the comparative benefits and costs of the possible adjustments. Furthermore, the Engineers apply the restricted benefit-cost formula for determining the justification of flood protective works rather than the broader view encompassed in the formula which uses advantage and disadvantage of site as well as benefit and cost of readjustment. In using this restricted formula, which precludes the evaluation of all available data, the Engineer Department has sought a degree of precision in measuring the ratio of costs to benefits which is not warranted by the coverage and reliability of the data measured.

Finally, in recommending action to reduce flood losses, the Engineer Department pays little or no attention to the desirability of the type of land occupance which will be promoted. "As a result, the national Treasury bears a large part of the costs of those who prefer to live on flood plains, and does so without inquiring as to whether or not such plains afford any pronounced advantages for such occupance."

Present policy often helps to stabilize uneconomic occupance. "Works for protection and abatement minimize the flood hazard at public expense for the most part, and in the process provide increments in land value to land owners, some of whom occupy the plain on a highly speculative basis." Some flood projects "have tended to embalm with public subsidies communities which have lost their part in regional and national life." At the same time, present policy often fails to offer any aid to economic occupance.

In areas where neither protection nor prevention is found to be economically feasible, the Federal Government assumes no responsibility for fostering types of adjustment other than public relief. It goes to great lengths to provide protection from floods if the cost-benefit ratio is favorable, but contents itself with helping merely to relieve and rehabilitate flood sufferers in areas where the ratio is unfavorable. Inasmuch as the cost-benefit ratio is no index of the economic vigor of a community, protection is given to some towns that are definitely decadent, while it is withheld from some areas where development, though recent, is highly promising.

Federal policy has been criticized particularly for failing to require proper State regulation of flood plain encroachment. In 1937 the Water Resources Committee stated:

Appropriate Federal, State, and local action looking toward the zoning of the flood plains of the rivers under discussion against undesirable and dangerous use is urgently needed . . . It is clear that social controls in the occupation and utilization of the flood plains of these rivers, especially in urbanized areas, may contribute much to a solution of the problem of their floods. If the reservoirs proposed in the past for tributaries of the Ohio were constructed, and if thereafter local interests at cities along the Ohio were to take advantage of the somewhat reduced flood heights that would result there, by occupying without restriction the banks of the river at lower levels than at present, then the value of the reservoirs to those cities might be reduced or nullified. In contrast, measures to *avoid* flood damage cannot fail to promote security. A comprehensive plan must utilize the potentialities of this field of action.[17]

Again in 1941 the subcommittee on national water policy, after examining the "fairly satisfactory experience" of the States of New Jersey, Pennsylvania, and Washington and that of some few municipalities in zoning their flood plains to prevent further unwise encroachment upon stream channels and to prevent uneconomic occupance hazardous to public health, concluded:

The public interest in these matters is great, and accordingly the Federal Government should promote in every way practicable the adoption of such regulatory measures as those indicated, in forms adjusted fairly to local conditions. The Federal Government invests heavily in the construction or rehabilitation of water projects that yield large local benefits. Without appropriate State or local regulations, Federal investments may be jeopardized. With them, the use of water resources by public agencies and by individuals alike will be greatly improved. It is recommended that this principle of action be incorporated in Federal policy, legislative and administrative.[18]

With respect to legislative policy, it was recommended specifically "that the Congress amend the Flood Control Act of June 22, 1936, as amended, so as to make further Federal contributions towards the cost of flood control projects conditional upon enactment by the States to be benefited of legislation prohibiting further undesirable encroachment upon stream channels."

Despite these several recommendations by committees of highly regarded experts, the Corps of Engineers has made no significant effort to obtain Congressional consideration of the desired legislative standards. In representing the executive establishment before Congressional committees concerned with flood control legislation, the Corps of Engineers has not mentioned most of these matters. With a few minor exceptions, survey reports of the Corps of Engineers have not contained recommendations that the standards be applied.[19]

As a consequence, it cannot be said with confidence that present Federal activities have the net effect of promoting sound land use . . . On the whole, present policy fosters an increasing dependence by individuals and local governments upon the Federal Government for leadership and financial support in dealing with the flood problem. While encouraging solicitation of further Federal aid and the establishment of types of occupance requiring such aid, the policy does not help or stimulate beneficiaries to explore the possibilities of making other adjustments with a view to promoting the most effective use of flood-plain resources.

FLOOD PROTECTION

It is evident, then, that the Engineer Department views the problem of preventing flood losses almost entirely in terms of engineering works for flood protection. Realizing the limitations of this approach, it is desirable nonetheless to examine briefly Engineer Department policies and procedures for planning these protective works, with special reference to the distribution of costs.

According to the repayment test of a sound water plan, the ultimate Federal contribution to any water project should be limited to amounts proportionate to the estimated national benefits, and State and local contributions should be required in proportion to benefits derived. Present flood control policy does not fulfill this requirement; and the USED has made no recommendations for change. Quite to the contrary, as a matter of fact, it has defended present policy against proposals which would bring it into accord with the desired principle.

The enactment of the Flood Control Act of 1936 was opposed by the National Resources Committee, in part, because of the provisions for local coöperation. These provisions required that State and local interests pay the costs of lands, damages, and operation and maintenance upon completion, and that the Federal Government pay the entire construction cost, except that if the cost of lands exceeded construction costs, the excess was to be divided evenly between the Federal and non-Federal agencies.

As early as July 1935, the chairman of the National Resources Committee reported to the Bureau of the Budget that the pending Flood Control Bill was unsatisfactory on these grounds. In the memorandum submitted by the NRC to the Budget Bureau, recommending that the President veto the enrolled bill, the chairman of the Water Resources Committee said, "the policy of allocation of costs proposed by the bill is inequitable and in the long run will tend to foster abuses of sound conservation principles. There is no logical reason for making the local and State contributions equal to and not to exceed the costs of rights-of-way, easements, and damages. In some projects these costs borne by local interests would amount to one-half the total cost of the project, and in other projects the local contributions would be two or three per cent only. These percentages bear no relation to the actual benefits received by local interests. Moreover, such a system of cost allocation would promote consideration of small-scale levee projects in which land and damage costs are relatively low, rather than of larger reservoir and cover-regulation projects having higher land costs. *The costs should be shared in part by local interests, but in proportion to the benefits received."*

Lt. Col. Edgerton of the Corps of Engineers and Mr. Tate of the Federal Power Commission, in dissenting from the WRC recommendations and in recommending that the President sign the bill, reasoned that although "the divisions of cost are not made upon the basis of the benefits that may accrue to the several interests affected, . . . such division is, at best, impracticable of precise determination, and it seems that simple rules of general application (such as those adopted in the bill) are practically necessary in legislation of this kind." The majority of the experts did not agree with Edgerton and Tate, for at a meeting of the executive committee of the WRC (of which Tate was not a member), called to discuss the dissent, the principles, policies, and criticisms of the chairman's memorandum were reaffirmed with the single dissent of the representative of the Corps of Engineers.[20]

Requirements for local coöperation were waived still further in the Flood Control Act of 1938. Because of difficulties in negotiating local contributions from groups of States benefiting from reservoir construction in a single State, and also in response to a desire of the public power groups to insure that full Federal authority to develop hydroelectric power at flood control dams would not be impaired by State control of reservoir operations (as contemplated in the proposed interstate compacts for the Connecticut and Merrimack Rivers), the financing of reservoir projects was made a complete Federal responsibility.[21] Local interests were no longer required to contribute lands and damages, nor to operate the projects upon completion. By this means, the major flood protection works proposed for many sections of the country became solely Federal in ownership and operation. Local requirements were removed for channel improve-

RESPONSIBILITY TO PROFESSION

ments, but they remained in effect for levees and other local protective works.[22]

The National Resources Committee opposed this legislation with even greater vigor for a number of reasons:[23]

First, the proposed provision would eliminate for reservoirs the principle of local participation.

The Committee [WRC] reaffirms the conclusions reached by itself and its predecessors on every occasion when the problems of local participation in the cost of water projects has been discussed. The principle of local participation in the cost of flood control and protection should be maintained in the interests of sound financial policy and of fundamental equity . . . Policy should . . . provide for allocation of costs in some fair proportion to the incidence of benefits. Federal contributions should normally be determined by and limited to the extent of national interest in the control and protection to be provided.

Second, the proposed provision would promote uneconomic projects.

It would remove the last real check against bold raids on the Federal Treasury for political but uneconomic projects. There are many reservoir projects for which local contributions could not be obtained because the benefits are slight, but which local groups would promote if they were to be financed wholly by the Federal Government. Local promoters would be encouraged to press for costly reservoirs in place of relatively inexpensive levees and channel improvements. The Kansas Cities, for example, under the proposed . . . amendment, doubtless would prefer a $51.8 million plan which would cost them nothing, to a proposed $10 million local levee plan which would cost them $5 million regardless of whether or not reservoirs, levees, or a combination of the two would best meet fundamental needs. (The reservoirs would have negligible power values.)

Third, the proposed provision would seriously affect the repayment principle in other water legislation.

The whole principle of local repayment for irrigation, water supply, low-water control, and other impounding projects would be destroyed, because every dam and reservoir has some flood control value, however slight. Such projects would soon be found creeping under the Federal flood control tent free of charge. The settlers of Federal reclamation projects almost certainly would refuse to repay their share of the costs of irrigation and power reservoirs if their neighbors were obtaining the same benefits from a reservoir built under the guise of flood control at no cost to the beneficiaries.

This prediction has been fulfilled with grim reality.

Fourth, the policy of local contribution should not be abandoned because of supposed difficulty in negotiating such contributions from groups of States benefiting from reservoir construction.

The Connecticut and Merrimack Valley flood control projects, cited as examples of delay, were not in fact delayed through failure to obtain local participation in costs. Agreements as to local participation were reached in less than a year following passage of the Flood Control Act. Local participation in costs has been assured in a number of other places throughout the United States, involving a cost of projects far exceeding the potentialities of budgetary allotment for the next three years.

Fifth, the policy of local contribution should not be abandoned because of difficulties in solution of collateral power issues. "The current controversy over these issues probably would have been avoided if the original Flood Control Act had adequately defined Federal policy with respect to them."

The NRC recommended Presidential veto; the War Department, approval. The President signed the bill. He apparently felt that the solution of the power problem was of paramount importance and that a politically feasible solution was at hand in the legislation.

The legislative policy for repayment of costs on flood control projects today, then, requires no local participation for dams and reservoirs, and local contribution of lands, damages, and maintenance and operation for local flood protection works, except for the great Mississippi River levees, floodwalls, and channel improvements for which no contributions are required. A few minor exceptions to this policy have also been authorized by the Congress from time to time for particular projects on the recommendation of the Chief of Engineers. The Engineer Department, however, has not used its discretionary authority of recommendation to promote in any significant manner the desired principle of local contributions in proportion to local benefits.[24] In those few cases where, for example, local contributions for land enhancement have been proposed, they have been inadequate. Thus, after reviewing the report of the Chief of Engineers on Green and Duwamish Rivers in Washington, the Bureau of the Budget wrote to the Secretary of the Army as follows:

... The estimates of [annual] benefits also include $405,000 for land enhancement which, as the reports correctly state, are direct benefits to the landowners warranting a substantial local contribution toward the first cost of the improvement. As these benefits constitute 45 percent of the total amount used in obtaining the benefit-cost ratio of 1.08, I do not believe that the $2,000,000 proposed in the report, or 10 percent of the total construction cost ($18,300,000), represents a "substantial" contribution by local interests. On the basis of information contained in the report, the actual monetary profit which will accrue to the landowners from the improvement is of sufficient magnitude to warrant local interests sharing at least equally the proportional part of the total costs of the work which land enhancement values bear to the total benefits ... In view of the above, I am authorized ... to advise you that, while there would be no objection to the submission of the report to the Congress, authorization of the recommended improvement on the basis of the amount of the proposed local contribution ... should not be considered to be in accord with the program of the President.[25]

Despite the Budget letter, the Green and Duwamish Rivers report was submitted to Congress by the Engineers with their recommendation that local contributions be kept at two million dollars; and Congress authorized the project in the Flood Control Act of 1950 in accordance with the USED proposals.[26]

As long as local contributions for large flood control projects remain relatively small, the recommended techniques for indirect assessment of private beneficiaries and for flexibility in repayment cannot apply in full force to Engineer Department procedures. The Corps has done nothing to encourage the formation of conservation or water use districts coterminous with the area of incidence of project benefits; nor, to the knowledge of this author, has it conducted any pilot studies to determine the utility of this device.[27] Where the Corps has required local contributions, these, with the exception of operation and maintenance expenses, have been made as lump-sum payments. As such, they inject an element of rigidity rather than flexibility into the repayment procedure, for there is no assurance that the means available to the local unit to finance its lump-sum payment will be sufficiently flexible to allow for the fluctuations in economic status of the beneficiaries.

The extent to which flood control policy meets the desired standards for advance of capital is somewhat confused by the fact that the functions of repayment and advance of capital are generally combined in a single action. One might say that the Federal Government, as recommended, advances capital for the construction of projects in which a substantial national interest is involved; and that, in the case of local protective works, a desirable joint participation in the advance of capital is promoted by requiring local contributions in kind, as with lands.

A major deficiency in flood control policy lies in its failure to limit either the amount of direct benefits that may accrue to any one individual from Federal river works or speculation in these benefits. The Corps of Engineers has not made recommendations to Congress with respect to the enactment of general provisions for these purposes. In its survey reports it has not recommended that State or local regulation of monopoly and speculation be made a requirement for Federal construction of projects. Corps survey reports do not, as a rule, identify *who* is to benefit from proposed Federal improvements — i.e., landownership surveys are not a part of the reports. The surveys may state how much land is to be protected, the value of the protection to be provided, and the population of the affected area; but the actual landowners, the size of their holdings, and the concentration or dispersion of benefits are seldom given attention. It is believed that close investigation would reveal for many projects a considerable concentration of benefits in few hands and for others, scandalous speculation in flood lands protected by Federal projects at Federal expense.

Some have held that speculation and monopoly controls are exceedingly difficult to apply to flood protection, as compared to irrigation, because flood protection does not involve a vendible service which can be withheld in the case of noncompliance. This same type of reasoning holds that application of the repayment principle is exceedingly difficult for flood protection. However, as in the case of repayment, it is believed that techniques for speculation and monopoly control can be devised for lands protected from floods by Federal projects. For example, we have held that the Federal Government should make contributions to water development projects contingent upon the enactment by States to be benefited of legislation designed to insure the most effective and full use of the project benefits. Under this principle, States or their political subdivisions — in this case, perhaps, conservancy districts — can be required to enact legislation or regulations to ensure the broadest distribution of benefits from projects financed with Federal funds.

As we shall see later, basic irrigation policy conforms more nearly to the desired principles for repayment and speculation control. The fact that a considerable gap separates flood control and irrigation policy in these respects creates certain basic inequities about which the National Resources Planning Board, among others, has complained. In its last regular report, the Board said:

> Existing differences in functional policies have widespread effects which are independent of basin boundaries. One of the most striking examples is the difference between the repayment provisions of the Reclamation Act of 1902 and the subsidy elements of the Flood Control Act of 1938. Under the provisions of the Reclamation Act, a farmer receiving water from an irrigation project must participate in the costs of the project through repayment of a specified sum over a 40-year period. In the same general region, perhaps not a hundred miles away, a farmer owning land in a frequently flooded overflow area may contribute nothing to the costs of a flood control reservoir to protect his lands. In each case the farmer involved is able to convert lands to more productive use, to more profitable cultivation. In the first instance the beneficiary pays his share of the direct project costs; in the second case he may or may not be required to contribute to the cost of the reservoir, depending on the size and character of the flood control project. Yet in both cases the Federal Government is instrumental in building and financing the work. The relation between the provisions of these two laws, and others in the water resource development field, promotes competition between Federal agencies, as well as between local groups interested in obtaining Federal assistance.[28]

Thus we conclude that Engineer Department policies and procedures for flood protection — with respect to repayment of costs and certain other features — fail to meet many established standards for professional responsibility. It must be remembered, however, that flood protective works are only one possible adjustment which might be made to the flood hazard and that, by considering this adjustment alone, the Engineer Department is more seriously failing in responsibility to profession.

Navigation

As broad problems of flood plain use form the framework within which Engineer Corps flood control policies must be examined, so the requirements of an integrated national land and water transportation system constitute the broader interest for USED domestic navigation policies. Although committees of transportation experts are notorious for their inability to come to agreement on important issues, there is general concurrence that waterway projects should be appraised as components of a general transportation system, not as separate entities.[29] Application of this principle would appear to involve four essentials described at some length in the material which follows.

Other transportation facilities. A sound domestic navigation policy should give full regard to the effect of navigation facilities upon the operation of other transportation facilities.

The effect of waterways on other types of transportation involves the complicated problem of the relative economy of the several types of carriers. It is axiomatic that the relative economy of a proposed waterway cannot be determined without a careful study of related transportation facilities in the area. Yet, the chairman of the Planning Board subcommittee on national water policy noted in 1940 that "no systematic study of a proposed waterway as a component of a transportation system involving water transport, rail transport, truck transport, and pipeline transport, has been made [by the Corps of Engineers] in any region, so far as known, in preparation for a decision with respect to Congressional action on the proposed waterway. No satisfactory technique has been announced, so far as known, for such a study." [30]

Furthermore, the prescribed USED procedure for evaluating benefits from proposed waterways fails to provide for a consistent consideration of relative efficiency. Benefits are estimated in terms of rate savings on expected traffic — i.e., the savings that will accrue to shippers if they use the waterway rather than the cheapest alternative means, usually railroads. Thus, existing rail rates are compared to the rates that will be charged by water carriers if the project is built. The comparative rates used by the Engineers, however, make no allowance for expenditures incurred by governments in providing transportation facilities and services. As governments incur large expenditures for waterways and relatively none for railways, the comparative rates, on which the economic justifications are established, do not reflect necessarily the relative economy of water and land transportation. "The significant costs in considering the relative economy of transportation on improved waterways obviously must include public costs as well as the carriers' costs; conclusions based on the latter costs only are bound to be misleading." [31]

The question of allowance for public costs, in turn, brings up the subject of user charges. The principle that users should pay the costs of public facilities for water transportation has been advocated for sound water development policy, sound transportation policy, and sound general national policy.

Considered from the point of view of water development policy, the Mississippi Valley Committee in 1934 and the Water Resources Committee in 1937 and 1941 have advocated toll charges.[32] The principle that beneficiaries should repay costs has been established as one of the tests of a sound water plan; and tolls represent an application of this test to the navigation use of water.

Viewed in the perspective of national transportation policy, the Interstate Commerce Commission in 1932; the Federal Coördinator of Transportation in 1938; the President's Committee of Six on the General Transportation Situation in 1938; the National Resources Planning Board in its report on transportation and national policy in 1942; Mr. Webb and the staff of the Board of Investigation and Research in 1945; Dearing and Owen in their report on transportation policy for the Brookings Institution and the Hoover Commission in 1949; and the Secretary of Commerce in a report to the President on transportation coördination in 1949 all have advocated or discussed in a favorable light the imposition of charges for the use of publicly financed waterway facilities.[33]

Finally, in terms of general national policy, President Roosevelt in his Budget message to the Congress of January 1940 said: "I have always believed that many facilities made available to our citizens by the Government should be paid for, at least in part, by those who use them . . . It would seem reasonable that some portion of these annual expenditures [for maintenance of dredged channels, etc.] should come back in the form of small fees from the users of our lakes, channels, harbors, and coasts." [34]

The special advantages of water user charges, particularly from the transportation point of view, are:

(1) They are a useful financial expedient in lieu of general taxes. "It is sound fiscal policy generally to require the recipients of special economic benefits from governmental activities to pay directly, at

least in part, for those benefits." [35] The important question here is whether the benefits of water transportation are so predominantly general and widespread as to justify their support by the general taxpayer; or whether they aid in large measure distinguishable economic groups, such as certain primary producers, carriers, industries, consumers. Water use statistics indicate that "while waterways, as public facilities, are theoretically available to all, only a comparatively few individuals and business enterprises find it practicable to take advantage of this opportunity." [36] The major industries are petroleum, coal, and iron ore.

There are in many instances collateral benefits that may well constitute a proper charge on the general taxpayer such, for example, as public subsidies to insure growth of newly developed industries. But the costs of providing these benefits should be met by subsidy grants specifically authorized by Congress and should not obscure the general principle of beneficiary repayment.

(2) User charges encourage the use of economic criteria in the planning and programming of navigation projects. By placing the burden of waterway costs directly on those who use the facilities, the collection of user payments would tend to promote sounder planning of waterway projects. It would "provide greater protection against agitation for wasteful navigation projects, and thus more effectively confine such public expenditures to those projects which have an economical place in a well balanced transportation system." It would "reduce pressures upon the Federal Government by individuals, commercial groups, and sections of the country whose interests center in having facilities of special advantage to them provided at the expense of the Nation as a whole." [37] And it would promote greater care in the prediction of benefits from proposed projects. If the Engineer Department knew that its estimates of expected waterway traffic, used as a basis for economic justification, could and would be measured in the future against actual toll receipts, then it would likely be more careful and more conservative in these estimates.[38]

(3) User charges establish a sounder basis for maintaining competitive relationships among transportation facilities. "That charging the user for public facilities should tend to reduce the inequalities among transport media, and thereby permit a more economic assignment of traffic, seems fairly apparent . . . The absence of

user charges, as on toll-free waterways, may mean that the allocation of traffic between waterways and other facilities is a function of the subsidy rather than any consideration of true economy." [39]

It is not claimed that inequalities among transport facilities would be eliminated by user charges. The differing methods of public financing for waterway improvements, and private financing for railway improvements present further problems which are not discussed here. Without question, though, user charges would reduce the inequalities significantly.

(4) User charges can eliminate or set the stage for elimination of uneconomic eccentricities in the transportation rate structure. The fact that waterway improvements are provided without direct charges to users contributes in an important way to these eccentricities. To compete with subsidized water transportation, the railroads, subject to whatever limitations are imposed by regulatory agencies, often depress to an uneconomic level their rates on freight that competes with waterways. They "lose" money on these out-of-pocket-costs rates, but may make up the loss by charging higher rates on freight for which there is no water competition. Thus, as Dearing and Owen point out, the shippers who are not in a position to utilize subsidized water competition are placed at a double disadvantage. As taxpayers they must contribute to the cost of improving waterways which they cannot use, and at the same time they must pay higher railroad rates in order to compensate for the railroads' uneconomic reduction in rates on traffic which competes with subsidized water transportation.[40]

As a consequence, neither the carriers by water nor their competitors are providing transportation at rates (or costs) which reflect the real economy of their respective operations. "Collection of charges to cover a proper share of the costs of waterway facilities would remove one of the significant factors which is now responsible for distortions in the existing structure of transportation rates." [41] If the collection of tolls were not to eliminate uneconomic rail rates automatically, then it would become the responsibility of the Interstate Commerce Commission to compel railroads to establish rates that truly represent their relative economies.

All advocates of user charges recognize that the imposition of tolls for waterways would introduce numerous problems. If the traditional policy in this matter were changed, it would seem to be desirable to (1) avoid an unduly abrupt and drastic reversal by a gradual transition for some waterways; (2) consider the necessary exemptions or other preferential treatment of any types of carriers, commodities, and traffic which may not have the ability to pay full costs; (3) allow a toll-free developmental period on new waterways which have not had a reasonable opportunity to develop a mature traffic; (4) exercise care to exclude in rate calculations past costs for improvements which are now obsolete and from which present users derive no benefits; (5) insure that users are not charged for collateral benefits which may constitute a proper charge on the general fund; and (6) weigh carefully the desirability of eliminating the use of public funds on those existing waterways which are uneconomic. If tolls are insufficient to cover the total annual expenditure to maintain and replace existing facilities, it does not necessarily follow that the waterways should be abandoned, since all the costs sunk in these enterprises would thereby be lost.[42]

Despite these problems, user charges are considered both desirable and feasible. "None of the limitations which qualify the self-liquidating principle, however, seems to possess sufficient long-run importance to modify the general conclusion that user charges for highways, waterways, and air facilities, in addition to being desirable, are feasible as a method of finance." [43]

The Corps of Engineers is opposed to including public costs, along with carrier costs, in comparing rail and water rates in order to establish the economic justification of projects, and to imposing any tolls or user charges on water carriers. The traditional inhibition of the Engineer Department with respect to making policy recommendations does not extend, apparently, to this issue. In discussing the proposed report on national water policy at a WRC meeting on 8 November 1940, General Schley referred to the recommendation on tolls for waterways and reminded the Committee that the Chief of Engineers had previously reported unfavorably on this to the President in a special report.[44] The statement on inland water transportation, prepared under the direction of the Chief of Engineers for the NRPB transportation study, recommends strongly against the consideration of public costs in economic justification and against tolls.[45]

The Engineers point out the traditional policy of the Government to treat waterways as free public highways. This policy found expression as early as 1787 in Article 4 of the Northwest Ordinance which stated: "The navigable waterways leading into the Mississippi and St. Lawrence, and the carrying places between the same, shall be common highways, and forever free, as well to the inhabitants of said territory as to the citizens of the United States, and those of any other States that may be admitted into the confederacy, without any tax, impost or duty therefor."

Since then the no-toll policy has been reaffirmed periodically. For example, the Rivers and Harbors Act of 1882 provided: "No tolls or operating charges whatever shall be levied upon or collected from any vessel, dredge or other water craft for passing through any lock, canal, canalized river, or other work for the use and benefit of navigation now belonging to the United States or that may be hereafter constructed." [46]

More fundamentally however, the Engineers attack the theory that tolls should be established in order to develop a sounder basis for competitive relationships among transportation facilities. Their argument is as follows:[47]

Cost of service is not the governing factor in fixing the rates of competitive railroads. Railroads establish uneconomic rates (out-of-pocket-costs rates) on freight that competes with waterways.

The effect of such differential rating is to keep freight that economically should travel on waterways, on the railroads instead, because of the better service which railroads can offer. Therefore, waterways are not used to the extent that they should be, economically, and as a result, unit costs are relatively high.

The most disastrous effect of the current system of permitting high cost, high grade carriers to compete, by means of unremunerative rates, with low cost, low grade carriers for low grade traffic, is the diversion from waterways, without profit to anybody, of traffic which they could serve adequately and economically. In thus curtailing water-borne tonnage it produces misleading unit cost statistics applied to the provision of channels and locks — statistics which are used with skill and effectiveness by opponents of the national waterway policy.

For these reasons, at least until such time as water-borne tonnage is allowed to swell to the predicted volume when permitted freely to seek water routes, uninfluenced by competitive rail rate depression, improvement costs should not be included in comparative rate figures for economic justification, and tolls should not be charged.

This argument is subject to criticism on several grounds. In the first place, the USED *Orders and Regulations* instruct all Engineers to estimate benefits for economic justification in survey reports by comparing *present* railroad rates with prospective water rates. Presumably the *present* rail rates — rates in effect before any water project is authorized — are not depressed. It is hard to see how the Engineer argument can support the practice of not including public improvement costs in water rates which are to be compared with undepressed rail rates to determine the economic justification of a project.

If water rate figures used in survey reports were revised to include both carrier costs and public improvement costs, the economic justification for any project would be determined by a simple comparison of rail and water rates. That is, assuming the water rates to be lower, the differential between the two rates would be multiplied by the amount of traffic (in ton-miles) which, after a development period, could be expected to move if asked to bear full costs. This would not give the same result as the Engineers now obtain by establishing a ratio between the annual costs of a project (derived by amortizing the investment and adding annual maintenance costs) and the annual benefits (derived by comparing rail rates to subsidized water carrier rates), for the simple reason that estimated volume of traffic is likely to be much greater where the rate comparisons are based on the lower subsidized water rates, which include no allowance for waterway improvement costs.[48]

In the second place, even if the *present* rail rates are already uneconomically depressed, or if it is feared that an uneconomic reduction in rail rates after a project is built will adversely affect its economic justification, then the duty of the Chief of Engineers as a *public* servant is not to recommend the construction of additional costly water projects on a justification which fails to include in water rates the public costs of improvements, but to estimate the traffic distribution which will result from rail and water rates, both based upon full cost of service, and then, if the project appears justified, to recommend its construction and at the same time to recommend that the railroads be made to establish fully economic rates by regulation if they fail to do so on their own accord.

A good example of the problems created by Engineer Department policies for determining the economic justification of navigation projects is found in a case study of the Lake Erie and Ohio River canal.[49] In 1934 the Chief of Engineers recommended a project for improving the Beaver and Mahoning Rivers in Pennsylvania and Ohio so as to provide a navigable canal from the improved Ohio River to Youngstown, Ohio — the so-called Beaver-Mahoning stub-end canal. In adopting this project in the Rivers and Harbors Act of 1935, the Congress provided that its authorization was to be subject to final approval by the Board of Engineers for Rivers and Harbors of a through canal from the Ohio River to Lake Erie, of which the stub-end canal would form one section.

On 24 January 1939, the Secretary of War submitted to the President "in compliance with your instructions" the report of the Chief of Engineers on the through canal. The construction of the long canal from the Ohio River through the Beaver, Mahoning, and Grand River Valleys to Lake Erie was recommended by the Board of Engineers and concurred in by the Chief of Engineers. The construction costs were estimated at $240 million — $226 million to the Federal Government and $14 million to local interests. The prospective traffic for the canal was 28 million tons per annum. The savings in transportation costs to users of the canal, figured by comparison of present rail rates to prospective subsidized water rates, would be approximately $20 million per annum, or 72 cents a ton as against a Federal and non-Federal annual cost of $12 million, or 43 cents per ton. This left a net saving of approximately $8 million, or 29 cents per ton, which was considered sufficient to justify the project.

If the railroads would permanently reduce their rates by an average of 29 cents per ton (on traffic which the Board of Engineers estimated would move on the canal) prior to the construction of the waterway, the through project would not be justified.

In view of the uncertainty as to the extent and effect of future rail rate reductions, it was recommended that the construction of the canal be made in two or three steps, the first being the improvement of the stub-end canal to Youngstown, for which a modification of the previously adopted plan was recommended. The estimated construction cost of the stub-end canal was $42 million — $38 million to the United States and $4 million to local interests.

"The extension of the waterway, in part or in full, to Lake Erie should be undertaken only if found advisable after the first section to Struthers (Youngstown) has been opened to traffic and after a

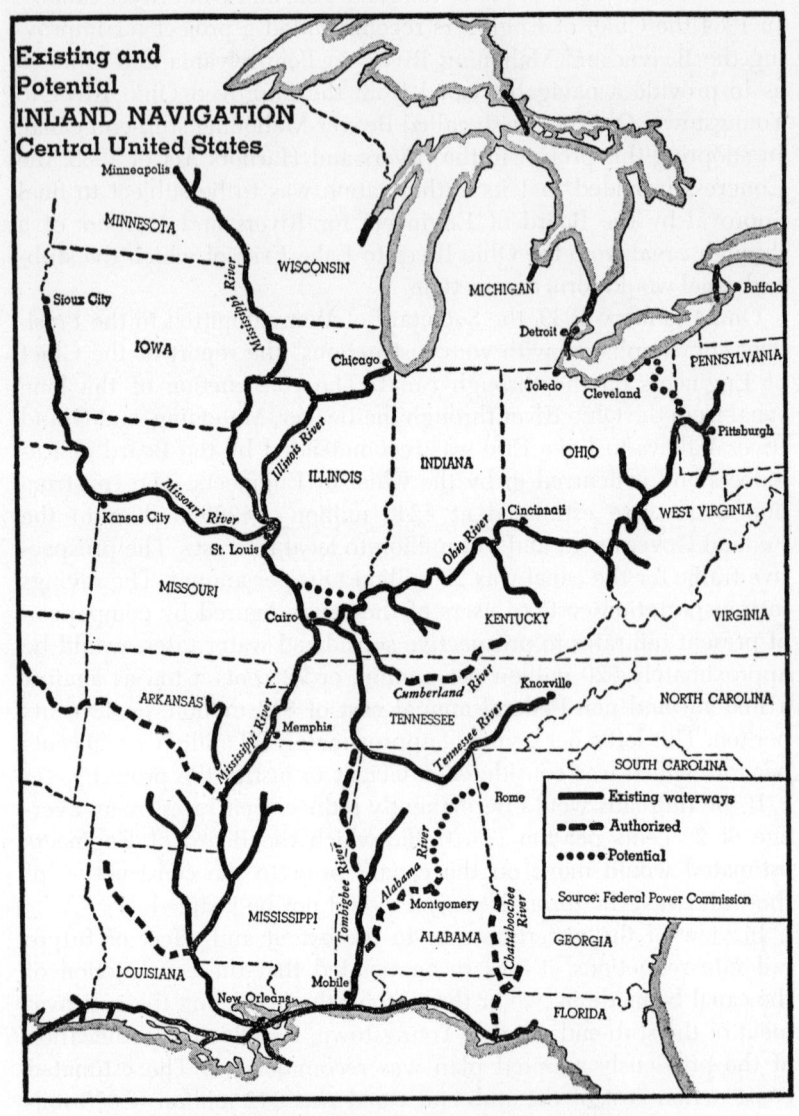

From the Report of the President's Water Resources Policy Commission (Volume II)

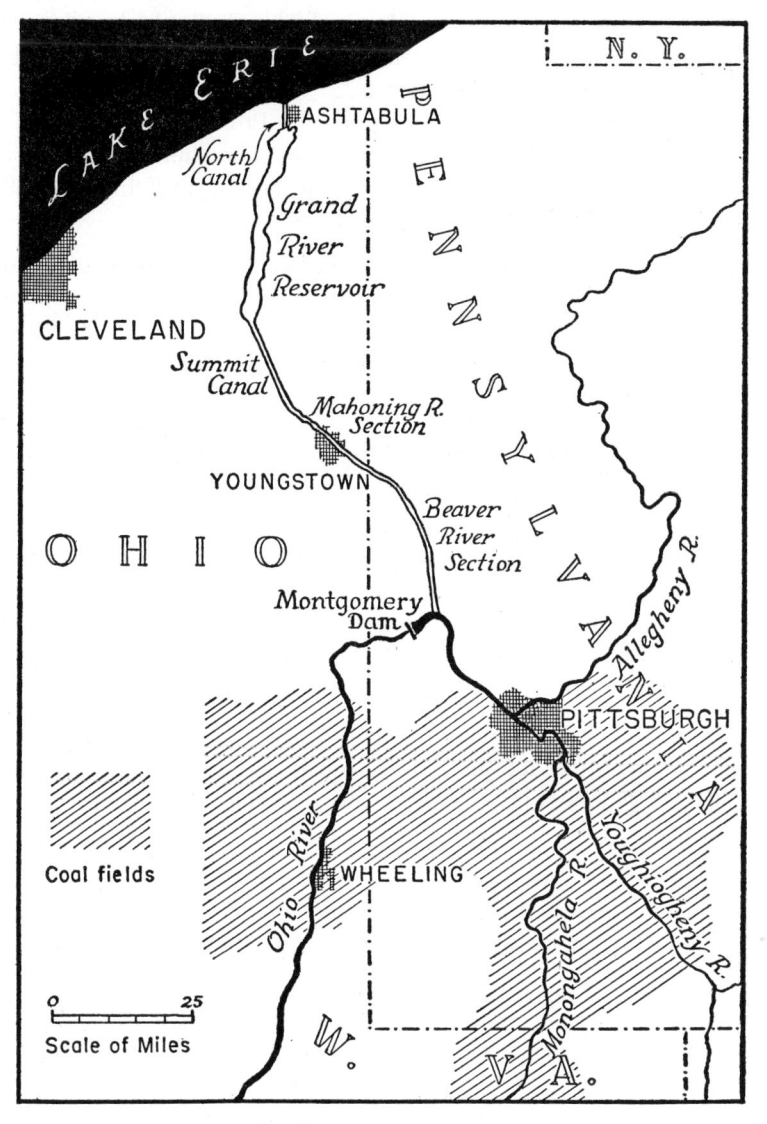

Proposed Lake Erie — Ohio River Canal

further determination of economic advisability, taking into consideration changes that result from the work already finished, and after the Chief of Engineers has been assured that adequate terminals will be constructed by local interests."

Upon receiving the Engineer report, the President sent it to the National Resources Committee for review. The staff and advisory committee of the NRC analyzed the report and on 16 February 1939 informed the President, in part as follows:

The [Rivers and Harbors] Board finds that "if the railroads would permanently reduce the rates by an average of 29 cents per ton prior to construction of the waterway the through project could not be justified." This raises a basic issue of policy. At a time when railroads generally are used far below capacity, is it making the most effective use of available construction funds to build a waterway to obtain benefits which might be obtained economically by readjustment in rail rates? This raises corollary questions. What would be the effect of the waterway improvement on the railways? What is the present capacity of the rail system? Would the proposed project encourage the further concentration of industry in the narrow valleys of the Youngstown-Pittsburgh-Wheeling area, and is such further concentration desirable?

These issues were not reported upon by the Board of Engineers for Rivers and Harbors. In this and all other reports on navigation projects a balanced analysis of the transportation needs and facilities of all types in the regions concerned is lacking. There is not even an accepted technique for determining the transportation needs of an area. The Advisory Committee feels that the study is inadequate and can be corrected only by an analysis from a broader viewpoint.

The advisory committee suggested that the President request the Interstate Commerce Commission to review the report. This suggestion was accepted immediately, and on 19 February 1939, the President, in a memorandum to the chairman of the ICC, stated:

In view of this report, I wish the Commission would undertake an investigation of rail rates in the area affected and review the report . . . so that the Commission may advise me on whether or not rate reductions of the magnitude and type noted above would be economically justified. I presume that such review would require consideration of the present railway and highway facilities in the area concerned, and of the effect which construction of the project would have on rail and motor carriers. These are problems which I should like to have examined before large Federal expenditures are made for the project.

It is interesting to note that for the first time in the history of inland navigation, the Commission was asked to review the findings of the Corps of Engineers from the standpoint of possible effects upon railroad freight rates.[50]

Under date of 26 October 1939, Chairman Eastman of the ICC transmitted to the President the Commission's report on "Certain Aspects of the Proposed Lake Erie-Ohio River Canal." The conclusions of the Commission were summarized at the close of the report as follows:

(1) Permanent rate reductions of the type and magnitude specified would not be economically justified *prior* to construction of the project, because they could not be confined to localities to be served by the waterway.

(2) If the waterway is built, a large volume of traffic, at least 56 million tons per year, would be affected and gross revenue loss of railroads would be $35 million or more.

(3) Railroads can ill afford now or in the future to lose revenues in such amount.

(4) Railroads have ample line and terminal facilities to carry any prospective traffic.

(5) The public has a vital interest in protection of revenues of the agency of transportation whose services are available the year-round to large and small shippers on equal terms.

(6) Motor carriers in a limited area would be adversely affected to some extent by construction of the waterway.

The President sent the ICC report to the Planning Board for further review. On 19 January 1940 Mr. Delano, chairman of the Board, asked the President for additional time to report on the matter. He sought by informal negotiations to work out an adjustment of rates on coal to the Youngstown district which would satisfy the steel interests at Youngstown, the principal proponents of the canal.

On 14 May, Mr. Delano reported to the President on the results of his negotiations.

We soon learned that the Youngstown interests were primarily interested in a "stub-end" canal to Youngstown rather than the through canal from the Ohio River to Lake Erie. They wished to reduce the transportation costs on coal from the mines to Youngstown in order to offset the advantage Pittsburgh enjoys in the low transportation costs of coal by water from the mines to Pittsburgh.

It was evident that if the railroads were able to make an adjustment of freight charges on coal to Youngstown satisfactory to these steel interests, the principal demand for the "stub-end" canal to Youngstown and also for the through canal to Lake Erie could be met without the necessity for heavy expenditures by the Federal Government both for the construction and operation of a canal.

I explored the situation with the railroad officials and the Interstate Commerce Commission, and also had several conferences with the Youngstown steel interests. As a result the railway officials expressed their willingness to make reductions on the rates on coal to Youngstown on condition that they would be confined, as I believed they should be, to the specific movement, and at my request, they conferred with the Youngstown people in an attempt to work out an adjustment. Unfortunately, however, these negotiations have thus far failed because the promised waterway has become so much of a Youngstown civic enterprise that the steel company officials do not feel justified in accepting any alternative adjustment of rates as a satisfactory solution.

For this reason, I am submitting my comments on the proposed Lake Erie-Ohio River canal briefly here . . .

My judgment is that the proposed Lake Erie-Ohio River canal, to cost the Federal Government $207,257,000 and local interests $12,472,000, is not economically justified. While I can appreciate Youngstown's interest in relief on the transportation of coal, I do not believe it should be through the construction of this unnecessary and costly facility.

Incidentally, if such a through canal were constructed, the optimum location for iron and steel manufacture would probably be at the junction of the canal with Lake Erie, since at that point coal and ore would meet by water transport and without the necessity of trans-shipment. Such a development might bring about drastic readjustments, seriously affecting Youngstown as well as other steel producing centers.

There still remains the question of the "stub-end" canal to Youngstown . . . The Chief of Engineers in his report on the Lake Erie-Ohio River canal does not estimate what average reduction in freight rates by the railroads would make the "stub-end" canal unjustifiable; nor does the report of the Interstate Commerce Commission give its views on the "stub-end" canal since the Commission reported only on the effects of the through canal.

For this reason, Mr. Delano suggested that the President request the Chief of Engineers to prepare a supplement to his report on the through Lake Erie-Ohio River canal estimating what reduction in freight rates by the railroads prior to the construction of the stub-end canal would make that project unjustifiable, either with or without tolls. When this supplementary report is completed, Mr. Delano proposed, the President should ask the ICC to estimate the effect on the revenues of the railroads (1) of the construction of the stub-end canal, and (2) of a voluntary reduction in freight rates prior to the construction of the canal which would make it unjustifiable.

The President approved the suggestion and on 20 May 1940 requested the Secretary of War to prepare the desired supplementary report. The report was completed more than one year later, in August 1941, and was transmitted to the President, who in turn sent it on to the ICC. In view of the many changes since the basic data for the 1939 report had been collected, including a sharp rise in construction costs, the lower cost of money, and changes in traffic movement and rail rates, a new traffic survey and a complete revision of cost estimates were made by the Engineers. Construction costs were boosted from $42 million to $55 million — $51 million to the Federal Government and $4 million to local interests. The prospective traffic for the stub-end canal was estimated at 5.5 million tons per annum. The savings in transportation costs to users of the canal, figured by comparison of present rail rates to prospective subsidized water rates, would be approximately $4.5 million per annum, or 82 cents per ton as against a Federal and non-Federal annual cost of $2.5 million, or 45 cents per ton. This left a net saving of approximately $2 million, or 37 cents per ton, which was considered sufficient to justify the project.

"Based on existing conditions for financing and on present trends of commerce and present construction costs, it is estimated that the proposed stub-end section of the Lake Erie-Ohio River canal will afford a means for the transportation of commodities to and from the Beaver River basin at a net cost approximately 36 cents below the present rail rate charges.[51] Reduction of present rail rates by 36 cents on the average for the prospective waterway movements would make the construction of the waterway unjustifiable at this time as a unit, either with or without toll charges."

The ICC, in response to the President's request, first estimated the effect on the revenues of the railroads of the construction of the stub-end canal. If the canal were constructed and operated on a toll-free basis, as was proposed by the Corps of Engineers, the total direct and indirect loss in rail revenues would be almost $10 million per annum. If the canal were operated on a toll basis, as had been proposed by Representative Kirwan of Ohio, the total loss would be $4 million per annum.

Second, the ICC estimated the effect on revenues of the railroads of a voluntary reduction in rates prior to the construction of the stub-end canal which would make it unjustifiable. For a toll-free canal the direct loss in revenues to the railroads of such a voluntary reduction would be $2 million. The indirect loss, or loss resulting from a reduction in rates on commodities which could not use the canal if it were built, but which compete in the same district with commodities which theoretically would use the canal, could be determined only after further investigation and hearings.

The ICC report of 2 December 1941 concluded with a clear summary of the industrial and transportation problems involved:

It is probably true, in the abstract, that if rail rate reductions aggregating $2,084,000 annually were made in the general area, no matter how thinly they might be spread, the economic justification for the canal, as measured by the [Rivers and Harbors] Board, would disappear. As a practical matter, however, we are well aware that any rate readjustment which failed to improve the position of Youngstown as a steel center, in relation to Pittsburgh, would not satisfy the proponents of the canal or lessen the demands for its construction. The principal traffic involved is coking coal moving to Youngstown from the Pittsburgh and adjacent mining districts.

The rail rates under which such coal is now carried form an integral part of a closely related structure covering practically the entire Appalachian region. They are short-haul rates and, as is true of short-haul rates generally, they are considerably higher per mile than the long-haul rates on similar traffic. While costs are higher, relatively, on short hauls than on longer ones, it is probable that the rates in question could be reduced and still return a profit to the railroads. But historically freight rates have never been made with a view to yielding the carriers a uniform profit from all their varied operations, and any attempt summarily to readjust the rate structures of the country on that basis, even though it were otherwise possible, would lead to industrial and economic dislocations so severe as to be intolerable.

Nevertheless, as those who have had occasion to follow our rate decisions in recent years know, the rise of competitive forms of transportation has caused and is causing readjustments of rail rates with closer reference to the costs of individual operations than was formerly the case; and it may be that the time has come when these short-haul rates to Youngstown should be reduced, not alone in the interests of the shippers and consumers but in the interests of the railroads as well. That question, however, . . . we could answer definitely only after investigation and hearings as provided by law.

In our prior report, after reviewing briefly the history of the rates in question, we said: "These comparatively recent changes in rates on coal to Youngstown are mentioned to indicate that . . . the rates are by no means immutable. They must and do change as conditions affecting transportation change; and if the Youngstown consumers, or the railroads serving them, feel that other rate adjustments tending to improve the competitive situation of the community can be justified by changed conditions or special circumstances not heretofore brought to our attention, we are prepared to consider carefully any evidence that they may wish to offer in support of that position in an appropriate proceeding."

In the two years which have since elapsed no proposal for a reduction has been made to us, by either shippers or carriers. We repeat that we stand ready to consider, promptly and in the light of possible changed conditions, any such proposal which may be placed before us.

The President again asked the National Resources Planning Board to review for him both the USED and ICC reports on the stub-end canal. Mr. Delano, for the Board, concluded, "it is my judgment that this stub-end canal . . . is no more economically justified than the through Lake Erie-Ohio River canal. On the other hand, I believe that the question of whether Youngstown should have relief in the transportation cost of coal through an equitable adjustment of freight rates is a matter of public concern." He recommended that the President request the ICC to *initiate* an investigation of these rates irrespective of failure of Youngstown interests to request readjustment in formal proceedings. The President agreed with this suggestion and on 9 May 1942 wrote to the acting chairman of the ICC as follows:

. . . I have noted the statement that the Commission stands ready to consider in the light of possible changed conditions any proposal which may be placed before it for a reduction in the rates of coal moving to Youngstown district mills. I understand, however, that the explanation of the failure of the affected groups to submit such a proposal is to be found in the conflict of interests in the district. While this failure of opposing interests to agree on a mutually satisfactory adjustment of these coal rates is understandable, it seems to me that it lies in the *public interest* for the Commission to undertake such an investigation on its *own initiative* [emphasis added]. As you know, this question of a possible reduction of rates has been raised in connection with the proposal to construct a stub-end canal connecting the Youngstown steel-producing district with the Ohio River. Inasmuch as this project would cost the Federal Government many millions of dollars, it is eminently desirable that the possible alternative of a reduction of rail rates on coal be thoroughly explored in due season. Such an investigation should, of course, include the broader subject of the general relationship in production costs among the steel-producing districts, with particular reference to post-war readjustments which the steel industry will face.

Accordingly, I should like to suggest that the Commission initiate the investigation when it can be done without interference with the essential war activities of the Commission and without undue burden on the carriers and shippers because of the war program. The problem is not a pressing one because of the present high level of activity in the Youngstown area, which will undoubtedly continue for the duration of the war, but it is desirable that the results of such an investigation should be available when we are faced with the review of the Youngstown proposal in relation to the post-war shelf of public works.

Before the ICC conducted its rate investigation, Senator Burton of Ohio made an effort to secure authorization of the revised plans for the stub-end canal in the Rivers and Harbors Bill of 1945. Hearings on the project were held by the Senate Committee on Commerce in early May 1944, and the Committee reported the project favorably. After lengthy debate on the Senate floor, relating in significant measure to the reports of the President and the ICC, the project was defeated by a vote of 52–16.[52]

In 1945 the ICC instituted on its own motion an investigation of the rates on bituminous coal to Youngstown and vicinity from coal mining districts in Pennsylvania, Maryland, and West Virginia. Although the investigation was initiated as a direct result of the President's request, it was conducted ostensibly with little reference to the relation of rail rates to the proposed canal. The Commission, according to the language of the Interstate Commerce Act, merely conducted an investigation to determine whether existing rates were "unjust or unreasonable" and therefore "unlawful."

The important fact is, however, that the investigation resulted in rate reductions on coal to the Youngstown district as follows:[53]

From	All-rail Distance to Youngstown (Miles)	Former Rate	New Rate	Reduction
		(Amounts per net ton)		
Pittsburgh district	95	$1.44	$1.37	$0.07
Leetonia district	35	0.94	0.89	0.05
Freeport district	94	1.44	1.32	0.12
Conway & Colona districts	(ex-river)	0.90	0.80	0.10

It is not known how these reductions will affect the economic justification for the stub-end canal; but it may be of note that no effort has been made to obtain authorization for the revised canal plans in rivers and harbors acts enacted since the ICC decision. Recent proposals to build a continuous belt for transportation of bulk materials, largely ore and coal, between Lake Erie and the Ohio River raise new problems for both the railroads and the supporters of the canal; but these will not be investigated here.

This case history illustrates, first, the inadequacies of USED survey procedures. "In this and all other reports on navigation projects a balanced analysis of the transportation needs and facilities of all types in the regions concerned is lacking. There is not even an accepted technique for determining the transportation needs of an area."

Second, the case history illustrates the difficulties entailed in rectifying inadequate survey procedures once a completed report, containing the favorable recommendations of the Board of Engineers for Rivers and Harbors, has been made. The USED report was transmitted to the President early in 1939. An alternative and economic solution to the problem — differential rail rate reduction — was not effected even partially until 1945. Mr. Delano might have been able to obtain reductions in 1940 had not the Engineer Corps' public recommendation for a through canal become "so much of a civic enterprise in Youngstown."

Third, this case illustrates the value of project clearance through a planning unit in the Executive Office of the President, particularly where agency techniques are inadequate. It was the Planning Board which advised the President to hedge on approval of the project until more adequate analysis could be made. It was the Planning Board which obtained, for the first time in history, ICC review of a proposed major public improvement in inland water transportation. It is likely that had it not been for the Planning Board, the through canal would be authorized and under construction today.

No attempt is made here to evaluate the attitude and actions of the ICC in this case.

Local contributions. In the absence of user charges, a sound domestic navigation policy should require local interests to contribute to the costs of navigation facilities in proportion to local benefits.

In reporting to the Congress on proposed waterways, the Chief of Engineers is required to make a statement of the local benefits that in his opinion will accrue to specific areas, and to recommend what local coöperation should be required. In general, Engineer policy on local participation has called for the contribution of lands, the payment of damages, and the provision of terminals. As such, the policy does not provide for participation in proportion to benefits. In commenting on this fact, the NRPB has said:

> Hereafter, greater use should be made of the principle of equitable participation by local beneficiaries. The relationship between general navigation benefits and local navigation benefits might well serve in many instances as a guide to the proper division of costs among the Federal Government and State and local bodies. If projects deserve Federal contributions, they certainly also deserve local contributions, and unless local interests are prepared to make appropriate contributions on their own behalf the Federal Government normally should not participate in the improvement they seek. The fact that a State or city wishes to save its own money cannot properly increase any Federal obligation to help it. The fact that a State or city claims to be unable to contribute anything toward a waterway project it seeks, might well lead to postponement of the undertaking until its economic status has improved. If all projects had to have appropriate local financial support as a prerequisite to adoption, they doubtless would not be urged unless the benefits were commensurate with the costs.[54]

The liberal interpretation which the Chief of Engineers gives to the local participation principle can be seen from a few illustrations:

The Rivers and Harbors Act of 1907 provided for a channel 3½ miles long and 18 feet deep from the Boston Harbor main ship channel to Commercial Point in Dorchester Bay, an area of shallow water lying south of Boston Harbor and of commercial importance largely for oil storage facilities on its shores.[55] In 1928 the Corps of Engineers recommended modification of this project to deepen the channel to 30 feet between the main ship channel and Cow Pasture, about half the distance to Commercial Point, providing local interests dredge at their own expense a 30-foot approach channel and turning basin in this vicinity. The proposal was adopted in the Rivers and Harbors Act of 1930, but it has never been built, as the local interests have been unwilling to make the required contribution.

Thus, in February 1939, the House Rivers and Harbors Committee adopted a resolution directing review of the 1928 report "with a view to determining if any modification in the existing project is advisable at this time." In his review report the District Engineer recommended abandonment of the 30-foot project and the provision instead of a 25-foot channel all the way to Commercial Point. "The character of the benefits to be expected from the proposed channel in Dorchester Bay points to the desirability of requiring substantial local cooperation. Since the oil interests at Commercial Point will be benefited promptly and materially by the improvement, they should be required to . . ." provide adequate terminal and storage facilities. In addition, "the expansion of activity at Commercial Point and the development of Cow Pasture, as they occur, will stimulate employment, increase property values and tax revenues and contribute generally to the industrial well-being of the community and the State, and it is, therefore, believed that the State or other local agencies should share in the cost of the Federal improvement to the extent of one-third of the initial cost, or approximately $100,000."

The Board of Engineers for Rivers and Harbors and the Chief of Engineers approved the revision of the project as proposed by the District Engineer, but decided that the local interests should be relieved of all monetary contributions to the cost of the Federal improvement, "thus giving them an opportunity to invest their available funds in the necessary terminal facilities, side channels, and basins."

For the President's Office, the NRPB Evaluation Committee reviewed the completed report and rated it "not recommended" unless the local contribution of $100,000 proposed by the District Engineer is forthcoming. The Chief of Engineers, ignoring this evaluation, recommended that Congress approve the project with no local monetary contribution, and Congress responded favorably in the Rivers and Harbors Act of 1945. Incidentally, this one act contained seventeen projects which had insufficient local coöperation according to the Executive Office of the President, but which were recommended nonetheless by the Chief of Engineers.

In early 1948 the Corps of Engineers completed a report on the St. Mary's River which forms the boundary between Georgia and Florida.[56] It recommended dredging a 28-foot channel from deep water in Cumberland Sound to a wharf at the mill of the St. Mary's Kraft Corporation, and a turning basin near that wharf. Local interests were to provide necessary lands, to agree to provide terminal facilities when needed, and to pay for damages. The Bureau of the Budget reviewed the report for the President's Office and informed the Corps, in part, as follows:

> It appears from the statements set forth in the report of the Chief of Engineers and accompanying papers that practically all of the benefits from the recommended 28-foot channel would be gained by a single private concern. As you know, and as past reports of the Corps of Engineers have indicated, it has been the policy of the United States, where major benefits from a navigation project accrue principally to a restricted area or to a single organization, to require a proportionately greater local participation in the improvement. On this basis, the local cooperation requirements proposed in the report of the Chief of Engineers would be wholly inadequate. I am, therefore, advising you that . . . authorization of the modification of the project to include a 28-foot channel in St. Mary's and North Rivers should not be considered to be in accord with the program of the President unless the local interests make an adequate cash contribution toward the initial cost of the work.

Yet the Chief of Engineers recommended that Congress adopt the project without further local contributions, and the Congress complied in the Rivers and Harbors Act of 1950.

Another interesting example is the 1948 report of the Corps on the improvement of Trenton Channel in the Detroit River, Michigan.[57] The benefits from the project would accrue from savings in transportation charges on the annual movement of one million tons of coal to be used by the Detroit Edison Company for the production of electric energy. The report required minimal local contributions and stated that the benefits would be general in nature, since savings in the cost of producing power would be passed on to the public through reduced power rates to the Detroit industrial area. After reviewing this report, the Budget Bureau informed the Corps:

> The fact that in this instance the benefits would accrue to a regulated public utility is not considered significant, since in the last analysis savings in the cost of doing business which accrue to any type of private enterprise, regulated or competitive in nature, as a result of public improvement should be considered as being passed on to the ultimate consumer. The important point is that the cost of improvements such as proposed in this report, when benefits accrue to only one establishment, are a proper charge against the production cost of the establishment. On this basis, the local cooperation requirements proposed in the report of the Chief of Engineers appear to be wholly inadequate . . . You are advised, therefore, that . . . authorization of the modification of the existing project should not be considered to be in accord with the program of the President unless the local interests make an adequate cash contribution toward the initial cost of the work.

Again the USED recommended that the Congress authorize the project in accordance with its original report, and Congress did so in the Rivers and Harbors Act of 1950.

Other navigation facilities. A sound domestic navigation policy should consider carefully how the improvement of one locality may affect the use of navigation facilities in other localities.

It would appear obvious that the development of one seacoast harbor or one waterway at public expense might draw traffic away from near-by harbors or waterways whose facilities, though improved, would be less adequate than those provided by the new development. And it would appear equally obvious that the economic justification for any such new development should evaluate not only the benefits from new traffic at the new location, but also the negative benefits (or costs) from loss of traffic at previously improved harbors or channels. Yet the Corps of Engineers, in keeping with its traditional policy of viewing projects in the light of highly localized effects, generally fails to take these factors into consideration in planning navigation developments.

A striking example is the harbors on the South Atlantic seaboard. There are five deep-water harbors along the Florida east coast. All of these compete more or less for the same business. Between 1941 and 1944, the Chief of Engineers recommended improvements at all five, as shown in the accompanying tabulation.

Harbor	Existing Project	Proposed Improvement	First Cost of Improvement (in thousands)	
			Fed.	Local
Jacksonville[a]	30 ft. channel	34 ft. channel	$3,200	(?)
Canaveral[b]	No previous project. Natural harbor with depths of 20–40 ft.	27 and 8 ft. channels	1,661	830
Palm Beach (Lake Worth Inlet)[c]	20 ft. channel and turning basin	25 ft. channel and turning basin	711	32
Hollywood (Port Everglades)[d]	35 ft. channel and turning basin	Enlarged 35 ft. channel and turning basin	786	1,384
Miami (Virginia Key)[e]	30 ft. main channel and harbor. None for Virginia Key	30 ft. harbor at Virginia Key	5,781	10,812 (incl. airport)

[a] H. Doc. 322, 77/1; S. Doc. 230, 78/2.
[b] H. Doc. 367, 77/1.
[c] H. Doc. 530, 78/2.
[d] H. Doc. 768, 78/2.
[e] S. Doc. 251, 79/2.

The recommended improvements at each harbor were based, in part, on estimates for increased commerce; but since the harbors are in competition with each other, increased commerce at one might well be at the expense of commerce diverted from another. The Hollywood and Miami harbors, in particular, are closely competitive. The Bureau of the Budget advised the Engineer Department that the authorization of *both* the Hollywood and Miami improvements would not be in accord with the program of the President. The Budget found the Hollywood project preferable and recommended against the Miami improvement. There is no question but that if the Hollywood harbor were authorized, it would operate to decrease the justification for the Miami improvement.

However, on the recommendation of the Chief of Engineers, the Congress in the Rivers and Harbors Acts of 1945 and 1946 authorized all five projects. Now that Jacksonville and Hollywood are to have harbors improved to a depth of from 34 to 35 feet, it can be expected that local interests in Miami will press for further improvement of their harbor, on the basis that increased traffic would result therefrom — though much of this traffic would, in all likelihood, be diverted from Hollywood and Jacksonville. And indeed, on 18 August 1944 the Senate Committee on Commerce adopted and transmitted to the Engineer Department a resolution proposed by Senator

Pepper calling for a review of report on Miami Harbor to determine advisability of increasing the depth from 30 to 35 feet.[58] The Engineers have not completed the review.

Additional illustrative material of the same nature might be developed by examining the relationship of the Florida harbors to other South Atlantic ports, such as Savannah, Georgia; Charleston, South Carolina; and Wilmington, North Carolina; but this will not be attempted here.

A more controversial example of Engineer planning for projects that compete with each other for the same traffic is found in the proposed waterway connecting the Tombigbee and Tennessee Rivers. The project provides for an improved waterway to permit barge traffic to pass from the improved Warrior-Tombigbee River system into the improved Tennessee River system, from where it can then pass into the Ohio-Mississippi River system. A nine-foot channel with eighteen locks is required.

The Board of Engineers for Rivers and Harbors in January 1939 concurred in the report of a special advisory board that the project was feasible and economically justified, and recommended its construction at a total estimated first cost to the United States of $66 million and an estimated annual cost of $500,000 for maintenance and operation.[59] The Chief of Engineers, however, took exception, among other estimates, to the allocation of annual benefits totaling $1 million from saving to upbound Mississippi River traffic to be diverted to the Tombigbee waterway. This diversion would occur because the new waterway would have the advantage of being a slack water route whereas upbound barge traffic on the Mississippi must move against currents. The Chief of Engineers said, "The estimate of saving of $1 million to up-bound traffic on the Mississippi results from a thorough study and I do not doubt that such a saving would result, but I doubt the wisdom of dependence upon diversion of any considerable part of the Mississippi River traffic to justify the new project, even though the credit is confined to the additional saving in transportation costs." General Schley did not specifically recommend authorization of the project, but stated that the decision must be made on the basis of intangible benefits which should appropriately be evaluated by Congress.

The National Resources Planning Board reviewed the Engineer Department report and submitted its evaluation to the Secretary of

War by special letter in April 1939. It recommended that further study be given to the estimated project benefits and that a broad review of transportation problems involved be made by the Interstate Commerce Commission before the project is authorized. This review was never made, and the NRPB evaluated the project again in May 1941, rating it "not recommended for authorization."

The House Rivers and Harbors Committee reported the project favorably in the Rivers and Harbors Bill of 1945.[60] However, on the recommendation of a committee minority, the House, in an unusual action, overrode the committee recommendation and struck the project from the bill. The matter here under consideration — crediting benefits derived by diverting traffic from a competing waterway — was only one of several reasons for the House action.

After the Congress rejected the project on the basis of the 1939 survey report, the Board of Engineers made a reëxamination in order to bring up to date the data with respect to economic benefits.[61] The total estimated first cost to the United States was revised upward to $117 million and the estimated Federal annual cost for maintenance and operation, to $811,000. The cost to local interests was set at $3.3 million. The allocation of annual benefits from saving to upbound Mississippi River traffic to be diverted to the Tombigbee waterway was revised upward to $1.2 million. This time the Chief of Engineers interposed no objection to the consideration of this annual benefit, without which the project could not have obtained a favorable cost-benefit ratio. He stated, "in addition, traffic already moving *advantageously* upstream against Mississippi River currents will be able to use the new waterway at additional savings estimated at $1.2 million annually."

For reasons not known, the Bureau of the Budget did not hold the new proposal contrary to the President's program, and the Congress authorized the waterway in the Rivers and Harbors Act of 1946.[62]

It should be noted that a policy of tolls would in all likelihood prevent the type of economic analysis found in these examples. The Corps no doubt had used the upbound Mississippi traffic to justify the improvement of that River. If it were required to prove out its justification by the collection of tolls, then the Corps could ill afford to divert the Mississippi traffic to a new waterway.

Evaluation of benefits and costs. A sound domestic navigation policy should require more careful evaluation of benefits and costs of proposed waterways prior to authorization, and periodic reëvaluations thereafter.

On the whole, the Engineers have been overoptimistic in their estimates of waterway traffic. According to a report of the Federal Coördinator of Transportation, in certain areas it would require more traffic than moves by all agencies of transport combined to bring waterway use up to effective working capacity.[63] The staff of the Board of Investigation and Research, after careful review of waterway use statistics, concluded that, "results attained on individual waterways are occasionally better — but more often worse — than predictions contained in the project documents. It is a fair generalization that the engineering cost estimates have been far superior to the traffic estimates. To some extent this situation is to be expected, in view of the complex issues presented in an attempt to foresee all of the influences affecting future traffic," such, for example, as uneconomic competitive railroad rates. However, any careful analysis of performance measured against predictions indicates clearly "the need for more realism in the initial traffic predictions on which decisions to construct waterways are largely based." [64]

Navigation projects have been justified often to meet the needs of an anticipated very general and large growth of traffic. This basis for planning projects had real validity in the early part of the century, but transportation economists are generally agreed that it does not represent the complex realities of modern transportation conditions. Striking changes have occurred in recent years; there are now vast facilities in railroads, highways, and pipe lines.[65] A realistic approach to the problem of the future aggregate demand for transport service will not, as a rule, justify waterway improvements to provide generally "needed" additions to the transport capacity. "Many years ago the objective of public promotion policy was simply to provide more facilities, for at that time the principal problem was the under supply of transportation service. Today, however, the problem has shifted from one of unlimited expansion to one of coordination, greater efficiency, and the correction of inadequacies." And yet, "Federal promotional policy continues to be concerned mainly with the promotion of more and more transportation capacity." [66]

Navigation projects have been justified at times on the basis of benefits attributed to national defense. The Corps has held that inland waterways promote the defense of the nation, especially when materials used for defense purposes are transported over them. Most transportation and water economists agree, however, that waterways are not unique in this respect.

Waterways as a class cannot properly be singled out for exceptional treatment on the grounds of essentiality to the exclusion of other means of transportation, unless a particular project serves a really unique function which places it in a position by itself in relation to the advancement of the national security and welfare. If part of the costs of improved waterways were to be charged expressly to national defense, simply because essential commodities are carried on them, similar and probably much greater allowances of the same character would have to be made in behalf of other forms of transportation; nor could this process logically stop with transportation, for it might as appropriately be extended to the whole complex of the Nation's essential industries and activities.[67]

The Tennessee-Tombigbee project offers an interesting illustration of the way in which the Corps has handled this problem. The special survey board and the Board of Engineers for Rivers and Harbors in 1939 allocated annual benefits totaling $600,000 for national defense.[68] The Chief of Engineers was somewhat wary of this, and other allocations for recreation and for enhancement of land values in the tributary area. He stated that these "intangible benefits" should appropriately be evaluated by Congress. The National Resources Planning Board, more wary than the Chief of Engineers, recommended that further study be given to these estimated project benefits by the executive agencies — a recommendation which was not accepted.

Congress turned down the Tennessee-Tombigbee in the Rivers and Harbors Bill of 1945, and the debate reveals that in doing so it in effect rejected the benefits claimed for national defense. Thus, in the reëxamination of the waterway conducted by the Board of Engineers in 1945, *all* of the "imponderable benefits of national defense, land enhancement, or recreation which had been objected to in the previous report" were eliminated.[69] It was this action which compelled the allocation of greater benefits to upbound Mississippi traffic, referred to above.

The imposition of user charges, or even the requirement of substantial local contributions, would encourage more careful benefit-cost evaluation. In the absence of these, systematic and periodic reviews of the use and costs of waterways might accomplish the same purpose, in part; and it has been proposed that every project be reviewed not less frequently than every ten years.[70] The more important advantages of such a practice would be:

(1) Needed restraints would be imposed upon unduly optimistic predictions regarding traffic on proposed waterway improvements.

(2) A more effective limitation of future public expenditures to those new and existing waterway projects which have a deserving place in the Nation's transportation system would be fostered.

(3) Greater attention would be focused on those projects which should be abandoned and on which additional expenditures cannot be made economically.

(4) Adjustments of some waterway improvements to changing needs and uses not contemplated in the original analyses of individual projects would be encouraged.

The Corps regularly collects commercial statistics on waterway traffic, but makes no use of these for the purpose of reëvaluating the economy of waterways. By failing to do this, the Corps avoids taking action that should lead both to greater economic soundness and to continued planning in relation to shifting economic and physical conditions.

We can conclude that with respect to four essentials of a sound navigation policy, the USED program for navigation improvements fails to meet many standards of professional responsibility, and in these respects does not promote the public interest.

This examination of navigation policy has been largely within the context of its broader interest — a national transportation system. That waterway projects must also be appraised in terms of complementary development of rivers for navigation and other purposes is of course of first importance. But this constitutes the multiple-purpose and basin relationship requirements for water development, which are not primarily under investigation here. However, the meaning of these requirements, as applied to a large and important waterway project, is illustrated by the canalization of the Ohio River, which has been characterized by the National Resources Planning Board as a "noteworthy" and "compelling" example of unrelated valley development. In the words of the Board:

This project, providing for cheap transportation of raw materials and bulk products, contributed to the great expansion of industrial operations in Pittsburgh and other areas adjacent to the Ohio River. Concurrently, and to some extent consequently, there was rapid growth of mining operations in western Pennsylvania, West Virginia, Ohio, and Kentucky. This, in turn, caused substantial increase in discharges of polluting effluents, particularly acids, from industrial and mining processes into receiving streams, thus adversely affecting the industrial and domestic water supplies. While few would claim that the cheap waterway transportation should not have been provided, such adverse complications as these could have been reduced or eliminated if the national policy had permitted recognition of conditions which might arise partly in consequence of the project, and had provided Federal and State agencies with authority to take initial steps towards remedial measures.[71]

Hydroelectric Power

The Corps has been concerned *primarily* with the development of rivers for the purposes of navigation and flood control. Other purposes — hydroelectric power and irrigation, for example — have been considered incidental, or *secondary*. As such, the Corps approach to river development does not conform to the true multiple-purpose test; this we have noted. Also, it becomes difficult to examine Corps policies for the "secondary" purposes in terms of professional responsibility. The Engineer Department just does not assume any responsibility for functional policies for these purposes, although it does take certain positions where benefits from these purposes will be derived from projects which it proposes to build. Thus examination of policies for power and irrigation in this context must be highly selective rather than comprehensive, for it is the activities of the Corps of Engineers in which we are interested.

The standards for production and distribution of hydroelectric power used in the analysis which follows represent a consensus of the proposals of the Mississippi Valley Committee in 1934; the National Resources Planning Board and its Water and Energy Resources Committees and Pacific Northwest Regional Planning Commission, from 1934 to 1943; the National Power Policy Committee in 1937 and thereafter; Presidents Roosevelt and Truman, particularly in connection with the important power provisions of postwar water legislation; the Department of Interior, as the Federal agency which has taken the lead in policy matters relating to development of public power; and the Federal Power Commission.[72]

A sound power policy should secure the optimum development and utilization of the power potentialities of water resources, consistent with other uses.

If power can be developed economically as a phase of the regulation of a river, it should be developed. "To waste it would be reprehensible. To sell it would not only help to serve the energy consuming public but would also help to defray the cost of controlling the river . . . The latent power resources of American rivers [should] be developed as rapidly as feasible."[73] To a large extent this policy requires Federal development of hydro power. Rivers must be developed for multiple purposes, not for the single purpose of power; and private industry in most cases cannot afford to build multiple-purpose projects nor to develop a river as a unit for multiple purposes. "While private business has done well some things in the field of water resources, nowhere has private development handled all of the things needed; and often what has been done privately was in conflict with other proper utilization of water resources . . . Since doing the job as a unit seems best, and since government must do part of it, government must carry on with the multiple purpose development."[74] That government takes priority over private industry in the development of the nation's rivers has been recognized in Federal legislation since the Water Power Act of 1920.

The Corps was first authorized to build multiple-purpose projects in the Flood Control Act of 1936. The Flood Control Act of 1938 specifically provided for the installation in Engineer Corps dams of penstocks for power development when approved by the Army, upon the recommendation of the Federal Power Commission. In connection with this provision, the Corps has developed working relations with the Commission, relying on the FPC for power marketing surveys, recommendations for the installation of power facilities, and estimates of benefits attributable to such installations.

The Commission has often differed with the Corps as to the amount of power that can be developed economically in proposed dams. The Corps has been slow to adjust to the policy of optimum power development, and as a result a number of river programs have been delayed. On occasion, differences between the USED and the Power Commission have been compromised, but more often they have been deferred by revising the Engineer Corps survey reports so as to make them sufficiently flexible to include greater or lesser power installations as desired in the future. Generally, however, and subject to the limitations stated, coöperation between the two agencies has been good, and the Commission has succeeded in getting the Corps of Engineers to add power facilities or provisions for future power installations at a number of dams.[75]

A notable and recent example of failure to plan adequately for power, however, can be found in the Corps' comprehensive report on the Cumberland River. The Cumberland Valley lies within a crescent formed by the valley of the Tennessee on the east, south, and west. The river rises in southeast Kentucky, flows through north central Tennessee, and empties into the Ohio just a few miles above Paducah, where the Tennessee empties. The physiographic, economic, and other characteristics of the Cumberland and Tennessee drainage areas are similar; and the resources problems created by these characteristics, closely interrelated. Due to this fact, Presidents Roosevelt and Truman, the NRPB, Federal Power Commission, and Department of Agriculture have supported legislation to include the Cumberland within the development area of the TVA. This legislation has not been approved by the Corps, whose supporters in Congress have helped block its passage.[76]

Here we are concerned primarily with optimum development of power on the Cumberland. In July 1946 the Secretary of War transmitted to Congress the Engineer Department's comprehensive report on this river.[77] The District Engineer had recommended improvements to provide a 9-foot channel to Nashville, flood protection for Nashville and other areas, and a power installation of about 840,000 kilowatts. The power would be supplied from projects to be built in three stages of development, as shown in the accompanying tabulation (see page 192).

The first stage provided for combined power and flood protection for Nashville and other areas. One project is on the river, some 460 miles from its mouth; the others, on its tributaries. At these first-stage projects 44 per cent of total estimated energy would be produced. The second stage provided for combined power and the 9-foot channel to Nashville. The power would be produced at a high dam on the lower Cumberland which would supply almost

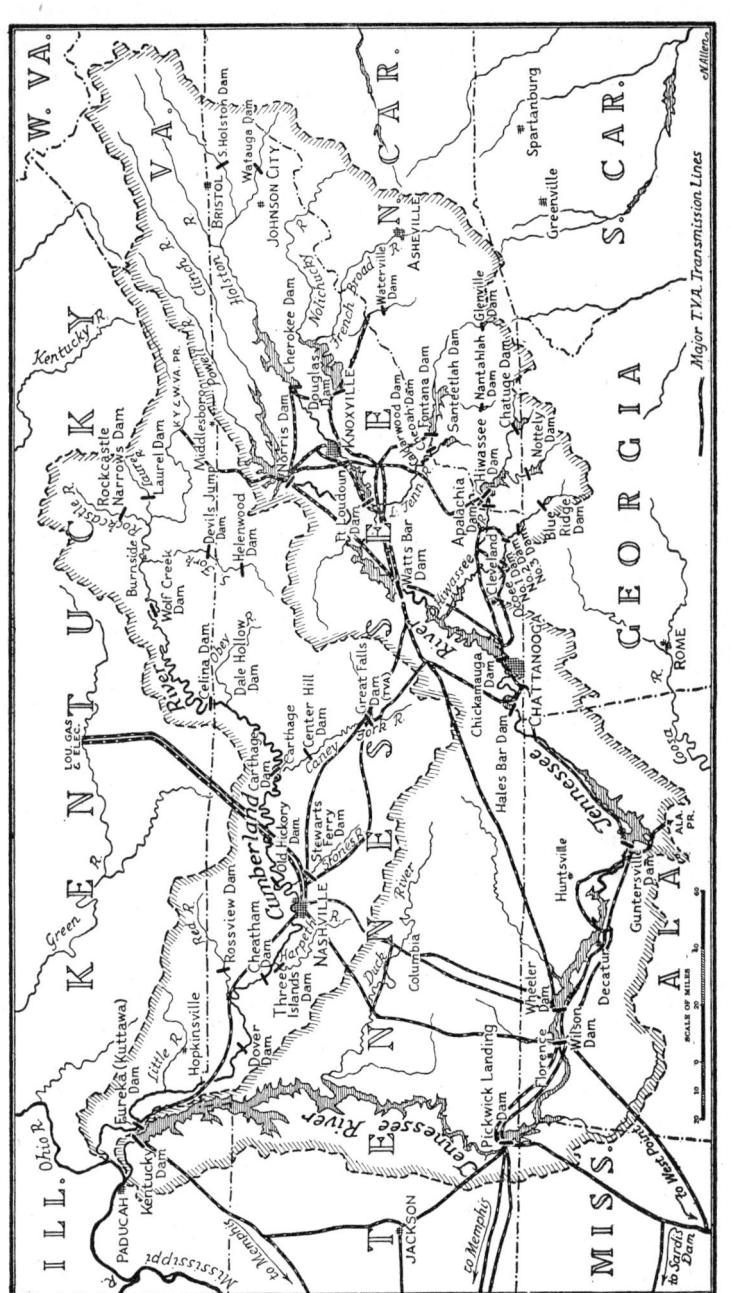

Water Resource Development, Cumberland and Tennessee River Basins

Project and Location	Purposes	Installed Generator Cap. in Kw[a]	Theoretical Total Energy Output in Av. Yr. Kw. Hr.[a]
First Stage			
Wolf Creek Cumberland R., 460 mi. above mouth	Power & flood control combined	270,000	867,000,000
Center Hill Caney Fork, 310 mi. above mouth of Cumberland	do.	90,000	328,000,000
Dale Hollow Obey R., 380 mi. above mouth of Cumberland	do.	36,000	120,000,000
Stewarts Ferry Stones R., 200 mi. above mouth of Cumberland	do.	13,500	52,000,000
Three Islands Harpeth R., 150 mi. above mouth of Cumberland	do.	10,000	45,000,000
Rossville Red R., 130 mi. above mouth of Cumberland	Flood control only	......	....
Second Stage			
Lower Cumberland Cumberland R., 30 mi. above mouth	Power & navigation combined	150,000	750,000,000
Cheatham Cumberland R., 150 mi. above mouth	Navigation only	......	....
Third Stage			
Celina Cumberland R., 385 mi. above mouth	Power	60,000	230,000,000
Carthage Cumberland R., 310 mi. above mouth	do.	90,000	343,000,000
Old Hickory Cumberland R., 215 mi. above mouth	do.	120,000	502,000,000
		839,500	3,237,000,000

[a] These figures taken from report of District Engineer. Later detailed plans have made some revisions.

one-fourth of the total power output of the river system. This dam and the reservoir behind it would correspond closely to Kentucky Dam and Lake on the Tennessee River, a very few miles to the west. The third stage provided for additional power — 33 per cent of the total — at main stem reservoirs between Nashville and Wolf Creek, with the possibility of installing locks for navigation if later conditions warrant.

Residents of the lower valley whose farms and homes would be inundated by the high dam opposed its construction. The Board of Engineers gave a hearing to these local interests and concluded that "the inhabitants of the valley both in Kentucky and Tennessee are strongly opposed to the taking of their homes and lands for the purpose of developing water power. Having given careful consideration to the views of local interests in this matter and to the effect of the extensive dislocations involved, the Board is of the opinion that the need for water power in the area is not now of sufficient importance to outweigh the local objections to a high dam." It, therefore, proposed construction, instead, of two low dams to provide navigation but no power, thereby eliminating about 25 per cent of the estimated power production for the river system. Otherwise, the Board concurred in the recommendations of the District Engineer; and the Chief of Engineers agreed with his advisory Board.

The TVA found the report, as modified by the Board of Engineers, highly unsatisfactory. The construction of two low dams in place of the originally recommended high dam on the lower Cumberland would mean "the loss for all time of the particular benefits inherent in that project." In regard to the originally proposed high dam for navigation and power, the Authority had recommended its operation for flood control in addition, by reserving the space between elevation 359 and the top elevation of 375 for flood storage. In this way it would be possible to eliminate two or three tributary dams and thereby save 30,000 to 45,000 acres of land from inundation. Futhermore, the 31,000 acres between elevations 359 and 375 on the high dam would have substantial value for agricultural purposes, as they could be farmed under proper management except during high flood periods. There is no indication that the Corps of Engineers gave any consideration to this TVA proposal. Finally, the TVA pointed out that the proposed multi-purpose projects should be designed and operated as part of an over-all regional plan embracing the combined Tennessee and Cumberland watersheds. According to the Authority, optimum integrated power planning would yield greater energy from the Cumberland than that contemplated even by the District Engineer. Thus, by way of example, TVA proposed the possibility of a canal connecting Kentucky Lake with the reservoir to be formed behind the high lower Cumberland dam, thus giving greater flexibility in the operation of either river system. There is no evidence that the District Engineer (even though he favored the high dam), the Board of Engineers, or the Chief of Engineers gave consideration to this possibility.

The Federal Power Commission had concurred in the original proposals of the District Engineer, but withdrew this approval upon being informed of the changes made by the Board of Engineers and approved by the Chief of Engineers.

The Executive Office of the President, after pointing out the positions of the TVA and the Federal Power Commission, advised that, "while the development of the water resources of the Cumberland River Valley is in keeping with the President's program and while there is no objection to your submitting to the Congress such report as you deem fitting, pending answers to the questions raised by the Federal Power Commission and the Tennessee Valley Authority as to the proposed development, no commitment is made as to the relationship to the program of the President of any particular feature recommended by the Chief of Engineers."

The USED deemed fit to submit its report to Congress without any further delay or revision; and Congress authorized it, on the recommendation of the Corps, in the Rivers and Harbors Act of 1946. The Corps has not yet begun to build the two substitute low navigation dams near the mouth of the river; and President Truman, apparently in an effort to forestall action, has asked the TVA to carry further its investigations of the Cumberland and to report to him. At this writing the TVA has a report in preparation which will propose again the construction of a high lower Cumberland dam for power and navigation. In the meantime, shortages of, and demands for, cheap power are growing rapidly in the Tennessee and Cumberland power market areas.[78]

Several conclusions can be drawn from this recent example. First, the Corps did not resolve its final plans in favor of comprehensive water resources development, nor optimum power development.

RESPONSIBILITY TO PROFESSION

The District Engineer had considered the alternative of low dams. He concluded, in discussing comprehensive development of the water resources of the basin, that "it would not be in the best interest of the Federal Government to ignore the large amount of hydro power which could be made available and the measure of flood control effected by construction of a dam to utilize most of the head potential between Nashville and the Ohio River." But the Board and Chief of Engineers struck this key project because of objections by those living within the reservoir site.

This leads to a second conclusion, namely that in the adjustment of the desires of local interests, the Corps often overemphasizes the highly localized effects of projects and fails to estimate their broad influences. In this case the local effect of the high dam is the displacement of families in the reservoir site; the broader influence, that resulting from optimum power development in the region. It is not meant to say that dislocation should be ignored; it is an economic and social cost and an important one which must be evaluated in any survey. The Corps did not evaluate it in the light of all relevant factors in this instance. This is indicated by the comments of TVA, an agency which has given serious attention to this problem in the past.

Third, the Corps did not plan Cumberland power development within that operating framework which would yield maximum benefits — i.e., integrated development with the Tennessee River.

Fourth, the Corps underestimated future demand for power. The District Engineer made no concrete estimate in his report, but assumed that future expansion in markets would absorb the power made available by the orderly development of the Cumberland in accordance with his recommendations. The Board of Engineers concluded that "need for water power in the area is not now of sufficient importance to outweigh the local objections to a high dam." This statement gives no estimate of power demands, but it is safe to say that the Board did not predict in 1946 the great demands for cheap power in the area that have developed in 1949 and 1950.

Finally, it should be noted that the Board of Engineers opposed the high dam because need for power in the area "is not *now* of sufficient importance." The implication is that if need developed in the future, then power would be provided. TVA took the Corps up short when it pointed out that construction of the two low dams in place of the high one would mean "the loss *for all time*" of the power. The nation just cannot afford to plan developments in terms of "now"; it must plan for the future.

With respect to distribution of public power, a sound policy should encourage the most widespread use of electric power in the public interest; secure for the ultimate consumer the benefits of low-cost power; and assure the most effective and efficient utilization of all energy resources.

The following paragraphs spell out in simplified manner agreed implications of these distribution objectives.

(1) Government policy should prevent monopolization, by limited groups, of energy produced at Federal projects.

(2) To prevent monopoly and thereby to effect widespread and efficient use of low-cost power by ultimate consumers at cheap rates, the Government should extend to municipalities, rural electric coöperatives, and other public and coöperative distribution agencies priority and preference in purchase of public power.

(3) To make this priority an effective one, the Government should sell power at wholesale at major load centers and build transmission lines to these centers. Only in this way can small utilities, including the publicly owned ones, take advantage of cheap public power. For Federal hydro plants are usually in headwaters, some distance from major centers of population, and only the largest private utilities can afford to build major transmission lines to the bus bars at these projects. Thus, with respect to a proposal to require that Federal power be sold at the bus bar and to prohibit Federal transmission lines, President Roosevelt said in 1944: "I would consider a restriction under which power must be sold at the switchboard as contrary to the public power policy repeatedly declared by the Congress during the last decade. So to restrict sales of electric power developed from the public resources with public funds might have the effect of depriving the public of an opportunity to obtain the many benefits that such low-cost electric energy should bring." [79]

(4) If the Government is to distribute to public and other utilities at load centers, then it must have available at these centers the optimum amount of firm public power to supply all or significant portions of their demands. If the Government is unable to supply firm power, then it may be forced to sell its power to private utilities

as secondary or dump power, and the private utilities alone will be in a position to service the preference customers at the load centers.

(5) To insure optimum firm power, the Government should integrate its own hydro facilities, where economic, by the construction of transmission lines which, along with the lines to major load centers, are often known as a backbone transmission grid. In addition, and where required (see next paragraph), the Government should build steam standby plants to firm up its hydro power.

(6) The Government should look toward the interconnection and integration of Federal systems with private power systems, but only under arrangements which will insure that public distribution objectives, as stated above, are realized. Thus, for example, the Government today should utilize private facilities for transmitting (wheeling) its power, providing these facilities constitute an equal or more advantageous method of supplying power than through Government construction of separate facilities, and providing other objectives of public distribution policy can be safeguarded in the wheeling arrangements.

(7) The objectives of power distribution policy should be an important consideration in setting power rates. As a first consideration, of course, rates should be set at a level which will insure repayment of project costs assigned to power, including interest. Generally, "postage stamp" rather than "mileage" rates should prevail. The former "will tend to contribute to the decentralization of new industries, the stabilization of existing communities, and should lessen the folly of competition between cities which will inevitably arise if the rates are graded in accordance with a series of distance zones with the cheapest rate at or near the generating sites." [80]

(8) Unified responsibility for Federal power marketing is generally desirable to insure uniform policies and administration. In this connection, President Roosevelt reported to Congress in 1944: "In the interest of economy and efficiency, it is desirable that the power marketing functions of the Government, with certain exceptions [the President was presumably thinking of TVA], be placed under common management, insofar as it is feasible to do so at this time." [81] The Hoover Commission Task Force on Natural Resources recommended that Federal power market functions, except for those of TVA, be consolidated in one Department.[82]

Many elements of this power distribution policy go back a great many years in Federal legislative and administrative history. For example, preference for publicly owned distribution systems is found in a reclamation act of 1906 and in the important Water Power Act of 1920 which established the Federal Power Commission.[83] As a guide for distributing large quantities of power developed at Federal projects, however, current policy took shape largely in the years 1936–1937 when legislation was drafted and enacted for sale of power from Bonneville and Grand Coulee Dams, then under construction.[84] It was during these years that the President appointed the National Power Policy Committee which, along with experts from the NRPB, the Federal Power Commission, and other agencies, perfected the policy.

The Corps of Engineers during these years opposed fairly consistently the policy proposals of the interagency committees and the Administration, and in doing so, supported, in effect, the private utilities in their opposition to Federal policy. Thus, for example, the Power Policy Committee, the NRPB, the President, and others were agreed that "postage stamp" rather than "mileage" rates should be set for power from the Columbia River dams.

So far as the Bonneville project is concerned, this latter zone system would be peculiarly ill-advised; first, because it would encourage the use of this energy in the heart of the Columbia River Gorge, where the topography and physical environment is primarily suited for recreation purposes and not for the building of industrial cities. There already exist within the Portland-Vancouver-Longview region many towns and cities now being served by expensive governmental functions — highways, schools, sewers, fire-police protection, etc. adequate to take care of the needs for considerable enlargements to their populations. It would be exceedingly wasteful, from the point of view of public economy, to encourage the building of new industrial towns next to the site of the Bonneville Dam. From the point of view of ultimate regional cohesion and goodwill, a policy based upon similar rates for large areas possesses distinct advantages.[85]

In order to facilitate establishing similar rates over large areas and for other purposes, the power experts also agreed to the necessity for a backbone grid system — a superpower network designed to serve existing and new generating and transmission facilities.

The representative of the Corps of Engineers reported to Congress that it would not be economically feasible to set uniform rates for the Pacific Northwest, because "it costs money to transmit power." And the Corps found that "the recommendation for the construction of a superpower network of transmission lines by the Government is questionable . . . If you superimpose an enormous transmission system or grid over that country with its present small population, relatively speaking, and large distances that you have to cover, and average up the cost so that it is the same all over, it will make your cost so much that you will never be able to sell to industry, and if you don't get industry, you don't get people, and if you don't get people, you can't sell power." [86]

The Engineer Department just did not comprehend the importance of low-cost power to the economic development of the Pacific Northwest. The standards which it proposed for rate making gave little emphasis to any social or economic objectives that might be obtained through power policy; they recognized only the necessary factor of reimbursement. The Corps representatives were among the calamity howlers of the thirties who feared the New Deal was erecting great white and power-full elephants in the West, particularly Grand Coulee. The rapid and complete utilization of power from these projects, the tremendous demand for more power, the current construction programs of the Corps and the Bureau of Reclamation on the Columbia to help supply this demand, and the orderly economic development of the area to date all attest to the wisdom and foresight of the interagency proposals of 1937.

The policies perfected in 1937 were made to apply generally to projects built by the Bureau of Reclamation by the Reclamation Project Act of 1939, although it should be noted that many of them had been in force on reclamation projects for a number of years. The 1937 policies were made to apply generally to projects built by the Corps of Engineers by Section 5 of the Flood Control Act of 1944; and it is in connection with this and related legislation that the activities of the USED should be examined.

After careful and lengthy consideration, the President and the Executive Office decided in early 1944 to request Congress to write the principles for power distribution, including that for unified management, into the pending Rivers and Harbors and Flood Control Bills, and thereby to apply national power policy to the large number of Corps power projects scheduled to be completed in the immediate and more distant future. The Department of Interior was selected as the marketing agency because it was known to be sympathetic to the policy objectives and had had experience in marketing power in accordance with these principles under the Bonneville, Fort Peck, and Reclamation Acts.

The USED did not support the President, although the need to incorporate national power policy in Corps legislation had been widely recognized among water and energy experts for a number of years. The Department had been informed of the President's decision in February of 1944, yet it submitted project survey reports to Congress in April, May, and June of 1944 recommending policies at variance with the President's.[87] In the case of the reports on Blakely Mountain Dam, Ouachita River, Arkansas and Louisiana and Des Moines River, Iowa, the Director of the Budget informed the Engineers that their recommendations for transmission and sale of electric energy should be reconsidered in the light of the President's stated policy that all power disposition from new Federal projects should be handled by the Department of the Interior. Again, the Engineers did not reconsider their recommendations. They were transmitted unchanged to the Congress, along with the advice received from the Executive Office of the President.

The President's proposal for a general provision in the Rivers and Harbors and Flood Control Bills appears to have enjoyed the opposition of the Engineer Department. The proposal was presented to Congress in a letter from the President to the chairman of the House Committee on Rivers and Harbors on 7 February 1944 after the Rivers and Harbors Bill had been reported out by the Committee.[88] When the bill was debated on the floor of the House, the Committee proposed an amendment to meet the President's policy, but this amendment failed of adoption.[89] Several days later the Flood Control Bill was reported to the House with no general provision for the marketing of power, and none was inserted when the bill passed the House on 9 May.[90]

In the Senate Committee on Commerce both bills were under the supervision of Senator Overton. The President was in direct communication with the Senator concerning the power marketing amendments.[91] The President was also in direct communication with the Secretary of War on this matter. The following curt note indi-

RESPONSIBILITY TO PROFESSION

cates, it is believed, that the Chief Executive was thoroughly dissatisfied with the lack of support he had received from the Engineer Department and that he expected a very definite change in attitude.

> THE WHITE HOUSE
> *Washington*
> *May 16, 1944*
>
> MEMORANDUM FOR THE SECRETARY OF WAR
>
> I want the Kings and Kern River projects to be built by the Bureau of Reclamation and not by the Army engineers. I also want the power generated at projects built by the Army engineers to be disposed of by the Secretary of the Interior. I hope you will see that the rivers and harbors and flood-control bills include appropriate provisions to effectuate these.
>
> /s/ F.D.R.

The Secretary of War transmitted the President's memorandum to the chairman of the Senate Committee on Commerce. He said in his letter of transmittal, "I accordingly recommend that your Committee give its earnest consideration to the desires expressed in that memorandum." The Secretary's letter and the President's memorandum were both inserted into the record of the Committee hearings on the Flood Control Bill, along with a number of other communications.[92] There was no discussion of the memorandum at the time. And an examination of the record of the Committee hearings on both the Flood Control and Rivers and Harbors Bills reveals no single occasion on which representatives of the Corps of Engineers supported the President's program in this respect. Sole executive support was provided by the President's Executive Office, and representatives of the Department of Interior. To be sure, the President's program prevailed in the long run, but the failure to support it constitutes additional grounds for questioning the administrative responsibility of the Corps of Engineers.

In the Eightieth Congress (1947), Representative Dondero (R., Mich.), chairman of the House Committee on Public Works, introduced legislation to amend Section 5 of the Flood Control Act of 1944.[93] His bill would return control over distribution of power from USED dams to the Corps. It would, with few exceptions, prohibit transmission of power to load centers and require sale at the bus bar, although it would permit interconnection of Federal dams. The Federal Power Commission would be charged with approval of contracts and rates for disposal of power.

Of his purpose, Mr. Dondero said at the hearings, "I am frank to say, for the purpose of the record, and so that the public may know, that I have viewed the operation of the Department of the Interior under Section 5 of the Flood Control Act, which I seek to repeal by this bill, as going far afield in the direction of competition with private enterprise in this country. That is my purpose in trying to stop it." The legislation was supported by representatives of the large private utilities, particularly of the Pacific Gas and Electric Company.

The President opposed the bill. His position was made known both by public addresses on the power issue in 1947 and by advice which was given to the executive departments by the Bureau of the Budget that the bill was not in accord with the President's program.

The position of the Corps of Engineers was that it favored the administrative provisions of the bill generally, though it would have preferred to see the FPC distribute the power; and that it could see no objection whatsoever to the sale of power at the bus bar. With respect to the administrative provisions, the following testimony is indicative:

> The Chairman [Dondero]. A question has been raised before this committee that if this bill is enacted that instead of simplifying the power question it would only complicate it by injecting the Army engineers into the picture. Do you think that is so?
>
> Col. Feringa [who represented the Engineers throughout]. No, sir. In answering that question I should state, however, that the Secretary of War in his report on this bill has suggested to the committee that consideration be given to the distribution of the power by the Federal Power Commission rather than by the Corps of Engineers . . .
>
> The Chairman . . . Do you see anything in the bill which would in any way complicate the administration or development and sale of this power if it is turned over to the Corps of Army Engineers of the War Department and the Federal Power Commission?
>
> Col. Feringa. No, sir; of course, we prefer that it be handled by the Federal Power Commission, but I will answer your question. No, sir.

The following interchange illustrates the Corps' attitude on sale of power at the bus bar:

The Chairman. I will simplify it. The objection is that if this bill is enacted as drawn, which requires the Federal Government to sell power at the bus bar, that it will destroy the economy of cheap power going to the people through the private utilities. Have you had any experience at any dam which the Corps of Engineers has constructed, along that line?

Col. Feringa. No, sir; we have had no such experience. I have read the bill, of course, and studied it and it seems to me that the Federal Power Commission would have the authority to fix the rates. So I don't see how the economy of power could be adversely affected . . .

The Chairman. Coming back to the question I asked you, Colonel, you do not have any fear that selling power at the bus bar . . . would make it possible for private industry to create a monopoly?

Col. Feringa. I have no such fear, Mr. Dondero. It could happen, of course, under certain conditions but I have no fear that it will happen with the Federal Power Commission controlling the rates . . .

The Chairman. Is there anything in the bill before the committee which you think will in any way hamper or retard the full development of power by the Federal Government at these dams we have been discussing here . . . ?

Col. Feringa. You say the full development of power, sir?

The Chairman. Yes. Power.

Col. Feringa. No, sir.

The Chairman. Whatever power is in those dams you are satisfied would be disposed of?

Col. Feringa. Yes, sir.

The Chairman. At the bus bar?

Col. Feringa. Yes, sir . . .

The Chairman. That brings me to this subject: In the Southeast we have a number of rivers already planned for generation of power, including Clark Hill, which we have all heard about.

Col. Feringa. Yes, sir.

The Chairman. I have introduced a bill which provides that the Army engineers will construct the dam and if the bill becomes law, that the power companies in the area will build the power house and install the machinery and continue in the generation and sale of electric energy.

Col. Feringa. Yes, sir.

The Chairman. Is there anything in that kind of arrangement that is at all detrimental to the Government, Colonel?

Col. Feringa. I cannot see that anything detrimental to the Government would be occasioned by such an arrangement . . .

As for the Colonel's reliance on FPC rate control to effect desirable power distribution, it should be pointed out that the Power

Commission under the bill would have no control over the rates which the ultimate consumer must pay for his power. All the Commission would do would be to determine the price which the private utility must *pay* for the power *at the bus bar,* not the price at which it *sells* the power to other utilities and to ultimate consumers.[94] Thus FPC rate control could not be relied upon to achieve the same objectives as are guaranteed by preference sales at load centers. Nor, as a matter of fact, was the bill intended by its sponsors to guarantee these same objectives.

In approving Mr. Dondero's proposals for power marketing in the Southeast, the Corps was apparently willing to go back not only to 1943 but to the Hoover Dam formula of 1927 — i.e., the Government sells falling water to utilities which install their own generators and are in full control of all power operations.

For reasons not understood by this writer, the Federal Power Commission also supported the bill. However, it did not get very far in the legislative mill, and President Truman made the bill and its objectives a major issue in his successful Western campaign tour of 1948.

Irrigation

As in the case of power policy, no comprehensive analysis of irrigation policy is undertaken here. We are interested essentially in the limited activities of the Corps in distributing irrigation benefits where these are a product of its multiple-purpose projects. And in this context, responsible policy dictates that irrigation features of Engineer Department projects be planned, constructed, and operated in accordance with reclamation law.

If this is not done, irrigation features of Corps multiple-purpose projects will be developed under conditions for repayment and delivery of water quite different from those for irrigation facilities developed by the Bureau of Reclamation. Such differences are bound to result in serious conflicts and competition between Federal water agencies and local groups interested in obtaining Federal aid, and in serious inequities to large groups of beneficiaries. As set out below, the provisions of reclamation law accord more nearly with the repayment and speculation control tests of a sound water plan than those of the Corps' flood control law. This is not to say that reclamation law fulfills all the requirements established at the start of this chapter; it has many serious deficiencies. Thus, to state that irrigation features of Corps projects should be operated in accordance with reclamation law is to state a *minimum* requirement. Ideally, these features, like those developed by the Bureau of Reclamation, should meet tests more nearly perfect.

With respect to *repayment,* reclamation law requires that water users, within their financial abilities, repay irrigation costs in periods up to forty years (with the addition of a developmental period not to exceed ten years), but free from interest. The water users, thereby, are charged for vendible benefits so as to repay those portions of project costs allocated to irrigation which are within their repayment abilities. On the other hand, where irrigation features of Engineer Department projects have been planned under flood control law prior to 1945, the provisions with respect to repayment have been largely indefinite and have not been dependent upon any consistent legislative standard. The amounts to be repaid by beneficiaries were the requirements for local contribution recommended by the Chief of Engineers in survey reports and approved by the Congress in authorizing the construction of projects in accordance with these reports. As a rule, water users would pay less and the Federal Treasury would recapture less under the local coöperation provisions of flood control law than under the repayment provisions of reclamation law.

Repayment contracts negotiated by the Bureau of Reclamation in accordance with reclamation law contain restrictions on water and land use which are lacking for projects constructed entirely under flood control law prior to 1945. In general, the reclamation law provides for significant Federal control over irrigation development whereas the Engineer Department policy has provided for local autonomy. The reclamation law contains *acreage limitations* designed to prevent land monopoly and to promote widespread ownership of land in family-size farms. No water in excess of that required to irrigate 160 acres, or 320 acres in community property States, may be delivered to a land owner until he has contracted to sell his excess lands.

Similarly, reclamation law contains provisions designed to protect the smaller working farmer from *land speculation* at his expense. For all projects constructed under reclamation law, the owner of excess lands, if he wishes to dispose of them in order that they may become eligible for delivery of water, must agree to sell on terms and conditions satisfactory to the Secretary of Interior and at prices based upon an appraisal made without reference to any increment of value due to Federal reclamation. These restrictions on acreage and speculation are in accord with the tests of a sound water plan. They should be applied to the irrigation features of all projects, no matter what agency constructs them.

Largely for these several reasons, the President, his Executive Office, the Bureau of Reclamation, and others have insisted that irrigation features of Engineer Department projects be planned, constructed, and operated in accordance with reclamation law. President Roosevelt in 1944 urged enactment of legislation which would insure that the Secretary of Interior be made responsible, under reclamation law, for the regulation of irrigation storage and the disposal of irrigation water from multiple-purpose projects built under authority of rivers and harbors and flood control acts. He wrote to the chairman of the House Committee on Rivers and Harbors as follows:

> Some of the projects to be authorized by the bill, particularly those affecting the arid and semi-arid areas of the West, may have substantial potential values for irrigation purposes. Obviously, where these values exist provision should be made for their eventual realization through the construction of irrigation works complementing the works constructed by the Corps of Engineers . . . It can hardly be questioned that the best way of accomplishing this objective is under the tested procedures of the Federal reclamation laws. Accordingly, I recommend that suitable provision also be made in the bill for the undertaking by the Bureau of Reclamation, in the form and manner prescribed by these laws, of reclamation works connected with or dependent upon projects covered by the bill.[95]

Such a provision, applicable to all navigation and flood control projects to be constructed in the future, was enacted as Section 8 of the Flood Control Act of 1944.

The Engineer Department has not favored this policy. Prior to enactment of Section 8, it had never recommended application of the reclamation standards to the planning and operation of irrigation features of its projects. To the contrary, recommendations in survey reports show that the Engineer Department much preferred to conduct the irrigation function under the almost nonexistent standards of flood control law. Even after the President had communicated with the Committe on Rivers and Harbors in early 1944, the Engineer Department transmitted to the Congress a number of survey reports, not in accord with the President's program, proposing development of irrigation without any regard for reclamation standards.[96]

The Corps of Engineers gave no backing to the President's recommendation in 1944. Numerous communications from the President and the Budget Bureau, and letters and testimony of the Department of Interior provided the support for the legislative policy.[97] The postlegislative history of Section 8 is one of conflict between the Corps and the Bureau of Reclamation in which the Corps has attempted by various means to limit and restrict its application. This story will be told in the concluding chapter.

Conclusion

Using as a guide a composite of professional views, such, for example, as that found in the reports of the Water Resources Committee of the National Resources Planning Board, we have attempted to hold the Corps of Engineers to a detailed accountability for Federal executive policy for flood control and navigation. With less precision, we have held the agency accountable for the manner in which it has conformed to approved power and irrigation policies in planning its multi-purpose developments. That the Engineer Department fails to live up to a great many of the accepted standards of professional responsibility in all of these respects has been pointed out. It remains to assess the total picture, to pull together conclusions on the responsibility of the Corps to the organized public, the Congress, the President, and to profession. This can be done best by the use of a concrete example, a case study. Thus, the concluding chapter is the case of the Kings River in the Great Central Valley of California.

FIVE

The Kings River Project in the Basin of the Great Central Valley[1]

IN FEBRUARY 1940 CONGRESS RECEIVED TWO SEPARATE reports recommending construction of a multiple-purpose reservoir on the Kings River in California — one prepared by the Corps of Engineers and the other by the Bureau of Reclamation. The reports were dissimilar in several important respects. Each report had acquired proponents and opponents among the local interests, and the two Federal agencies were put in competition with each other to obtain the support of the California beneficiaries.

Why did two Federal water development agencies plan similar multiple-purpose projects on the same river? Why were not the conflicts between the two agencies reconciled at an early stage in the planning process, and the competition between the two put to an end by the President's office? What have been the results of this uncoördinated conflict? What has been the effect on the public interest of agency competition to win the support of local groups of water users? This case history of the Kings River project is designed to illustrate some of the causes and results of uncoördinated water resource development.

DESCRIPTION OF AREA

California is traversed lengthwise by two parallel ranges of mountains — the Sierra Nevada on the east and the Coast Range on the

KINGS RIVER PROJECT

west — which converge at Mount Shasta on the north and are joined by the Tehachapi Mountains on the south to enclose the Central Valley Basin. The Basin is nearly 500 miles long, averages 120 miles in width, includes more than one-third of California. The main valley floor, comprising nearly one-third of the basin area, is a gently sloping, practically unbroken, alluvial area 400 miles long and averaging 45 miles in width. Sacramento River drains the northern portion of the Basin and San Joaquin River the southern portion. The confluence of these two streams is in the Sacramento–San Joaquin Delta from which they find a common outlet to the ocean through San Francisco Bay.

Water supply and water requirements in the Central Valley Basin are unbalanced geographically. Available water supplies decrease from north to south. Conversely, the water requirements are greater in the south by reason of larger irrigable areas, less rainfall, and greater evaporation. As a result, the total runoff into Sacramento Valley far exceeds its ultimate water requirements, while in the southern or Upper San Joaquin Valley local supplies are inadequate to meet local demands. On the east side of the Upper San Joaquin Valley irrigation has reached a stage where dependable stream flow has long since been completely used and in many cases the draft on ground water greatly exceeds the natural replenishment. An alarming lowering of the ground water table has brought this overdraft forcibly to the attention of the water users of the area. For some time it has been realized that unless additional water is secured, pumping depths will become so great that considerable areas of land now irrigated will have to be abandoned because of excessive water costs.

One of the principal objectives of the Central Valley Project of the Bureau of Reclamation is to remedy this situation. An initial phase of the Project, now under construction and in partial operation, is designed to effect a transfer of surplus water from the northern to the southern portions of the Basin. The Delta-Mendota canal and two additional canals proposed for future authorization and construction will carry surplus Sacramento River water 120 to 140 miles southerly from the Delta to Mendota Pool on the San Joaquin River. Here the water will be used to meet the demands of crop lands on the west side of the San Joaquin River now irrigated by diversions from the San Joaquin.

By this exchange of water the runoff of the San Joaquin River can be stored in Millerton Lake behind Friant Dam, on the east side of the Valley near the headwaters of the San Joaquin, and from there it can be made available for diversion north and south, through the Madera and Friant-Kern canals, to irrigate lands in east side Upper San Joaquin Valley.

Friant Dam, Madera, and Friant-Kern canals are initial units of a comprehensive plan prepared by the Bureau of Reclamation for utilizing practically the entire runoff tributary to the southern Central Valley Basin. Additional features include planned reservoirs on each of the principal streams flowing west from the mountains into the Basin, south of Friant Dam and the San Joaquin River. The primary objective of the prospective reservoirs is temporary storage of surplus winter and snow-melt runoff until it can be released to existing and prospective canals for direct irrigation use or for ground water replenishment. Such water regulation will be of value not only for irrigation but also for flood control. The principal flood damage in the area results from large volumes of water which in wet years flow into the closed basin of Tulare Lake, south of the San Joaquin River. Extensive areas of agricultural land are flooded, but the water is subsequently used beneficially for irrigation. The reservoirs and canals proposed for east side Upper San Joaquin Valley would greatly reduce this damage by temporarily storing, and then diverting for irrigation use, water which would otherwise cause flood damage in the Tulare Lake area. Reservoirs are proposed for the Kings, Kaweah, Tule, and Kern Rivers which are all tributary to Tulare Lake, except that Kings River can be diverted in part by means of control works either north to San Joaquin River or south to Tulare Lake. It is with the project on the Kings River that we are primarily concerned in this case study.

Early Planning[2]

As early as 1937 both the Corps of Engineers and the Bureau of Reclamation undertook investigations of the Kings River area. The investigation of the Corps of Engineers was initiated under the Flood Control Act of 1936; that of the Bureau of Reclamation, under an allotment from an appropriation under the National Industrial Recovery Act. Both investigations were requested originally by the same water users' association in the Kings River area. The

EXISTING AND PROPOSED
WATER DEVELOPMENTS
IN THE STATE OF CALIFORNIA

**FEATURES CONSTRUCTED
OR UNDER CONSTRUCTION**
■■■■■■■■ PROPOSED FEATURES

MAJOR

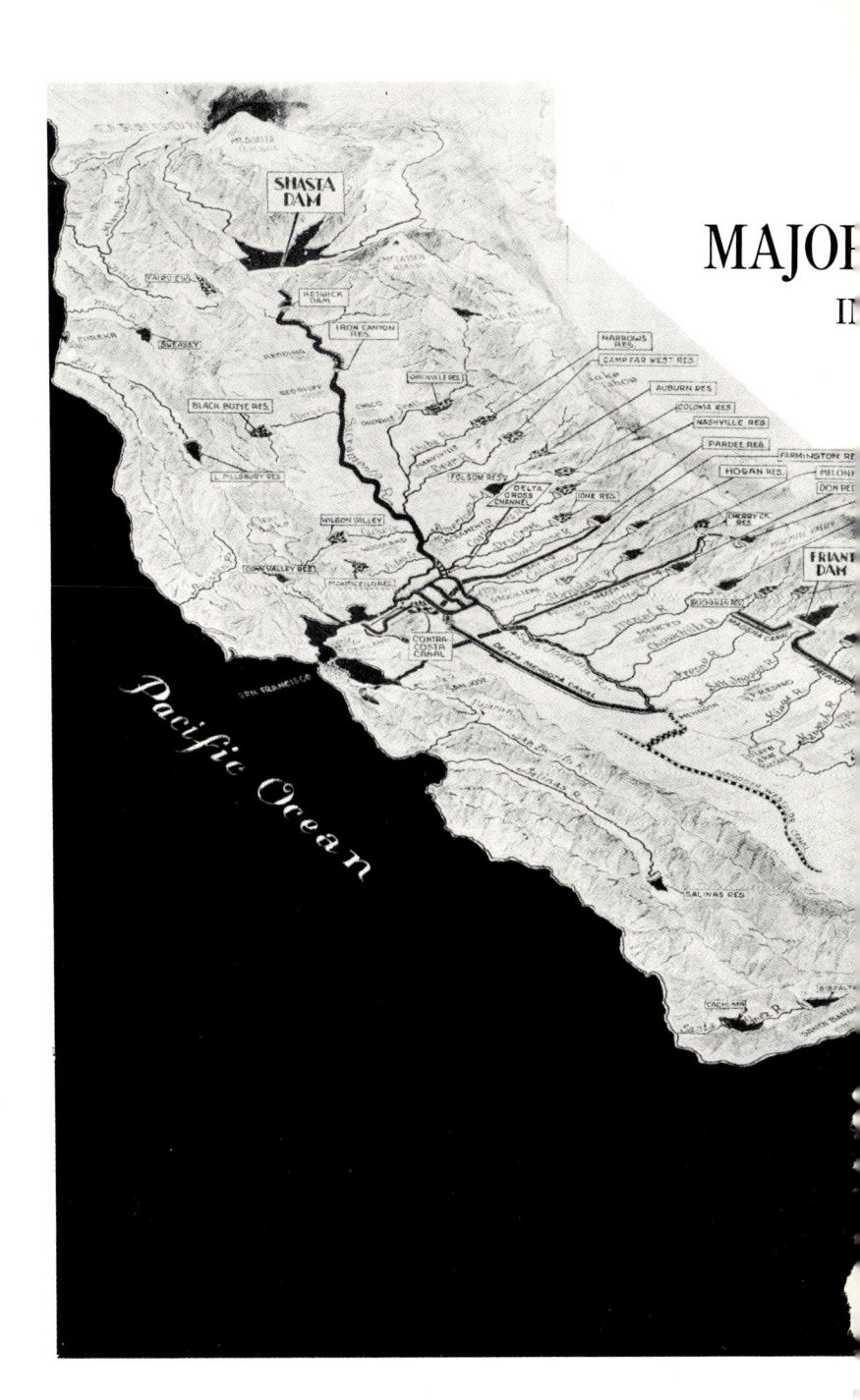

association members apparently wanted to see what each agency would propose so that they would be in a position to express a preference for that plan which would afford them, as existing water users, the greatest benefits at the least costs.

The likelihood of controversy between the two Federal agencies developed soon thereafter. Although the engineers of the Corps and Bureau effected an exchange of physical data, separate field investigations were conducted and each agency developed its conclusions and recommendations independently.

Through its drainage basin committee for the Central Valley area, the Water Resources Committee of the National Resources Planning Board was made aware of the developing agency conflict before the field reports were completed. The Water Committee was very much opposed to the submission of separate reports by the two agencies; its members preferred that the survey organizations coöperate to deliver a single report reflecting the combined judgment of the water experts in the executive branch of the government. From experience they knew that integration of investigations is far more likely to be effective if undertaken at the initiation and field study stages of project investigations before findings are crystallized; it is largely and necessarily perfunctory if delayed until the basic conclusions have been reached independently by those concerned.

The Committee, however, was unable to stop the competition. The field reports were completed and the Valley water users, learning of the conflicting recommendations of the two agencies, began to take sides for the Bureau or for the Corps. The survey report of the District Engineer was submitted to Washington in April 1939, and soon thereafter the tentative field report of the Bureau of Reclamation was transmitted to Washington headquarters.

Either through the National Resources Planning Board, or the Secretary of the Interior, President Roosevelt was made aware of the developing conflict in the area. The President viewed the Kings River controversy with such concern, particularly as regards any precedent it might set for irrigation and flood control policy, that he instructed the two agencies to keep their reports confidential insofar as their contents had not already become known to local interests and requested a conference in his office on the problem on 19 July 1939.

At this conference the President indicated his concern over the duplication of water development functions in the Central Valley and similar areas and stated his firm desire and intention to eliminate similar duplication in the future. As for the Kings River project, the President agreed to an arrangement whereby the two agencies would coöperate in preparing independent reports, but these reports should contain agreement on both design and economic features of the project. As for future areas of potential conflict, the President instructed the Departments of War, Interior, and Agriculture, in coöperation with the National Resources Planning Board, to draw up a memorandum of agreement which, by insuring consultation in the early stages of project planning, would preclude the possibility of similar conflicts.

The interagency agreement, negotiated in response to this request, was the Tripartite Agreement, which, as we have noted, authorized free interchange of information between the three agencies in the field in the preparation of reports on multiple-purpose projects, and joint consultation in the field and in Washington on any such reports. At the time the Agreement was negotiated the National Resources Planning Board felt that it fell short of the requirements of the situation and of the desires of the President. Experience under the Agreement confirmed these fears. Although it did contribute to some improvement in field coöperation, the Agreement did not eliminate conflicts and divergencies in later reports.

The Planning Board would have preferred that the arrangement on the Kings River project provide for the submission of a joint report by the two agencies rather than of separate, but reconciled, reports. However, the President requested the agencies to submit their revised reports to him, giving them to understand that the reports would then be reviewed for the President by the Water Resources Committee before they were made public or submitted to the Congress. In this way some of the advantages of a joint report might be realized.

On 23 January 1940, the Secretary of Interior submitted to the President, through the National Resources Planning Board, the revised report of the Bureau of Reclamation. Four days later the Director of the Board informed the Chief of Engineers that the Secretary of Interior had forwarded his report on the project "to the President through the Board" and stated that, "When your report on the project is received, the Board will then have an opportunity to comment upon any points of difference which may exist between the two sets of recommendations. This we will do promptly."

On 31 January the Chief of Engineers acknowledged receipt of the Director's letter in writing and stated that he understood that the Reclamation report had been forwarded to the President, through the National Resources Planning Board. The Chief of Engineers, however, did not state that the report of his Department had been completed nor that it had been sent *directly* to the President on the preceding day. By the time the National Resources Planning Board heard that the Engineer Department report had been sent directly to the White House, and communicated with the President's executive clerk to catch up with it, they found that it had been allowed to pass directly to the Congress. Thus, the recommendations of the Engineer Department were made public without any opportunity for review by the Water Resources Committee and before they had been fully reconciled with those of the Bureau of Reclamation.

As for the action of the White House in allowing the War Department report to pass directly to the Congress, no definite explanation is available. However, it is believed that approval for transmission of the report to Congress was the result of a clerical error; that the White House was under the impression that the report had cleared the Planning Board. As for the action of the Chief of Engineers, it may well be that the instructions of the President at the July conference had been to submit the revised and reconciled reports to him; but the Engineers knew that the reports were not fully reconciled and they knew that the Secretary of Interior had transmitted the Reclamation report to the President through the National Resources Planning Board where it was being held, awaiting receipt of their report. Thus it seems that from the standpoint of the Engineer Department the complete by-passing of the National Resources Planning Board was merely a fortunate accident, which the Department considered to be no part of its duty to prevent. The failure to mention transmittal of the report to the President in the letter of 31 January may or may not be taken to indicate there was no active desire on the part of the Engineers for coördination.

Even if the final handling of the Engineers' report was not in any way a product of the jurisdictional competition with the Bureau of Reclamation, this competition may very well have been responsible for a significant variation from the uniform procedure for the preparation of Engineer survey reports. The procedure, as descibed in Chapter I, requires that the District Engineer conduct the survey in the field and that the Division Engineer, the Board of Engineers for Rivers and Harbors in Washington, and the Chief of Engineers, each review the survey report and state their conclusions and recommendations in an endorsement to the District Engineer's report. In this case, however, the report of the District Engineer, which was transmitted to Washington in April 1939, never saw the light of day nor did any revision of this report which might have been made after the President's conference. Instead the Chief of Engineers used as the basis for his report a very brief interim report of the Board of Engineers which had been prepared in Washington in June 1939, before the original conference with the President, and which made no reference to the District Engineer's survey.

To this brief interim report the Chief attached his own recommendations, containing those revisions in project design which had been agreed to jointly by the Office of the Chief of Engineers and the Commissioner of Reclamation. It is difficult to understand this procedural variation unless it can be attributed to a desire on the part of the Engineers to act quickly, a desire growing from the jurisdictional competition. More important, however, the President and the Congress were provided with a report which, though designed to serve as the basis for action upon a highly controversial project recommendation, was seriously lacking in basic data.

Upon learning that the Engineer report had gone to Congress, the Chairman of the National Resources Planning Board, on 2 February 1940, wrote to the President:

We understand that the Army report has already gone to the Congress. In justice to the Secretary of the Interior and the Bureau of Reclamation, it now seems desirable that the Interior Department report should also go to the Congress even though the Army and Reclamation recommendations have not yet been completely reconciled.

And so, in February 1940, the Congress received two separate reports from the Federal agencies, each recommending construction of a reservoir at Pine Flat site on the Kings River. The reports were generally reconciled on features of engineering design but were far apart on matters of water economics. The conflicting recommendations became a matter of public record. They attracted ardent proponents and opponents. The Planning Board scheme of insuring integration prior to the crystallization of findings and recommendations had failed.

Future events were to confirm the conviction of the Board that integration which is delayed until basic conclusions have been reached and published independently by those concerned is extremely difficult, if not impossible, of effective attainment.

Basic Differences in Plans[3]

The reports of the Bureau of Reclamation and the Corps of Engineers were in agreement as to the design of the project. They both recommended construction of a multiple-purpose reservoir with a storage capacity of one million acre feet at the Pine Flat site on the Kings River and of channel improvement works to regulate the flow passing into Tulare Lake. After some differences of opinion, the agencies reached agreement on estimates of cost — $19,500,000 for the Pine Flat Reservoir, exclusive of any power development, and $200,000 for the channel improvement works.

The basic differences in the reports which remained unreconciled when they were submitted to Congress related to major questions of policy rather than to design.

Basically at difference were the water use philosophies of the two agencies. The Bureau of Reclamation has viewed the development of the Kings River area as part of a comprehensive plan for the development of the Central Valley Basin, with emphasis on water conservation and maximum water use. The Corps of Engineers on the other hand had little interest in any basin-wide comprehensive plan at the time and considered the development of the water resources of the Kings River almost entirely from the point of view of local flood protection. Thus, for example, the Division Engineer at San Francisco told the Central Valley drainage basin committee, during the preparation of the Kings River survey report: "There seems to be a conflict as to how the water should be handled. The Army investigations have been only from the standpoint of flood control." [4]

As mentioned, the reports of the District and Division Engineers on the project were never released, and the brief reports of the Board of Engineers for Rivers and Harbors and the Chief of Engineers which were transmitted to Congress did give some consideration to water conservation. But the conflicting water use philosophies of the two agencies, as we shall see, were bound to produce significant disagreements.

Stemming from this basic conflict, the independent recommendations of the two agencies and their later modifications have revealed the following important areas of conflict:

(1) Should the project be built in accordance with flood control law or irrigation law? The most significant differences between the two laws as they have been applied by the two agencies relate to the matters of repayment, distribution of benefits, and project operation.

The differences in *repayment* and *distribution of benefits* have been analyzed in Chapter IV. In the Kings River report the Bureau of Reclamation recommended that the water users repay the entire cost allocated to irrigation ($9,750,000) over a period of forty years without interest. The Corps of Engineers, on the other hand, recommended that local interests contribute a lump sum of $4,710,000 for irrigation benefits, which if borrowed by the local interests at an interest rate of three and one-half per cent per annum would make their total pay-out roughly equal to that under the Reclamation plan. The Bureau of Reclamation would apply to the Kings River project the restrictions of reclamation law on acreage and speculation. The Corps of Engineers, by constructing the project under flood control law, would exempt the project beneficiaries from these restrictions.

There are differences in the *operation* of completed irrigation facilities between those developed by the Bureau of Reclamation in accordance with reclamation law and those developed by the Engineer Department in accordance with flood control law. Works constructed by the Corps of Engineers are often turned over to local interests for administration, with only general control by the Corps; works constructed by the Bureau of Reclamation are ordinarily operated by it for a period of years, and some works remain under its jurisdiction indefinitely.

Most irrigation projects require a dam and reservoir to retain and store water and supplemental irrigation canals, ditches, and spreading works to distribute the water. Where landowners fail to comply with the requirements of reclamation law, it is a simple engineering matter to cut off water deliveries. In areas like the Upper San Joaquin Valley, however, additional irrigation water may be provided by the

KINGS RIVER PROJECT

construction of dams without the necessity of supplemental Federal works. Existing privately owned canal and distribution systems are fed from the main river channels; and water in the channels and canals, not required for immediate use, can seep into the ground water table from which it can be pumped when needed for irrigation purposes. Any operation of the completed reservoirs will allow more water, formerly wasted to the sea, to be diverted into ground water for later use by irrigators through pumping. Where these dams and reservoirs are of multiple-purpose character, particularly difficult operation problems and controversies are bound to arise; and such controversies are inevitably sharpened when two Federal agencies promote different basic proposals for project operation and maintenance.

This is the case in the Kings River project. Because the project is part of a basin-wide plan for the Central Valley, the Bureau of Reclamation recommended that it be operated by the Federal Government in harmony with other developments in the Valley. The Bureau reported:

> The complexities of irrigation uses, the potentially conflicting interests of irrigation and flood control, the coordination of power production by the Kings River and the Central Valley projects, and the prospect of sale of water from the Central Valley project to portions of Kings River service area, make it highly advisable for the government to operate the contemplated Kings River project works, leaving the operation of the canals and the distribution of water in local hands. Water releases, except in rare cases, must conform to vested irrigation rights.

The Corps of Engineers, on the other hand, recommended that the project be turned over to local interests for operation. They reported:

> It is noted that water rights in the area under consideration are complex and involved, and that local interests have expressed a willingness and desire to maintain and operate the proposed improvements in accordance with regulations to be prescribed by the Secretary of War. Such an arrangement is desirable as it would relieve the United States of the responsibilities involved in the operation of conservation storage.

Through these conflicting recommendations, the related issues of "Federal domination" and of local water rights entered into the controversy between the Bureau and Corps in the Central Valley.

With respect to water rights, local records and the report of the Bureau of Reclamation disclosed "overschedule water" or water in excess of entitlement in Kings River to which present water users, represented by their water associations, asserted a right and claim based on use and necessity. The Corps of Engineers, by turning operation of the project over to local interests — the water users' associations — would have allowed the present water users to arrange disposition of the "overschedule water" themselves. The report of the Bureau of Reclamation recognized the validity of vested irrigation rights, but proposed to retain operation of the project under Federal control, and thereby to deny to present water users the one hundred per cent control over all releases from the reservoir which they sought in their own interests.

A fourth difference between flood control and reclamation law which bears on this case study should be mentioned: that of authorization. The rules of Congress provide that no money can be appropriated except for activities that have already been authorized by Congress. Under the reclamation law, a project is considered to be authorized when the Secretary of Interior determines that it is economically and engineeringly desirable and feasible under the standards set in the statute. No additional legislative authorization is required, though Congress must appropriate money for the specific project before construction can begin. Under flood control law, on the other hand, the Congress must authorize each separate project, on the basis of an Engineer Department survey report, before an appropriation can be provided.

Thus, with respect to the Kings River project, the report of the Secretary of Interior submitted to Congress in February 1940 constituted in effect authorization for the project under reclamation law. The report of the Chief of Engineers constituted a recommendation that Congress authorize the project under flood control law.

(2) Should the development of power be initiated as part of the irrigation improvement, or should provision be made for future development under license by the Federal Power Commission? In its report, the Bureau of Reclamation recommended the construction of a power plant, with provision for an ultimate capacity of 45,000 kilowatts, but an initial installation of 15,000 kilowatts; and the provision of transmission lines to connect with lines of the Central Valley

Project. The Bureau considered the power development to be essential to the proper and most beneficial utilization of conserved waters. The initial power installation was needed to meet the immediate local requirements of pumping and would constitute the most favorable immediate step in the full development of power on the Kings River.

The Corps of Engineers, on the other hand, did not propose the immediate development of hydroelectric power, but suggested that provision be made for the installation of penstocks for possible future development of power, under Federal Power Commission license. The Corps considered that the development of power was not an essential part of the flood control and irrigation improvement and that the public interest would be best served by development under private license.

The largest water users' association in the area preferred the Army scheme because it planned to file with the FPC for the license to develop the power and then to set power rates which would yield sufficient revenues to help retire the local contribution for irrigation benefits. In other words, it would use power primarily as a means of obtaining cheap water. If the Bureau of Reclamation developed the power and tied it in with the Central Valley Project, power rates would be set in the light of a combination of economic, social, and other objectives rather than in the light of cheap water alone.

(3) What should be the allocation of project costs and benefits as between flood control, irrigation, and power? Flood control improvements are largely constructed at Federal expense; irrigation improvements (when constructed under reclamation law) must be paid for by project beneficiaries over a period of forty years, but without interest; power improvements must be paid for by power users with interest. Thus, where a multiple-purpose project involves these three uses, the allocation of costs is a matter of vital concern to the local interests. Where two agencies propose to construct the same multiple-purpose project and at the same time propose different cost allocations, the project beneficiaries will naturally align themselves with the agency which proposes the greater allocation to flood control (a one hundred per cent Federal contribution for reservoirs) and the lesser allocation to irrigation.

The survey reports of the Corps and Bureau submitted to Congress in February 1940 were in general agreement on cost allocation. Half of the reservoir costs of $19,500,000 were to be allocated to flood control and half to irrigation. The costs of river control works ($200,000) were to be allocated to flood control, and those of the Pine Flat power plant and transmission lines, proposed in the Bureau report only, to power.

This agreement on cost allocation did not hold for long, however. As soon as construction costs began to rise and the two agencies were required to reëxamine total project costs and allocations, they failed to continue any agreement and their recommendations came into sharp conflict. As we shall see, the agency which recommended the greater allocation to flood control — the Corps of Engineers — received thereby the bulk of the local support.

Turning from cost allocations to estimates of the distribution of benefits, the reports were in disagreement from the very beginning, as the following tabulation indicates:

Annual Benefits from	Corps of Engineers 1940 Report	Bureau of Reclamation 1940 Report
Irrigation	$ 995,000	$1,255,000
Flood Control	1,185,000	1,185,000
Power	None	683,000

These differences are important not only because they are reflected in cost and repayment allocations, but because they raise a question as to the primary or dominant purpose of the project when considered alone.

(4) When should the project be built (a) in relation to other projects in the area and to the six-year construction programs of the Corps and Bureau, and (b) in relation to the negotiation of repayment contracts? The problem of timing in terms of the year in which a project should be built is subject to a complexity of factors, among them the authorization procedure, the priority of the project in the agency's six-year construction program, the speed with which definite plans and specifications can be completed, problems relating to land acquisition and the fulfillment of requirements for local contributions, the appropriations made available by the Congress, etc. Where two agencies have planned construction of the same project, but are subject to different procedures for authorization, use different criteria for programming based on different philosophies of water

use, and receive different treatment from the Congress in regard to appropriations, it is to be expected that they will differ on the exact timing of a project. The local interests will naturally support the agency which promises to build first.

The problem of timing in relation to the negotiation of repayment contracts is quite another matter. If the Kings River project were constructed as originally recommended by the Corps of Engineers under flood control law, the local interests would have to satisfy the Chief of Engineers that they had made or were prepared to make the cash contribution of $4,710,000 before construction was begun. If, on the other hand, the Kings River project were constructed as originally recommended by the Bureau of Reclamation under reclamation law, the constructing agency would have to negotiate repayment contracts with the prospective irrigation beneficiaries before the project was begun. This is true because the Kings River area is one in which the construction of a Federal water distribution system is not required in order to deliver the irrigation benefits. It would be almost impossible to secure repayment contracts or to enforce acreage limitations and speculation controls after a reservoir is in operation, for there would be no effective and economical means of denying irrigation benefits to those who failed to comply. As we shall see, this aspect of the timing of construction became the center of controversy between the two agencies six and seven years after the original reports were submitted to the Congress.

The Growing Controversy, 1940–1944 [5]

Once the survey reports were published without restriction, the controversy between the two agencies and their supporters in California broke wide open. Secretary Ickes expressed concern lest a decision on the basic differences in the two reports be left entirely to the most directly interested groups. If the controversy were to be settled on the basis of which Federal agency could acquire the preponderant support of local interests in the Kings River area, then such a settlement might well not be in the public interest. The Secretary therefore proposed to the President that the National Resources Planning Board review both reports with a view to recommending to the President a reconciliation in the national interest. The Secretary's letter follows:

March 7, 1940

My dear Mr. President:

With respect to the separate reports submitted by the Bureau of Reclamation and the Corps of Engineers on the Kings River project in California, I believe your attention should be called to the fact that a local controversy has developed and is growing more heated in the area. This controversy revolves around the question as to which report proposed the most attractive development judged solely by the cost of water to prospective irrigators, and without regard to the ability and responsibility of the irrigators to pay as a result of benefits to be received.

Reports from the area indicate that the plan proposed by the Army and the plan proposed by the Reclamation Service each have supporters who are organized and intend to fight.

I cannot believe that it is in the public interest to leave the decision to interested groups for a settlement on the basis indicated. I would not attempt now to guess what the eventual outcome might be if this controversy should be permitted to develop and to run its course, but I have no reason to believe that the Reclamation project would not be chosen. It seems doubtful, however, whether any decision would be made in several years, and much unnecessary bitterness might result. I do not believe that representatives of either the Corps of Engineers or of the Bureau of Reclamation are participating in the contest.

I would not want the project built by the Bureau of Reclamation if I felt that the local, interested groups had been responsible in having it so for the selfish reason that by adopting the Reclamation project they could shift an undue burden to the Federal Government. On the other hand, I would be greatly disappointed if the Reclamation plan were to be rejected solely because the irrigators of the Basin felt that the Army plan would cost them less and the United States more.

The situation described has developed largely because of the circumstances which resulted in submission of the two reports to the Congress without a review by the National Resources Planning Board and with no indication of preference by the Administration for either plan or for a division of responsibility in connection with the project.

I suggest, therefore, the advisability of a review of the two reports by the National Resources Planning Board, even though the reports already have been submitted to the Congress. The National Resources Planning Board would make such a review and would report if requested to do so by you. The report of the National Resources Planning Board, when approved by you, could be submitted to the Congress. This should be instrumental in having the questions revolving about the 2 proposals decided in the national interest.

I am submitting, therefore, for your consideration, a draft of a letter to

KINGS RIVER PROJECT

the National Resources Planning Board requesting a review and report on the Kings River project plans.

Sincerely yours,
HAROLD L. ICKES
Secretary of the Interior

Copy for National Resources Planning Board
Washington, D. C.

The Corps of Engineers did not express any similar concern over reaching a settlement within the executive branch. It urged its own proposals on the Congress without reference to the views of the Secretary of Interior and the President; and it took the position that the issues could be decided properly on the basis of local support.

The President agreed to the suggestion of Secretary Ickes, and the Water Resources Committee undertook to analyze the two reports carefully and to point up the major areas of disagreement: power development, agency to construct project, method of repayment, method of operation.

Before the WRC could complete its analysis, the House Committee on Flood Control conducted hearings on the Kings River project in April 1940. The Engineers testified in favor of authorization of the project under flood control law and in accordance with their report. The Commissioner of Reclamation presented the views of his agency. The three representatives of local interests who testified all favored the Army, though there were petitions from groups on both sides. The House Committee reported out a Flood Control Bill in early May 1940, recommending among other projects that the Kings River project be authorized for construction by the Corps of Engineers. However, the Bill was never considered by the House, so no final congressional action was taken in 1940.

In the meantime, the Water Resources Committee completed its analysis, and the President, on 29 May 1940, made a decision which was intended to serve as the Administration policy on the matter and to put an end to the unseemly squabbling among two executive agencies. The President wrote to the Secretary of Interior, with a copy to the Secretary of War, as follows:

With respect to these matters, it seems to me that the project is dominantly an irrigation undertaking and is suited to operation and maintenance under the reclamation law. It follows, therefore, that it should be constructed by the Bureau of Reclamation, and that the portion of the project cost to be charged to irrigation should be financed on the basis of the prevailing Federal policy of 40 annual payments by irrigation beneficiaries. The project should be maintained and operated by the Bureau of Reclamation, but operation for flood control should be in accordance with regulations prescribed by the Secretary of War.

So as to publicize the Administration policy, the Secretary of the Interior transmitted the President's letter to Congress, where it was printed as a House Document.

The decision of the President, however, does not appear to have had any effect whatsoever on the position taken by the Corps of Engineers. As we have noted, the Engineers have traditionally held that they, as the engineer consultants to Congress, are "an agency of the legislative branch"; and in accordance with this traditional position, they resisted this attempt by the President to intervene in the direct relations between the Corps and the Congress.

When the House Committee on Flood Control reopened hearings on the Kings River project in April 1941, the Engineers once more testified in favor of constructing the project under flood control law. They never once mentioned the President's policy in the matter. They stated that the project was primarily for flood control and did not mention that the President had found the project "dominantly an irrigation undertaking." At the hearings the Commissioner of Reclamation supported the President's policy, which favored his agency and the reclamation program.

As these hearings reopened the entire controversy, the President took the matter up at a Cabinet meeting. The decision reached at that meeting, representing a reaffirmation of the previously determined Administration policy, is stated in the following letter of 5 May 1941 from the President to the Secretary of War:

> Recalling the discussion at the recent Cabinet meeting, I believe it wise to record for reference the decision made with respect to the interests of the Corps of Engineers and of the Bureau of Reclamation in proposed developments on the Kings River and on the Kern River in California.
>
> The Kings River and the Kern River projects are dominantly irrigation projects and as such they should be built at the appropriate time by the Department of the Interior through its Bureau of Reclamation rather than by the War Department through the Corps of Engineers. My letter to the Secretary of the Interior of May 29, 1940, which is published in part 2 of House Document 631, Seventy-sixth Congress, third session, clearly

stated my decision on the policy which should be applied to the Kings River project. This decision is applicable to the Kern River project as well. I do not consider it wise to authorize these projects, or any project dominantly for irrigation for construction by the Corps of Engineers.

I am writing to Chairman Whittington of the Flood Control Committee of the House of Representatives to inform him on this matter. By thus clearing doubts which may have persisted with respect to the scope of the fields of operation of the two outstanding construction agencies of the Government it is my hope that unnecessary duplication of work will be avoided and that potential sources of friction will be eliminated.

Copies of this letter are being sent to the Secretary of the Interior, to the Director of the Bureau of the Budget, and to the Chairman of the National Resources Planning Board for their information.

In writing to the chairman of the House Committee on Flood Control on the same day, the President proposed, as a basis for delineating the jurisdictions of the Corps of Engineers and the Bureau of Reclamation, the dominant interest theory:

A good rule for Congress to apply in considering these water projects, in my opinion, would be that the dominant interest should determine which agency should build and which should operate the project. Projects in which flood control or navigation clearly dominate are those in which the interest of the Corps of Engineers is superior and projects in which irrigation and related conservation uses dominate fall into the legitimate field of the Bureau of Reclamation.

On this basis, the President said:

Good administration continues to demand that projects which are dominantly for irrigation should be constructed by the Bureau of Reclamation, Department of the Interior, and not by the Corps of Engineers, War Department. The Kings River project is authorized for construction by the Bureau of Reclamation at this time . . . Neither of these projects [the letter also concerned the Kern River project], therefore, should be authorized for construction by the Corps of Engineers, to do so would only lead to needless confusion.

The project was not put in the Flood Control Bill of 1941 as reported and passed by both Houses because of the President's known opposition. However, a separate bill, authorizing the Kings River project in accordance with the Army plans, was reported favorably by the House Flood Control Committee in August 1941. The Committee report stated:

> The Committee felt that inasmuch as Congress had authorized the Chief of Engineers to examine the project and inasmuch as the land owners affected and the citizens interested, after carefully considering the project as proposed by the Commissioner of Reclamation and the project proposed by the Chief of Engineers, approved the project of the Chief of Engineers, the bill should be reported to provide for construction by the Chief of Engineers.
>
> In deference to the views of the President of the United States and the Secretary of the Interior, the project was not included in the flood control bill . . . The Committee, however, felt that in all the circumstances, the bill should be favorably reported, and that the public interest would be promoted by the construction of the project by the Chief of Engineers of the War Department, as prayed for by the citizens' interest.

The special bill was not considered further by the Congress.

The Bureau of Reclamation, considering the Kings River project authorized under reclamation law, requested funds for the commencement of construction for fiscal year 1942 and again for fiscal year 1943; but each time the Bureau of the Budget denied the request, as the project was not considered to be of immediate value to the national defense and war programs, and all such public works projects were to be deferred for postwar construction.

During the war, however, certain control works on lower Kings River, to permit the deflection of flood waters away from Tulare Lake, were constructed by the Corps of Engineers. As the Kings River project had not been authorized under flood control law, the Army built this small unit of the project under the authority of a war emergency flood control appropriation for repairs and maintenance. This procedure was seriously questioned by some members of the executive branch and of the Congress. More important, the move itself put the Corps of Engineers to work for the first time in the Kings River area, and naturally was likely to leave the impression locally that future work would be under the same auspices. Although the particular works constructed and repaired were relatively minor and were primarily for flood control, they did provide some irrigation benefits, and these benefits were made fully nonreimbursable under the emergency flood control appropriation — a welcome gift to the local beneficiaries from the Federal Government.

The Showdown — 1944

In 1944 the controversy between the partisans of the Corps and the Bureau was fought out in Washington on three legislative proposals: the Interior Department Appropriation Bill, the Flood Control Bill, and the Rivers and Harbors Bill.

Interior Department Appropriation Bill for Fiscal Year 1945 [6]

Apparently to forestall authorization of the Kings River project by the Congress in the Flood Control Bill then under preparation in the House of Representatives, the President, in March 1944, transmitted to Congress a budget request of $1,000,000 for the Bureau of Reclamation to cover plan preparation, preconstruction explorations, purchase of rights-of-way, and clearing on the Kings River project. The Congressman from the district and the master of the Kings River Water Association appeared before the House Appropriations Committee in opposition to the budget request. The Committee did not approve the estimate. It called attention to the local opposition and to the fact that the House Committee on Flood Control had included the project for Army construction in the pending Flood Control Bill.

The Senate Appropriations Committee restored the full estimate, and reported as follows:

> The committee has reinstated the Budget estimate of $1,000,000 . . . The committee is impressed by the statement in the hearings that it is more advantageous to the government to have the Kings River project constructed by the Bureau of Reclamation because of the indefinite provisions with respect to repayment contained in the pending flood control bill, H. R. 4485, which proposes authorization of the construction of the project by the Corps of Engineers. That bill provides no legislative standard for repayment by the beneficiaries and leaves the repayment obligation of the local interests entirely at the discretion of the Secretary of War. If the Secretary of War should adopt a recommendation made by the Chief of Engineers in House Document 630, Seventy-sixth Congress, third session, the cost to the landowners would be only $4,710,000 as compared to repayments of $9,750,000 which are provided in the Reclamation Bureau plan. The landowners would gain and the reclamation fund would thus lose $5,040,000.
>
> Another effect of the proposed transfer of constructing the Kings River project from the Reclamation Service to the Corps of Engineers would be

to escape from the provisions of section 46 of the Reclamation Adjustment Act of 1926 . . .

Under existing law, as above quoted, reclamation project water is available to any landowner regardless of the size of his holdings provided that he agrees to sell any irrigable land in excess of 160 acres when and if an opportunity occurs at a price not in excess of its fair appraisal value. This law has been in effect for 18 years on more than 60 reclamation projects and there is excellent proof that it operates in a reasonable and equitable manner and is achieving the purpose for which it was intended. It does not require sudden or precipitate breaking up of real estate holdings but, in an orderly and gradual way, it prevents land monopoly and speculation in benefits created by the expenditure of Federal funds. Most of all, it assures that there will be opportunities for men to secure farms and make homes and livelihood for themselves and their families without incurring a ruinous debt because of the wild gambling of land speculators.

The Committee's statement that landowners would gain and the reclamation fund would lose five million dollars if the project were constructed under flood control law was only half true; the reclamation fund would lose, but the landowners would not gain. Under flood control law the landowners would have to borrow money to meet their lump-sum contribution, and it was estimated by the Board of Engineers that, at an interest rate of three and one-half per cent, the total pay-out by the beneficiaries under the flood control law would be roughly the same as that under reclamation law.

The conference committee of the two Houses agreed to eliminate the budget request, so that the Bureau of Reclamation was denied funds to proceed with detailed plans for its project in fiscal year 1944.

FLOOD CONTROL BILL OF 1944 [7]

The House Committee on Flood Control had commenced hearings on the Kings River project on 9 February 1944 in connection with the important Flood Control Bill of that year. In order to preclude consideration of the project for authorization under flood control law, the Secretary of Interior had written to the Secretary of War on 20 January as follows:

My dear Mr. Secretary: I understand that Chairman Whittington of the House Committee on Flood Control is preparing to hold hearings on a bill to authorize the construction of the Kings River project in California by the Corps of Engineers. I know that you cannot control the actions of the congressional committee and its chairman.

It will be embarrassing to both our Departments, however, if the hearings could bring about authorization for construction of the project by the Corps of Engineers, since the project is already authorized for construction by the Bureau of Reclamation under the reclamation law.

You may want to review the history of this project. The War Department report was printed as House Document No. 630, Seventy-sixth Congress, third session, and the Interior Department report was printed as House Document No. 631, Seventy-sixth Congress, third session. You will find printed in this document a letter by the President authorizing me to submit my report.

On May 29, 1940, the President sent another letter to me assigning the project to the Department of the Interior. This letter is printed in full in House Document No. 631, part 2, Seventy-sixth Congress, third session, and the body of it reads as follows: . . . [letter not reproduced here]

On several occasions since this decision was made by the President and since the project was authorized under the reclamation law, the Flood Control Committee has held hearings for the purpose of considering bills to authorize the project for construction by the War Department. I believe it would be helpful if you should call the status of this project to the attention of the Chief of Engineers in order that he might be prepared to set the committee right with regard to your Department's position with respect to it.

When there is so much to be done, I can see no profit in preparing lengthy presentations to be made at hearings that serve no useful purpose. This hearing, at best, could only reopen a controversy that would be troublesome to us both and which was settled nearly 4 years ago.

Sincerely yours,
HAROLD L. ICKES
Secretary of the Interior

The reply of the Secretary of War did not indicate that his Department would in any way oppose favorable consideration of the project for authorization under flood control law:

January 26, 1944

Dear Mr. Secretary: Reference is made to your letter of January 20, 1944, regarding prospective hearings by the House Committee on Flood Control with respect to the proposed Pine Flat Dam on the Kings River, Calif. In your letter you state that the project is already authorized for construction by the Bureau of Reclamation under the reclamation law and you ask me to call the status of the project to the attention of the Chief of Engineers in order that he may be prepared to advise the committee relative to the position of this Department with respect to the project.

As you mention in your letter the Flood Control Committee has considered the Pine Flat project in public hearings on several occasions, the most recent having been in June of 1943. The record of these hearings indicates very clearly the status of the Pine Flat project both as pertains to the War Department and the Interior Department. I have requested the Chief of Engineers to present your letter of January 20 to the Flood Control Committee if he or his representatives are called upon for further testimony on the subject of the Kings River project.

Sincerely yours,
HENRY L. STIMSON
Secretary of War

Two days before Representative Whittington opened hearings on the project the President wrote him in an attempt to avert favorable action by the Congressman's committee. The President said:

February 7, 1944

My Dear Mr. Whittington: Over 2 years ago, on May 5, 1941, I wrote to you about the Kings River project and the Kern River project in California. Your committee was then considering the authorization of both of these projects for development by the Corps of Engineers under the jurisdiction of the Secretary of War.

The schedule of hearings on the Flood Control bill of 1944 indicates that proposals for authorizing these projects as undertakings of the Corps of Engineers will be considered again on February 9, 1944. I shall appreciate it if you will read this letter into the record at that time.

In my letter of May 5, 1941, I said, in part: "Good administration continues to demand that projects which are dominantly for irrigation should be constructed by the Bureau of Reclamation, Department of the Interior, and not by the Corps of Engineers, War Department. The Kings River project is authorized for construction by the Bureau of Reclamation at this time. The proposed project on the Kern River . . . is dominantly an irrigation project . . . Neither of these projects, therefore, should be authorized for construction by the Corps of Engineers. To do so would only lead to needless confusion." That letter is applicable today.

These projects should be constructed by the Bureau of Reclamation and that portion of their cost to be charged to irrigation should be financed on the basis of the prevailing Federal policy of 40 annual payments by irrigation beneficiaries. These projects should be maintained and operated by the Bureau of Reclamation, but operation for flood control should be in accordance with regulations prescribed by the Secretary of War.

In my letter of May 5, 1941, I suggested that a sound policy in connection with these water projects would consist of selecting the construc-

KINGS RIVER PROJECT

tion agency by determining the dominant interest. Projects in which navigation or flood control clearly dominate are those in which the interest of the Corps of Engineers is superior and should be so recognized. On the other hand, projects in which irrigation and related conservation dominate are those in which the interest of the Bureau of Reclamation in the Department of the Interior is paramount and should be so recognized. No matter which agency builds a multiple-purpose structure involving in even a minor way the interests of the other, the agency with the responsibility for that particular interest should administer it in accordance with its authorizing legislation and general policies. For example, the Bureau of Reclamation in the Department of the Interior should administer, under the Reclamation laws, and its general policies, those irrigation benefits and phases of projects built by the Corps of Engineers. These suggestions are, to my mind, even more pertinent today. For today we gird for peace. Confusion over jurisdiction ought not to be allowed to disrupt the great preparations now being made for post-war construction of vital public works.

Sincerely yours,
FRANKLIN D. ROOSEVELT

At the hearings, the representative of the Corps of Engineers read into the record the letters reproduced above and answered all questions asked by Committee members. At no time did he advance any support for the President's policy. The Commissioner of Reclamation presented the views of the Administration and of his agency.

After the hearings on the project had been concluded, Representative Whittington wrote to the President that the Kings River project was in fact dominantly a flood control project. The Congressman implied that the President had been misinformed in believing that the project was for the primary purpose of irrigation and that a strict application of the President's own dominant interest theory would dictate its authorization under flood control law. In the hearings, the representative of the Chief of Engineers and several members of the Committee had given emphasis to the fact that the report of the Chief of Engineers allocated the greater percentage of project benefits (54 per cent) to flood control and only 46 per cent to irrigation. It will be remembered that the Reclamation report, on the other hand, allocated the greatest benefits (40 per cent) to irrigation; 38 per cent to flood control; and 22 per cent to power. Representative Whittington's letter follows:

I gladly read your letter of February 7, 1944, into the record of hearings now being conducted by the Flood Control Committee on February

9, 1944, when the multiple-purpose projects on the Kings and Kern Rivers, California, were under consideration. The committee had previously given most careful consideration to your letter of May 5, 1941.

The reports on these projects were submitted by the Chief of Engineers of the United States Army in response to the authorization in the Flood Control Act of June 22, 1936.

The Chief of Engineers and the Commissioner of Reclamation were heard by the Committee on Flood Control. I think it is a fair statement to say that aside from either the statements or reports of the Chief of Engineers or the Commissioner of Reclamation the testimony given at the hearings, including the testimony of consulting engineers of outstanding merit and reputation, shows conclusively that flood control is the dominant interest in the Kings and Kern River projects, and that these projects have no direct relation to the Central Valley project, including the Mt. Shasta and Friant Dams and related works, under construction by the Bureau of Reclamation.

I think it proper also to report to you that the testimony shows that there are no Federal Reclamation projects nor have there ever been any such projects along the Kings and Kern Rivers. The local interests have constructed and maintained through the years reclamation projects without federal aid. The testimony shows that no public lands are involved and that very little, if any, new land is to be brought under water.

The hearings also disclose that there is a definite flood problem and that the local interests without federal contribution have constructed local protective works. Recent excessive floods have demonstrated that these works are inadequate.

The local interests, seeking flood protection through the construction of the projects in question, have over many years acquired adequate water rights under California laws and, as stated, have established and operated their own irrigation systems. The citizens and the landowners with one accord object as disclosed by the hearings to being brought under the restrictions of the Reclamation Act.

I beg to assure you that the policies as outlined in your letter of February 7, 1944 will be fully considered by the Committee on Flood Control in the light of the facts developed at the hearings.

In reply, the President emphasized the importance of viewing the Kings River project as a multiple-purpose element in a basin-wide plan, rather than as an isolated project. In other words, the President hit at the very fundamental difference in water use philosophies of the Corps of Engineers and the Bureau of Reclamation, and stated his conviction that the most favorable development of water resources can result only from an approach which emphasizes basin-wide planning and development. The President interpreted his own dominant interest theory to apply to the principal objective of a closely integrated basin-wide plan, rather than to the principal objective of a single multiple-purpose project considered in vacuum. The President said:

March 7, 1944

My dear Mr. Whittington:

I have received your letter of February 17, 1944, in which you discuss the proposed Kern River, California, multiple-purpose project. It may well be, as you state in your letter, that, when the structure proposed by the Chief of Engineers is considered alone, the benefits are predominantly flood control. However, I feel that neither the Kern River project nor the Kings River project can properly be viewed without regard to the development of the Central Valley of California as a whole.

It seems to me that the multiple-purpose projects proposed by the Chief of Engineers on the Kings and Kern Rivers are only two elements in a basin-wide plan for the development and use of the water resources in the Great Central Valley of California, and that the primary and dominant objective of that plan, especially in the southern part of the Valley, is the provision of water supplies for domestic, municipal, industrial and irrigation uses. It would appear that, if any such plan is to be successful, the operation of all units of the plan should be fully coordinated on a regional basis. Such coordination, insofar as the projects undertaken by the federal government are concerned, can best be obtained by a single agency constructing, operating and maintaining the multiple-purpose elements of the plan, particularly those projects involving water conservation. Since the Congress has already authorized the construction and operation by the Bureau of Reclamation of certain multiple-purpose elements of the Central Valley plan involving water conservation, from the standpoint of good federal administration it would follow that the Bureau of Reclamation should also be authorized to construct and operate the other multiple-purpose elements, such as the projects proposed on the Kings and Kern Rivers by the Chief of Engineers, with appropriate care exercised, of course, to observe the existing local irrigation rights established by usage, decrees, and agreements.

I know that you will understand that my expression of views arises from my desire to obtain what I believe to be the best method of federal participation in the over-all plan for the development of the Central Valley, and not from any intention of interfering with the proper consideration of this matter by the Congress.

Sincerely yours,
FRANKLIN D. ROOSEVELT

Despite the firm Administration policy, the Committee on Flood Control reported the Kings and Kern River projects favorably, and they were approved by the House. The Committee stated that it had adhered to the policy of reporting projects only where the dominant interest is flood control. "Differences of opinion in executive departments as to the dominant interests respecting a few of the projects included in the bill exist. All interests were heard, and only those projects where the preponderance of the testimony showed that flood control was paramount are contained in the pending bill." The Committee justification for these Central Valley projects was generally similar to that contained in Representative Whittington's letter to the President.

The President was not content to accept this verdict and apparently was no better pleased with the attitude of the Corps of Engineers. On 16 May 1944, soon after the Flood Control Bill had passed the House, he wrote to the Secretary of War:

> I want the Kings and Kern River projects to be built by the Bureau of Reclamation and not by the Army engineers. I also want the power generated at projects built by the Army engineers to be disposed of by the Secretary of the Interior. I hope you will see that the rivers and harbors and flood-control bills include appropriate provisions to effectuate these.

It will be remembered that this memorandum was quoted and discussed in connection with the analysis of power policy in Chapter IV. The Secretary of War transmitted the memorandum to the Chairman of the Senate Committee on Commerce, who saw that it was inserted in the record of the hearings on the Flood Control Bill, along with a number of other communications. There was no discussion of the memorandum at the time. And while an examination of the record of the Committee hearings reveals no expressed opposition to the President's position, it likewise shows no single occasion on which representatives of the Corps of Engineers, in testifying on the Central Valley projects, supported the President's program in this respect. Support was provided by the Bureau of the Budget and the Department of Interior.

The Senate Committee on Commerce voted to leave the Kings River project in the bill. Senator Overton informed the President of this decision, and the President responded as follows on 7 August 1944:

The dam and reservoir projects in the Central Valley of California, which would be authorized by H.R. 4485 for construction by the Army engineers, should, for purposes of sound administration and coordinated operation, be constructed by the Bureau of Reclamation in the Department of the Interior. These projects constitute logical extensions of the existing Central Valley project of the Bureau of Reclamation. California, in common with the other Western States, has a flood-control problem and a need for water. The basic and best solution of her flood control problem lies in the maximum storage and use of water for irrigation. Every flood control project and every navigation project in the West should therefore be made, so far as practicable, to play its part in the great scheme of conservation of water for beneficial consumptive uses.

It may well be that testimony before your Committee in favor of the construction of these projects by the Corps of Engineers was a reflection of the desire of certain large land interests in California to obtain irrigation and other benefits without being subjected to the repayment requirements and to the other public safeguards that are a part of the reclamation law, but I do not believe that this should be allowed to obscure the fundamental objectives of that law.

. . . I hope, therefore, that the Congress will see fit to place in the Bureau of Reclamation the authority and the responsibility for accomplishment of the great objectives that the Federal Government should achieve in California.

Despite this strong stand, the Senate failed to strike the Kings River project from the legislation, so that the Flood Control Act of 1944 included authorization of that project and several similar ones in the Upper San Joaquin Valley.

However, this same Flood Control Act contained a general provision with respect to the irrigation features of projects built and operated by the Corps of Engineers which was designed to accomplish Administration policy at least in part. This was Section 8, discussed in relation to irrigation policy in Chapter IV, and providing that irrigation features of Corps dams be planned, constructed, and operated by the Bureau of Reclamation in accordance with reclamation law.

When it became apparent that, despite Administration policy, the Congress was going to authorize the Kings River and other Central Valley projects under flood control law, Administration supporters sought to make certain that the new policy of Section 8 would apply to them, so that the irrigation benefits of these projects would become subject to repayment under reclamation law and to the acreage and speculation restrictions of that law. They feared that some question might arise with respect to the Central Valley projects because these projects did not require the construction of additional Federal works for the distribution of irrigation water and because of the nature of the language of the Bill relating to these specific projects.

The following interchange on the floor of the Senate between Senator Hill (Ala.), the acting Majority Leader, and Senator Overton (La.), chairman of the subcommittee on flood control of the Committee on Commerce and floor manager of the Bill, can leave no question, however, as to the intent of Congress that the reclamation law be made applicable to all Central Valley projects:

Senator Hill. There still seems to be confusion on the part of some Senators with reference to the application of reclamation laws in regard to some of these projects.

I heard the distinguished Senator from Louisiana, when the bill was under consideration, and I think he made it very clear. However, I wish to ask this question: Is it not a fact that section 8 of this bill, as agreed to in conference, makes some reclamation laws applicable to the handling of irrigation water of any of the projects, including California projects, where it is found that irrigation may be carried out? I ask the Senator in charge of the bill whether it is not a fact that the President wanted the California projects in this bill constructed under the Bureau of Reclamation so that the water policies would conform to reclamation laws?

Senator Overton. The Senator is correct with respect to the projects in the so-called Central Valley of California. The President wrote me and the chairman of the subcommittee in this regard. However, in view of the fact that the Senate amendment made not only the California projects but all such projects subject to irrigation laws, and in view of the fact that the House concurred in this action by agreeing to section 8 of the Senate bill, I am sure that the President will feel that we have met the problem which he raised. Section 8 of the bill clearly places reclamation uses of water from these projects under the Secretary of the Interior and under the applicable reclamation laws. No project in this bill which may include irrigation features is exempted from the reclamation laws.

Senator Hill. I thank the Senator.

Senator Overton. The Senate amendment made not only the California projects, but all such projects subject to the irrigation law. In view of the fact the House concurred in that action by agreeing to section 8 of the bill, I am sure the Senator from Alabama will feel that we have met the question which he has raised. As I stated a while ago, section 8 of the bill clearly places reclamation uses of waters from all projects authorized in this bill under the Secretary of the Interior and under the applicable reclamation laws.

With this assurance that the irrigation features of the Central Valley developments would be subject to reclamation law, Secretary Ickes recommended that the President sign the Flood Control Bill. He said:

. . . I recommend that the President approve H.R. 4485.

. . . Were H.R. 4485 to be approved, the situation of the California projects would be as described below. The Corps of Engineers would be authorized to build a number of projects in the Central Valley area of California, including the Kings River project and the Kern River project. However, the power generated at those projects would be disposed of by the Secretary of the Interior in accordance with the provisions of section 5 of the bill, an excellent incorporation in law of the public power policy of the President. Under section 8 of the bill, the use of water from those projects for irrigation purposes would be subject to the jurisdiction of the Secretary of the Interior and would be governed by the Federal reclamation laws. In net effect, therefore, while the Corps of Engineers would be authorized to construct the projects and to operate them for flood control purposes, their use for reclamation and power purposes would be governed by the reclamation laws and by the public power provisions of section 5, and their administration for these purposes would be vested in the Secretary of the Interior. Hence these projects can and will be integrated into the Central Valley Project. I believe that the undertaking of physical construction by the Corps of Engineers, instead of by the Bureau of Reclamation, if that ultimately becomes necessary, is a price worth paying for the sweeping defeat of the California interests who oppose the power policies and the land policies of the Administration. True the matter of construction is not without significance in the programming of further development of public power and reclamation in the Central Valley of California. However, if the California interests attempt to hinder a construction program that is in the public interest, their attempts can be dealt with when they are made.

The President signed the Bill on 23 December 1944, but immediately instructed the Secretary of War to make no allocation of funds, or submit any estimate of appropriations, either for the construction or for the preparation of detailed plans for the construction of projects authorized by the Bill, until such proposed allocations of funds or estimates of appropriations had been taken up with the Bureau of the Budget for the President's approval. This instruction was designed to insure that no further work be done on the Central Valley projects and certain others until the interests of the Departments of Interior and War were fully reconciled.

RIVERS AND HARBORS ACT OF 1945 [8]

Immediately when it became apparent that the Kings River and other Central Valley projects, though authorized by flood control law, were to be made subject to the reclamation law for irrigation benefits, those interests in California who had worked hardest to obtain Engineer, rather than Reclamation, construction and operation of the projects in the Upper San Joaquin sought exemption of the Central Valley from the acreage and speculation restrictions of the reclamation law. Representative Elliott of Kern, Kings, and Tulare Counties pressed hard for such an exemption in the pending Rivers and Harbors Bill. The House enacted the exemption. In the light of determined Presidential opposition to the provision and an aroused public concern over the distribution of benefits from Federal expenditures, the Senate eliminated the exemption. The Congress came to an end with the two Houses deadlocked over the so-called Elliott rider. The new Congress in 1945 hurriedly enacted the Rivers and Harbors Bill without the controversial provision.

APPROPRIATIONS FOR PRECONSTRUCTION OPERATIONS, 1945 [9]

As of 1 January 1945, then, the Kings River project was authorized for construction by both the Bureau of Reclamation and the Corps of Engineers. The conflict between the two administrative agencies thus became one over appropriations. Whichever bureau could first obtain funds from the Congress for preconstruction and construction operations would thereby in effect be designated as constructing agency.

The President still favored construction by the Bureau of Reclamation. In his budget for fiscal year 1946, submitted to Congress in January 1945, the President approved an item of $490,000 for the Bureau of Reclamation for preliminary work on the Kings River project; he did not submit any request for the Engineers for this project. However, before the House Committee on Appropriations had reported out the Interior Department Appropriation Bill, the Congress had added to the President's budget request for the Corps of Engineers an amount to cover the preparation of detailed plans for the

Kings River project by the Engineer Department. In signing the War Department Civil Functions Appropriation Bill, President Roosevelt stated his serious objection to the Corps of Engineers' commencing preconstruction operations on the Central Valley projects. He said:

> I have approved reluctantly H.R. 2126, the War Department civil functions appropriation bill, fiscal year 1946.
>
> Notwithstanding the fact that the bill contains appropriations for certain worthwhile purposes, I have been reluctant to sign it because of the fact that it contains also appropriations for work by the Corps of Engineers in connection with projects in the Central Valley area of California, such as the projects in the Kings and Kern Rivers and tributaries.
>
> On a number of occasions, I have expressed the opinion that these projects, which are predominantly irrigation projects, should be constructed and administered under the Federal reclamation laws. The provision of funds now for plans for their construction by the Corps of Engineers may affect adversely existing Federal reclamation work in the Central Valley area and has a tendency, in my judgment, to undermine the established policy which seeks, through Federal reclamation projects, to create farm homes while providing, to the fullest practicable extent, for reimbursement of costs.
>
> I am convinced that the Congress, which has sought by all appropriate means in the past to preserve and to extend the 40-year-old Federal reclamation policy, will realize, as I do, that all of these projects in the Central Valley area of California are, in fact, interrelated units, comprising one scheme of Federal reclamation; that the construction and operation of some of them by the Army engineers, while others are under construction and operation by the Bureau of Reclamation, leads to conflicts of policy and jurisdiction and to operation difficulties — adding up to an administrative headache — and resulting in depriving not only California but the Nation of ultimate benefits which should be derived from vast expenditure of public funds in connection with the Central Valley reclamation plan.
>
> Accordingly, I propose in the near future to submit to the Congress recommendations for legislation transferring jurisdiction over all of these projects in the Central Valley of California to the Bureau of Reclamation, Department of the Interior.

After considerable debate the Congress denied the appropriation requested for the Bureau of Reclamation. The Secretary of the Interior, in May 1945, submitted to the new President a draft message to Congress designed to effectuate President Roosevelt's proposal to transfer jurisdiction over all Central Valley projects to the Bureau of

Reclamation. President Truman deferred action on this message pending further negotiations between the two Departments on the whole Central Valley matter and pending the completion by the two Departments of comprehensive basin reports on the Sacramento and San Joaquin Rivers.

Application of Section 8 to Central Valley[10]

If the Corps of Engineers were to build the Kings River project, and if the reclamation law were made to apply to the irrigation benefits to be derived therefrom, it would be essential that the Bureau of Reclamation make all required arrangements with local interests, including the negotiation of repayment contracts, *before* actual construction of the dam was undertaken. The Kings River area, like most of the Upper San Joaquin, is one in which the very construction of a reservoir and the release of water therefrom will yield irrigation benefits without the necessity for the construction of supplemental irrigation delivery works. Thus, it would be almost impossible to secure repayment contracts or to enforce acreage limitations and speculation controls after the reservoirs are in operation, for there would be no effective and economical means of denying irrigation benefits to those who failed to comply.

President Truman had this situation in mind when he wrote to the Secretary of War in June 1945 concerning all projects authorized under flood control law but involving irrigation benefits. The President desired that (1) the Department of Interior be given full opportunity to participate; (2) the Department of Interior be given full opportunity and a sufficient period of time in which to negotiate repayment contracts *before* any construction is begun; and (3) the Engineer Department, in discussing any project plans with other authorities, make it perfectly plain that the water users can receive water only under reclamation law, including all requirements for repayment. The pertinent paragraph of the President's letter follows:

> I recognize that in this as in other areas the conflict among Federal agencies arises in part from the different laws under which the various agencies operate. I believe, nevertheless, that the disharmony could be reduced through the conscientious effort of those engaged in the work. In this connection, in consonance with the Flood Control Act of 1944 which clearly established the intent of the Congress to support and maintain the

KINGS RIVER PROJECT

principles of the Federal reclamation laws for all irrigation uses of water in connection with flood-control projects, I desire that, in connection with the development and construction of any flood-control projects in which irrigation features may have a direct relation, the Department of the Interior be given full opportunity to participate and that, before any construction is begun or contracts for construction advertised or awarded, that Department be given full opportunity and a sufficient period of time in which to negotiate such repayment contracts as are inherent in the plan of development. It is my desire that in discussing such plans or projects with other authorities it be made perfectly plain that the water users can receive water only under the reclamation laws, including the requirement that they make appropriate reimbursement to the Federal Government for all waters received in consequence of the construction or operation of flood-control projects.

Despite these specific instructions from the Chief Executive, the Chief of Engineers proposed to commence construction of the Kings River project as soon as labor and materials became available after the war; he did not propose to wait for the Bureau of Reclamation to negotiate. In the face of the legislative history of the provision and of the instructions of the President, the Chief of Engineers held that Section 8 of the Flood Control Law had no application to projects in which additional Federal works for distribution of irrigation water were not needed; that instead jurisdiction over payments by local interests for water conservation benefits in the San Joaquin Valley was vested in the War Department.

In the fall of 1945, General Robins, the Deputy Chief of Engineers, went to the West Coast and delivered several widely reported public addresses in which he informed California water users that Section 8 of the Flood Control Law did not apply to the lower Central Valley projects; that water users, therefore, would not be subject to the 160-acre law and other limitations of reclamation law, and that the Corps of Engineers planned to commence construction of some of the projects, including the Kings River project, as soon as funds were made available.

The Sacramento *Bee* of 21 August 1945 reported:

Major General Thomas M. Robins, deputy chief of the U. S. Corps of Army Engineers, told Sacramento civic leaders yesterday the people of the central valleys have been denied flood control by a "lot of arguments that are neither here nor there" on what should be done with the water behind proposed dams.

"If Californians would wake up and get the water first and then decide what to do with it she would be better off," General Robins declared. He added that by the time water problems are settled "we may all be dead."

The Fresno *Bee* of 17 August 1945 reported:

> General Robins said . . . Section 8 does not apply to projects in the upper San Joaquin Valley and could not without jeopardizing users of water from the streams now.

The General won great favor for his organization among California water users on this field trip to the Central Valley. The promise to provide irrigation benefits with none of the restrictions of reclamation law, despite Section 8 of the Flood Control Law, was a happy one for present landowners in the area.

Similarly, the Chief of Engineers in a letter to the Governor of California of 3 December 1945 stated: "The actual agreements for such repayment will be between local interests and the War Department. It is not mandatory under the law that these agreements comply with the provisions of the Reclamation Acts . . ."

Without going into details of later developments, it should be noted that, due to constant pressure from the President, the Chief of Engineers subsequently withdrew from his position with respect to the applicability of Section 8 to the Kings River project. However, he has maintained that position with respect to other Central Valley projects. As late as July 1948, the Chief of Engineers, in a supplemental report on the Sacramento-San Joaquin River Basins, stated with reference to the Flood Control Act of 1944, "In substance, the law provides that the Secretary of the Army will make agreements for repayment to the United States for conservation storage when used. Under instructions from the President, a somewhat different procedure is actually being followed in the case of the Kings River Project in California in determining repayment under the Flood Control Act of 1944."

Furthermore, the Chief of Engineers did not change his position with respect to a number of Central Valley projects, including the Kings River project, that they should be built immediately, allowing no delay for the Bureau of Reclamation to negotiate repayment contracts.

Appropriations for Construction, 1946 [11]

The President's budget requests for postwar public works did not include any funds for the beginning of construction on the Upper San Joaquin multiple-purpose projects. "In order that there may be no misunderstanding of the Bureau of the Budget action on these . . . estimates and that War Department witnesses testifying before the appropriation committees of Congress may have full knowledge thereof," the Director of the Budget informed the Secretary of War that the Engineer Department request for funds for the Kings and Kern River projects had been eliminated, pending completion by the War and Interior Departments of their comprehensive reports on the Central Valley and "in advance of a decision by him [the President] as to the course to be followed on these works."

Without waiting for any further decision from the President, the representative of the Corps of Engineers nevertheless stated before the Senate Appropriations Committee, with respect to the San Joaquin River projects, that "we are ready to make a definite recommendation to undertake the construction . . . and we included that in the estimates to the Bureau of the Budget." The Senate Committee added to the War Department Civil Functions Appropriation Bill two million dollars to commence construction on both the Kings and Kern River projects with the proviso that none of the appropriation for the Kings River be used for construction of the dam "until the Secretary of War has received the reports as to the division of costs between flood control, navigation, and other water uses from the Bureau of Reclamation and local organizations and shall have made a determination as to what the allocation shall be." The reports were to be made not later than nine months from the enactment of the Appropriation Bill.

While the Bill was in conference, the President on 30 March 1946 sent letters to the majority leaders of the House and Senate recommending that the appropriation of two million dollars be deleted, but that if it were allowed to remain, satisfactory provision be made to insure repayment under reclamation law.

The President's request for elimination of the appropriation aroused some public sympathy as the following editorials reveal.

From San Francisco *News*, 4 April 1946:

President Truman exercised wise statesmanship yesterday in asking congressional leaders to hold up final action on appropriations for dams on the Kern and Kings Rivers until settlement of the conflict between the Army Engineers and the Reclamation Bureau over development of the Central Valley project.

There is need for adjustment between the 2 federal agencies. Conflicting statements emanating from both have confused the situation in the public mind and, we fear, also in the minds of some of the representatives of the 2 services. It was for this reason that the President called upon both to report in detail their plans for development of California's inland waters. These reports either are in his hands or soon will be. He should have a chance to study them before Congress acts upon recommendations contained therein.

The Army Engineers insist that there is no difference between them and the Reclamation Bureau. With respect to the type and size of the proposed dams on the Kern and Kings Rivers, that is true. But with respect to other features, such as repayment of the cost of the dams from use of water for irrigation and power, and the 160-acre limitation feature, the Reclamation Bureau indicates a decided difference of opinion. And it is naive to claim no controversy exists over other parts of the Central Valley Project. The Reclamation Bureau has made known its positive assumption that the undertaking is primarily concerned with reclamation — not flood control and navigation, the fields to which the Army Engineers are limited.

So long as these two federal services are not in agreement upon principles governing the development of California's valuable inland waters the danger of improper development will continue to exist. If that danger should become reality, California's resources might suffer permanent injury.

Hence the News is glad to see President Truman's move to intervene and hold up construction until the differences can be adjusted.

From *Washington Post*, 30 March 1946:

. . . Similarly, it was the clear purpose of the Senate when it passed the 1944 Flood Control Act authorizing these dams, among others, to apply the reclamation laws to all flood control projects where any irrigation water would be developed. But the assistant chief of the Army Corps of Engineers, Major General Thomas M. Robins, says flatly that if his agency does the job the 160-acre provision will not apply.

We do not suppose that more than a few members of the Senate understood this or recognized its grave implications when they passed the appropriation measure adding the Kern and Kings River dams to those for which the House appropriated. The measure is now in conference. We hope that the conferees will kill this slick deal of their own accord. If they fail to do so, a Presidential veto is in order. For the whole basis of the reclamation program is threatened by this shoddy evasion of it. Whether, in the end, the Army Engineers or the Bureau of Reclamation builds these dams, the reclamation laws should be rigorously applied to the lands enriched by them.

While the Appropriation Bill was under consideration by the Senate-House conference, the Chief of Engineers, on a field trip to California, publicly urged immediate construction of the disputed dams by his organization. The San Francisco *Chronicle* of 3 April 1946 reported:

Immediate construction of flood control dams in California was urged yesterday by Lt. Gen. Raymond A. Wheeler, Chief of the Army Engineers. "These dams should have high urgency because of their immediate need for flood control," he said.

Approximately $2,000,000 has been voted by the Senate for start of construction on low level flood control dams on the Kern and Kings rivers but has not yet been approved in the House.

The conference committee eliminated the appropriation for the Kern River but retained that for the Kings River and modified the language to insure that allocation of costs be made by the Secretary of War *with the concurrence of* the Secretary of Interior.

In signing the appropriation measure the President issued a special statement impounding the funds appropriated for the Kings River project pending (1) determination of allocation of costs and (2) the making of necessary repayment arrangements. The President's statement follows:

The War Department civil functions appropriation bill, 1947 (H.R. 5400), which I approved on May 2, 1946, makes appropriations for a number of thoroughly worthwhile projects that will further the development of the water resources of the nation. I am also glad to note that the Congress, by the addition of certain provisos to the item for the Kings River project, California, has afforded an opportunity for assuring that the Federal reclamation policy, including repayment and the wide distribution of benefits, will apply to that project. This is in accordance with the view that I have heretofore expressed and the position repeatedly taken by the late President Roosevelt. It is consistent with the policies laid down by the Congress in the Flood Control Act of 1944.

Consistently with the action taken by the Congress on the Kings River project, I propose in the near future to send to the Congress my recommendations regarding an over-all plan for the development of the water resources of the Central Valley area in California. I am withholding action in that regard pending receipt of comments from the Governor of California. The over-all plan for the Central Valley area of California will include means for achieving comprehensive development and utilization of its water resources for all beneficial purposes, including irrigation and power, and it will provide adequately for flood protection. It will have regard for the need for integrated operation of reservoirs which is essential for complete utilization of the land and water resources of the area. It will provide for application in the Central Valley area of the Federal reclamation policy — including repayment of costs and the wide distribution of benefits. I hope that the Congress will, by the adoption of that plan, act to put an end to a situation which, in California and in Washington, has been productive of administrative confusion as well as confusion to the general public.

In the meantime, in view of the legislative history of the provisos in the Kings River item, and in view of the disadvantageous position in which the government would be placed if repayment arrangements were unduly postponed, I am asking the Director of the Budget to impound the funds appropriated for construction of the project, pending determination of the allocation of costs and the making of the necessary repayment arrangements.

Determination of Allocation of Costs and Repayment Arrangements[12]

Release of funds for construction of the Kings River project, then, was not to be made until the Corps and the Bureau had come to an agreement on the allocation of costs and until adequate repayment arrangements had been negotiated.

With respect to division of costs, the various agencies recommended as follows:

	Irrigation	Flood Control
Department of the Interior	$14,250,000	$19,250,000
Corps of Engineers	13,232,000	20,268,000
State of California	10,000,000	23,500,000
Local water users	10,000,000	23,500,000

After considerable negotiation, the Secretary of War agreed to accept the Reclamation figure as the ceiling on the amount to be repaid by water users. In a letter to the President, he said:

> In arriving at his recommended allocation the Chief of Engineers has given careful consideration to views of both Federal and local irrigation

interests; and in the normal case I would consider that he had arrived at a solution equitable to both of those interests. The Secretary of the Interior is firmly convinced that any repayment less than $14,250,000, which he has found to be well within the repayment ability of the water users, would adversely affect adjacent Federal reclamation programs in the Central Valley of California; and because irrigation features are involved in this project I feel that the views and requirements of the Department of the Interior must be weighed carefully. Likewise the local agencies, on the basis of actual experience with irrigation in this area, present strong support for their lower evaluation of irrigation benefits and for their offer of repayment of $10,000,000. Although differences are relatively small, there is no agreement on a specific figure. Obviously any division of cost, to be of practical value and in the public interest, must be one agreed to by water users who must pay the bill and by the Bureau of Reclamation which you have charged with making repayment arrangements. I therefore determine, in order to meet the requirements of existing law, that the division of cost to irrigation should be set at an amount not to exceed $14,250,000, the exact amount to be as agreed upon between the Bureau of Reclamation and the local agencies concerned.

By placing a ceiling on the amount to be repaid by water users rather than a fixed allocation, the report of the Secretary of War would appear to conform to neither the law nor the President's instructions. However, the Secretary of Interior concurred in the proposal, and the President transmitted it to Congress on 17 February 1947.

No explanation has ever been offered for the acceptance by the Secretary of Interior and the President of this allocation proposal which was presumably not wholly satisfactory to the former and which was clearly in contravention of the instructions issued by the latter. The President, to be sure, was faced with a proposal approved by two members of his Cabinet who had previously been in disagreement on the matter. If the President refused to concur, he would be reopening a dispute that had been resolved.

Behind this specific factor may have lain other influences deriving from a change in administrative environment. Secretary Ickes had resigned in February 1946 and had been succeeded by Secretary Krug in March 1946. On taking office Krug made known his firm distaste for the jurisdictional disputes to which his predecessor had never shown any great aversion.

Whatever the influence of factors such as this, the acceptance of the allocation proposal remains surprising. Even more surprising, however, is the action of the President and Secretary Krug with respect to the repayment provisions of the Secretary of War's report. The necessity for the completion of repayment negotiations *before* construction of the Kings River project has been emphasized. The Chief of Engineers, however, was not willing to wait for the Bureau of Reclamation to negotiate repayment contracts before he started construction. In the report on allocation, the War Department proposed "that the Kings River project be constructed *immediately* and operated *initially* for flood control. The project will not be operated for irrigation until agreement has been reached between the Bureau of Reclamation and local water users on the division of cost and on repayment arrangements." However, due to the physiographic and hydrologic characteristics of the area, this was not physically possible. It was estimated that at least fifty per cent of the irrigation benefits would result from the very construction of the dam, whether or not its operation was limited to flood control. And once the dam was constructed it would be difficult, if not impossible, for the Army, even if it were so inclined, to resist the pressure from local interests to release water in the most economical manner from the point of view of downstream water users.

These circumstances were well known to the Secretary of Interior and the President. Nevertheless, for reasons not presently apparent the Secretary finally concurred in the recommendations of the Secretary of War; and on the day the President transmitted the report to Congress he released the $1,000,000. Soon thereafter construction was commenced. In releasing the funds, the President instructed the Secretary of Interior "to continue work in connection with repayment agreements to the end that full benefits of the project can be attained promptly upon completion of construction and that Federal reclamation policies can be carried out."

The Bureau of Reclamation, however, is experiencing difficulty in negotiating any repayment contracts whatever. The attitude of the landowners is about as follows: "Let's just wait and see how this project is operated for flood control only. Then, if there would appear to be significant advantages to our land in a change in project operation, we can consider negotiating contracts. But even then, we shall have to balance the advantages of whatever needed additional water can be provided by a change in project operation against the dis-

KINGS RIVER PROJECT 249

advantages to us, as present landowners, of application of the acreage restrictions and speculation controls of the reclamation law." As recently as July 1950 the Commissioner of Reclamation reported to Congress that his agency had been unable to negotiate any repayment contract with the Kings River interests. It may well be that the Federal Government will never receive a penny for a large part of the irrigation benefits provided by this project, and the benefits will accrue to the present owners of land rather than to the small independent farmer around whom the whole philosophy of Federal reclamation has been built.

A CHANGE IN THE ALLOCATION OF BENEFITS — WHY? [13]

In 1940 the Corps of Engineers informed Congress that the Kings River project was dominantly a flood control project. The distribution of annual benefits was calculated to be $1,185,000 for flood control and $995,000 for irrigation — a ratio of 1.19 to 1 for *flood control*.

On the basis of this analysis in part, the House Committee on Flood Control determined that the project was properly one for authorization and construction under flood control law.

In 1948, with the project well under way, the Engineer Department recalculated prospective annual benefits as follows: for flood control, $2,126,000; for irrigation, $3,382,000 — a ratio of 1.59 to 1 for *irrigation*. According to this later analysis, then, the project ceased to be primarily a flood control project, even using the Engineer Department criterion — ratio of prospective benefits allocated to different purposes for each individual project. And yet it is being built and will be operated by the Corps of Engineers.

The progressive changes in benefit allocations are illustrated in the following table based on the Corps of Engineers reports on the Kings River Project:

	Preliminary Draft Report 1939	Report Submitted to Congress, 1940	Cost Allocation Report, 1946	Supplement to Comprehensive Report, 1948
Flood Control	$1,185,000	$1,185,000	$3,377,000	$2,126,000
Irrigation	430,000	995,000	2,179,000	3,382,000
Ratio: Flood Control to Irrigation	2.75:1	1.19:1	1.55:1	0.63:1

The reasons for this complete reversal in benefit calculations are not known. However, it might be pointed out that the flood control benefits from the Kings River project accrue largely to the Tulare Lake area; that three other streams on which the Corps of Engineers is authorized to build multiple-purpose projects (Kaweah, Tule, Kern Rivers) also flow into the closed basin of Tulare Lake and contribute to flood damages there; that there exists the possibility of shifting the distribution among the four projects of the total flood benefits that will result in the Tulare Lake area when all four dams are built; that there is no longer a compelling necessity for the Corps to show flood control benefits greater than irrigation benefits for the Kings River project, as the dam is already being constructed under their supervision, whereas there may be a greater necessity to show a favorable ratio of flood control to irrigation benefits for certain of the other projects.

Kings River and the Central Valley[14]

For illustrative purposes this case study has been concerned with the Kings River project. The history of this project, however, is not unique. Very much the same story is true of other river developments in the Upper San Joaquin — Isabella Reservoir on the Kern River, Success Reservoir on the Tule River, and Terminus Reservoir on the Kaweah River. Large parts of the case history have application to multiple-purpose projects planned or authorized by both agencies elsewhere in the Central Valley (such as New Melones Reservoir on Stanislaus River, Folsom Reservoir on American River, Bullards Bar or Narrows Reservoir on Yuba River, Monticello Reservoir on Putah Creek, Indian Valley Reservoir on Cache Creek, Iron Canyon or Table Mountain Reservoir on Sacramento River, Black Butte Reservoir on Stony Creek), as well as to river developments in the arid and semi-arid West outside of the Central Valley of California.

All of the Central Valley projects are discussed in the two separate comprehensive basin-wide reports prepared recently by the Corps and the Bureau for the Central Valley. These two reports were submitted to the Governor of California and to the Executive Office of the President in November 1945. As the reports were obviously in conflict, the Executive Office (Budget Bureau) returned them to the originating agencies for reconciliation of differences — it was hoped, through the Federal Inter-Agency River Basin Committee. The failure of the Committee to achieve this reconciliation has been pointed out in Chapter III. As a result, in July 1948, almost three years after the President had sent back the comprehensive surveys, there were submitted to him four separate reports — the final comprehensive reports of the Chief of Engineers and the Secretary of Interior and separate statements by each on the differences between these reports.

Finally, in August 1949, the President's Office completed review of these documents. The President concluded that the content of the reports of neither the Corps nor the Bureau justified the approval of either as a comprehensive valley plan; but he authorized the agencies to submit their reports to Congress along with a statement of his reconciliation of their differences. President Truman directed that the so-called Folsom formula be applied to the entire Central Valley. This formula provides that *all multiple-purpose projects* are the responsibility of the Bureau of Reclamation, and dams and other works *exclusively* for flood control are the responsibility of the Corps of Engineers. To effectuate this policy, the President recommended that multiple-purpose projects under construction or nearing construction by the Corps be transferred to the Bureau of Reclamation after completion of construction; that existing construction authorizations of the Corps for other multiple-purpose projects within the Valley be transferred to the Bureau; and that Congress in future not authorize the Corps to build multiple-purpose projects in the Central Valley.

For Folsom Dam, Congress has passed a law providing for transfer of the works to the Bureau upon completion of construction by the Corps, and for integrating the development with the Central Valley Project. No other projects have enjoyed similar treatment. Legislation has been introduced to apply the Folsom formula to the Kings River. Initial hearings were held by the House Committee on Public Lands in June 1950, but the taking of testimony has not been completed at this writing (July 1950). The bill has been opposed vigorously by the Kings River water users.

This same legislation would authorize Federal construction of Pine Flat power plant, as proposed originally by the Bureau of Reclamation in 1939; construction of one reservoir and two power plants above Pine Flat on the North Fork of Kings River; and Federal acquisition and expansion of Pacific Gas and Electric Company's Balch power plant on the North Fork. The North Fork proposals were contained in a new Bureau of Reclamation survey report, which called for unified operation of the entire proposed Kings River power installation of 101,500 kilowatt capacity.

Prior to completion of the North Fork report, however, and prior to hearings on the Kings River bill in Congress, the Pacific Gas and Electric Company had applied to the Federal Power Commission for a private license to develop additional power facilities on Kings River, and the Fresno Irrigation District had applied for a preliminary permit to secure priority while perfecting its application for a license for a hydro development on the same river. The Bureau of Reclamation opposed these applications, because the Federal Government proposed to construct the power facilities involved as part of the comprehensive plan for development of the water resources of the entire Central Valley. The FPC trial examiner in November 1948 recommended that the Commission decide in favor of Federal development and reject the applications of PG&E and Fresno Irrigation District. One year later, in November 1949, the Power Commission, after hearings, overruled the trial examiner and authorized licenses for expansion and new development of power facilities on the North Fork by PG&E and a preliminary permit to Fresno Irrigation District for investigation of the proposed power plant at Pine Flat Dam. The Secretary of Interior applied for a rehearing in December 1949; this request was granted; and at this writing the final FPC decision has not been handed down.

Thus, legislation to apply the Folsom formula to Kings River is tied up with an extremely complex power problem, which, incidentally, is to a significant degree the product of Corps, rather than Bureau, construction of the Pine Flat Dam.

It is not proposed to develop in greater detail the history of the North Fork projects. The case study in its present form will serve its intended purpose — by use of a concrete example, to derive conclusions which will lead to an estimate of the total administrative responsibility of the Corps of Engineers as an agency of Government.

Results of Failure to Resolve Central Valley Conflict

(1) It is still questionable whether the water resources of the Kings River are being developed in accordance with the most economic and beneficial use of all water and related land resources of the San Joaquin Valley and the Central Valley Basin.

(2) The Kings River project will cost the Federal Government

considerably more than it should. First, duplication of planning has added an unnecessary charge to the Federal budget. Second, a significant portion of the irrigation costs, as yet not subject to precise evaluation, will in all likelihood never be repaid to the Federal Treasury.

(3) Some of the beneficiaries of the Kings River development may be able, for all time, to avoid acreage, land speculation, and full repayment provisions of Federal law. Furthermore, the outcome of the conflict will in all likelihood favor the owners of large tracts of land and the present users of large quantities of irrigation water. Prospective and small landowners and water users will not benefit proportionately. (This finding has greater application to the Kern River and other areas to the south than to the Kings River area, where there are a number of relatively small landowners.)

(4) The easing of repayment, speculation, and acreage requirements of Federal reclamation law with respect to the Kings River project has resulted in considerable pressure on the Federal Government to make equivalent concessions to other existing and proposed irrigation developments. Such pressure, if it succeeds, will undermine reclamation law and increase the cost to the Federal Government of water resource programs by hundreds of millions of dollars. In this connection, the Hoover Commission Task Force on Natural Resources stated: "Interagency rivalry has fostered a sort of Gresham's law with respect to Federal financial policies, the tendency being for higher standards of repayment by State, local, and private beneficiaries to be replaced by lower." [15]

(5) The conflict has tended to prevent development of sound water policies. The differences in policy which now exist have assumed certain institutional values to the agencies involved. Most proposed changes in policy are now appraised by each agency in the light of effects on its jurisdictional position rather than in the light of merit.

(6) The Kings River project has been delayed unreasonably. Seven years elapsed between the time the agencies first submitted their project reports to the Congress and the time President Truman released funds for commencing construction. Although a large part of this delay can be attributed to the intervening war years, a significant portion is due to the conflict.

(7) Controversy over the Kings River project has meant a great

loss of time of executives, from the field level all the way up to the President, and of Members of Congress. An unreasonable amount of time was given to problems of coördination in both the White House and the Bureau of the Budget. Similarly, department and agency heads and their top assistants devoted much effort to these problems, effort which could be better used in developing unified programs in the first instance.

(8) The intensity of the conflict over the Kings River project has led to embarrassing and unbecoming conduct on the part of both the Corps of Engineers and the Bureau of Reclamation, and a consequent loss of confidence by the public at large in the activities of the Federal Government in the field of water resources. There are, of course, many expressions of "confidence" in one or both of these agencies by special interest groups. But in the eyes of the general public, the Government has lost caste.

Causes of Continuing Failure to Resolve Central Valley Conflict

(1) The basic cause of failure lies in the fact that two Federal water resource agencies are operating in the same river basin, each planning multiple-purpose water control projects. It may well be that in situations such as that in the Central Valley, where two agencies are doing the *same* job in the *same* area, coördination cannot succeed. Coördination implies the relating of *similar*, but not wholly duplicative, tasks. There can be coördination when two agencies are doing the same or similar jobs in different places; in that case the function of coördination is to insure reasonable uniformity of policy. There can be coördination also when two agencies are performing different tasks, but tasks that are related to each other and impinge on each other. In that case the function of coördination is to secure coöperative operating programs. But the case of the Corps of Engineers and the Bureau of Reclamation in the Central Valley falls under neither of these headings. As long as we accept the principle of "one river, one problem," we can only conclude that in fact the Corps and the Bureau are performing the same tasks where each is building multiple-purpose projects in the same area.

Although their analysis is not in the same terms, the Hoover Commission and its Task Force on Natural Resources reached the same conclusion as to the basic cause of failure in all past attempts at

KINGS RIVER PROJECT

coördination. The Task Force concluded: "There is simply no escaping the fact that so long as the present overlapping of functions exists with respect to the Corps of Engineers, the Bureau of Reclamation, and the Federal Power Commission, costly duplication, confusion, and competition are bound to result. It has been demonstrated time and again that neither by voluntary cooperation nor by executive coordination can the major conflicts be ironed out." [16]

(2) The basic water use philosophies of the Corps of Engineers and the Bureau of Reclamation, as revealed by their plans for the Kings River, are in sharp contrast. The Bureau gives primary emphasis to closely integrated, multiple-purpose drainage basin development. The social objectives to which the Bureau subscribes are those related to the wide distribution of Federal land improvement benefits among small independent landholders and of Federal power benefits among all ultimate consumers — rural and urban. The Corps gives primary emphasis to the cost-benefit ratio of the individual water projects which Congress has requested it to investigate. The major concern of the Corps is flood control and navigation, and it places little emphasis on social objectives related to the wide distribution of benefits.

(3) Failure in coördination results, in part, from the different laws under which the two agencies operate. Statutory inconsistencies are important, but care must be taken not to lay full blame on this cause. As President Truman has said in a letter to the Secretaries of War and Interior, disharmony, often attributed to statutory differences, could be reduced by the conscientious effort of those engaged in the work.

The Hoover Commission Task Force on Natural Resources found that statutory differences, requiring extended and usually unsuccessful efforts at coördination, were encouraged by the division of water development responsibilities between the Corps and the Bureau. "The committee believes that one of the foremost obstacles to the formulation of a consistent policy, namely, absence of a focal point of administrative responsibility, will be removed if its recommendations regarding unification of functions is carried out." [17]

(4) The two agencies hold conflicting concepts of administrative responsibility. Through the Secretary of Interior the Bureau holds itself directly responsible to the President and, through the President, responsible to the Congress. The Corps holds itself directly

responsible to the Congressional committees which handle its legislation and hardly responsible to the Secretary of War and the President at all. This basic difference makes effective coördination within either the legislative or executive branches extremely difficult.

Major differences between the two agencies resolve themselves into controversies between the Chief of Engineers, a commissioned officer of the United States Army with the rank of major general, and the Secretary of Interior. The dissimilarity of the status of these two officers of Government presents further difficulties in effecting any coördination within the Cabinet, the Executive Office, or the Congress.

(5) The dominant interest theory, as a means of achieving coordination, has failed. All parties have accepted the statement of the theory but have failed to agree on its application. New questions raised by the application of the theory include: (a) Should the theory be applied to each individual project or to an entire basin-wide plan? (b) Should the dominant interest be determined solely by a comparison of prospective benefits to be derived from each purpose of a multiple project or should other factors be taken into consideration? (c) Where estimates of benefits prepared by the Corps and the Bureau differ, which figures are to be adopted? (d) What agency has dominant interest in the control of water for power, drainage, municipal and industrial water supplies, and salinity control?

(6) The Corps and the Bureau have failed to decentralize adequately their responsibilities for planning. This failure is a contributing cause to the lack of success in interagency coördination. At the same time, it is, to a marked extent, a result of the fact that both agencies are in competition with each other in the same river basins. When important problems have arisen relating to jurisdiction over river developments, application of acreage limitations, policies for distribution of power, and the like, the regional representatives have referred them to their superiors in Washington. And these superiors, involved as they are in a constant struggle for jurisdiction and for acceptance of their contradictory policies, could hardly be expected to authorize their regional men to make firm commitments on these important issues by negotiation in the area.

With respect to decentralization and division of responsibility,

KINGS RIVER PROJECT

the Hoover Commission Task Force on Natural Resources concluded:

> The committee feels that the unfortunate results of divided responsibility have been intensified by the necessity of referring disputes to Washington for settlement. The development agencies of course have elaborate field office structures, and actual operations are heavily decentralized. Authority to make the most important decisions, however, rests with the central offices. The committee does not suggest that central review of decisions made by field offices is undesirable, but it believes that existing arrangements make inadequate provision for delegation of authority to units organized around river basins. This defect impedes cooperative relations with other Federal agencies and with State and local authorities, and has constituted an obstacle to basin-wide water planning and development.[18]

(7) There are serious defects in executive coördinating procedures and machinery. As indicated previously, the problems and issues raised by the fact that two agencies are competing for the same jobs in the same areas are by their very nature extremely difficult, if not impossible, to resolve through executive coördinating machinery. Recognizing this, it is desirable to point out certain characteristics in the functioning of the machinery which would jeopardize its success even under more favorable conditions.

(a) Efforts to coördinate policy matters have failed at the initiation of investigations. Integration of investigations is effective if undertaken at their initiation before findings are crystallized. It is largely and necessarily perfunctory if delayed until the basic conclusions have been reached independently by those concerned.

(b) The procedure whereby the Corps of Engineers and the Bureau of Reclamation have announced to local interests the tentative recommendations contained in field survey reports, before these recommendations are fully reconciled with those of other Federal agencies, has made effective reconciliation more difficult. The recommendations acquire partisan support and opposition among local interests who attach themselves to, and provide support for, one Federal agency or the other.

(c) The two survey agencies have been allowed to submit separate reports — on both the Kings River and other individual projects and on the comprehensive basin plan — rather than a single coordinated report reflecting the combined judgment of the water experts of the executive branch of the Government.

(d) Since the abolition of the National Resources Planning Board, the Executive Office of the President has taken little positive action to facilitate the reconciliation of conflicting agency recommendations. The Office has taken a stand for the President and has required agencies to inform Congress of the President's program, but it has avoided the assumption of leadership in the organization of joint planning efforts.

(e) The Federal Inter-Agency River Basin Committee has been ineffective as a means for reconciling conflicting agency policies. In practice the Inter-Agency Committee takes action only when there is unanimous consent of the members. This prevents, of course, any resolution of issues if even one interested party is opposed, and has thus effectively prevented the Committee from accomplishing any major coördination of plans. In fact, the unanimity rule has prevented issues from even being presented to the Committee by its members, because the members know in advance that the Committee cannot take effective action. And with the Bureau and Corps in competition in the same river basins, it can be said that the unanimity rule is almost inherent in committee operation.

Short of a major reorganization, most of these characteristics can be improved only by a basic reorientation on the part of the USED in its water use philosophy and its theories of responsibility; and it is doubtful that such a reorientation can be made.

(8) Lack of uniformity in consideration by Congress of authorizations and appropriations for projects recommended by the Corps and the Bureau has abetted the conflict between the two agencies and made interagency coördination more difficult. The programs of these two agencies are handled by separate Congressional committees. The Senate and House Public Works Committees handle Corps of Engineers legislation, while the House Committee on Public Lands and the Senate Committee on Interior and Insular Affairs deal with the Bureau of Reclamation. Also, in each House separate Appropriations subcommittees consider the funds for the Corps and the Bureau.

In failing to sign and concur in the important report on national water policy of the Water Resources Committee, General Robins complained that the document did not portray adequately the current procedures of the Federal agencies — that "it emphasized instances of improper planning and neglected the many instances of proper planning." [19] It can be predicted that the representatives of the Corps of Engineers will have similar objections to this study. They will complain that sufficient emphasis has not been given to the real advances in water planning which have been made since 1934.

There is no question that significant improvements have been made; and, it is hoped, these improvements have been pointed up. But the progress has in no way kept pace with the increasing complexities of multiple-purpose river-basin development. If the major water projects under development today were similar to the single-purpose projects of fifteen years ago, the present procedures of the Corps of Engineers would approach more nearly the requirements of administrative responsibility. Since 1936, however, the Engineer Department has become increasingly involved in very complex operations the manner of whose execution has the most profound effects upon the social structure and economic welfare of large regions and of the nation as a whole — "a seamless web: the unity of land and water and men." The Corps has failed to grow to the task.

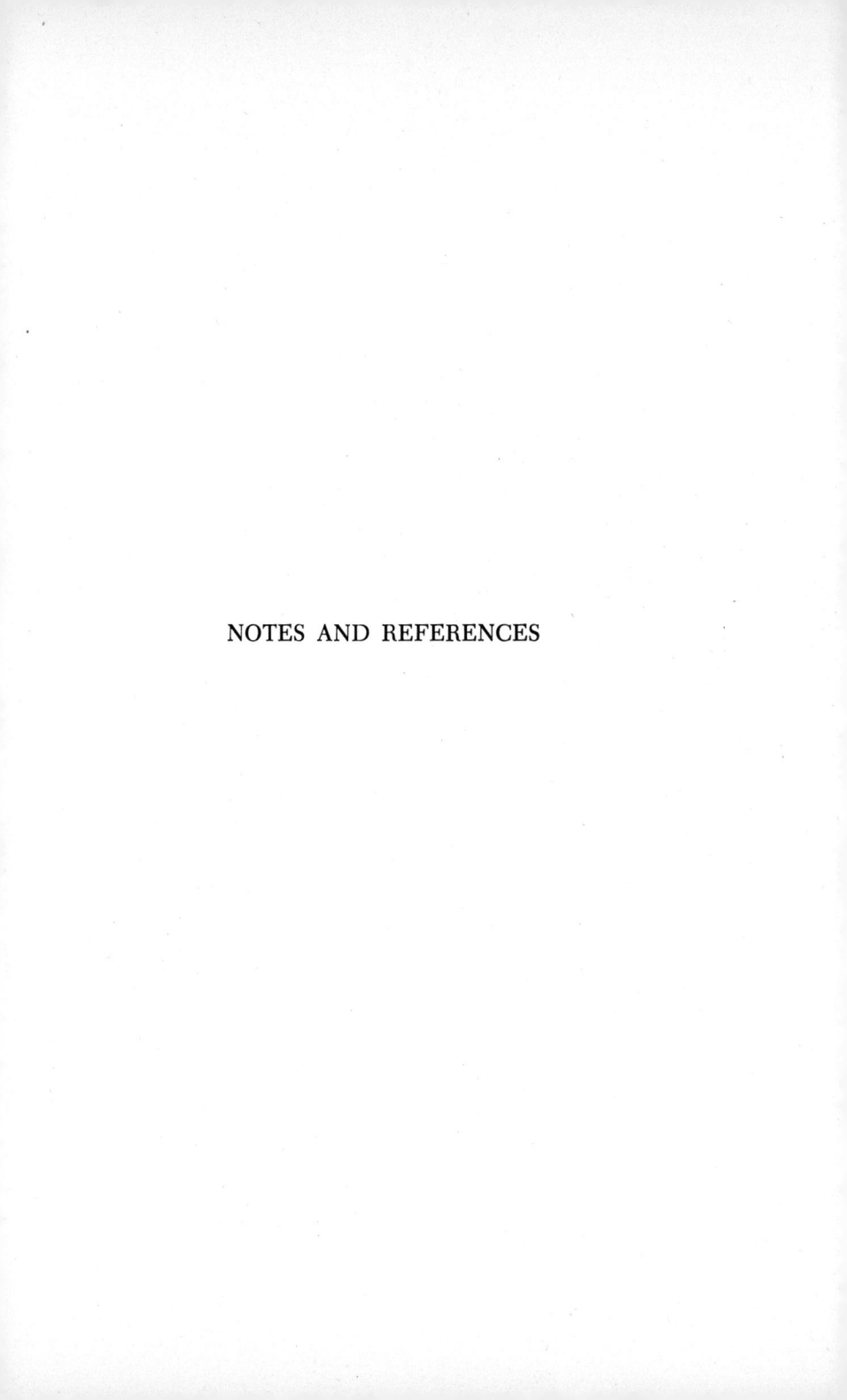

NOTES AND REFERENCES

Abbreviations and Statute References

A list of abbreviations used in the notes and in certain cases in the text follows.

APSR	American Political Science Review
BB	Bureau of the Budget
BI&R	Board of Investigation and Research for Transportation
CBIAC	Columbia Basin Inter-Agency Committee
CL	Circular Letter, Corps of Engineers
CR	Congressional Record
CVA	Columbia Valley Administration
EO	Executive Order
ERC	Energy Resources Committee, National Resources Planning Board
FIARBC	Federal Inter-Agency River Basin Committee
FPC	Federal Power Commission
HR	House Bill
ICC	Interstate Commerce Commission
MVC	Mississippi Valley Committee
NA	National Archives
NPPC	National Power Policy Committee
NRB	National Resources Board
NRC	National Resources Committee
NRPB	National Resources Planning Board

O&R	Orders & Regulations, Corps of Engineers, 1948
PAR	Public Administration Review
PG&E	Pacific Gas and Electric Company
PL	Public Law
PNRPC	Pacific Northwest Regional Planning Commission
PWA	Public Works Administration
R&H	Rivers & Harbors (referring to Corps of Engineers' circular letters)
S	Senate Bill
Stat.	Statutes at Large
USED	United States Engineer Department
WRC	Water Resources Committee, National Resources Planning Board

Where statutes are referred to frequently, the citation is given in the notes the first time but not thereafter. For ready reference, a table of the statutes referred to most often is given.

Name of Statute	Citation
Flood Control Act of 1936	49 Stat. 1570
Flood Control Act of 1938	52 Stat. 1215
Flood Control Act of 1939	53 Stat. 1414
Flood Control Act of 1941	55 Stat. 638
Flood Control Act of 1944	58 Stat. 887
Flood Control Act of 1946	60 Stat. 641
Flood Control Act of 1950	64 Stat. 163
Rivers & Harbors Act of 1910	36 Stat. 630
Rivers & Harbors Act of 1922	42 Stat. 1038
Rivers & Harbors Act of 1925	43 Stat. 1186
Rivers & Harbors Act of 1927	44 Stat. 1010
Rivers & Harbors Act of 1935	49 Stat. 1028
Rivers & Harbors Act of 1937	50 Stat. 844
Rivers & Harbors Act of 1938	52 Stat. 802
Rivers & Harbors Act of 1942	56 Stat. 703
Rivers & Harbors Act of 1945	59 Stat. 10
Rivers & Harbors Act of 1946	60 Stat. 634
Rivers & Harbors Act of 1950	64 Stat. 163
Water Power Act of 1920	41 Stat. 1063

Notes

Upon abolition of the National Resources Planning Board, its files and those of its predecessor agencies were turned over to the National Archives by direction of Congress. At the Archives most of the files are available for public inspection, and they have been used extensively for this study. In citing material from the files, the name and date of the document have been followed by the abbreviation for National Archives (NA), a dash, the abbreviation for National Resources Planning Board (NRPB), and the file number. Thus:

Prelim. rpt. on conservation of waterfowl, 4 April 1937, NA-NRPB 123.4.

INTRODUCTION

GAUGING ADMINISTRATIVE RESPONSIBILITY

1. This Introduction has appeared in 9 PAR 182 (1949) under the joint authorship of Arthur A. Maass and Laurence I. Radway.

Most references and sources for this Introduction are found in the following bibliographical note.

METHOD OF APPROACH: The general approach is suggested by Herbert A. Simon, *Administrative Behavior; A Study of Decision-making Processes in Administrative Organization* (New York, 1947), especially chapter 2.

RESPONSIBILITY — A GENERAL AND HISTORICAL VIEW: Friedrich's analysis of bureaucracy forms the basis of the discussion. See Carl J. Friedrich, *Constitutional Government and Democracy* (Boston, 1941), especially chapters 2, 18, 19. The citations are from this text.

See also Max Weber on bureaucracy in H. H. Gerth and C. Wright Mills (translators), *From Max Weber* (Oxford, 1946), chapter 8; and in Talcott Parsons (editor), *Max Weber: The Theory of Social and Economic Organization* (Oxford, 1947), chapter 3.

RESPONSIBILITY FOR WHAT? The following deal with responsibility for formulating as well as executing public policy: Carl J. Friedrich, "Public Policy and the Nature of Administrative Responsibility," in Friedrich and Edward S. Mason (editors), *Public Policy, 1940* (Cambridge, 1940); V. O. Key, "Politics and Administration," in Leonard D. White (editor), *The Future of Government in the United States* (Chicago, 1942); Don K. Price, "Democratic Administration," in Fritz Morstein Marx (editor), *Elements of Public Administration* (New York, 1946); Wayne A. R. Leys, "Ethics and Administrative Discretion," 3 PAR 10 (1943); Edwin E. Witte, "Administrative Agencies and Statute Law Making," 2 PAR 116 (1942); Elisabeth McK. Scott and Belle Zeller, "State Agencies and Lawmaking," 2 PAR 205 (1942).

RESPONSIBILITY TO THE PEOPLE — PRESSURE GROUPS: The need for such responsibility is seen and defended by E. Pendleton Herring, *Public Administration and the Public Interest* (New York, 1936); John Dickinson, "Democratic Realities in Democratic Dogma," 24 APSR 283 (1930); Avery Leiserson, "Interest Groups in Administration," in Morstein Marx, *Elements of Public Administration;* V. O. Key, *Politics, Parties, and Pressure Groups* (New York, 1947), chapter 7.

The role of advisory groups in recent administration is discussed by William H. Newman, "Government-Industry Cooperation That Works," 6 PAR 240 (1946).

RESPONSIBILITY TO THE LEGISLATURE: The argument for indirect responsibility is taken from Friedrich, "Public Policy and the Nature of Administrative Responsibility," in Friedrich and Mason, *Public Policy;* Price, "Democratic Administration," in Marx, *Elements of Public Administration;* John M. Gaus, *Reflections on Public Administration* (University of Alabama, 1947); V. O. Key, *Politics, Parties;* and "Politics and Administration," in White, *The Future of Government;* Leonard D. White, "Legislative Responsibility for the Public Service," in *New Horizons in Public Administration* (University of Alabama, 1945); President's Committee on Administrative Management, *Report . . . with Studies* (Washington, 1937). The quotation on p. 11 is from this last report.

Some of the forms of responsibility to legislature are discussed by Joseph P. Harris, "The Future of Administrative Management," in White, *The Future of Government*.

RESPONSIBILITY TO THE CHIEF EXECUTIVE: Problems of staffing the presidency are analyzed in Don K. Price, "Staffing the Presidency," in Fritz Morstein Marx (editor), "Federal Executive Reorganization Re-examined: A Symposium I," 40 APSR 1154–68 (1946); and V. O. Key, "Politics and Administration," in White, *The Future of Government*.

RESPONSIBILITY TO PROFESSION: Friedrich in particular has emphasized this aspect of administration. See "Public Policy and the Nature of Administrative Responsibility" and *Constitutional Government and Democracy,* especially chapter 19. In this connection, see also Fritz Morstein Marx, "Administrative Responsibility," in Morstein Marx (editor), *Public Management in the New Democracy* (New York, 1940); and Reinhard Bendix, "Bureaucracy and the Problem of Power," 5 PAR 194 (1945).

The dangers of heavy reliance on professional responsibility are pointed up by Herman Finer, "Administrative Responsibility to Democratic Government," 1 PAR 335 (1941); Marshall Dimock, "Bureaucracy Self-Examined," 4 PAR 197

(1944); Key, "Politics and Administration," in White, *The Future of Government*.

2. "Many of the most severe breakdowns in contemporary administration, accompanied by violent public reactions against irresponsible bureaucracy, will be found to trace back to contradictory and ill-defined policy . . ." Carl J. Friedrich, "Public Policy and the Nature of Administrative Responsibility," p. 4.

3. Leiserson also observes cogently that the administrator may endanger his whole program by too meticulous an effort to resist group pressures. Both the agency and the pressure group are part of the same community, and legislative support for the achievement of the agency's aims depends on its ability to get the support of vocal groups. See his "Interest Groups in Administration."

4. This is merely one form of what Friedrich has termed "the rule of anticipated reactions." See *Constitutional Government and Democracy*, pp. 589 ff. It is impossible to overestimate the general importance of this "rule" as a restraint on power of all types.

5. There are some exceptions, notably those relating to professional groups. Appleby vigorously opposes any tendency to delegate public power to private groups, since it is difficult to hold them responsible. See Paul H. Appleby, *Big Democracy* (New York, 1945).

6. General analysis of the broader questions of the relative effectiveness of cabinet and presidential government is beyond the scope of this work. Similarly, proposals to establish other types of executive-legislative relations, e.g., the interpellation and the joint legislative-executive council, are not analyzed since they cannot provide criteria for gauging administrative responsibility in the United States today. For a convenient summary of such proposals see George B. Galloway, *Congress at the Crossroads* (New York, 1946), especially chapter 7.

7. ". . . in the future, legislatures perforce must deal with administration on the basis of principle and generality if they are to deal with it effectively and in the public interest." Leonard D. White, "Legislative Responsibility for the Public Service," p. 6.

8. Too often, alas, the "rule of anticipated reactions" here dictates that an agency request more money than it really wants in order that it will not be granted less than it actually needs. But though this practice is common, and to some extent inevitable, astute officials are aware that it may "backfire" with disastrous consequences.

9. No effort is made to establish a separate set of criteria for measuring the responsibility of subordinate officials to the heads of their own agencies. However, these will not differ substantially, *mutatis mutandis*, from the criteria for measuring the responsibility of agency heads to the chief executive.

10. In this connection, Pendleton Herring has questioned whether too close a responsibility of the chief executive for the actions of administrative agencies is desirable. He raises practical arguments against pushing the current shibboleths too far. "If the President were held to a closer accountability, he would inevitably become laden with an accumulation of grievances. Is this compatible with an official elected for a fixed term of years?" If the President is to remain effective, he must to some extent be guarded "from the frictions that his administration creates." *Presidential Leadership* (New York, 1940), pp. 114 ff.

11. Failure to make such adaptation should be an occasion for disciplinary action, but direct political ties between the offending agency and individual legislators often prevent the required measures. This points up the importance of the final criterion of responsibility set forth in the preceding section.

12. Deviations can, of course, be justified when the legislature demands information which may be contrary to the chief executive's program.

13. It is realized that information concerning a conflict may be suppressed and that such suppression should not be considered evidence that the conflict has been resolved. However, unless the chief executive purposefully presents the conflict to the legislature or to the people for their determination, or unless the legislature demands the facts in the case, the administrative agencies should not publicize the unresolved issues.

14. For many reasons, such a sense is "not a firm part of the American heritage of public administration. . . . Not even the literature of public administration has yet described what are respectable standards of administrative discipline . . ." Leonard D. White, "Field Coordination in Liberated Areas," 3 PAR 192–3 (1943).

15. This does not imply that an official may sabotage a legislative or executive policy simply because *he* happens to deem it undemocratic. The remedy must be sought "through channels," and, should this fail, outside of channels, i.e., by severing his official relationship with the authority which promulgated the policy he condemns and indulging his passion for "higher law" from another vantage point.

CHAPTER ONE

THE CIVIL FUNCTIONS OF THE CORPS OF ENGINEERS

1. 2 Stat. 137.
2. 39 Stat. 950.
3. 49 Stat. 1570. For a somewhat detailed history of the development of the early programs, see W. Stull Holt, *The Office of the Chief of Engineers of the Army*, Institute for Government Research, Service Monographs of the United States Government, No. 27 (Baltimore, 1923).
4. These figures do not represent total Federal investment in national water resource development, but only that investment made under the Corps of Engineers. Other Federal agencies, for example, the Bureau of Reclamation and the Tennessee Valley Authority, have invested billions more for irrigation, hydroelectric power, and general multiple-purpose river development. See *Annual Report of Chief of Engineers, U. S. Army*, 1948, pt. I, vol. 1, p. 22. See also, NRPB, *National Resources Development Report*, 1943, pt. III, pp. 47–53; Robert W. Hartley and Maynard M. Hufschmidt, "Rural and Regional Development," in Dewhurst and Associates, *America's Needs and Resources* (New York, 1947), pp. 444–445; Commission on Organization of Executive Branch of Government (Hoover Commission), *Report of Task Force on Natural Resources* (1949), p. 16.
5. For organization of USED see O&R 1003–1007.
6. In addition there is a Beach Erosion Board, directed by law to make investigations for preventing erosion of shores and determining most suitable methods for protecting and restoring beaches. The Board is composed of seven members of whom four must be officers of the Corps and three must be selected from among the State agencies coöperating with the Corps in beach erosion.
7. Prior to the reorganization of Congressional committees in 1947, these matters were handled as follows:

CIVIL FUNCTIONS OF ENGINEERS 269

	House
Rivers and harbors	Committee on Rivers and Harbors
Flood control	Committee on Flood Control
	Senate
Rivers and harbors	Committee on Commerce (Subcommittee on Rivers and Harbors)
Flood control	Committee on Commerce (Subcommittee on Flood Control)

8. This theory was stated by Rep. Mansfield, then chairman of the House Committee on Rivers and Harbors, 79 CR 13718.

9. USED, CL 4325, 25 March 1947; House Com. on Public Works, 80 Cong., 2 Sess., Legislative Calendar.

The general procedure of requiring Congress to specifically authorize the conduct of an examination and survey for each individual project has been modified to a certain extent by the famous "308" report. The Rivers and Harbors Act of 1925 (43 Stat. 1186) authorized the Corps of Engineers, in cooperation with the Federal Power Commission, to study and report on the cost of surveys on all streams where power development appeared feasible, with a view to effective development of these streams for navigation, potential water power, flood control, and irrigation. The report made in response to this instruction was published as House Doc. 308, 69 Cong., 1 Sess. In the Rivers and Harbors Act of 1927 (44 Stat. 1010) Congress authorized the Corps of Engineers to conduct surveys on all streams covered in House Doc. 308 and thus, presumably, gave the Engineers full power and authority, without further individual authorization in each case, to survey every stream in the country whereon power appeared feasible and practical. At the close of fiscal year 1948, surveys on 191 streams had been completed under this authority and reports thereon transmitted to Congress (*Annual Report of Chief of Engineers,* 1948, p. 2971).

10. O&R 4202.03.

11. As of 30 June 1948, there was a grand total of over one thousand outstanding authorized investigations of all types. However, many of these may never be made and many others can be combined (*Annual Report of Chief of Engineers,* 1948, p. 2973). The only breakdown of preliminary examination and survey funds in the justifications for appropriations is one which allocates among the District Offices the total sum requested for examinations of rivers and harbors. No such allocation is presented for flood control investigations.

12. O&R 4202.06.
13. O&R 4202.06.
14. O&R 4202.08–4202.13.
15. O&R 4202.07, 4202.13.
16. O&R 4202.15, 4205–4207.
17. O&R 4202.22.

18. For a good statement of the relation of the Chief of Engineers to the Board of Engineers for Rivers and Harbors, see testimony of Brig. Gen. George B. Pillsbury, Office of Chief of Engineers, before House Com. on Rivers and Harbors, 75 Cong., 1 Sess., Hearings on HR 6150.

19. Clearance with Federal agencies is facilitated by the Federal Inter-Agency River Basin Committee, to be discussed in greater detail in Chapter III.

20. 32 Stat. 372; 37 Stat. 826; 39 Stat. 948. The twelve-month provision was

not law, but a committee rule; it could be, and was, disregarded on occasion. See, for example, history of preliminary examination, survey, and review of Sebastian Inlet, Florida. An unfavorable report was submitted to Congress, 5 August 1941, and a review resolution passed the House Committee on Rivers and Harbors, 8 August 1941.

21. USED, CL 4325, 25 March 1947; House Com. on Public Works, 80 Cong., 1 Sess., Legislative Calendar.

22. USED, CL 4325, 1947; resolutions adopted by Senate Com. on Public Works, 80 Cong., 1 Sess., unpublished.

23. O&R 4209.

24. O&R 4202.03.

25. O&R 4202.17, 4206, 4208.

26. In the case of "308" reports (see footnote 9 *supra*), the Corps may conduct a reëxamination of survey on its own initiative. The Rivers and Harbors Act of 1935 (49 Stat. 1048) provided that these reports may be supplemented by such additional study or investigation as the Chief of Engineers finds necessary to take into account important changes in economic factors as they occur, and additional stream flow records, or other factual data.

27. House Com. on Rivers and Harbors, 75 Cong., 3 Sess., Hearings on the Improvement of Delaware River between Philadelphia and the Sea, p. 14. Mr. John H. Small, a former member of Congress, was representing the Atlantic Deeper Waterways Association before the committee of which he had once been chairman.

28. Flood Control Act of 1946 (60 Stat. 641). In order to insure the adoption of projects based only on recent engineering reports, the Rivers and Harbors Act of 1922 provided "That hereafter no project shall be considered by any committee of Congress with a view to its adoption, except with a view to a survey, if five years have elapsed since a report upon a survey of said project has been submitted to Congress pursuant to law." (42 Stat. 1043). This requirement, also, may and has been circumvented by introducing an amendment on the floor of the House to authorize a project based on a survey report more than five years old.

29. House Com. on Rivers and Harbors, 75 Cong., 1 Sess., Hearings on HR 7015; House Com. on Flood Control, 76 Cong., 1 Sess., Hearings on HR 9640.

30. 49 Stat. 1570.

31. National Rivers and Harbors Congress, *Proceedings of the Luncheon Meeting*, 34th Annual Convention, Washington, 23 March 1939.

32. O&R 4214.

33. War Dept. Civil Functions Appropriation Bill for 1943, 56 Stat. 220.

34. As a matter of administrative detail it should be noted that the District Engineer does not commence the definite project report immediately upon receipt of the allotment. He must first submit to the Chief of Engineers for approval a "subproject," which is a letter report of the proposed distribution of funds under the allotment.

35. O&R 4214.

36. House Com. on Appropriations, 76 Cong., 3 Sess., Hearings on War Dept. Civil Functions Appropriation Bill for 1941, p. 132.

CHAPTER TWO

ADJUSTMENT OF GROUP INTERESTS

1. Walter Lippmann, "Roosevelt Is Gone," editorial in *New York Herald Tribune*, reprinted in Donald Porter Geddes, *Franklin Delano Roosevelt — A Memorial* (New York, 1945), p. 76.
2. House Com. on Appropriations, 80 Cong., 1 Sess., Hearings on War Dept. Civil Functions Appropriation Bill for 1948, p. 492.
3. House Com. on Appropriations, 75 Cong., 3 Sess., Hearings on War Dept. Civil Functions Appropriation Bill for 1939, p. 135.
4. 87 CR A5610.
5. Unpublished manuscript on Waterways, prepared within the NRPB in 1935 from memoranda submitted by Adah L. Lee, NA-NRPB 578, p. 19.
6. *Annual Report of Chief of Engineers*, 1946.
7. The Atlantic Deeper Waterways Association, with headquarters in the Widener Building, Philadelphia, publishes *Reports and Resolutions* of its annual conventions, and up until September 1942, published periodic *President's Letters*.
8. 59 Stat. 10.
9. For example: Rep. John W. Small (N. C.), one time chairman of the Rivers and Harbors Committee, served for years as vice-president-at-large of the Association after leaving the House. Sen. Moses (N. H.) and Sen. Hastings (Del.) have served as State vice-presidents of the Association after leaving the Senate. Reps. Peter G. Ten Eyck (N. Y.) and Robert G. Houston (Del.) have served as directors of the Association after leaving the House.
10. Atlantic Deeper Waterways Association, *Resolutions of the 34th Annual Convention*, Miami, 12 November 1941, p. 6.
11. Atlantic Deeper Waterways Association, *Report of the Proceedings of the 25th Annual Convention*, Philadelphia, 1932, p. 72.
12. House Com. on Rivers and Harbors, 75 Cong., 1 Sess., Hearings on HR 6150 for Completion of Construction of Atlantic-Gulf Ship Canal, Florida, p. 117.
13. House Com. on Rivers and Harbors, 75 Cong., 3 Sess., Hearings on the Improvement of Delaware River between Philadelphia and the Sea, p. 18.
14. Letter of J. J. Mansfield, chairman, House Com. on Rivers and Harbors, to J. Hampton Moore, president, Atlantic Deeper Waterways Association, dated 7 November 1939, in Atlantic Deeper Waterways Association, *Extracts from Proceedings of 32nd Annual Convention*, Philadelphia, 13–14 November 1939.
15. The Ohio Valley Conservation and Flood Control Congress, with headquarters at 2141 Micklethwaite Road, Portsmouth, Ohio, gives a Washington address at the Raleigh Hotel. The quotation is from a letter of Alan N. Jordan, executive secretary of the Congress, to Mr. Pendleton Herring, Harvard University, Cambridge, Massachusetts, dated 30 November 1940, and is used here by permission of Dr. Charles E. Holzer, president of the Congress.
16. The Congress has headquarters at 1720 M St., N.W., Washington, D. C. In addition to material issued by the Congress, see the following: Robert de Roos and Arthur A. Maass, "The Lobby That Can't Be Licked," *Harpers*, August 1949, p. 21; Leslie A. Miller, "The Battle That Squanders Millions," *Saturday Evening Post*, 14 May 1949, p. 30; Benton J. Stong, "The Rivers and Harbors Lobby," *New Republic*, 10 October 1949, p. 13.

17. National Rivers and Harbors Congress, *National Rivers and Harbors Congress and Its Work* (Washington, 1940).
18. The recommendations of the Hoover Commission are discussed at pp. 112 ff., *infra*.
19. 86 CR A1446.
20. 93 CR A2424.
21. National Rivers and Harbors Congress, *National Rivers and Harbors News*, vol. VI, no. 4 (April 1940).
22. National Rivers and Harbors Congress, *Proceedings of the Luncheon Meeting*, 34th Annual Convention, Washington, 23 March 1939.
23. National Rivers and Harbors Congress, *National Rivers and Harbors News* (April 1940).
24. National Rivers and Harbors Congress, *National Rivers and Harbors Congress and Its Work* (Washington, 1940).
25. See, for example, resolutions adopted at the 39th Annual Convention in Washington, 8–9 April 1949, in 95 CR A2793–4.
26. National Rivers and Harbors Congress, *National Rivers and Harbors Congress and Its Work* (Washington, 1940).
27. Quoted by Stong, "The Rivers and Harbors Lobby," *New Republic*, 10 October 1949; emphasis added.
28. S. 555, 79 Cong., 1 Sess. See hearings on this bill before Senate Committees on Irrigation and Reclamation and on Commerce.
29. Information on this organization may be found in the mimeographed material issued by its Washington headquarters at 1720 M St., N.W.; and in Senate Irrigation and Reclamation Com. Hearings on S 555, 79 Cong., 1 Sess., pp. 648 ff.
30. Information on this organization may be found in the material issued by its Washington headquarters, 1215 16th St., N.W., especially *Summary & Proceedings* of the 2nd Conference in Kansas City, Missouri, 18–19 September 1947.
31. The effects of this procedure in relation to national water policy are considered at greater length in Chapter IV, pp. 181 ff.
32. For material relating to this report, see: House Doc. 359, 77 Cong., 1 Sess.; House Com. on Flood Control, 77 Cong., 1 Sess., Hearings on Flood Control Plans and New Projects (HR 4911), pp. 593 ff.; House Rpt. 759, 77 Cong., 1 Sess.; Sen. Com. on Commerce, 77 Cong., 1 Sess., Hearings on Flood Control (HR 4911), pp. 30 ff.; Sen. Rpt. 575, 77 Cong., 1 Sess.; 87 CR 5434 ff.
33. "Project flood" refers to the maximum flood for protection from which a project has been planned. In this case, it is a flood of greater dimensions than the 1927 flood, the most serious flood recorded to the date of the report.
34. This indication of preference for plan 5 is supported by the following statement from the report of the House Com. on Flood Control with reference to this project (House Rpt. 759, 77 Cong., 1 Sess.): "While no specific recommendation was made as to which of the alternative plans should be adopted, it was apparent from the conclusion of the report that protection against the maximum [plan 5], rather than the project [plan 4] flood, with future determinations was looked on with favor."

The following exchange between the chairman of the House Flood Control Committee and General Tyler is also instructive in this respect (House Hearings, p. 976):

"The Chairman (Mr. Whittington, Miss.). And if those hazards are to be assumed you are leaving it to the Congress of the United States to provide

for their assumption in building a lot higher levees because you are recommending no particular plan here in this report?
"General Tyler. I wouldn't say that we have quite done that, Mr. Chairman.
"The Chairman. Tell me what you have done so I will be more accurate.
"General Tyler. I wouldn't say that in this report we have left the implication that if the Congress sees fit to adopt a 'levees only' plan [plan 4] we wish to place the responsibility for the engineering on the Congress. In other words we are not trying to dodge our responsibility.
"The Chairman. Wherever the responsibility be placed, whether it be on the Congress or elsewhere, is it not a fair statement that the plan here that undertakes by levees to protect the greatest number of acres carries with it the greatest hazards?
"General Tyler. I think it does; yes, sir.
"The Chairman. So that for my part we can strike out about the responsibility."
35. House Com. on Flood Control, Hearings on Flood Control . . . , p. 697. The following excerpts from the same hearings (pp. 972, 974) further illustrate the unwillingness of General Tyler to commit the Engineer Department despite consistent prodding by members of the Committee.
"Mr. Norrell (Ark.). Now, if you can't construct the floodway — and we have had a floodway on our statutes since 1928 — then as our engineer in charge of work, what do you recommend, if anything, should be done?
"General Tyler. We make no recommendation, sir . . .
"Mr. Norrell. Now, in all fairness and serious dealing with all citizens of the United States alike, since that is all true as established by your report, I am wondering if the Army engineers could not give serious consideration to trying to make a recommendation, if this can be done — back in 1928 they took the floodway plan as a decree because they didn't think there was any other way around it.
"You do care to comment on that statement — I don't want to get you out too far.
"The Chairman. Put him just as far out as you can.
"General Tyler. The confinement of the floodwaters increases the hazard to the east side of the river and you can expect, perhaps, a great many of the people there to resist that method just as the west side resisted the construction of the floodway.
"Mr. Norrell. How about the United States Government getting up and doing the thing that is physically and feasibly possible and equally safe and will be beneficial to the greatest number of citizens and the largest area of land, as plan No. 4, as you say it will do.
"General Tyler. Plan No. 4 protects the greatest area with a certain factor of safety, but plan No. 5 protects a certain area with a greater factor of safety.
"Mr. Norrell. But putting them all together?
"General Tyler. There is still the conflict of interests."
36. Sensitiveness to Congressional opinion may be largely responsible for the attitude taken by the Engineer Department. Sen. Overton (La.), chairman of the Subcommittee on Flood Control of the Senate Committee on Commerce, and Rep. Norrell (Ark.), member of the House Committee on Flood Control, had introduced companion bills (S 705, HR 3064, 77 Cong., 1 Sess.) to eliminate the floodway and build equal grade levees on both sides of the river — essentially plan 4 of the Mississippi River Commission. These two influential Members of Congress intended to press hard for this legislation. On the other

hand, Rep. Whittington (Miss.), chairman of the House Committee on Flood Control, and as far as flood control legislation in the House was concerned, by far the most influential Member of Congress, represented the east-bank interests and was aggressively opposed to the Overton-Norrell bills and to plan 4.

37. 87 CR 5436.

38. Another classic example in which the Chief of Engineers failed to make any recommendation on a controversial project and deferred to "the wisdom of the Congress" is found in the 1939 report on the Tennessee-Tombigbee waterway. In this case, however, the Board of Engineers for Rivers and Harbors did make a recommendation. See: House Doc. 269, 76 Cong., 1 Sess.; Committee on Rivers and Harbors, 76 Cong., 1 Sess., Hearings on Rivers and Harbors Bill (HR 6264); House Rpt. 614, 76 Cong., 1 Sess.; Sen. Rpt. 630, 76 Cong., 1 Sess.

39. See p. 35, *supra*.

40. Since this administrative practice is so unique, its origin should be mentioned. By the Rivers and Harbors Act of 1866 (14 Stat. 70) the Secretary of War was required to submit in the case of each work provided for in the bill, along with other information, the amounts that could be profitably expended during the next fiscal year. This provision applied only to the works mentioned in the act. However, the rivers and harbors bill of the next year repeated the same provision, and it became customary to include such information in the annual report whether specifically requested by law or not. This information served a very useful purpose before adoption of the consolidated executive budget (Budget and Accounting Act in 1921). After that date, however, there appears to have been little excuse for publishing such a statement, however useful it may be in presenting the Department's requests before the Budget Bureau.

41. Engineer Department estimates taken from *Annual Report of the Chief of Engineers*, 1946, p. 20; Budget estimates, from *Budget of the United States* for fiscal year 1948, Table 10.

42. House Com. on Appropriations, 76 Cong., 1 Sess., Hearings on War Department Civil Functions Appropriation Bill for 1940, p. 157.

43. National Rivers and Harbors Congress, *Proceedings of the Luncheon Meeting*, 34th Annual Convention, 23 March 1939; speech of Sen. Josiah Bailey.

CHAPTER THREE

RESPONSIBILITY TO THE EXECUTIVE AND LEGISLATIVE ESTABLISHMENTS

1. Statement of President Roosevelt in vetoing a rivers and harbors bill in 1939, 84 CR 11228.

2. See Holt, *The Office of the Chief of Engineers*, p. 21. Stimson testimony from House Select Com. on the Budget, 66 Cong., 1 Sess., Hearings on the Establishment of a National Budget System, p. 641.

3. Sen. Doc. 325, 60 Cong., 1 Sess.

4. 36 Stat. 630.

5. Sen. Newlands of Nevada, a member of the Commission, introduced Sen. Bill 500, 60 Cong., 1 Sess.; Sen. Bill 10900, 61 Cong., 3 Sess.; and an amendment to the Rivers and Harbors Bill of 1910.

6. See Arthur B. Darling, editor, *The Public Papers of Francis G. Newlands* (New York, 1932), II, 187–329; also a memo on "National Water Planning, The Newlands Decade," by John F. Finerty, Jr., 18 March 1940, NA-NRPB 578.

7. Finerty, "National Water Planning," p. 6.

8. See Sec. 18, Rivers and Harbors Act of 1917, 40 Stat. 269.
9. 41 Stat. 1063.
10. Prior to the Hoover plans two legislative proposals for transfer of the civil functions of the Corps of Engineers to other agencies had met with quick death. A bill to transfer to the Department of the Interior the public works functions of the Federal Government, including the nonmilitary functions of the Corps of Engineers, was introduced in the 70th Congress (HR 8127, 70 Cong., 1 Sess.). Extensive hearings were held on this bill in March and April 1928 by the House Committee on Expenditures in the Executive Departments. Tremendous opposition to the rivers and harbors and flood control aspects of the bill developed, and it was never reported out of committe.

A bill to set up a Public Works Administration to include, among others, the nonmilitary functions of the Corps of Engineers, was introduced in the 72nd Congress in 1932 (HR 11011, 72 Cong., 1 Sess.). Again, hearings were held by the House Committee on Expenditures in the Executive Departments. This bill was reported, as amended in committee (House Rpt. 989, 72 Cong., 1 Sess.), but never came to a vote on the floor of the House. The only important amendment to the bill made by the Committee was one which excluded from its provisions all works relative to rivers and harbors and flood control. Of a total of twenty-two members of the committee, only three signed a minority report objecting to this exclusion.

For the Hoover plans see House Doc. 493 (EO 5959-5969), 72 Cong., 2 Sess.; House Com. on Expenditures in the Executive Departments, 72 Cong., 2 Sess., Hearings on President's Message on Consolidation of Government Agencies; House Rpt. 1833, 72 Cong., 2 Sess.; 76 CR 2110 ff.

11. The following material is largely from NRPB, *Resource Development Report*, 1942, pp. 95–99; NRPB, *Development of Resources*, 1941, pt. 3, pp. 23–31.

12. For an example of applicable criteria, see NRPB, *Development of Resources*, 1941, pt. 3, pp. 29–30.

13. For a more detailed analysis of the review function in water resources, see *Report of Task Force on Natural Resources* (Hoover Commission), pp. 89–93.

14. See Report of President's Committee on Waterflow, House Doc. 395, 73 Cong., 2 Sess. Emphasis added in quotations from report.

15. The National Resources Board succeeded the National Planning Board. The National Planning Board was established in July 1933 by the Administrator of Public Works at the direction of the President and consisted of three members: Frederic A. Delano, chairman; Charles E. Merriam; and Wesley C. Mitchell. The National Resources Board was established by the President in June 1934 (EO 6777) to supersede the National Planning Board. The new Board consisted of the Secretary of the Interior, chairman; the Secretaries of War, Agriculture, Commerce, and Labor; the Federal Emergency Relief Administrator; Frederic A. Delano, Charles E. Merriam, and Wesley C. Mitchell. For a detailed statement of the legal status of the Board see NRPB, *Progress Report*, 1939, pp. 161 ff.

16. NRB, *Report*, December 1934; Mississippi Valley Committee, *Report*, October 1934. The MVC was a special committee set up by the Federal Emergency Relief Administrator to investigate water problems in the Mississippi Valley. This Committee became the Water Planning Committee of the National Resources Board.

17. Secretary of War, letter to chairman NRB, 28 September 1934, NA-NRPB old file, not numbered.
18. Chairman NRB, letter to Secretary of War, 11 October 1934, NA-NRPB old file, not numbered.
19. Secretary of War, letter to chairman NRB, 23 November 1934, NA-NRPB old file, not numbered.
20. President's message to Congress, 24 January 1935, printed in Sen. Rpt. 974, 74 Cong., 1 Sess.
21. Notes re Sen. Bill 2825, 1935, NA-NRPB 071.1. Also, Sen. Com. on Commerce, 74 Cong., 1 Sess., Hearings on National Planning Board of 1935 (S 2825); Sen. Rpt. 974, 74 Cong., 1 Sess.
22. Failing to obtain permanent status through legislation, the National Resources Board was reëstablished by the President as the National Resources Committee in June 1935. (EO 7065, issued under authority of the Emergency Relief Appropriation Act of 1935, 49 Stat. 115.) The membership of the Committee was the same as that of the Board. The Committee abolished the Water Planning Committee, establishing in its place a new Water Resources Committee which consisted of eight representatives of Federal agencies (Corps of Engineers, Soil Conservation Service, Biological Survey, Geological Survey, Bureau of Reclamation, Public Health Service, Federal Power Commission, TVA) and four non-Federal experts, including two representatives from State water resources agencies. The new membership indicates a greater emphasis on the coördination of Federal activities in the field of water resources development.
23. House Com. on Public Lands, 74 Cong., 2 Sess., Hearings on Establishment of a National Resources Board (HR 10303 and 11105).
24. Memo in NA-NRPB 071.6. President's letter printed in House hearings on HR 10303 and 11105.
25. Executive officer NRC, memo to Under Secretary of Interior, 3 March 1936, NA-NRPB 071.1. Also, various letters of members of House Public Lands Committee, March and April 1936, same file.
26. Secretary of War, letter to chairman NRC, 11 April 1936, NA-NRPB, old file, not numbered, entitled Flood Control, General.
27. See, in particular, statements by Reps. DeRouen and Wadsworth, Hearings on HR 10303, pp. 25, 62.
28. 80 CR 7706–7710.
29. Executive officer NRC, memo for chairman advisory committee, 22 May 1936, on NRB Bill, NA-NRPB 070.8.
30. Executive officer NRC, letter to director of research President's Committee on Administrative Management, 25 June 1936, NA-NRPB 071.1.
31. House Joint Res. 541, 74 Cong., 2 Sess.
32. Unless otherwise indicated, information on flood control studies in 1936 is obtained from the following two files: NA-NRPB old file, not numbered, entitled Organization, Flood Control; NA-NRPB old file, not numbered, entitled Flood Control, General.
33. See footnote 26, *supra*.
34. HR 8455 and House Rpt. 1223, 74 Cong., 1 Sess.; 79 CR 14174–14199, 14285–14305.
35. Sen. Rpt. 1963, 74 Cong., 2 Sess.
36. See executive officer NRC, memo to chairman advisory committee, 14 May 1936, on conference with the President and Sen. Carl Hayden, NA-NRPB 079. 80 CR 7573–7601, 7675, 7690, 7696, 8636, 8642, 8851, 8857, 8863.

RESPONSIBILITY TO EXECUTIVE AND LEGISLATURE 277

37. Information on veto recommendation from various documents, 29 May to 24 June 1936, in file NA-NRPB 079.
38. Executive officer NRC, memo to chairman advisory committee, 24 June 1936, NA-NRPB 079.
39. *N. Y. Times,* 30 June 1938; 52 Stat. 1215.
40. NRC, *Public Works Planning,* 1936.
41. House Joint Res. 175 and Sen. Joint Res. 57, 75 Cong., 1 Sess.
42. The letter of the Secretary of War is printed in Committee report on the bill, House Rpt. 798, 75 Cong., 1 Sess.
43. Secretary of War, letter to President, 8 April 1937, NA-NRPB 597.7.
44. House Com. on Flood Control, 75 Cong., 1 Sess., Hearings on Ohio River Basin, p. 2.
45. 81 CR 7831.
46. 81 CR 7831.
47. See pp. 97–101, *infra.*
48. 81 CR 7835.
49. 81 CR 7822–7841, 5654, 7963.
50. Memo on House Joint Res. 175 and Sen. Joint Res. 57, 9 August 1937, NA-NRPB 079.
51. President, letter to Frederic A. Delano, 12 August 1937, NA-NRPB 076.
52. For veto message, see Sen. Doc. 95, 75 Cong., 1 Sess.
53. NRC, *Drainage Basin Problems and Programs,* 1937 revision, p. 154.
54. See pp. 88–90, *supra.*
55. From the foreword by the NRC, *Drainage Basin,* 1937, p. vi.
56. President's Committee on Administrative Management, *Report with Special Studies,* 1937. It is interesting to note that the President appointed this Committee at the suggestion of the NRC. For recommendations on planning see pp. 28–29.
57. The President's letter to Sen. Byrnes was made public through NRC press release no. 064, 13 February 1939, NA-NRPB 089.5. The Reorganization Act is found at 53 Stat. 561.
58. Executive officer NRC, memo to advisory committee, 21 February 1939, covering copy of Rep. Cochran's letter to P. H. Elwood, Ames, Iowa, 31 January 1939, NA-NRPB 070.1.
59. National Rivers and Harbors Congress, *Proceedings of the Special "Council of War" Meeting,* 26 April 1938, Washington, p. 8.
60. The agencies exempted in the 1938 Senate bill (S 2331) were: (1) the independent regulatory commissions; (2) Board of Governors of Federal Reserve System; (3) Board of Tax Appeals; (4) municipal government of the District of Columbia; (5) the General Auditing Office, to be established; (6) Engineer Corps of the Army and the Mississippi River Commission.
The agencies exempted in the 1939 Reorganization Act (53 Stat. 561) were: (1) the independent regulatory commissions (except CAA); (2) Civil Service Commission; (3) Coast Guard; (4) Engineer Corps of the Army and the Mississippi River Commission; (5) General Accounting Office; (6) Board of Tax Appeals; (7) Employees' Compensation Commission; (8) Tariff Commission; (9) Veterans' Administration; (10) National Mediation Board and National Railroad Adjustment Board; (11) National Railroad Retirement Board; (12) Federal Deposit Insurance Corporation and Board of Governors of Federal Reserve System.
61. House Rpt. 120, 76 Cong., 1 Sess., pp. 5–6.

62. Sen. Com. on Judiciary, 79 Cong., 1 Sess., Hearings on Government Reorganization (S 1120).

63. 59 Stat. 613. The three categories of exempted agencies are as follows: (1) Agencies which Congress refuses to consider appropriate for any reorganization: civil functions of the Corps of Engineers. (2) Agencies for which Congress refuses to consider reorganization plans except transfers to them of other functions: Interstate Commerce, Federal Trade, and Securities and Exchange Commissions; National Mediation, National Railroad Adjustment, and Railroad Retirement Boards. (3) Agencies for which Congress desires separate consideration in any plans for reorganization: Federal Communications and U. S. Tariff Commissions; Federal Deposit Insurance Corporation; Veterans' Administration.

64. See statement by Rep. Whittington, 86 CR A1450. 52 Stat. 802, 53 Stat. 1415, emphasis added.

65. House Doc. 261, 75 Cong., 1 Sess.

66. Sen. Com. on Agriculture and Forestry, 75 Cong., 1 Sess., Hearings on Creation of Conservation Authorities (S 2555, introduced by Sen. Norris). House Com. on Rivers and Harbors, 75 Cong., 1 and 2 Sess., Hearings on Regional Conservation and Development of Natural Resources (HR 7365, introduced by Rep. Mansfield; HR 7392 and HR 7863, introduced by Rep. Rankin).

67. President's message to special session of Congress called in November 1937 to deal with the recession, 82 CR 11. House Rpt. 2030, 75 Cong., 3 Sess., on HR 10027, which had been introduced as a substitute measure.

68. House Com. on Rivers and Harbors, 75 Cong., 2 Sess., Hearings on Regional Conservation, pp. 717–729.

69. Reorganization Plan No. 1 (House Doc. 262, 76 Cong., 1 Sess.); EO 8248, 8 September 1939.

70. NRPB, *Progress Report,* June 1941, pp. 33–34. For text of Agreement see USED, CL R&H No. 42, 11 August 1939.

71. EO 8455, 26 June 1940.

72. Pp. 127–129, *infra.*

73. Members of the subcommittee were as follows: Harlan H. Barrows, University of Chicago, chairman; M. S. Eisenhower, Land Use Coördinator, Dept. of Agriculture; James L. Fly, Chairman, Federal Communications Commission (formerly TVA); Leland Olds, Chairman, Federal Power Commission; John C. Page, Commissioner, Bureau of Reclamation; Brig. Gen. T. M. Robins, Assistant to Chief of Engineers; Clifford H. Stone, Director, Colorado Water Conservation Board.

74. NRC, WRC, subcommittee on national water policy, minutes of executive session, 15 January 1940, NA-NRPB 578.1; emphasis added.

75. NRC, WRC, subcommittee on national water policy, minutes of 5th meeting, 28–30 November 1940, pp. 5, 6.

76. Gen. Robins is noted as the single dissenting member of the subcommittee in the final printing of the report. See NRPB, *Development of Resources,* 1941, pt. 3, p. 21; also Robins' letter to Barrows, 6 November 1940, NA-NRPB 578.1.

77. NRC, WRC, minutes of 66th meeting, 8 November 1940, NA-NRPB 582.2; emphasis added.

78. Chief of Engineers, letter to chairman WRC, 19 November 1940, NA-NRPB 578.

79. NRPB, *Development of Resources,* 1941, pt. 3, p. 21. The additional dissent of Dr. Barrows from the WRC report, although he signed the subcom-

RESPONSIBILITY TO EXECUTIVE AND LEGISLATURE

mittee report, is attributable to certain changes made by the WRC in the subcommittee report which had the effect of making the recommendations more general and less specific in nature. WRC draft letter of transmittal to chairman NRPB, 24 December 1940, NA-NRPB 578.1.

80. For Work Relief Appropriation Act of 1938, see 83 CR 6794, 7806–7816; 52 Stat. 816. For Emergency Relief Appropriation Act of 1939, see 53 Stat. 927.

81. For 1941 appropriation see following, all 76 Cong., 3 Sess.: House Rpt. 1515; Sen. Rpt. 1177; Sen. debate, 86 CR 1050–1060; Conf. report, House Rpt. 1958; House debate on conf., 86 CR 4450–4459. Also, executive officer NRPB, memo to Board, 27 February 1940; chairman NRPB, memo to President, 4 March 1940, NA-NRPB 076. Emphasis added in quoting.

82. Another significant conflict bewteen the NRPB and the Engineer Department developed in 1942 with respect to a recommendation by the President and the NRPB that the Congress authorize and appropriate a planning fund for the preparation of surveys and detailed plans and specifications for a shelf or reservoir of projects to be undertaken when defense and war requirements permitted. (President's recommendations quoted in Sen. Rpt. 961, 77 Cong., 2 Sess.) In order to effectuate this recommendation, legislation was introduced in both the Senate and the House authorizing the President to allot funds for these purposes to agencies of the United States and to make advances to the States and their agencies and political subdivisions. The Senate Committee on Education and Labor and the House Committee on Labor both reported the legislation favorably (Sen. Rpt. 961 and House Rpt. 1478, 77 Cong., 1 Sess.). However, when it came up for consideration in the House, it was roundly defeated by a vote of 252 to 104 (88 CR 1486–1494). Opposition to the bill was led, for the Army's rivers and harbors bloc, by the Democratic chairman of the Committee on Flood Control and, for the Republicans in general by Reps. Dirksen (Ill.) and Hoffman (Mich.). Charges against the bill were manifold, including statements that the planning activities envisioned by the bill would supplant the activities of the Corps of Engineers and that the bill would continue, make permanent, and provide more money for both the NRPB and the State planning agencies. The first charge was untrue; the second might have been true in part. The final vote on the bill shows that the Democratic chairman of both the Rivers and Harbors and Flood Control Committees voted against the legislation.

Further evidence of the importance of opposition to the bill engendered by Engineer Corps supporters is found in the fact that later legislation, introduced by the Administration to accomplish the same purpose — i.e., advances of planning funds to States and local governments and allotments to Federal agencies — specifically exempted the Corps of Engineers, and that agency only (HR 7782, 77 Cong., 2 Sess.; S 846 and HR 1898, 78 Cong., 1 Sess.).

It should be noted that the opposition to this legislation by the friends of the Corps did not represent opposition to the idea of preparing in advance plans for public works projects, but opposition to the Planning Board and to any opportunity for it to interfere in the direct relations between the Corps of Engineers and the Congress. Faced with what was interpreted as a threat of competition from the NRPB, the Army Engineers got busy and obtained for themselves appropriations for preparing advance plans for postwar projects, although the President had not recommended any funds for them for this purpose (War Dept. Civil Functions Appropriation Bill for 1943, 28 April 1942, 56 Stat. 219).

83. On returning from his important trip to Africa, the President heard of the action of the House Appropriations Committee in omitting the NRPB from

the Independent Offices Appropriation Bill for 1944. He wrote a long personal letter to Rep. Cannon (Mo.), chairman of the Appropriations Committee, stating at length why, in his opinion, the appropriation should be restored. FDR letter to Cannon, 16 February 1943, NA-NRPB 079.

84. All of these factors played a part. Those who were closely connected with the Board have never come to any agreement as to the relative importance of any one factor. See, for example, John Millett, *The Process and Organization of Government Planning* (New York, 1947); Rex Tugwell's review of this book in 8 PAR 49 (1947); Charles E. Merriam, "The National Resources Planning Board," 38 APSR 1075 (1944).

85. 89 CR 1048.
86. 89 CR 4926.
87. EO 9384, 4 October 1943.
88. 90 CR 845.
89. For 1945 appropriation see the following, all 78 Cong., 2 Sess.: House Com. on Appropriations, Hearings on Independent Offices Appropriation Bill for 1945, p. 939; House Rpt. 1023; 90 CR 845. Congressional action on a prior supplemental estimate for this purpose for fiscal year 1944 is inconclusive (First Supplemental National Defense Appropriation Bill, 1944).
90. FIARBC, *Statement on FIARBC*, 26 May 1949 (mimeo.). The Dept. of Commerce signed the Agreement and was admitted to the Committee, 27 September 1946. The effectiveness of the Committee is discussed in greater detail at pp. 119 ff., *infra*.
91. FIARBC, *Statement*.
92. 58 Stat. 887, sec. 1. This provision has been repeated in subsequent navigation and flood control legislation.
93. Although this manuscript was in general completed before the Hoover Commission reported to Congress and for the most part deals with developments prior to 1949, the Commission's recommendations are considered of such significance with respect to this study that they have been included.
94. Hoover Commission, Report on the Department of Interior and Report of Task Force on Natural Resources.
95. Report of Task Force on Natural Resources, pp. 89–94. The procedure set out at the beginning of this chapter was written before the Task Force prepared its report.
96. Report of Task Force on Natural Resources, p. 35.
97. Hoover Commission, Report on the Department of the Interior, p. 81.
98. In addition, the Task Force on Public Works recommended a similar consolidation.
99. Commissioners McClellan and Manasco dissented. Commissioner Forrestal abstained from participation in the discussion and formulation of recommendations relating to the Corps of Engineers because of his relationship, as Secretary of Defense, to the Corps in the National Military Establishment. (Hoover Commission, Report on the Department of the Interior, p. 10, n. 7.)
100. Hoover Commission, Report on the Department of the Interior, p. 29.
101. Hoover Commission, Report of Task Force on Natural Resources, pp. 26–27.
102. Hoover Commission, Report on the Department of the Interior, p. 31.
103. The writer is Avery Leiserson, "Political Limitations of Executive Reorganization," 41 APSR 73 (1947).
104. Hoover Commission, Report of Task Force on Natural Resources, p. 67.
105. For documentation on Reorganization Act of 1949, see the following,

all from 81 Cong., 1 Sess.: House Com. on Expenditures, Hearings on Reorganization Act of 1949; House Rpt. 23; Sen. Com. on Expenditures, Hearings on Reorganization Act of 1949; Sen. Rpt. 232; House Rpt. 843; PL 109.

106. Senate Hearings on Reorganization Act of 1949, p. 78.

107. Press conference of 7 February 1949, as quoted in *N. Y. Herald Tribune* of 8 February and most other daily papers.

108. See 95 CR, temp., 1364–5 (17 February 1949), 2836–9 (19 March), 3857 (4 April).

109. Secretary of War, letters to Sen. Lodge, 15 March 1949 (95 CR, temp., 2839) and 1 April (95 CR, temp., 3857).

110. Sen. Rept. 232, 81 Cong., 1 Sess.

111. 95 CR, temp., 7584 (8 June 1949).

112. See various publications of the Citizens' Committee for the Hoover Report.

113. President's Committee on Waterflow, *Development of Rivers;* Mississippi Valley Committee, *Report,* 1934; NRC, *Drainage Basin Problems and Programs,* 1936, and 1937 revision.

114. The USED participated in all of the drainage basin committees. It participated also in a number of special basin studies organized by the Planning Board. Although serious diffcrences between the Board and the Engineer Department developed with respect to the special reports on the Pacific Northwest (NRC, *Regional Planning,* pt. I, May 1936) and on Ohio-Mississippi River regulation (NRC, *Drainage Basin,* 1937, pp. 69–75), relative success was enjoyed in the preparation of special joint reports on the Red River of the North (NRC, *Regional Planning,* pt. V, August 1937), the Northern Great Plains (Great Plains Drought Committee, *The Future of the Great Plains,* December 1936; and NRPB, *Regional Planning,* pt. IX), the Pecos River (NRPB, *Regional Planning,* pt. X), and the Arkansas Valley (NRPB, *Regional Planning,* pt. XI). Joint investigations of the Gila River Basin and Platte River Basin were not completed when the NRPB folded, and they have not been completed since. The Corps of Engineers was not a participant in the joint investigation of the Upper Rio Grande (NRC, *Regional Planning,* pt. VI).

115. For documentation on the Columbia River investigations, see the comprehensive report of the Department of Interior (House Doc. 473, 81 Cong., 2 Sess.), especially the letters of transmittal; and that of the Corps of Engineers (House Doc. 531, 81 Cong., 2 Sess.); also the hearings of the Senate and House Committees on Public Works on CVA legislation, 81 Cong., 1 Sess. The analysis which follows is based on a careful review of pertinent documents, including the minutes of the CBIAC and Norman Bacher's master's thesis on CBIAC (Stanford Univ., 1949). The analysis does not confirm certain statements of the Chief of Engineers and the Commissioner of Reclamation as to coördination achieved insofar as these statements refer to matters of major policy and over-all program.

116. For documentation on the Central Valley investigations see the comprehensive report of the Department of Interior (Sen. Doc. 113, 81 Cong., 1 Sess.); that of the Corps of Engineers (House Doc. 367, 81 Cong., 1 Sess.); and Chapter V.

117. This letter of 31 January 1945 is referred to in President Truman's letter to Secretary of War, 2 June 1945, and printed in Sen. Com. on Appropriations, 79 Cong., 2 Sess., Hearings on War Department Civil Functions Appropriation Bill for 1947, p. 521.

118. Message to Congress in approving the Rivers and Harbors and Flood

Control Bill of 1950. Printed in N. Y. Times, 23 May 1950.

119. President's letter of 3 July 1941, quoted in NRPB, Resources Development Report, 1942, p. 35.

120. Although the 1944 Flood Control Act called for clearance of reports with Governors of affected States and, in certain cases, with the Department of the Interior, it did not direct joint investigations.

121. See Chapter V; also executive officer NRPB, letter to executive clerk White House, 18 July 1939; secretary WRC, letter to chairman advisory committee NRPB, 28 July 1939, both in NA-NRPB 579.7.

122. See Chapter V.

123. For Hell's Canyon, see House Docs. 473, 531, 81 Cong., 2 Sess.; for Jamestown, see, in particular, report of the Sen. Appropriations Committee on Army Civil Functions Appropriation Bill for 1950, Sen. Rpt. 361, 81 Cong., 1 Sess.; for San Luis Valley, see executive officer NRC, letter to executive clerk White House, 18 July 1939 and WRC, letter to chairman advisory committee, 28 July 1939, NA-NRPB 597.7.

124. See hearings of both House and Senate Committees on Public Works on Flood Control Act of 1949, 81 Cong., 1 Sess.

125. For Russian River, see Sen. Com. on Public Works, 81 Cong., 1 Sess., Hearings on Flood Control Act of 1949, pp. 1064 ff. For Humboldt River, see Hearings on Flood Control Act of 1949, pp. 935 ff. For Neches Waterway, see Sen. Doc. 98, 76 Cong., 1 Sess.; and sec. 104 of the Rivers and Harbors Act of 1948, 62 Stat. 1171.

126. Re Rio Grande order, see NRC, Progress Report, 1936, p. 44; re PWA project review, see Brookings Institution report on Government activities in the field of public works and water resources, Sen. Doc. 1275, 75 Cong., 1 Sess., p. 288; re emergency flood control projects, see NRC, Drainage Basin, 1937, p. 59; re total cost of applications, see NRC, Progress Report, 1939, p. 11.

127. See pp. 88–90, supra. N. Y. Times, 7 April 1937.

128. The general confusion over review between 1937 and 1939 is described in chairman WRC, memo to advisory committee NRC, 28 April 1939, on review of War Department reports submitted for the NRC's comment, NA-NRPB 579.7.

129. Re short-circuiting of FIARBC, see Sen. and House Coms. on Public Works, 79 Cong., 2 Sess., Hearings on Flood Control Act of 1946 (HR 6597).

130. The evaluation subcommittee was superseded in October 1942 by a new Project Review Committee of the NRPB.

131. Statistics developed by Budget Bureau for use of Hoover Commission Task Force on Natural Resources. See Task Force Report, Appendix 3.

132. P. 108, supra.

133. NRC, Progress Report, 1936, pp. 3–4.

134. The Federal Employment Stabilization Board had collected from Federal agencies six-year programs of public works construction between 1932 and 1934, when it ceased activities due to lack of funds.

135. For the criteria see NRPB, Development of Resources, 1941, pt. 3, pp. 29–30.

136. President, memo to Congress, 17 March 1941, in transmitting report of NRPB on Development of Resources.

137. Various correspondence, January–February 1941, in NRPB public works committee files, NA-NRPB.

138. EO 9384, 4 October 1943.

RESPONSIBILITY TO PROFESSION

139. See, for example, House Com. on Appropriations, 79 Cong., 2 Sess., Hearings on War Department Civil Functions Appropriation Bill for 1947, pp. 148, 275.

140. Statement by the President in approving HR 6407 and HR 6597, 24 July 1946.

141. Several recent examples can be found among the Engineer Department projects in the Central Valley of California; see Chapter V.

142. As a recent example, President Truman was forced to yield to Congressional pressure and modify an anti-inflationary reserve set up for rivers and harbors and flood control appropriations, whereas similar reserves set up for other appropriations were not modified at that time. See *N. Y. Times*, 28 September 1946. The quotation is from National Rivers and Harbors Congress, *National Rivers and Harbors News*, January 1940.

CHAPTER FOUR

RESPONSIBILITY TO PROFESSION

1. David E. Lilienthal, *TVA–Democracy on the March* (New York, 1944), p. 58.

2. (a) Among Federal representatives, the following have been included: *From the Corps of Engineers:* G. E. Edgerton, J. P. Dean, E. M. Markham, W. A. Snow, P. A. Feringa, M. Reber, A. B. Jones, J. L. Schley, M. C. Tyler, C. W. Kutz, J. J. Kingman, E. Reybold, G. E. Textor, J. W. Kimbel, T. H. Robins. *From the Bureau of Reclamation:* J. C. Page, P. I. Taylor, W. R. Nelson, C. E. Fix, R. M. Patrick. *From the Geological Survey:* N. C. Grover, H. Stabler, G. L. Parker. *From the Fish and Wildlife Service:* W. B. Bell, E. Higgins, I. N. Gabrielson. *From other bureaus in the Department of Interior:* A. C. Fieldner, C. L. Wirth, J. D. Wolfsohn, E. F. Preece, E. C. Fortier, L. Muck. *From Soil Conservation Service:* H. H. Bennett, A. L. Patrick, H. G. Calkins, W. C. Lowdermilk, W. A. Hutchins, J. C. Jarvis. *From Forest Service:* E. N. Munns, T. W. Norcross. *From other bureaus in the Department of Agriculture:* S. H. McCrory, S. A. Rohwer, M. Eisenhower, H. H. Wooten, J. T. Wendzel, E. H. Wiecking, M. Regan, B. W. Allin, C. P. Barnes, P. Glick. *From TVA:* S. Woodward, B. M. Jones, C. H. Paul, A. E. Morgan, T. B. Parker. *From Federal Power Commission:* T. R. Tate, L. Olds, J. C. Beebe, W. W. Gatchell, R. B. McWhorter. *From Public Health Service:* R. E. Tarbett, L. L. Williams, J. K. Hoskins. *From Weather Bureau:* W. R. Gregg, M. Bernard. *From Federal Works Agency:* P. Fellows, W. N. Carey. *From Federal Communications Commission:* J. L. Fly (formerly TVA).

(b) Among State representatives, the following have been included: Edward Hyatt, State engineeer of California; Abel Wolman, chief engineer, Maryland State Department of Health; Clifford Stone, Director, Colorado Water Conservation Board; S. B. Morris, Department of Water and Power, Los Angeles, California.

(c) Private consultants and university professors have included: Thorndike Saville, New York University; Abel Wolman, Johns Hopkins University; Donald Baker, consulting engineer, Los Angeles; H. K. Barrows, Massachusetts Institute of Technology; W. W. Horner, consulting engineer, St. Louis; Joseph Jacobs, consulting engineer, Seattle; Royce Tipton, consulting engineer, Denver; J. J. Doland, University of Illinois; Carroll Merriam, Pennsylvania Water Power Co., Baltimore; Harlan Barrows, University of Chicago; Baldwin M. Woods, University of California; P. H. Cornick, Institute of Public Administration; Charles A. Lory, Estes Park, Colorado; Gordon M. Fair, Harvard University; and many other drainage basin consultants.

3. WRC, report on national water policy, in NRPB, *Development of Resources,* 1941, pt. 3, pp. 24 ff. Much of the material on tests (pp. 135–145 of this Chapter) is taken from this report. Where quotations on the tests are not otherwise credited, they are from pp. 24–44 of this report.

4. Analyses have been made also of planning for land drainage; protection and development of fish and wildlife; water pollution; recreational uses of water; and municipal and industrial supplies. Space limitations prevent their presentation here.

5. A subcommittee of the FIARBC has published a report recently (May 1950) entitled *Proposed Practices for Economic Analysis of River Basin Projects.* This section on economic soundness has been revised to reflect the findings of the subcommittee. However, it should be noted that these findings are almost identical with those of the WRC in 1941, though they are spelled out with considerably greater precision.

6. FIARBC, *Proposed Practices,* p. 24.

7. FIARBC, *Proposed Practices,* p. 37.

8. The problems of allocation of joint costs are not considered here. For a good discussion see FIARBC, *Proposed Practices,* p. 153.

9. If the standard of ability to repay, rather than benefits received, were adopted for the general repayment principle, then national benefits would have to be defined as those over and above the ability to repay of all other identifiable beneficiaries.

10. These quotations and other quotations in this section on flood control, unless otherwise indicated, are from Gilbert F. White, *Human Adjustment to Floods* (Chicago, 1945), pp. 205–211, 129, 2–3, 140. In several instances of enumeration White's text is followed closely without the use of quotations. Dr. White's book is largely an expansion and refinement of basic flood policy concepts accepted by the WRC. See, for example, NRC, *Drainage Basin,* 1937, pp. 68–79. Dr. White was for a time secretary of the Water and Land Committees of the NRPB and its predecessors.

11. Because this point is considered controversial by some, additional references are given: (a) Statement of C. P. Barnes, associate land use coördinator, Department of Agriculture, in House Com. on Flood Control, 78 Cong., 2 Sess., Hearings on Flood Control (HR 4485), p. 1119; (b) various articles by Bernard Frank in coöperation with others, for example, Frank and George R. Phillips, "To Help Control Floods," in *Trees,* 1949 Yearbook of Department of Agriculture, pp. 610–613.

12. NRC, *Drainage Basin,* 1937, p. 70.

13. Statement by chairman, subcommittee on national water policy at 3rd meeting, 11 December 1939, NA-NRPB 582.2.

14. Chairman NRPB, letter to President, 2 July 1940, on Report of Chief of Engineers on Thames River, Conn. and Mass., NA-NRPB 597.7.

15. This example is cited by White, *Human Adjustment,* p. 132.

16. The authority is contained in the Flood Control Act of 1938. USED reports on the Ohio Valley flood of 1937 gave some consideration to this alternative. In a few other reports it has been suggested that relocation might be desirable for occupance which could not be protected by levees. For example, report on Choctawhatchee River, Fla., House Doc. 242, 72 Cong., 1 Sess. See White, *Human Adjustment,* pp. 14–15, 188–189.

17. NRC, *Drainage Basin*, 1937, p. 71.
18. NRPB, *Development of Resources*, 1941, pt. 3, pp. 41, 43.
19. In several instances during 1940–41 the Chief of Engineers, in recommending local flood protection works, made as one of the conditions of Federal participation the enforcement by local interests of adequate measures to prevent further encroachment upon stream channels. None of these recommendations has thus far been adopted by the Congress in authorizing the construction of projects. (See White, *Human Adjustment*, p. 196.) In a report on the Missouri River (House Doc. 821, 76 Cong., 3 Sess.) levees were recommended for construction from Sioux City, Iowa, to Kansas City, Missouri, subject to the condition that the States having a common boundary on the River would, as a condition precedent to initiation of construction, establish by interstate compact floodway boundary lines and floodway regulations. However, in authorizing construction of the project in the 1941 Flood Control Act, Congress specifically eliminated such a requirement. It was eliminated first by the Senate Committee on Commerce, which in its report said only that this had been done "to facilitate the fulfillment by local interests of the requirements of local cooperation" (Sen. Rpt. 575, 77 Cong., 1 Sess.). The Committee hearings reveal that Senator Butler (Neb.) presented a short statement requesting deletion of the requirement due to the general difficulty of negotiating interstate compacts. The Engineer representative present at the hearing was not called upon, nor did he volunteer, to speak in defense of the proposal, and Senator Butler was not questioned by members of the Committee (Hearings on Flood Control Bill of 1941, p. 117). There was no significant discussion on the Senate floor (87 CR 6351) nor later in the House.
20. See pp. 83–86, *supra*.
21. These issues are brought out in the following documents: chairman NRC advisory committee, letter to acting director Budget Bureau, 8 December 1937, and enclosures, NA-NRPB 079; chairman NRC advisory committee, letter to President, 18 April 1938, and enclosure, NA-NRPB 077.21; chairman NRC advisory committee, letter to director Budget Bureau, 22 June 1938, and enclosure, NA-NRPB 075.6.
22. The Flood Control Act of 1941 reinstated the requirement of local contribution of lands, rights-of-way, and damages for channel improvements.
23. All quotations from sources cited in note 21, *supra*.
24. See, for example, USED, CL 3575, 23 February 1945.
25. House Doc. 271, 81 Cong., 1 Sess.
26. PL 516, 81 Cong., 1 Sess.
27. In this connection, A. E. Morgan, supported by his successful experience with the Miami Conservancy District, prepared a proposed Federal statute to insure beneficiary repayment through the organization of water control districts. This proposal was presented to the WRC (see S. Thompson memo, Toward a National Water Policy, 11 January 1940, NA-NRPB 578.1) and to the House Committee on Rivers and Harbors (see House Com. on Rivers and Harbors, 75 Cong., 2 Sess., Hearings on Regional Conservation).
28. NRPB, *National Resources Development*, 1943, pt. I, p. 49.
29. For example, the Transportation Committee of the National Resources Planning Board was unable to come to full agreement in its report on national transportation development policy before World War II made it inopportune to hold further meetings. A summary statement of findings and recommendations was prepared by the director of the study and published, along with contributions by committee staff specialists and by agencies within the Government

(*Transportation and National Policy*, May 1942). The Board of Investigation and Research, appointed under the Transportation Act of 1940, has published a report on public aids to domestic transportation (*Public Aids to Domestic Transportation*, House Doc. 159, 79 Cong., 1 Sess.). However, the report consists of a statement of a few recommendations agreed to by both Board members, lengthy separate statements of the two members, and a staff report which was neither accepted nor approved in full by either member, but largely for differing reasons. However, there are some points on which almost universal agreement has been reached and others on which a significant number of the experts are in accord.

30. Chairman, subcommittee on national water policy, comments on national policy concerning inland navigation, minutes 4th meeting of subcommittee, 13–15 January 1940, NA-NRPB 582.2.

31. BI&R, *Public Aids*, p. 24; Mr. Webb and the staff both emphasize this point. Similarly, the summary report of the NRPB transportation study states that "proper allowance should be made . . . for expenditures incurred by governments in the provision of facilities and services." (p. 7). The Transportation Task Force of the Hoover Commission agrees with this conclusion. Although the Task Force report has not been published, its authors, Charles L. Dearing and Wilfred Owen, have published a book, *National Transportation Policy* (Washington, 1949), based on their report. See Chapter XVI. See also Secretary of Commerce Sawyer's report to the President, entitled *Issues Involved in a Unified and Coördinated Federal Program for Transportation*, 1 December 1949, pp. 43–46.

32. Mississippi Valley Committee, *Report*, 1934, p. 41. NRC, *Drainage Basin*, 1937, p. 97. NRPB, *Development of Resources*, pt. 3, p. 36.

33. ICC in *Annual Report*, 1932, pp. 3, 18–19. Federal Coördinator of Transportation in *Public Aids to Transportation* (1938), vol. i, pp. vii, 55–58; and vol. iii, pp. 121–127. Committee of Six, *Report of Committee*, pp. 4, 19. This Committee, it should be pointed out, was composed of three railroad executives and three representatives of railway labor. NRPB, *Transportation*, pp. 9, 10, 257 ff. BI&R, *Public Aids*, recommendations and statement by Mr. Webb, pp. 3, 20 ff.; staff report, Chapter V. Mr. Childe opposes tolls, pp. 38, 961 ff. Dearing and Owen, *National Transportation Policy*, pp. 358–360, 377–378. Secretary of Commerce, *Issues Involved*, pp. 45–46.

34. Message of the President, accompanying Budget for Fiscal Year 1941, 3 January 1940.

35. BI&R, *Public Aids*, staff report, p. 413.

36. BI&R, *Public Aids*, statement of Mr. Webb, p. 24. Mr. Childe dissents from this conclusion, p. 858.

37. BI&R, *Public Aids*, staff report, p. 414.

38. As a warning, however, it should be noted that "while financing through user charges should promote a more economic use of public funds, this method does not provide an automatic guide by which the justification of investment can be determined. For although private outlays are deemed to be worth making if the result has a value sufficient to cover the cost, it cannot be said that public outlays are justified if costs are covered by user charges, since the user charge as a guide to investment has . . . defects . . . No one would argue that the amount a monopoly can exact under conditions of inelastic demand automatically determines justifiable investment. And in the case of transport facilities, not only is demand inelastic because of the generally essential nature of transportation, but the charge for using public facilities would in most cases be so small

RESPONSIBILITY TO PROFESSION 287

a part of total costs that it would possess 'the importance of being unimportant.' " (NRPB, *Transportation*, staff report on promotional policy, p. 258.)
39. NRPB, *Transportation*, staff report on promotional policy, pp. 257–259.
40. Dearing and Owen, *National Transportation Policy*, p. 367.
41. BI&R, *Public Aids*, staff report, p. 416.
42. These problems are pointed out by the BI&R (*Public Aids*, p. 3) and the staff of the NRPB (*Transportation*, pp. 262–263).
43. NRPB, *Transportation*, p. 264.
44. NRPB, WRC, minutes of 66th meeting, 8 November 1940, NA-NRPB 582.2.
45. "Inland Water Transportation," in NRPB, *Transportation*, pp. 443–446.
46. Act of 2 August 1882.
47. "Inland Water Transportation," in NRPB, *Transportation*, pp. 443–446.
48. The Engineers, of course, recognize this fact. See NRPB, *Transportation*, p. 446: "If agreement could be had on the volume of traffic involved . . ." etc. Note the use of *if*.
49. Unless otherwise cited, all information on this case study is from file NA-NRPB 734.121 and House Doc. 178, 76 Cong., 1 Sess.
50. NRPB, *Progress Report*, 1941, p. 33.
51. The Engineers use both the 37 cents and 36 cents figures. The use of both can be explained.
52. Sen. Com. on Commerce, 78 Cong., 2 Sess., Hearings on Rivers and Harbors Omnibus Bill (HR 3961), pt. 2; Sen. Rpt. 903, 78 Cong., 2 Sess.; 90 CR 8793–8820, 8873–8874.
53. 263 ICC 683 (2 October 1945) and 264 ICC 347 (4 March 1946).
54. NRC, *Drainage Basin*, 1937, p. 97. This conclusion is concurred in by the NRPB staff report on promotional policy (*Transportation*, pp. 267–268) and the BI&R staff report on *Public Aids*, p. 412.
55. For this project see House Doc. 394, 77 Cong., 1 Sess.; and NRPB evaluation sheets in NA files.
56. For this project see House Doc. 680, 80 Cong., 2 Sess.
57. For this project see Sen. Doc. 30, 81 Cong., 1 Sess.
58. Sen. Com. on Public Works, 80 Cong., 2 Sess., Legislative Calendar, 9 July 1948, p. 58.
59. House Doc. 269, 76 Cong., 1 Sess.
60. House Rpt. 1000, 78 Cong., 2 Sess.
61. House Doc. 486, 79 Cong., 2 Sess. Emphasis added in quotation that follows.
62. House Rpt. 2009 and Sen. Rpt. 1508, 79 Cong., 2 Sess.; 92 CR 6414, 6422, 8322.
63. Federal Coördinator of Transportation, *Public Aids*, vol. i, p. 79.
64. BI&R, *Public Aids*, staff report, pp. 398–399.
65. To be sure, there was a transportation shortage during the war, and there is an apparent threat of one today; but "the reason is not difficult to discover." It is not lack of railways and waterways. "Obviously it is not enough to provide a transportation system; it must be operated as a system. The Federal Government . . . has neglected to provide for such operation." (NRPB, *Transportation*, staff report on public promotional policy, pp. 272–273.)
66. NRPB, *Transportation*, summary report, p. 9. Mr. Webb and the staff of the BI&R agree in this conclusion: "It is apparent that the nature of this problem has changed in important respects. The policy of extending aids to transportation was begun when the primary aim was simply to increase trans-

portation facilities. Viewing the problem broadly from the standpoint of the public interest, it is clear that what is needed now is a policy which will give proper recognition to the influence of public aids upon the functioning of the domestic transportation system as a whole." (*Public Aids*, p. 6.)

Federal transportation legislation reflects this change. Thus, the Transportation Act of 1920 places emphasis on the *further development* of water transportation (sec. 500), whereas the Transportation Act of 1940 stresses *preservation* of the inherent advantage of each mode of transport.

67. BI&R, *Public Aids*, staff report, pp. 401–402.
68. House Doc. 269, 76 Cong., 1 Sess.
69. House Doc. 486 and Sen. Rpt. 1508, 79 Cong., 2 Sess.
70. Among others, the members and staff of the BI&R have proposed this. See *Public Aids*, pp. 398–399.
71. NRPB, *Resources Development Report*, 1943, pt. 1, p. 48.
72. MVC, *Report*, 1934, pp. 43–55. NRC, WRC, *Drainage Basin*, 1937, pp. 55–57. NRC, ERC, *Energy Resources and National Policy*, 1939, pp. 25–28, 274–281; and "Energy Development Policies," in *Development of Resources*, 1941, pt. 3, pp. 53–59. PNRPC, *Regional Planning Part I, Pacific Northwest*, 1936. NPPC, *Report*, published as Sen. Doc. 21, 75 Cong., 1 Sess. For Presidents Roosevelt and Truman, see later references in this section to Flood Control Act of 1944. For Department of Interior, same. For Federal Power Commission, see especially Federal Power Acts of 1920 and 1935.
73. NRC, *Drainage Basin*, 1937, p. 9.
74. NRC, *Energy*, pp. 276–277.
75. An example of delay is Norfork Dam, White River, Ark. (see WRC draft report on national water policy, 8 October 1940, p. 8, NA-NRPB 578.1). Also, FPC, *Annual Report*, 1939, p. 18; Robert D. Baum, *The Federal Power Commission and State Utility Regulation* (Washington, 1942), pp. 127–130.
76. For legislation to place Cumberland River under TVA, see the following: House Doc. 107, 79 Cong., 1 Sess.; Sen. Com. on Agriculture & Forestry, 77 Cong., 1 Sess., Hearings on Including Cumberland River Basin in TVA (S 1539); Sen. Rpt. 567, 77 Cong., 1 Sess.; 87 CR 6790, 7445.
77. House Doc. 761, 79 Cong., 2 Sess. All information that follows on the comprehensive report is taken from this document or House Doc. 107, 79 Cong., 1 Sess. Emphasis added.
78. See, for example, periodic reports in Nashville *Tennesseean* in 1950.
79. President, letter to Rep. Mansfield, 7 February 1944. Copy available in Franklin D. Roosevelt Library, Hyde Park, New York.
80. NRC, Pacific Northwest Planning Commission, *Regional Planning Part I*, p. xvii.
81. President, letter to Rep. Mansfield, 7 February 1944.
82. Task Force Report, pp. 70–71.
83. 34 Stat. 116; 41 Stat. 1063.
84. Bonneville Power Act of 1937, 50 Stat. 731.
85. NRC, Pacific Northwest Planning Commission, *Regional Planning Part I*, p. xvii.
86. Secretary of War, letter to chairman NRC, 11 April 1936, NA-NRPB, old file not numbered, entitled Flood Control General. Also House Com. on Rivers and Harbors, 75 Cong., 1 Sess., Hearings on Bonneville Project (HR 7642, etc.), pp. 52 ff., esp. p. 60; Sen. Com. on Agriculture & Forestry, 74 Cong., 2 Sess., Hearings on Columbia River (S 869, etc.), pp. 15–16, 223 ff., 249–250.
87. House Doc. 647, 78 Cong., 2 Sess., Blakely Mountain Dam; House Doc.

KINGS RIVER PROJECT

651, 78 Cong., 2 Sess., Des Moines River; Sen. Doc. 189, 78 Cong., 2 Sess., Santee and Congaree Rivers, N. C. and S. C.; House Doc. 650, 78 Cong., 2 Sess., Roanoke River, Va. and N. C.; House Doc. 652, 78 Cong., 2 Sess., Yadkin-Pee Dee River, S. C.; House Doc. 657, 78 Cong., 2 Sess., Savannah River, Ga.

88. President, letter to Rep. Mansfield, 7 February 1944.
89. 90 CR 2764, 2846–2848.
90. House Rpt. 1309, 78 Cong., 2 Sess.; 90 CR 4114–4150, 4194–4232.
91. For example, see the President's letters of 11 May 1944 (Sen. Com. on Commerce, 78 Cong., 2 Sess., Hearings on Rivers and Harbors Omnibus Bill, HR 3961, pt. 6, p. 993); and of 13 June 1944 (90 CR 6370).
92. Sen. Com. on Commerce, 78 Cong., 2 Sess., Hearings on Flood Control Bill of 1944 (HR 4485), p. 11.
93. House Com. on Public Works, 80 Cong., 1 Sess., Hearings on Section 5 of Flood Control Act (HR 3036). The quotations from the hearings can be found at pp. 58, 440, 441, 457–459.
94. Of course, FPC has authority under Sec. 205 of its basic statute (49 Stat. 835) to regulate rates for wholesale interstate transmission of all power; but this authority is not in question here. The Dondero bill would not increase or decrease this authority.
95. President, letter to Rep. Mansfield, 7 February 1944.
96. See, for example, reports on Kern River, Calif. (House Doc. 513, 78 Cong., 1 Sess.), transmitted 20 March 1944; Littlejohn Creek and Calaveras River Stream Groups, Calif. (House Doc. 545, 78 Cong., 2 Sess.), transmitted 17 April 1944; Kaweah and Tule Rivers, Calif. (House Doc. 559, 78 Cong., 2 Sess.), transmitted April 1944; Sacramento River and Tributaries, Calif. (House Doc. 649, 78 Cong., 2 Sess.), transmitted 30 May 1944. All of these projects in the Central Valley are not in accord with the President's program primarily because they should be part of a closely integrated basin plan in which the dominant interest is water conservation under the jurisdiction of the Bureau of Reclamation. If, however, the Engineer Department chose to disregard this fact and nonetheless recommend the projects to Congress, then it can be further criticized for not providing that the irrigation features of the projects be administered under reclamation law.
97. After a provision for control by Department of Interior of irrigation features of Engineer Department dams had passed the House and was being considered for minor amendment in the Senate Committee on Commerce, the following exchange took place:

"Sen. Millikin. Perhaps I can short circuit my further examination by asking whether you approve or disapprove of those amendments [perfecting amendments to the provisions already enacted in the House bill]?

"Col. Reber. I see no objection, Senator Millikin, to either of these two amendments as they stand in front of me right here." (Sen. Com. on Commerce, 78 Cong., 2 Sess., Hearings on Flood Control (HR 4485), p. 728.)

But this statement can hardly be interpreted as support for the President's program for irrigation development.

CHAPTER FIVE

THE KINGS RIVER PROJECT IN THE BASIN OF THE GREAT CENTRAL VALLEY

1. This case study was prepared originally for the Hoover Commission Task Force on Natural Resources (Task Force Report, Appendix 7). It has since been

revised and published as a public administration case study by the Committee on Public Administration Cases, Washington, D. C. The case here presented differs in some respects from the earlier versions.

2. Most of the information on early planning was obtained from the following: (a) NA-NRPB 516.22, 579.7; (b) House Com. on Flood Control, 76 Cong., 3 Sess., Hearings on Comprehensive Flood Control (HR 9640), pp. 560–562; (c) The printed survey reports of the two agencies: Corps of Engineers, House Doc. 630, 76 Cong., 3 Sess.; Bureau of Reclamation, House Doc. 631, 76 Cong., 3 Sess.

3. Most of the information on basic differences was obtained from the following: (a) The agency survey reports: Corps of Engineers, House Doc. 630, 76 Cong., 3 Sess. and Bureau of Reclamation, House Doc. 631, 76 Cong., 3 Sess.; (b) Letter from Secretary of the Interior, 10 June 1940, transmitting to Congress communication from President concerning Kings River project, House Doc. 631, 76 Cong., 3 Sess., Part 2; (c) Memos on project reports dated 12 April, 15 May, and 20 May 1940 in files of NRPB, NA-NRPB 579.7; (d) Report on allocation of costs of Kings River, 31 January 1947, House Doc. 136, 80 Cong., 1 Sess.

4. From minutes of a meeting of the California Central Valley–Central Coast Drainage Basin Committee at Hanford, Calif., 14 April 1939, NA-NRPB 516.22.

5. Most of the information on the period 1940 to 1944 was obtained from the following: (a) NA-NRPB 579.7; (b) House Com. on Flood Control, 76 Cong., 3 Sess., Hearings on Flood Control Plans (HR 9640), pp. 517–578, 950–956; House Rpt. 2103, 76 Cong., 3 Sess.; (c) House Com. on Flood Control, 77 Cong., 1 Sess., Hearings on Flood Control Plans and New Projects (HR 4911), pp. 93–114, 159–166, 176–195; (d) House Rpt. 1174, 77 Cong., 1 Sess.; (e) House Com. on Flood Control, 78 Cong., 2 Sess., Hearings on Flood Control Plans and New Projects (HR 4485), pp. 636–638.

6. Most of the information on the Interior Dept. appropriation request was obtained from the following: (a) House Doc. 480, 78 Cong., 2 Sess.; (b) House Com. on Appropriations, 78 Cong., 2 Sess., Hearings on Interior Dept. Appropriation Bill for 1945, pp. 730–735, 1138–1148; House Rpt. 1395, 78 Cong., 2 Sess.; (c) Sen. Com. on Appropriations, 78 Cong., 2 Sess., Hearings on Interior Dept. Appropriation Bill for 1945, pp. 216–218, 335–337, 372–373, 663; Sen. Rpt. 899, 78 Cong., 2 Sess.; (d) House Rpt. 1678, 78 Cong., 2 Sess.

7. Most of the information on the Flood Control Act of 1944 was obtained from the following: (a) House Com. on Flood Control, 78 Cong., 2 Sess., Hearings on Flood Control Plans and New Projects (HR 4485), pp. 611–652, 737–768; House Rpt. 1369, 78 Cong., 2 Sess.; (b) Sen. Com. on Commerce, 78 Cong., 2 Sess., Hearings on Flood Control (HR 4485), pp. 11–14, 201–264, 276–340, 362–364, 449, 452–455, 459–465; Sen. Rpt. 1030, 78 Cong., 2 Sess.; (c) House Doc. 545, 78 Cong., 2 Sess., pp. xi–xii; (d) 90 CR 4119 ff., 7882–3, 8185 ff., 9264.

8. Most of the information on the Rivers and Harbors Act of 1945 was obtained from the following: (a) 90 CR 2921–4, 8875, 9478, 9493, 9745, 9787; (b) Sen. Com. on Commerce, 78 Cong., 2 Sess., Hearings on Rivers and Harbors (HR 3961), pt. 4, p. 529, pt. 5, pt. 6, p. 993; Sen. Rpt. 903, 78 Cong., 2 Sess.; (c) Sen. Rpt. 22 and House Rpt. 63, 79 Cong., 1 Sess.; (d) 91 CR 1381.

9. Most of the information on the appropriations for preconstruction operations was obtained from the following: (a) House and Senate, 79 Cong., 1 Sess., Hearings, reports, and debate on the War Dept. Civil Functions Appropri-

KINGS RIVER PROJECT

ation Bill for 1946 (HR 2126); (b) House and Senate, 79 Cong., 1 Sess., Hearings, reports, and debate on Interior Dept. Appropriation Bill for 1946 (HR 3024); (c) House and Senate, 79 Cong., 1 Sess., Hearings, reports, and debate on First Deficiency Appropriation Bill for 1945 (HR 2374); (d) Sen. Com. on Appropriations, 79 Cong., 2 Sess., Hearings on War Dept. Civil Functions Appropriation Bill for 1947 (HR 5400), pp. 521–523.

10. Most of the information on application of Section 8 of the Flood Control Act of 1944 was obtained from the following: (a) Sen. Com. on Appropriations, 79 Cong., 2 Sess., Hearings on War Dept. Civil Functions Appropriation Bill for 1947 (HR 5400), pp. 521–523; (b) Proceedings of California Water Conference, 6–7 December 1945, State Capitol, Sacramento, Calif., pp. 72–75; (c) House Doc. 136, 80 Cong., 1 Sess.; (d) House Doc. 367, 81 Cong., 1 Sess.

11. Most of the information on appropriations for construction was obtained from the following: (a) House and Senate, 79 Cong., 1 Sess., Hearings, reports, and debate on First Deficiency Appropriation Bill for 1946 (HR 4805); (b) House and Senate, 79 Cong., 2 Sess., Hearings, reports, and debate on War Dept. Civil Functions Appropriation Bill for 1947 (HR 5400); (c) House and Senate, 79 Cong., 2 Sess., Hearings, reports, and debate on Interior Dept. Appropriation Bill for 1947 (HR 6335).

12. Most of the information on allocation of costs and repayment arrangements was obtained from the following: (a) House Doc. 136, 80 Cong., 1 Sess.; (b) 96 CR (temp.) 11645–6 (1 August 1950). Emphasis added in quotation.

13. Most of the information on benefit allocations was obtained from the following: (a) NRPB file NA-NRPB 579.7; (b) House Doc. 630, 76 Cong., 3 Sess.; (c) House Doc. 136, 80 Cong., 1 Sess.; (d) Bureau of Reclamation, Transcript of public meeting on Kings River Project, Fresno Memorial Auditorium, Fresno, Calif., 30 July 1946; (e) House Doc. 367, 81 Cong., 1 Sess.

14. Most of the information on the Central Valley comprehensive plans was obtained from the following: (a) House Doc. 367, 81 Cong., 1 Sess.; (b) Sen. Doc. 113, 81 Cong., 1 Sess.; (c) House Com. on Public Lands, 81 Cong., 2 Sess., Hearings on Kings River (HR 5264, 6919); (d) House Doc. 537, 81 Cong., 2 Sess.; (e) FPC Opin. No. 183, 9 November 1949, on Projects Nos. 1925, 175, 1988; (f) 38 Calif. L. Rev. 630–636, 689, 717–728.

15. Task Force Report, p. 23.
16. Task Force Report, p. 29.
17. Task Force Report, p. 28.
18. Task Force Report, pp. 24–25.
19. NRPB, subcommittee on national water policy, minutes of 5th meeting, 28–30 November 1940, NA-NRPB 578.1.

Index

For identification of abbreviations, see pages 263–264.

Acreage limitations, 144, 205, 216, 221, 228, 235–236; in Kings River project, 238, 241, 244, 249, 253
Adjustments, flood hazard, types, 146–147; evaluation, 148; most effective, 149
Administrative responsibility: criteria for gauging, 1–19; and group interest adjustment, 37–60; overemphasis on local interests, 51–57; avoidance, 52, 56–57; shifting, 57–60. *See also* Agency responsibility, Bureau of Reclamation, *and* United States Engineer Department
Advance of capital, construction projects, 157–158
Agency responsibility: public policy, 3–4; in mediation, 4; to electorate, 4–5; information, 5; to pressure groups, 5–8; to legislature, 8–13; to chief executive, 8, 9, 13–15, 101–102; to political parties, 16; to profession, 16–18, 134–207; to courts, 18–19; in conflicting obligations, 19. *See also* Administrative responsibility *and* United States Engineer Department
Allen, Rep. A. Leonard, 48, 55, 56
Amendments, to project bills, 32–33
Amortization, uniform, 139–140; deferment of charges, 143
Annual Report of Chief of Engineers, 35, 57–58
Appropriations: rivers and harbors, 21; flood control, 21; Army Department Civil Functions Appropriations Bill, 34; public works coördination, 109–110; projects construction and timing, 220; Interior Department Appropriations Bill, 1945, 227–228, 238; Kings River project, 238–240, 243–246
Arkansas and Louisiana, and Des Moines River project, 200
Arkansas, water plan, 92
Army. *See* United States Engineer Department
Army Department Civil Appropriations Bill, 34
Army-Interior Agreement, limitations, 119–120
Atlantic Deeper Waterways Association: objectives, 41; officers, 41, 42, 43; relations with USED, 41–42; relations with Congress, 42–43; effectiveness, 43

Atlantic Intercoastal Waterway, 41, 42
Authorization, Congressional, projects construction, 30–33; effect on group interest adjustment, 52; effect on USED responsibility to Congress, 63; flood control and irrigation projects, 218; and timing, 220

Backbone transmission grid, 197; purpose, 198; USED views, 199; Dondero amendment, to Flood Control Act of 1944, 201–204
Bailey, Sen. Joseph William, cited, 32, 59
Barkley, Sen. Alben, 44–45, 105, 106
Barrows, of WRC, 103
Basin-wide plans, sound, 118–122, 136–137; preparatory steps, 69–71; identification of problems, 69; determination of objectives, 69–70; interpretation of basic data, 70; formulation of development plan, 70; translation into specific projects, 70, 122–124; construction program, 70–71, 129–132; interagency coöperation, 71; review, 124–129; failure of USED in Lake Erie-Ohio River Canal, 167–177; principles, USED violations, 187, 188; USED failure in Cumberland dam project, 194–195; Roosevelt letter on, 233
Beaver Canal project, 167
Beaver River Basin. *See* Lake Erie-Ohio River Canal
Benefit-cost evaluations, 184–188; increased traffic, 185; national defense, 186; effect of user charges on local contributions, 186; review of use and cost, 187
Benefits, incremental, 140; of flood abatement, 146; relation to costs, 148; limitation, 158; navigation projects, USED estimates, 160–161, 166–167; local, proportionate contributions for, 178; in St. Mary's River project, 180; Federal policy, 180; crediting, 183, 184; water projects, relation to costs, 138–139, 148–149; national, 141–142; distribution in Kings River project, 216; allocation, Kings River project, 249–250. *See also* Flood Control Acts, United States Engineer Department, *and individual projects*
Bills, projects, drafting, 31
Black Butte Reservoir, 250
Blakely Mountain Dam, project, 39, 200

Board of Engineers: review of survey reports, 29; approval of project reports, 32; recommendations on Nashville power dam, 193
Board of Engineers for Rivers and Harbors: function, 22; action in unfavorable reports, 26; hearings, 26; review of preliminary examination reports, 27; recommendations to Chief of Engineers, 27; approval of revision of Commercial Point project, 179; recommendation of Tombigbee project, 183; report on Kings River project, 214
Board of Impartial Analysis, 112
Board of Investigation and Research, 161, 185
Bonneville Dam, 198, 200
Budget: agency, legislative committee review, 12; of Chief of Engineers, 35; President's, 1946, 238. *See also* Bureau of the Budget
Budget, Director of the, 200, 243
Bulkheads, emergency, 147
Bullards Bar, 250
Bureau of Agricultural Economics, and Tripartite Agreement, 101
Bureau of the Budget: clearance, agency programs, 15; unfavorable preliminary examinations, 27; clearance, survey reports, 30; approval of projects, 34; advice on total projects sums, 35; rules on appropriations requests, 57; USED violation of rules, 57-59; action on USED-Congress relations, 68; clearance of Secretary of War's report on SJR 57, 85); failure to notify NRC, 88; fiscal planning, 99; executive order on agency responsibility to chief executive, 101-102; USED conflict with, 1943-1950, 108-112; and public works coördination, 109-110, 111; Task Force findings on clearance procedure, 114; review of agency reports, 126, 127; 6-year programs, 129, 130-131; in President's office, 129; resources development budget, 130; letter on Green and Duwamish rivers project, 157; review of USED reports, 180, 181; position on Hollywood and Miami projects, 182; action on Kings River projects, 226, 234, 237, 250
Bureau of Reclamation, 45; action on USED-Congress relationship, 68; and Tripartite Agreement, 101; proposals of Task Force on, 113; conflict with USED, 114; competition with USED on basinwide planning, 122; WRC evaluation committee, 126; power policies, 199, 218-219, 252; irrigation policies, 204-207; support of reclamation law, 207, 235; report on Kings River project, 208, 211, 214; objectives in Kings River project, 209, 215-221; water use philosophy, 215, 255; support of Administration policy, Kings River project, 224, 231; construction of Kings River project, 238; negotiation of repayment contracts, Kings River project, 248-249; plan for Pine Flat power dam, 251; Folsom formula, 251; concept of administrative responsibility, 255-256; planning, 256
Bureaucracy, significance and influence, 2-5, 9-10, 17-18
Burton, Sen. Harold Hitz, 176
Byrnes, Sen. James Francis, 95, 105

Cabinet Resources Board, 75
California, flood control, 48; cost allocation, in Kings River project, 246. *See* Kings River project
Caney Fork power project, 190
Cape Canaveral Harbor project, 48, 182
Caraway, Sen. Hattie Wyatt, 87
Carthage power project, 190
Case, Rep. Francis Higbee, 46, 108, 109-110
Celina power project, 190
Center Hill power project, 190
Central Valley projects: USED and Reclamation reports, 121, 250; Basin described, 208-210; water needs, 209; Roosevelt letter, 233; application of reclamation law, 235-237; unity, 239; application of Section 8, 240-243; President's plan, 246; Kings River and, 250-252; conflict, 252-259. *See also* Kings River project
Channel improvements, 146, 149; provisions, Flood Control Bill of 1938, 154-155; present financing policy, 156
Charleston Harbor improvement, 48
Cheatham power project, 190
Chesapeake and Ohio Canal, building, 21
Chief of Engineers: responsibility to Secretary of War, 21-22; assistance, 22; cost estimates, preliminary examinations, 23; action on preliminary examinations, 27, 28; priority assignments, 29, 71-72; survey recommendations to Congress, 29, 30; allotment of lump-sum appropriations for projects, 34; approval of projects reports, 34; reports to Atlantic Deeper Waterways Ass'n, 42; failure to resolve conflicts, Mississippi flood control project, 55, 56; *Annual Report*, 57-59; provisions of final reorganization bill on, 96; report on Kings River

INDEX

project, 213–214. *See* United States Engineer Department
Chief executive: and agency-legislative liaison, 4, 8; agency responsibility to, 5, 10, 11, 13–15, 61–68; relations with legislature, 9; freedom from Congressional sanction, 9; role in coördinating agency programs, 10; agency conformance to program, 13; resolution of conflicting agency obligations, 19; shifting of responsibility to, by USED, 57–60; value of direct agency responsibility to, 61; criteria of USED responsibility to, 61–62, 73–74; denial of veto, 62; failure to break USED-Congress relations, 62; relation with USED and Congress in flood protection policy, 84. *See* Executive Office of the President, Roosevelt, Truman
Citizens' Committee for the Hoover Report, 118
Civilian Conservation Corps, 125
Clark Hill power project, 203
Clearance, agency, inadequacies, 15; projects, 30, 85, 167–177
Cochran, Rep. John Joseph, 95
Columbia Basin Inter-Agency Committee, 110–111; Department of Interior Report, 119–120; failure to evolve unified plan, 119–120
Committee on Administrative Management, 94
Committee on Agriculture and Forestry (Senate), 98
Committee on Appropriations (House): action on agency budgets, 12; action on NRPB appropriation, 104–105; hearings on Interior Appropriations Bill, 1945, 227; hearings on Kings River project, 238
Committee on Appropriations (Senate): action on agency budgets, 12; action on NRPB appropriations, 104–105; and USED, in Kings River project, 227–228; hearings on Kings River project, 243
Committee on Commerce (Senate): procedures on tabled reports, 27–28; and USED, 63; domination of NWC, 66; hearings on permanent planning board bill, 77; action on Flood Control Bill of 1935, 83, 84; USED relations with, 100; review of Miami Harbor report, 182–183; hearings on Flood Control Bill of 1944, 200–201, 234
Committee on Expenditures, 67–68
Committee on Flood Control (House), 30, 87; procedures on tabled reports, 27–28; and USED, 62, 89–90, 100; hearings on Kings River project, 223, 224, 228; report on Kings River project, 225, 227, 234; and Kern River project, 234; hearings, Pine Flat Dam project, 229, 230, 231–232; authorization, Kings River project, 249
Committee on Public Lands (House), 77, 78, 251
Committee on Public Works (House), 201; policy on preliminary examinations, 23; projects review, 23; reëxamination of survey reports, 30
Committee on Public Works (Senate): policy on preliminary examinations, 23; projects review, 23; failure to revise procedures on tabled reports, 28; reëxamination of survey reports, 30; referral of projects bills to, 32; hearings on Army-Interior Agreement, 120
Committee on Rivers and Harbors (House): consideration of tabled reports, 27–28; review resolutions, 1935, 40; and USED, 62, 100; domination of IWC, 66; opposition to transfer of USED's civil functions, 67–68; hearings on conservation proposals, 97–98; on Commercial Point project, 179; Tombigbee project report, 184; action on power policy legislation, 200; Roosevelt letter to, 206
Committee on Waterflow, President's, 1934, 72–74, 118
Committee resolutions, Congressional, 38–40, 62
Committees: interdepartmental, 15; intraagency, 15; Congressional, relations with National Rivers and Harbors Congress, 49; USED relations, 62, 63; attitude on NRB, 80
Congress: loss of power, 9; authorization of projects, 22; local requests for project surveys, 23; reports of unfavorable preliminary examinations to, 27; approval of projects, 34; transfer of responsibility in group interests adjustment, 38, 52; pressure techniques, 38–40, 63; relations with USED, 40, 62–63; committee responsibility, 62; USED responsibility to, 63, 74, 88–89, 99, 100, 101, 117–118, 119; attitude on USED's project investigations, 123; authorization of USED projects conflicting with President's program, 128; authorization of USED relocation contributions, 150; response to USED recommendations, 179, 180, 181, 182; response to Budget Bureau recommendations on cost benefits, 179–180, 187; authorization of USED report on Cumberland River project, 194; action on Kings River project, 236–237, 238–239; effect of multiple committees on interagency conflict, 258

Connecticut Valley project, 156
Consent, public, agency programs, 5–6, 7; limitations on, 6; USED techniques, 52, 56, 57
Conservation legislation, regional, 1937, 97–101; report by USED, 98–99
Construction programs, 129–132
Consultation, interagency, 211–212
Coördination, interagency: need, 14–15; of related government programs, 61; position of Theodore Roosevelt, 65; procedure for, 69–72; organization for, 69–72; Task Force recommendations, 112; pattern for, 118–132; failure, water projects, 255–259; defects, 257–258
Coöperatives, distribution, 144
Copeland, Sen. Royal S., 44, 77, 80
Cost-benefit ratio, projects: analysis by field engineers, 29; formula, 148; use in New Creek report, 150; USED use in flood protection justification, 150–151; in Kings River project, 219–220
Costs: incremental, 140; water and rail rates compared, 160–161, 163, 165; allowance for public, 161; relation to rates, 162, 163; USED policy 164–165; damages payments, 178. See also Estimates
Courts, agency responsibility to, 9, 18–19
Cumberland River power development: conflict, 190, 193–196; Cumberland and Tennessee River basins (map), 191; list of projects and purposes, 192
Cumberland Road continuation, 21

Dale Hollow, power project, 190
Damages, payment, as cost contribution, 178
Davenport, Fred M., 68
Dearing Report, 161, 163
Decentralization, of planning responsibility, 256–257
Definite projects reports: aims, 33; machinery, 33–34
Delano, Frederic A., 77, 107; Roosevelt letter to, 93; report on Youngstown steel negotiations, 171–173, 175, 177
Delta-Mendota Canal, 209
Department of Agriculture: USED coöperation with, 25; submission of unfavorable reports to, 27; coöperation with War Department, flood control studies, 83; objections to emergency flood control legislation, 1935, 84; investigation of upstream watershed protection, 123; representation on WRC, evaluation committee, 126; position on Cumberland-TVA project, 190; and Tripartite Agreement, 212

Department of Interior: USED coöperation with, 25; submission of unfavorable reports to, 27; proposed transfer of waterways activities to, 67; abolition, proposed by Task Force, 113; proposal for consolidation of water functions with USED's, 113; standards for hydroelectric power, 188; as power marketing agency, 200; policy on irrigation land sales, 206; proposed transfer of irrigation projects to, 206; support of reclamation laws, 207; and Tripartite Agreement, 212; Appropriations Bill, 1945, 227–228, 238; views on Kings River project, 234: cost allocation, Kings River project, 246
Dern, Secretary of War: opposition to interagency coördination on water use, 73–74; opposition to President's attempt to break direct USED-Congressional relations, 74; letter to Ickes, 75; attitude on NRB, 75, 76, 77, 78–80; opposition to WRC program, 82–83
Detroit Edison Company, 180–181
Detroit River. See Trenton Channel project
Dislocation, of residents, evaluation, 195; objections of Cumberland Valley residents, 193
Distance zone, effect on power rates, 197
District engineer, 22; role in preliminary examinations, 24; survey of rivers and harbor projects, 29; report of changes in local interest, 29; 6-year funds programs, 35; assignment of project priorities, 35; preparation of part of *Annual Report of Chief of Engineers,* 35; public hearings by, 37, 38, 39; appeals for Congressional hearings, 38–39; relations with Members of Congress, 63; survey of Kings River project, 214
Diversions, 146
Division engineers, 22; review of survey reports, 29; review of definite project reports, 34
Dockweiler, Rep. John Francis, cited, 39
Dominant interest theory, projects construction, 225, 230–231, 233; failure in interagency coördination, 256
Dondero, Rep. George Anthony, cited, 100; proposed repeal of Section 5, Flood Control Act of 1944, 201–203, 204
Drainage basin committees, aims, 118–119
Drainage Basin Problems and Programs, WRC report, 91–92, 118; 1937 revision, 93
Driver, Rep. William, cited, 58–59, 95–96
Dump power, 196–197

Easements, procurement, 53
Eastman, 171

INDEX

Economic justification: principles, in water project plans, 138–141; of flood control measures, formula, 147–148; formulas, 148, 151; benefits estimates by USED, 166–167; in Lake Erie and Ohio Canal project, 167–177; competitive navigation facilities, 181–187, 185, 186; based on overrated traffic increases, 185; based on national defense needs, 185–186; Tombigbee project, 186; hydroelectric power, 189

Economy Act of 1932, 67; House disapproval of Hoover's executive orders under, 67–68

Edgerton, Lt. Col., 84; flood control studies program, 81–82; "about-face" on Flood Control Bill, 85; dissent from WRC position on Flood Control Bill of 1936, 154

Elliott, Rep., on Kings River project, 238

Elliott rider, Rivers and Harbors Act of 1945, 238

Engineer Corps. *See* United States Engineer Department

Englebright, Rep. Harry Lane, cited, 90

Erosion control, 146

Estimates, of cost-benefit ratio of projects, 29; annual budget, of USED, 34; on projects costs, by District Engineers, 35

Eudora floodway, 53–54

Evacuation, temporary, value, 149

Executive-legislative relationships, laws, 3–4, 5–6, 8–10; in agency administration, 10; budget, 12

Executive agencies: coördination, 13; USED relations, 63. *See* Chief executive, Executive Office of the President, *and individual agencies*

Executive Office of the President, 194; budget rules, 57; USED violations of rules, 57–59; USED relations with, 63; attempts to break USED-Congress direct relations, 68; attempts to improve water planning procedures, 101–102; review of project plans, 112; final review reports to, 126; clearance of USED reports, 127; tabulation of reports, 128; ineffectiveness in imposing planning views on USED and Congress, 128; budgetary techniques, 130–132; action on Central Valley projects, 250, 251; avoidance of planning leadership, 258. *See also* Bureau of the Budget

Executive Orders: No. *8455,* 126, 129–130; No. *9384,* 127

Federal Coördinator of Traffic, 185
Federal Coördinator of Transportation, 161
Federal government: taxing power, 142–143; contribution to water developments, 141–142; advance of capital for construction, 143; state regulatory measures, 144; criticisms of flood plain occupance policy, 151–152

Federal Inter-Agency River Basin Committee, 110; Task Force report on, 113–114; lack of basin-planning staff, 119; informed of USED and Reclamation reports on Columbia Basin plan, 121; failure to resolve differences in Central Valley reports, 121, 250–251; failure to resolve conflicts in reports, 126; USED attitude toward, 126; estimate of economic life of project, 139; effect of unanimity rule on agency coördination, 258

Federal Power Commission: USED coöperation with, 25; submission of unfavorable reports to, 27; establishment, 67, 198; omission, in SJR *57,* 91; Task Force proposals, 113; overlapping of functions with USED, 114; representation on WRC evaluation committee, 126; hydroelectric power standards, 188; recommendations on penstocks, 189; relations with USED, 189–190; position on Cumberland-TVA project, 190, 194; shaping of Federal power policy, 198; favored by USED for power agency, 202, 203; support of Dondero amendment, Flood Control Act, 1944, 204; limitations on control of consumer rates, 204-205; licensing power, 218, 219; recommendations, Central Valley project, 252

Feringa, Col., cited, 202–203

Flood abatement, 146; emergency measures, 147; survey of measures, Department of Agriculture, 150; stimulus to uneconomic occupance, 151. *See also* Flood control

Flood control, 145–146; appropriations and authorization, 21; adjustment of occupance, 146–147; USED policy appraised, 149–153

Flood Control Act, 1936, 21, 123, 210; cost provisions, 153–154; first authorization of multiple-purpose projects, 189

Flood Control Act, 1938: Roosevelt's reservations, 86; financing of reservoir projects, 154; penstocks provisions, 189

Flood Control Act, 1939, 97

Flood Control Act, 1941, 56

Flood Control Act, 1944, 123; controversy, 111; advance in water planning, 127; Section 5, 199; Dondero amendment, 201-204; Section 8, 206, 235–237, 240–243, 244, 245

Flood Control Act, 1950, 157

Flood control acts, 45

Flood Control Bill, 1935, 83–84; defects, 84–85
Flood Control Bill, 1936, and NRC bill, 80; USED-NRC conflict, 81
Flood Control Bill, 1941, 225
Flood Control Bill, 1944, 200, 201, 227, 228–238; Commerce Committee hearings, 200–201, 234, 235; provisions of Section 8, 235–237; application of Section 8 to Central Valley projects, 240–242; Truman comment, 240–241; Major Robins' interpretation of Section 8, 241, 242; newspaper comments, 241, 242, 244, 245
Flood control bills, machinery, 23. *See also* Flood Control Acts
Flood control law, contrasted with irrigation law, 216–218
Flood control projects: expenditures, 43; regional sponsorship, 40–45; national group sponsorship, 45–50; emergency, review, 125; submission of plans, 125–126; formula for sound policy, 146–149; USED policy, 149–153, 157–159; present policy, defects, 153, 157–159; violations of sound policy, 153–157; USED objectives in Kings River project, 215
Flood control studies, USED recommendations, 81; and allied problems, 81–82; approved by Roosevelt, 82
Flood losses, causes, 145–146; prevention, 145–147, 149, 150; insurance, 147, 149; best means of reducing, 146; USED policy of prevention, 153
Flood plain occupance, 145; types of adjustment, 146–147; evaluation of adjustments, 147–148; most effective, 149; uneconomic occupance, 150–151, 153; WRC policy, 151–152; Federal policy, 152
Flood protection, 153–159; zoning legislation in flood plain, 144, 147, 149, 151–152 means and evaluation, 46; defect, 149; defects in USED policy, 155–159; present financing policy, 156. *See* Flood Control Acts
Folsom Dam, legislation, 251
Folsom formula, provisions, 251
Folsom Reservoir, 250
Forest planting, 146
Forest Service, 113
Forestry Service, 83
Fort Peck Act, 200
Freight rates, differential, 162–167, 177
Fresno *Bee*, cited, 241–242
Fresno Irrigation District, 252
Friant Dam, 210
Friant-Kern Canal, 210

Geological Survey, 83
Grand Coulee Dam, 198; USED opposition, 199
Grand Prairie–Bayou Meto development, 124
Green, Rep. Robert Alexis, cited, 48–49
Green–Duwamish Rivers projects, 156–157
Griffith, Rep. John K., 48
Group interests, adjustment, 5, 37–60; activity of Members of Congress, 38–40, 45; activity of local groups, 40; activity of regional groups, 40–45; activity of national groups, 45–50; USED, 51–57

Hackensack River, improvement project, 48
Hansen, Alvin, 108
Harpeth River power project, 190
Harris, Rep. Oren, cited, 39
Hayden, Sen. Carl, 80
Hearings, public: rivers and harbors projects, 26–27, 37–38, 40, 41–42; Congressional, 31, 32; on unfavorable survey reports, 30; on projects, by subcommittees, 32
Hell's Canyon, 124
Hendricks, Rep. Joseph Edward, 48
Hill, Sen. Lister, cited, 236
Hollywood (Port Everglades), project, 182
Hoover, Herbert: Economy Act of 1932, 67; criticism of USED, 115, 116
Hoover Commission on Organization of the Executive Branch of the Government. *See* Hoover Report
Hoover Dam, formula of 1927, 204
Hoover Report, 112–118; Task Force recommendations, 112–118; position on user charges, 161; recommendations on Federal power marketing, 197; on interagency rivalry, 253, 254–255; on unification of agency functions, 255; on divided agency responsibility, 257
House Documents, *630, 631,* 76th Congress, 3rd Session, 229
House Resolution, *2126,* 239; *4485* (1944), 235, 237; *5400,* 245–246
Humboldt River, project report, 124
Hydroelectric power, 188–204; rate policies, 142, priority, 144; state regulatory legislation, 144; sound policy, 189, 196–197; standards of NRPB and NPPC, 188; FPC and USED relations, 189–190; inadequate planning, Cumberland projects, 190–196; TVA regional planning, 193–194; shortage in Cumberland-Tennessee areas, 194; future demand, 193, 194, 195–196; in Kings River project, 218–219. *See also* Power distribution policy

INDEX

Ickes, Harold, 44, 77; sponsorship of NRB, 75, 76, 77; letter to Secretary Dern, 75–76, 78, 228–229; "supporters" in opposition to NRB bill, 80–81; letter to Roosevelt on Kings River project, 222–223; support of HR *4485*, 237; support of Flood Control Bill, 1944, 237
Incremental benefits and costs, 140
Indian Valley Reservoir, 150
Information project, sought by USED, 24–25
Inland waterways, Atlantic, 41
Inland Waterways Commission, 65–66
In-service training programs, 18
Insurance, flood losses, 147, 149
Interest groups adjustment: discretion, 4; agency responsibility, 5–8; representation on multiheaded boards, 7, 8; information on survey reports, 29–30; USED techniques, 37–60; Members of Congress, 38–40, 45; local interests, 40, 45, 51–57; regional, 40–45; national, 45–50; avoidance of commitments, 52, 55–57; shifting of decisions, 57–60. *See also* Pressure groups
Interest rates, uniform, 139
International Boundary Commission, 91
Interstate Commerce Commission, position on user charges, 161; review of USED report on Lake Erie-Ohio River Canal project, 171, 172, 173–176
Investigations, legislative: of agencies, 12; of projects, 71
Irrigation law: limitations on land benefited, 144; state regulatory legislation, 144; present legislative policy, 159; responsible policy, 204–207; contrasted with flood control law, 216–218. *See also* Acreage limitations, Reclamation law, *and* Speculation controls
Iron Canyon Reservoir, 250
Isabella Reservoir, 250

Jacksonville Harbor project, 182
Jamestown Reservoir, 124
Jennings, Rep. John, 48
Jordan, of Ohio Valley Conservation and Flood Control Congress, cited, 44–45

Kaweah River, 210; project, 250
Kentucky Dam and Lake, power project, 190; TVA proposal, 194
Kern River, 210
Kern River project, 250; President's letter on, 201, 224–225; elimination of appropriation, 245
Kings River project, 124, 201; case history, 208–259; area described, 208–210; early planning, 210–215; USED and Reclamation Bureau plans compared, 215–221; controversy over, 221–238; USED construction, 226; preconstruction operations appropriations, 1945, 238–240; application of Section 8, 240; construction appropriations, 1946, 243–244; funds impounded by President, 245; allocation of costs and repayment arrangements, 246–249; funds released, 248; change in allocation benefits, 249–250; Kings River and Central Valley, 250–252; bill to apply Folsom formula, 251; results of failure to resolve Central Valley conflict, 252–254; causes of continuing failure to solve conflict, 254–259
Kirwan, Rep. Michael Joseph, 174
Krug, Secretary Julius A.: testimony on Army-Interior Agreement, 120; appointment, 247; and Kings River project, 247–248

Lac Qui Parle project, 49
Lake Erie and Ohio River Canal: and Youngstown Canal, report, USED, 167, 170; NRC review of report, 170; ICC study of rail rates, 170–171; NRPB negotiation on rail rates, 171–172; USED supplementary report, 172–173; ICC review, 173–176; NRPB review of USED and ICC reports, 175; effects of investigations, 177
Lake Worth Inlet, project, 182
Land, contribution, as participation in projects cost, 178
Land elevation, 146
Land speculation, reclamation law. *See* Speculation controls
Land use, and flood control, 145–149; readjustment, 147, 149. *See also* Adjustments, Flood plain occupance, Reclamation law
Legislation: origin in administrative agencies, 4; by committee resolution, 38–40. *See* Appropriations Acts, Flood Control Acts, *etc.*
Legislative controls, of executive branch, laws, 3–4, 5–6, 8–13; budget, 12
Legislature: mandate to agency, 3–4, 5–6; agency responsibility to, 8–13, 61; need to adapt organization to current needs, 9; relations with administrative agencies and chief executive, 9; difficulty of checking minorities in, 10; confirmation of agency appointments, 13; danger of minority control over agency affairs, 13; committee resolutions on review of unfavorable reports, 27; criteria of USED responsibility to, 61–62; direct responsibility of USED, 1934, 63; effects of USED direct responsibility, 63–68; at-

tempts to break USED-Congress direct relationship, 68
Levees, 146, 149, 153; emergency, 147; local requirements, Flood Control Bill, 1938, 155; present financing policy, 156
Lilienthal, David, cited, 134
Lippmann, Walter, cited, 37
Lobbies. *See* Pressure groups
Lobbying, USED, demands for investigation, 115–116
Lodge, Sen. Henry Cabot, Jr., 115–116
Long-range construction programs, 129, 130, 131
Lower Cumberland, power project, 190

McClellan, Rep., 87
McClellan, Sen. John, 46, 112, 113, 114–115, 116
McCormick, Rep. John William, 117
McGann, Joseph H., cited, 42
Machinery, oil protection, 147
MacKenzie, General Alexander, 66
McLean, Rep. Donald Holmes, 90
McMillan, Rep. Clara G., 48
Madera Canal, 210
Manasco, Rep. Carter, 112–113, 114–115
Mansfield, Rep. Joseph Jefferson, 43, 67–68
Mansfield, Judge, 106; cited, 30–31
Markham, Maj. Gen., 75, 76, 87
Maverick, Rep. Maury, 77, 78
Mendota Pool, 209
Merriam, of NRB advisory committee, 77
Merrimack River project, 48
Merrimack Valley flood control project, 156
Miami Conservancy District, 44, 143
Miami (Virginia Key) project, 182
"Mileage" power rates, 197; opposed for Columbia River dams, 198
Millerton Lake, 210
Minnesota, and Red River Basin, plans, 92
Mississippi River: navigation improvements, 21; flood control project, 52–54
Mississippi River Commission, 22; report on Mississippi flood control project, 53, 55
Mississippi Valley Association, opposition to reorganization bills, 115
Mississippi Valley Committee: report, 74, 75; demonstration of basin-wide planning, 118; on toll charges, 1934, 161; standards for hydroelectric power, 188
Missouri Basin Inter-Agency Committee, 110–111, 119
Missouri River, conflict over irrigation and navigation uses of, 111
Mitchell, of advisory committee of NRB, 77
Monopoly control, lack, in present flood control policy, 158
Monticello Reservoir, 250
Moore, J. Hampton, 41, 42, 43

Moreland, Capt. J. W., 49
Morgan, Arthur, 44
Multiple-purpose, water development: balanced, 135–136; USED policy, 145; USED planning violations, 187–188; need of Federal direction, 189; TVA plan for Cumberland power projects, 193–194; interagency competition over, 208, 211, 213–214; application of Tripartite Agreement, 212; allocation of costs benefits, 219–220; Central Valley, 250; Folsom formula provisions, 251
Muskingum Conservancy District, work, 44
Muskingum Valley Project, 44

Narrows Reservoir, 250
Nashville Channel project, 190
Nashville power project, 193
National flood control policy, 44; ideal, 146–149
National Industrial Recovery Act, 210
National interest, in project, WRC definition, 143–144
National planning, under SJR 57, 92
National Planning Board: recommendations of NRC, 86–87; appropriations, 104–105; legislation, 1938 to finale, 104–108; President's appeal for, 106–107: House vote, 107; abolition, 107; effect of abolition on basin-wide planning, 119; inventory of water projects, 129
National Power Policy Committee, standards for hydroelectric power, 188; appointment, 198
National Reclamation Association, 45
National and Regional Land and Water Organizations' Coördinating Committee, 50
National Resources Board, 74, 75, 76; creation, 74; sponsorship by Roosevelt, Ickes, 75–76, 77; opposition by Secretary of War, 75, 76, 77, 78–80; attitude of Congressional Committees, 80; USED attitude, 80, 98–99; conflicts with USED, 86; proposed functions and scope, 98
National Resources Board (permanent), scope defined by Committee on Administrative Management, 94; ignored in final reorganization bill, 95; USED opposition, 95; legislation, linked with conservation legislation, 97–98
National Resources Committee: correlation of flood investigation work, 82; recommendations on flood control activities, 83; objections to emergency flood control legislation, 1935, 84; coördinating agency in flood control project selection, 85–86; and report on *Public Works Planning*,

INDEX

86; recommendations on national planning board, 86–87; memorandum opposing SJR 57, 91–93; supported by Rep. Cochran, 95; opposed by Rivers and Harbors bloc, 95; conflict with USED, 100–101; review of upper Rio Grande Basin plan, 125; review of projects for 1936 and 1937, 125; review board for flood control proposals, 125–126; preparation of 6-year public works programs, 129; opposition to Flood Control Act of 1936, 153–154; to Flood Control Act of 1938, 155–156; review of USED Beaver-Mahoning Canal project, 170. See National Resources Board

National Resources Planning Board, manuscript from, 39–40; executive order providing for direct agency responsibility to chief executive, 101–102; organization of subcommittee of WRC on national water policy, 102; and USED relations, 105–106, 107, 108; review of agency reports, 126, 127; in President's office, 129; adjustment and review of 6-year programs, 130; annual reports, defects, 130–131; complaints on USED flood control policy, 149; report on USED survey of Thames River, 149–150; position on user charges, 161; review of USED report on Beaver-Mahoning Canal project, 171–172; achievements in Lake Erie-Ohio River Canal project, 177–178; comment on local contributions to costs of navigation facilities, 178; review of USED report on Tombigbee project, 183–184; report on Ohio River canalization project, 187–188; standards for hydroelectric power, 188; position on Cumberland-TVA project, 190; shaping of Federal power policy, 198; action on Kings River project, 211, 212–213, 214, 215, 222–223; abolition, 258

National Resources Planning Board Evaluation Committee, 179–180

National Rivers and Harbors Congress, 45–50, 112–113; objectives, 45; membership, 45–46; membership of Engineers in, 45–46, 51; Members of Congress, officers, 46; relations with Engineers, 46–47; work of Projects Committee, 47–49; relations with Congressional Committees, 49; Engineers' reports, 49; policy on Engineers' reports, 49; policy on other projects, 49; influence, 49–50; opposition to reorganization bills of 1949, 115

National Water Conservation Conference, 50

National water development policy: lack of, 1934, 64; proposals for, 65; effort to develop, 1939–1941, 102; lack of USED coöperation in, 102–118, 119

National Waterways Commission, results, 66

Natural resources projects, coördination, Task Force recommendations, 112

Navigation projects, 159–188; expenditures, 43; facilities, rate policies, 142; essentials of sound policy, 160–164; relations to other facilities, 160–162, 181–184; user charges, 162–163, 164; USED policies, 164–167, 181, 182, 187; local contributions, 178–181; Florida harbor projects, 181–183; competitive facilities, 181–184; evaluation of benefits and costs, 184–188

Neches Waterway report, 124

New Creek, Staten Island, USED report on, 150

New Jersey Ship Canal, 41; authorized in Rivers and Harbors bill, 1945, 41

New Melones Reservoir, 250

Newlands, Sen. Francis Griffith, 66, 67

Newlands amendment, repeal, 67

Nonvendible services, charges, 142–143

Norrell, Rep. William Frank, cited, 56

Norris, Sen. George William 72, 90

Norris-Rankin valley authority bills, 90

North Dakota, and Red River Basin plan, 92

North Fork report, 251–252

North River. See St. Mary's River project

Northwest Ordinance, no-toll policy, 165

Oakdale and Harriman Dams project, 48

Obey River power project, 190

Office of Price Administration, 8

Ohio Conservancy Law, 44

Ohio-Lower Mississippi River regulation, WRC report on, 88, 89, 91, 94

Ohio River, navigation improvements, 21; canalization project, 187–188

Ohio Valley Conservation and Flood Control Congress, objectives, 43–45

Old Hickory power project, 190

O'Mahoney, Sen. Joseph, 80–81, 111

O'Mahoney Amendment, to Flood Control Act of 1944, 111

Omnibus authorization bills, 30; unrecommended projects in, 31; mention of survey reports in, 31; defects of, 64

Omnibus flood control bill of 1939, hearings, 31

Orders and Regulations of the Corps of Engineers, 25; 1934, 63, 124; 1949, 124

Oregon, Willamette Valley plan, 92

Osmers, Rep. Frank C., 48

Ouachita River project, USED report, 200

"Overschedule water," defined, 218

Overton, Sen. John Holmes, 46, 56, 200; position on NRPB, 105, 108; statement on committee's attitude toward NRPB and Budget Bureau, 128–129; report of Commerce Committee decision on Kings River project, 234; cited on Kings River project, 236
Owen, report on transportation policy, 161, 163

Pacific Gas and Electric Company, 202, 251, 252
Pacific Northwest Regional Planning Commission, standards for hydroelectric power, 188
Palm Beach (Lake Worth Inlet), project, 182
Participation: local, 50–51; Federal, water projects, 141–142; local contributions principle, violation, 153–156; present legislative principles, 156; violation in Green and Duwamish Rivers project, 156–157; USED policy, 157, 178–181; in Commercial Point project, 178–179; in St. Mary's River project, 180; and timing of project construction, 220
Parties, political, 5, 16–18
Penstocks, legislation, 189
Pepper, Sen. Claude D., 182–183
Personnel, agency: professional status, 17–18; total, USED, 22
Pine Flat Dam, 228–230, 251, 252
Pine Flat Reservoir, 214, 215, 220
Planning: social, 3–4; after project authorization, 33–36; group interest adjustment, 37–60; basin-wide, 69–71, 118–129, 136–137, 187–188, 233; organization for coördination of, 72–118; national, under SJR 57, 92; technical and fiscal, 99; USED concept, 99–100, 149–153; efforts at revision, 1939–1940, 101–102; duplicate, 121, 122, 123, 124, 238; tests of sound water plan, 135–149; USED policy evaluated, 149–207. See also Basin-wide plans, Projects, and Water project planning, Planning board. See National Planning Board and National Resources Planning Board
Policy, administrative: formulation, 3–4, 134; role of chief executive in integrating, 10; outlining broad issues, 11; agency conformance to, 13–15; USED avoidance of policy making, 104, 105; role of Congress in, 107
Port Everglades project, 182
"Postage-stamp" power rates, 197; recommended, Columbia River dams, 198
Power distribution policy, 196–197; prevention of monopoly, 196; purchase priority to public agencies, 196; Federal transmission lines, 196; sale at bus bar, 196; firm power at load centers, 196–197; mileage rates, 197; integration of Federal hydroelectric facilities, 197; integration of Federal and private systems, 197; setting rates, 197; unified responsibility for Federal power marketing, 197; history of Federal policy, 198–204, 218–219, 252; Dondero amendment, 201–202, 203, 204; USED position, 202, 203; Section 5, Flood Control Bill, 1944, 237
Powers, Rep., testimony, 58–59
Preliminary examinations, projects: House committee policy, 23; purpose, 24; priority, 24; public hearings, 24; field reconnaissance, 24–25; reports, contents, 25; review, 25–26; return of report to District Engineer, 25, 26
President. See Chief executive
President's Committee of Six, 161
President's Committee on Waterflow, 1934, 72–74, 118
Pressure groups: role in administrative responsibility, 5; agency responsibility to, 5–8; Members of Congress as, 38–40, 45; local, 40–45; regional, 40–45; national, 45–50
Price levels, uniform, 140
Priorities, in preliminary examination, 28; in programs, 71–72
Professional standards, agency responsibility to, 16–18; of USED, 134–207. See Water project planning, professional standards
Projects: inception, 23; preliminary examination, 24–28; reports, 25–26, 30; survey, 28–30; Congressional authorization, 30–33; approval by Chief of Engineers, 30–31; public hearings, 31; planning after authorization, 33–36; definite project report, 33–34; appropriation process, 34–36; expenditures, 43, 129; attempts to revise procedures, 65, 101–102; need of interagency coöperation, 71; selection, acceleration, and deceleration, 71; review, 71–72, 124–129; programming-budgeting, 130–132; uneconomic, 155; reviews, advantages, 187. See also Basin-wide plans, Planning, and Water project planning, professional standards
Public interest, and USED project practices, 59–60; and direct responsibility to chief executive, 61; in water project plans, 138
Public Works Administration, 76, 125, 129
Public Works and Drainage Basin Reports, 1936, 86–87

Quadrupartite Agreement, 109, 110, 123, 126

INDEX

Railroads, rates: out-of-pocket cost rates, 163, 165; investigations, Lake Erie-Ohio area, 170–172, 173, 174–176; short-haul and long-haul rates, 174, 175; basis of ICC readjustments, 174–175; Roosevelt letter to ICC on Youngstown rates, 175–176; ICC investigation, Youngstown, 176–177

Railroads, revenues, effect of Lake Erie-Ohio River Canal, 171; toll-free basis, 173–174; with toll, 174; indirect losses, 174

Rate policies, water use, 142–143; USED estimates on rate savings, 160–161, 165; transportation rate structure, 163–164, 165; recommended revision, 166. *See* Power distribution policies, Railroads, rates, *and* Repayment

Rayburn, Rep. Sam, 107

Reber, Maj., 56

Reclamation Act, 200

Reclamation Adjustment Act, 1926, 228

Reclamation law, 204; on irrigation projects, 204–207, 216–218; Roosevelt letter on, 206; application to Kings River project, 235–237; Truman's views, 240–241; undermined, in Kings River project, 253

Reclamation Project Act, 1939, 199

Red River Basin, sample survey report, 31; power project, 48, 49, 190

Red River of the North, drainage area, tri-state plan, 92

Reëxaminations of projects, 38–40; number of, 1935, 1946, 40

Rensselaer Polytechnical School, 20

Reorganization Act: (1939), 97; (1945), 97; (1949), 115–118

Reorganization bills, controversy, 95; special treatment of USED in, 96, 97; Truman appeal for, 97, 115; Hoover appeal for, 115; opposition of USED, 115

Repayment, water projects, 141–143, 153; flexibility, 143; USED defense of unsound policy, 153, 154, 157; provisions of Flood Control Acts of 1936 and 1938, 153–156; present legislative policy, 156; provisions of Flood Control Act of 1950, 157; inflexibility in present USED policy, 158; USED and Reclamation policies, 204–205; Reclamation and USED plans, Kings River project, 216; Senate Appropriations Committee views, 227–228; Truman views, 240; contracts, Kings River project, 241–245, 248–249

Reservoirs, 146, 149, 153; financing in Flood Control Bill of 1938, 154–155; present financing policy, 156

Resolutions, Congressional, force, 38–40; 62. *See* House Resolutions

Resources development, 130. *See* Multiple-purpose water development, National Resources Planning Board, *and* Reclamation law

Review resolutions, Congressional, 38–40, 62

"Rights," defined, 145

Rivers and Harbors Act: (1882), 165; (1907), 178–179; (1910), 66; (1930), 179; (1935), 167, 176; (1938), 97; (1945), 123, 238; (1946), 184, 194; (1950), 180, 181

Rivers and Harbors Bill: (1937), 31; (1945), 184, 186

Rivers and harbors bills, machinery, 23

Rivers and harbors and flood control bills, and power distribution policy, 199–200; USED opposition, 200, 201; Executive Office and Interior support, 201

Rivers and harbors improvement, 21; appropriations, 21; Board of Engineers for Rivers and Harbors, 22; Mississippi River Commission, 22; special organizations charged with, 22; House Committees on, 30. *See also* Committee on Rivers and Harbors

Robins, Maj. Gen. Thomas M., 102–103, 241–242, 258–259

Rogers, Rep. Edith Nourse, 48

Roosevelt, Franklin Delano: cited, 61; approval of NRB, 77–78; objection to emergency flood control laws, 1935, 84; reservations on Flood Control Act, 1938, 86; letter on USED report on flood control, 89–90, 94; message to Congress on TVA's, 90; veto message, SJR 57, 93; appeals for NRPB appropriations, 104–107; statement on USED basin policy, 122; position on USED Ohio-Mississippi Rivers reports, 125; on user charges, 161; instigation of rail rates investigation, 170, 171, 172, 173, 175; on hydroelectric power, 188; position on Cumberland-TVA project, 190; report on Federal power marketing, 197; appointment of NPPC, 198; request for Federal power laws, 199–200, 201; plea for reclamation laws on irrigation projects, 206; conference on Kings River project, 211–212; letters on Kings River projects, 223–224, 224–225, 230–231, 233, 235; statement on HR *4485* (1944), 235

Roosevelt, Theodore, cited, 65; support of Newlands plan, 66

Rossville power project, 190

Rousseau River project, 49

Russian River project reports, 124

Sacramento *Bee,* cited, 241–242

Sacramento River, 209

Sacramento-San Joaquin Delta, 209
Sacramento-San Joaquin River Basin, report, 242
St. Mary's Kraft Corporation, 180
St. Mary's River project, 180–181
San Francisco *News,* cited, 244
San Joaquin River, 209
San Luis Valley project, 124
Sanctions, on administrative responsibility, 2–3; lack of Congressional, 9; Congressional investigations, 12
Santa Monica Harbor project, 39
Saville, Thorndike, 84
Schley, Maj. Gen. Julian, 55, 56; cited, 46; testimony on planning legislation, 98–100; objections to WRC report on national water policy, 103–104; on user charges, 164; on Tombigbee waterway, 183
Secretary of Army, Agreement with Secretary of Interior, on Columbia River Basin report, 119
Secretary of Interior: interest in western rivers, 111; agreement with Secretary of Army on Columbia River Basin plan, 119; report to CBIAC, 119–120; report on Kings River project, 212–213; role in irrigation projects, 236, 237. *See also* Department of Interior, Ickes, Krug
Secretary of War: responsibility of Chief of Engineers to, 21–22; opposition to NRB, 75, 76, 77, 78–80; opposition to WRC, 82–83; endorsement of SJR *57,* 87–88; letter to Roosevelt on USED flood control plan, 88–89; national planning duties under SJR *57,* 92; allocation and repayment plans, Kings River project, 245, 246–247. *See also* Dern, Stimson, *and* War Department
Senate Joint Resolution *57,* 1937, 87, 113; endorsed by Secretary of War, 87–88; endorsed by House Flood Control Committee, 88; NRC memorandum, 91–93; Roosevelt veto message, 93
Sheppard, Rep. Harry R., 48
Simpson, Rep. Sid, 46
Small, President of Atlantic Deeper Waterways Association, 42, 43
Snyder, Rep., testimony, 58–59
Soil Conservation Service, 83
South Dakota, and Red River Basin plan, 92
Speculation, controls, Federal projects, 144; lack, in present flood control policy, 158; reclamation law on, 205–206, 216, 221, 228, 235–236; in Kings River project, 235, 240, 241, 244, 249, 253
States: submission of project reports to, 25; reports of unfavorable preliminary examinations to, 27; and taxing power, 142–143; regulatory measures on water use, 144, 158–159; regulation of flood plain occupance (recommended), 151–152
Statutes, drafting: agency advice, 11–12; revision, 11; covering work of USED, 1852, 21; Flood Control Act, 1936, 21
Steam standby plants, 197
Stewarts Ferry power project, 190
Stimson, Henry, testimony, 64; letter on Kings River project, 229–230
Stones River power project, 190
Storm warnings, value, 149
Success Reservoir, 250
Survey reports, 29, 30, 31

Table Mountain Reservoir, 250
Taft, Howard K., support of Newlands plan, 66
Task Force on National Resources. *See* Hoover Report
Tate, Thomas R., 84, 85, 154
Taxes, direct, Federal, 142–143; for waterways benefits, 161–162
Tehachapi Mountains, 209
Tennessee River drainage area, 190
Tennessee Valley Authority: omission in SJR *57,* 91; proposals for Nashville power project, 193–194
Terminals, local, 178
Terminus Reservoir, 250
Thames River, USED survey, 149–150
Three Islands power project, 190
Tolls. *See* User charges
Tombigbee waterway, 183–184; justification, 186
Traffic distribution, as economic justification, 160–161, 166
Transportation costs, savings, USED estimates: on navigation projects, 162–167; on Lake Erie-Ohio River Canal, 167, 170, 171, 172, 173, 174; on Trenton Channel project, 180–181; on Tombigbee waterway, 83
Transportation facilities, and navigation facilities, 160–162; competition, 162–163; rate structure, 163, 164, 165
Trenton Channel project, 180–181
Tripartite Agreement, 101, 123, 126; USED position, 108; provisions, 212
Truman, Harry S.: appeal for reorganization legislation, 97; support of Hoover Report, 118; recommendations on Columbia River Basin plans, 119; statement on USED basin policy, 122; plea for interagency project planning, 123; standards for hydroelectric power, 188; position on Cumberland-TVA project,

INDEX

190, 194; action on Ickes' message on Kings River project, 240; letter on flood control-irrigation projects, 240–241; attitude on Kings River project appropriations, 243–244, 245–246; action on Secretary of War's cost allocation and repayment plans, Kings River project, 247–248; action on Central Valley projects reports, 251

Tulare Lake, 210, 215; flood control construction, 226; and Kings River benefits, 249–250

Tule River, 210; project, 250

United States Engineer Department: motto, 20; history, 20; civil functions, 20, 21–35; appropriations, 21; military functions, 21; organization and scope, 21–22; project planning, 22–36; coöperation with Federal and state agencies, 25, 27; review of unfavorable preliminary examinations, 27; reports on preliminary examinations, 28; group interests adjustment, 37–60; membership of officers in pressure groups, 45–46; submission to Congress on controversial projects, 52, 55; responsibility to executive and legislative departments, 52, 57–60, 61–133; and appropriations process, 57–58; procedure and policies, 1934–1949, 68–133; opposition to attempts to break USED-Congress relationship, 68–69, 74, 88–89, 99, 100, 101, 117–118, 119, 132–133, 224; opposition to creation of national planning agencies, 72–133; about-face tactics on flood study proposals, 75, 83, 85; special treatment in Reorganization Acts, 1939, 1945, 97; conflict with NRC, 100–101; and Tripartite Agreement, 101–102; and NRPB, 105, 106, 107, 108; conflict with Budget Bureau, 1943–1950, 108–112; action on Interior's western rivers reports, 111; Task Force and Hoover Commission proposals, 113, 114; position on executive coördinating procedures, 113, 119; action on reports conflicting with President's program, 114; opposition to reorganization laws, 115; opposition to transfer of civil functions, 116–117; report on Columbia River Basin plan, 120–121; "308" reports, 122; basin-wide planning, 122; position on joint project reports, 123; coöperation with other agencies, 124; survey reports review, 125; representation on WRC evaluation committee, 126; action on FIARBC, 126; coöperation with NRPB and Budget on flood control and navigation construction, 131; procedures and policies, 1950, 132–133; responsibility to profession, 134–207; flood control viewpoint, 145, 149–153, 157–159; action on change in land use, 152–153; defective waterway evaluation, 160, 164, 165; policy on user charges, 164, 165–167; illustration of survey procedures, 167–177; policy on local participation in projects costs, 178–181; traffic predictions, 185; navigation policy, 187; policy on multiple-purpose river development, 188; relations with FPC, 189–190; report on Cumberland-TVA project, 190, 194; opposition to Federal power policy in 1936–1937, 198, 200; overemphasis on local effects, 195; position on uniform rates, Pacific Northwest, 199; Ouachita River report, 200; failure in administrative responsibility, 201; position on Section 5 of Flood Control Act of 1944, 202; on Dondero amendment, 204; opposition to President's irrigation policy, 206–207; plans on Kings River project, 208, 210, 213, 214, 215–221, 221–226; water-use policy, 215, 255; views on hydroelectric power, 218–219; repayment and timing plans on Kings River project, 221; failure to support President's policy on Kings River project, 231, 234; cost allocation, Kings River project, 246; calculation of benefits, Kings River project, 249; responsibilities under Folsom formula, 251

United States Public Health Service, 91
Upper Rio Grande Basin plan, 125
Upper San Joaquin Valley, 209, 216–217
User charges, 161;· advantages, 161–163, 164; recommended changes in policy, 163–164; USED policy, 164–165; criticism of USED policy, 166–167

Vendible services, charges, 142
Veto, 15; denied chief executive, 62; proviso in Reorganization Bill, 1949, 116, 117
Virginia Key project, 182

Walter, Rep. Francis Eugene, 77
War Department: attitude toward NRB, 75, 76; and Tripartite Agreement, 212; Civil Functions Appropriation Bill, 1947, 239, 243, 245–246. *See also* Secretary of War *and* United States Engineer Department
War Production Board, 8
Washington *Post,* cited, 244–245
Water and Energy Resources Committee, standards for hydroelectric power, 188
Water Development Service, proposed, 113
Water law, western states, 145

INDEX

Water Planning Committee, report, 1935, 74, 75
Water Power Act, 1920, 189, 198; Section 29, 67
Water project planning, professional standards: review, 124–129; multiple purposes, 135–136; basin relationships, 136–137; planning for shifting conditions, 137; broader problems, 138; economic soundness, 138–141; economic life, 139; repayment of costs, 141–143; advance of capital, 143–144; prevention of speculation, 144; state regulatory measures, 144–145; legal rights, responsibilities, 145; flood control, 145–149; USED policy appraised, 149–153; flood protection, 153–159; navigation, 159–188; hydroelectric power, 188–204; irrigation, 204–207; effect of interagency conflict, 253
Water Resources Committee: opposition to program, 82–83; investigation of flood control, 83; opposition to Flood Control Bill, 1935, 84; recommendations for coördinated national water plan, 87; Ohio-Lower Mississippi report, 88, 89, 91, 94; report on flood control, 89; report on drainage basin problems and programs, 92; and national water policy, 102–104; project review, agreement with PWA, 125; evaluation subcommittee, 126; development of criteria for programs, 130; reports, and USED responsibility to profession, 135; definition of national interest, 143–144; complaint on USED flood problem policy, 149; statement on occupance of flood plains, 151–152;
recommendation of toll charges, 161, 164; views on Kings River reports, 211, 212, 213, 223; report on national water policy, 258–259
Water resources development: lack of national policy, 1934, 64; proposals for, 65; activities, Western, survey, 123–124; long-range program, 130; budget for, 130; USED policy, 134, 149–153, 155–159, 164–167, 181, 182, 187; priority of government over private industry, 189. *See also* Water Resources Committee
Water rights, in Kings River project, 217–218
Waterways Commission, 66, 67
Webb, of Board of Investigation and Research, 161
Wheeler, Lt. Gen. Raymond A., 245
Wherry, Sen. Kenneth Spicer, 46
White, Gilbert F., cited, 145–146
Whittington, Rep. William Madison, 46, 56, 57; opposition to changes, 67–68, 115; on planning agencies, 90; and Kings River project, 231–232
Wilson, Woodrow, 66
Wolf Creek power project, 190
Wolman, Abel, 84, 103
Woodrum, Rep. Clifton Alexander, 106–107
Works Progress Administration, 125

Youngstown Canal, 167. *See also* Lake Erie-Ohio River Canal

Zoning restrictions, in flood plain, 144, 147, 149; WRC statements on, 151–152; enforcement, 152